Recovering the U. S. Hispanic Literary Heritage

Edited by
Ramón Gutiérrez and Genaro Padilla

Arte Público Press
Houston
Texas
1993

The publication of this book is made possible through support from the AT&T Foundation. Support for the conference from which these articles were drawn was provided by the Rockefeller Foundation. The supporters of Arte Público Press include the National Endowment for the Arts (a federal agency), the Lila Wallace-Reader's Digest Fund and the Andrew W. Mellon Foundation.

Arte Público Press
University of Houston
Houston, Texas 77204-2090

Cover design by Mark Piñón

Recovering the U.S. Hispanic literary heritage / edited by Ramón Gutiérrez and Genaro Padilla.
     p.   cm.
    ISBN 1-55885-063-5 : $34.95. — ISBN 1-55885-058-9 (trade pbk.) : $17.95
     1. American literature—Hispanic American authors—History and criticism. 2. Hispanic American literature (Spanish)—History and criticism. 3. Hispanic Americans—Intellectual life. 4. Hispanic Americans in literature. I. Gutiérrez, Ramón A., 1951– . II. Padilla, Genaro M., 1949– .
    PS153.H56R43   1993   92-45114
                                                     CIP

The paper used in this publication meets the requirements of the American National Standard for Permanence of Paper for Printed Library Materials Z39.48-1984. ∞

Contents

Recovering the U. S. Hispanic Literary Heritage

Nicolás Kanellos
Project Director

Julián Olivares
General Editor

Foreword

This volume is a product of the Recovering the U. S. Hispanic Literary Heritage, a project whose purposes include locating, rescuing from perishing, evaluating, disseminating and publishing collections of primary literary sources written by Hispanics in the geographic area that is now the United States from the Colonial Period to 1960. The ten-year project will focus on the implementation of the following programs:

     I.   An on-line data base
    II.   A periodicals recovery program
   III. A consortium of Hispanic archives
   IV. Grants-in-aid and fellowships for scholars
    V.   A publishing program
   VI. Conferences and dissemination of information

This is the largest project of its kind undertaken in the history of scholarly efforts to study Hispanic culture in the United States. Its importance lies in filling the large gap which exists in American literature: the Hispanic contribution. The broad scope of the project includes recovery of all conventional literary genres as well as such forms as letters, diaries, oral lore and popular culture by Cuban, Mexican, Puerto Rican, Spanish and other Hispanic residents of what has become the United States.

The project will have an immediate as well as long-lasting impact on education and on our knowledge about a large and important dimension of U. S. culture. It will shape for decades to come academic scholarship in the disciplines of literature and history and it will have a major influence on the curriculum and teaching of English, Spanish and bilingual education in K-12 schools as well as in institutions of higher education.

As a natural result of the work that the scholars represented in this volume have been developing over a twenty-year period, the Rockefeller Foundation provided funds to the center for U. S. Hispanic Literature at the University of Houston to bring together in two conferences those scholars to plan the extensive program to recover the U. S. Hispanic literary heritage. During the first conference held at the National Humanities Center on November 17–18, 1990, and subsequently during the second meeting of the Board of Editorial Advisors on May 17, 1991, guidelines were established for the Recovery Project. The programs outlined below are the priorities selected by the participating scholars.

I.   The On-Line Data Base will:
   A.   Centralize and make accessible all data referring to texts for researchers, including their dates of production, current location, current physical condition, sex and ethnicity of the authors, and the themes of the works.
   B.   Index and catalog all data.
   C.   Prepare data for publication in diverse forms:
      1.   Microform and CD-ROM publication of the complete databank
      2.   Bibliographies
      3.   Indices
      4.   Other reference works
   D.   Use the databank to locate and study works for possible editing and publication.

II.   The Periodical Literature Recovery Project
   Because of the historical importance of newspapers and other periodicals in publishing a significant portion of Hispanic literature of the United States, this activity will focus on the recovery of periodicals. Much of this literature is in danger of being lost due to decay. The periodicals themselves exist in widely disperse collections around the world and in varying degrees of preservation, from decaying newsprint to microfilm. The program will support the work of researchers whose task is locating, preserving, indexing and making accessible Hispanic literature published in periodicals from the early nineteenth century to 1960.

III.   An Archival Consortium will:
   A.   Create and/or stabilize existing Hispanic archives.
   B.   Collect, index, safeguard and make accessible materials generated by the project.
   C.   Assist in acquiring, preserving and safeguarding materials at large that are inaccessible and in danger

of perishing.

IV. Grants-in-aid and Fellowships for Scholars will procure the funds necessary for the support of work by scholars who will be searching for, collecting, micro-filming, indexing, editing and publishing the materials.

V. A publishing consortium composed of university presses in the United States, Mexico, Puerto Rico and Spain will be established to publish recovered works in critical editions, in electronic, print and microform media as individual works, anthologies, textbooks and entire hardbound library collections.

VI. Conferences, communications networks and publications will be established to disseminate information to scholars, graduate and undergraduate students and educators at all levels.

Nicolás Kanellos
Project Director

imposed by "outsiders"—by persons and entities who are not members of these communities—, "Hispanic" may tend to obliterate the diversity of Latino ethnic and national communities in the United States.

We are fully cognizant of how politically charged the term "Hispanic" currently is in some circles, but we have chosen to employ it here as a broad cultural term that most succinctly captures the history of the diaspora of Spain's peoples, institutions and language throughout the American hemisphere. The Latin etymological root of the word Hispanic is *hispania,* the ancient Roman appellation for what became the modern nation-state of Spain. Within decades of Christopher Columbus' 1492 mooring in the Indies, the men and women who journeyed across the sea to this land that became known as *las Américas,* thought of themselves as Spaniards or *españoles.* And not too long after that, *Hispanoamérica* became the common name for Spain's former colonies in North and South America. The term Hispanoamérica, thus, includes the Spanish and New World identities in one term, a sort of fusion that is representative of the *mestizaje* or racial and cultural mixing that took place. Furthermore, there is abundant documentary evidence from newspapers and other sources that "Hispanic" was a term used in cosmopolitan communities in New York, Los Angeles, San Francisco, etc., during the early part of this century and results from the self-identifier "hispanoamericanos," which is used throughout the Hemisphere (as opposed to "Latin American," a term created in the United States to lump together all of the countries south of the border). Also, there are millions of Hispanics who self-identify themselves today (as opposed to outsiders calling them) as "Hispanics" when they refer to their relationship with other ethnic nationality groups of Hispanic-American origin. It is with this very long and profound cultural genealogy in mind, then, that we have set out here to recover and restore the Hispanic literary heritage of the United States.

The Hispanic presence in what is now the United States dates to 1513, a fact that largely has been overlooked and is only now being better understood. Well over a century before Jamestown was founded in 1607 and before the 1620 landing of the Pilgrims at Plymouth, Spain's citizens had explored Florida by 1513, beheld the majesty of the Grand Canyon in Arizona by 1540, sailed into San Diego Bay in California by 1542, and established outposts in the Kingdom of New Mexico by 1598. From primitive huts first constructed on the island of Española (Santo Domingo) beginning in 1508, Spanish explorers left for Puerto Rico, Cuba, Jamaica, Florida, and then for Mexico and New Mexico until each were conquered, Christianized and colonized. At the beginning of the eighteenth century, Texas and Arizona, and much later in the century California, were settled in similar fashion. In each of these regions, Spanish culture and institutions were firmly established.

Over time, distinct regional subcultures developed that eventually produced the differentiation of regions into the states and nation-states of Spanish America.

The Spanish *conquistadores* who settled the Americas were largely young and single men. Some brought their families, but the majority did not. And as those who came alone cast their own fate with that of their budding colony, they took American Indian and African slave women as lovers, concubines and occasionally as legal brides. It did not take long for a cultural *mestizaje* (mixing) to develop, a syncretic culture created through biological, linguistic and social mixing.

A Spaniard and an Indian produced a *mestizo*; a Spaniard and a mestizo engendered a *castizo* (good breed); a Spaniard and a black begot a *mulato* (dark half-breed), and so on, stated the Régimen de Castas (Regulation of Breeds), the legal code that measured one's genealogical proximity to those that were stigmatized by conquest and forced into subjugation and toil. In the eighteenth century, Spanish colonial America was sharply differentiated according to these racial and legal color categories. One's social class and position in the division of labor was easily and quite visibly assessed by one's physical color. This consciousness of color—what some scholars have called Spanish America's "pigmentocracy"—is one of the enduring lamentable legacies of Spain's conquest of America's native peoples.

Despite the cultural hybridity that evolved in each of Spain's American possessions, her colonials persistently maintained that they were *españoles* or Spaniards. Some, like the *criollos*, even proclaimed that their blood was pure and aristocratic. But these were largely cultural fictions used to create social boundaries and hierarchies of prestige. For by calling themselves *españoles* the colonists sharply differentiated themselves as overlords from *indios* and African slaves they subjugated and forced to toil, and from the mixed progeny they begot, be it on the islands of Cuba and Puerto Rico, in Florida's swampy marshes or in the desiccated deserts of Arizona, California and New Mexico.

The Spanish ideology of racial superiority was given expression in the Spanish narratives of conquest that described the military feats of the *españoles* in every corner of the hemisphere, in the ecclesiastical visitations (*visitas*) of the empire's center and margins, and in the personal writings of settlers from Cuba to California. And whether it was in the eighteenth century, the nineteenth, or our own, issues of race and color remained central preoccupations in the literary imaginations of writers who first identified as Spaniards, and only later called themselves Mexicans, Mexican-Americans, Chicanos, Latinos, Puerto Ricans, Nuyoricans and Cubans.

By the mid-eighteenth century as well, there developed in the Spanish communities of what is now the United States, a strong consciousness of place, a *consciencia de sí*, and an identification with the *patria chica*, or the "small fatherland." Residents in Spain's various kingdoms long had thought of themselves as Castilians, as Catalans, as Leonese and as Galicians. But as the various kingdoms of the Iberian peninsula were forged into the modern nation-state of Spain after 1492, loyalty to the region was partially supplanted by loyalty to the nation. The amalgamation in the Americas of persons from Spain's various regions truly gave meaning to the word "Spaniards." It was only after several centuries of relatively autonomous development and through intermixing with Native Americans and black slaves that loyalty as Spaniards dissipated and regional identities were reborn and invigorated anew.

By the early 1800s one sees the Tejanos proclaiming their uniqueness. The Californios reveling about their pastoral ways. The Tucsonenses (residents of Tucson, then Arizona's major settlement) describing the aridity of their terrain. The Nuevo Mexicanos celebrating their long residence in America and the very distinct regional culture they had created. In the Caribbean, too, the residents of Havana became known as *habaneros* and residents of Cuba's Oriente province called themselves *orientales*. In Puerto Rico, identity increasingly became tied to one's city as residents of Ponce called themselves *ponceños*.

Ultimately, Spain's colonial empire in the American hemisphere came to an end. Between 1810 and 1821, most of Spanish America, save Puerto Rico, the Dominican Republic and Cuba, gained its independence. Where once loyal Spanish subjects had offered fealty to their monarch, now Mexican, Peruvian and Argentine citizens pledged allegiance to independent republics. In 1848 one-third of Mexico's national territory was taken by the United States of America at the end of the U.S.-Mexican War—as the spoil of Manifest Destiny. And as the global empire of the United States expanded, by 1898, so too Cuba, the Dominican Republic and Puerto Rico became independent of Spain, but firmly planted under the umbrage of the United States.

The various regional wars of independence against Spain, and the wars of resistance against territorial annexation by the United States gave literary voice to numerous men and women. In ruminations, encoded as narratives, poems, novels, essays, memoirs and folk songs, they asserted their right to autonomy, decried the tyranny of domination, and waxed nostalgically about the way things used to be. In many of their mental and verbal utterances committed to paper and some to print they resisted the discourses and textual politics of political conquest that aimed to silence them and, if not that, to subordinate their voices.

From the streets of New York City to those of Tampa and Key West, exiled Cubans dreamed and plotted of a return to an independent Cuba free of tyranny. Many putschist, revolutionary and filibustering tracts for the retaking of Mexican, Puerto Rican and Latin American territory were written by Hispanic exiles in the United States. Many tearful letters of hardships and just as many of joy and plenty filled the mail bags to Havana, to Guadalajara and to San Juan as Cuban, Mexican and Puerto Rican immigrants described what they had found in the United States. Some, particularly the political refugees, eventually returned to their homelands, but many more stayed, creating homes in the United States. It was in this process of sinking roots and of fashioning a hybrid culture that was particularly attuned to issues of power that the Hispanic literary consciousness of Cubans, Puerto Ricans, Central Americans, Mexicans, South Americans and Chicanos living in the United States was born.

The long forgotten editorials these men and women wrote, their manifestoes for better wages and better working conditions, their private thoughts and emotions committed to diaries, their moral tales disguised as comedies and farces, their tersely measured lyrical poems, and their pauses and silences in the textual record are the collective object of our study. Our endeavor is recuperative; our project is restorative. Our mission and goal is nothing less than to recover the Hispanic literary heritage of the United States, to document its regional and national diversity, to view from various perspectives and angles the matrix of power in which it was created, and to celebrate its hybridity, its intertextuality and its polyvocality.

The essays in this volume all address these central issues in various ways and from numerous perspectives. Part I of this anthology offers a set of essays outlining the literary histories of Hispanic literatures in the United States which, as a group, overturn the all too pervasive notion that Hispanic literary production is a recent phenomenon. Raymund Paredes' essay provides a broad overview of the formation of Mexican American literature from the mid-nineteenth century through the more contemporary period. His work shows that indeed our literary production has a complex and dialectical richness, with regional, class and gender distinctions that should not be overlooked. "Cuban literature, Cuban exile literature, Cuban American literature: where does one end and the other begin?" Rodolfo Cortina poses a crucial question for the study of a literature that has sustained dual citizenship between Cuba, for which the imagination always longs, and the United States, where Cubans have resettled for well over a century. Cortina, however, refuses to anguish over the question and instead presents a bibliographically rich essay surveying the literary production of Cubans in the United States from the 1820s when the first Cuban American newspapers appeared in Philadelphia, New York, and New Orleans. The question with which Cortina opens his essays appear especially pertinent for such writers as José Martí who was, according to Cortina, "a Cuban writer, an exile writer, but also a Cuban American writer. There is no law that forbids literary historians from including the same figure in several categories ... when the author lives a transnational reality."

Juan Flores' essay also opens with a question, but for Flores a question that speaks to the general American ignorance: "Can anyone name the great Puerto Rican novel?" Flores argues that among the "ethnic" and "minority" literatures of the United States, "Puerto Rican literature has drawn the least critical interest and the fewest readers." Flores's essay opens the rich terrain of Puerto Rican writings that begins with late nineteenth-century anti-Spanish exile poetry, personal narratives, diaries and letters, and, "the popular songs of the migration, the hundreds of *boleros*, *plenas* and examples of *jíbaro* or peasant music dealing with Puerto Rican life in the United States." Flores proposes that this literature is one "of straddling, a literature operative within and between two national literatures and marginal to both."

Part II explores the history of various Hispanic regional communities in the United States through their literary production. In "Truth-Telling Tongues," Luis Leal surveys the "uninterrupted tradition" of bilingual poetry that dates all the way back to the early Spanish colonial period in Mexico, where Nahuatl and Spanish were used interchangeably in various works. After 1848, Mexican and Mexican American poets incorporated English into their work, not as a sign of their acceptance of a new social order, but as a form of resistance to strange looking and strange sounding foreigners and as a critique of the social and linguistic accommodations some *mexicanos* made to Americans. In his essay Nicolás Kanellos reconstructs the history of Hispanic newspapers in the United States. He explores the roles these newpapers played in providing basic information, contesting misinformation, helping to preserve cultural identity through the use of the Spanish language, educating local communities on world affairs, and sometimes serving as publishing houses for aspiring writers. Kanellos argues that, while Hispanic newpapers in the Southwestern part of the United States were primarily involved in the defense of their communities against Anglo domination, newpapers in the Northeast that served Cuban and Puerto Rican communities were more involved in protecting civil rights so that the Hispanic immigrants in this century could pursue the American Dream, just as had European immigrants before them.

The long forgotten and recently discovered works of several nineteenth-century New Mexican writers is the topic of Erlinda Gonzales-Berry's essay. The literary works of these authors deserve sustained attention, she argues, because of the sense of displacement, grief and disillusion that permeates their poetry and novels. In the works of Vicente Bernal, for example, one detects his psychological ambivalence over assimilation and acculturation as a recent colonial subject of the United States. In his essay, Genaro Padilla also takes up the larger issue of displacement through an analysis of the major autobiographical texts produced in the Southwest in the decades after the end of the U.S.-Mexico War in 1848. Here Padilla not only chronicles a long historical tradition of autobiographical expression, but he also focuses our attention on the textual articulation of a contestatory Mexican-American culture that emphasizes resistance, both open and covert, to Anglo-American domination. Finally, Edna Acosta-Belén chronicles the history of Puerto Rican writers and activists in New York City between 1890 and 1950. She focuses on the publishing enterprises of Bernardo Vega and Jesús Colón, but also on lesser known feminists writers, poets and playwrights. Here is a rich and varied history of a community that previously was dismissed as monolithic and uninteresting.

In Part III, the question of canon formation and the socio-literary implications of this recovery project for future scholars is discussed in essays situated within the larger debate on the canon and but finely focused on issues local and specific to Hispanic literary production. In "Some Considerations on Genres and Chronology for Nineteenth-Century Hispanic Literature," Chuck Tatum notes that the project for recovering Hispanic literature of the United States is "at once exciting and daunting." Exciting because we are shaping "an intellectual enterprise of great magnitude," daunting because we will be "defining and delimiting" an entire body of literature. Tatum suggests that, if anything, we "should err on the side of openness" in our recovery of literary material, and that our interpretation should recognize the diversity of material, regional and socio-historical experiences.

In "Canon Formation and Chicano Literature," María Herrera-Sobek cautions that in establishing a new literary canon we be "as inclusive as possible and keep an open policy with respect to the publication of materials from the colonial period to the present." Herrera-Sobek ties issues of canon formation in Chicano literature to larger debates about the ideologies underlying canon formation in Western Europe and the United States, reminding us that aesthetic purity alone does not account for established literary hierarchies. Western canon formation has been "inextricably linked to nationalistic concerns." In a similar fashion, Chicanos and Chicanas likewise must be free to "insist on the specificity and socio-historical context of our literature."

In "Reconstructing a Literary Past," Francisco Lomelí challenges the ethnocentric assumption of American literary historians who have ignored, or dismissed, the historically continuous Mexican-American literary tradition, either because it was written in Spanish or, worse, because Americans casually regarded their cultural production as superior. Lomelí argues that a literary discourse of the Spanish Colonial and Mexican period must be recovered: Gaspar Pérez de Villagrá's epic of 1610, *La Historia de La Nueva México*, and the work of late nineteenth-century *sociedades literarias*, as well as numerous other literary documents must no longer be ignored. In "Nationalism and Literary Production," Ramón Gutiérrez explores the history of Hispanic textual production in the United States and focuses on two periods of literary nationalism, 1898 to 1945 and 1967 to 1991. He argues that the first period was marked by state nationalism from above, as Spain tried to rehabilitate its former empire textually. Gutiérrez then looks at Chicano ethnic nationalism in the late 1960s, showing the textual politics of this nationalism from below.

Part IV of this collection is intended to introduce both the expert and the neophyte to the numerous sources that are available to chronicle the literary imagination of Hispanics in the United States. José Fernández examines the vast array of documents—*relaciones, testimonios, visitas, derroteros, causas, expedientes*—that were produced by Spaniards in what is now the United States as part of this country's early Hispanic literary heritage. Fernández lists those texts that have the greatest literary value and that most contribute to our understanding of the history of Hispanics in the United States. Antonia Castañeda, in her essay "Historical Documents as Literary Text," questions that strict definition of genres that has dominated literary histories. She argues here that when dealing with subordinated groups, such as women—the same would also hold for American Indian groups and members of ethnic and racial minorities—that we must seek other sources to obtain authentic voices from the past. Using civil and ecclesiastical court dockets, Castañeda shows the richness of these for recovering aspects of female personal and public life. Rosaura Sánchez's essay explores the history and textual production of the Californio narratives that were collected by Hubert H. Bancroft and his editorial assistants at the end of the nineteenth century. These narratives tell the story of the Californios' territorialization and their bitter dispossession in the decades following the end of the U.S.-Mexican War in 1848. Sánchez argues that these texts are rich literary documents, which are always dialogic and double-voiced, recording the thoughts of the informant as transcribed by interviewers, and at times also heteroglossic, revealing several layers of editing, translating and correcting. Clara Lomas documents the existence of several feminist newpapers in Mexico during the period of revolutionary upheaval, 1910-1917. Lomas demonstrates that these newpapers, edited largely by women, often gave radically different accounts of the revolution. Writers for these feminist newspapers constantly challenged patriarchal rule, questioned the strict gender division of space between the household and politics, and offered visions of female emancipation. And finally, the essay by Ramón Gutiérrez describes a massive bibliography project on Mexican American literary culture in the United States that was conducted by UCLA Professor Raymond Paredes.

All these essays chronicle how we have imagined and studied the Hispanic literary past. They challenge us to critically examine anew issues of nomenclature, periodization, genres, the politics of textual production and reproduction, the primacy of written over oral forms of literature and, most importantly, the silence and resistance of female and subaltern voices.

PART I

The History of Hispanic Literature in the United States

Mexican-American Literature: An Overview

Raymund A. Paredes

Mexican-American literature began to exhibit a distinctive character in the last third of the nineteenth century, a generation after the Treaty of Guadalupe Hidalgo ended the Mexican War and transformed over 80,000 Mexicans into residents of the United States. Before this time, Mexican-American culture, including literature, was indistinguishable from that of Mexico: rooted in Spanish colonialism, formed and expressed in Spanish and faithful, more or less, to Catholicism. Certainly, the great distance from the Mexican heartland of Texas, New Mexico, California and the other northern provinces ceded to the United States in the Guadalupe Hidalgo Treaty of 1848 had always stimulated some slight degree of cultural particularity but, for the most part, the institutions of Mexican Americans, for some time after the Treaty, were the institutions of Mexico. However, the planting of *yanqui* capitalism, political practices, education and religion gradually transformed the lives and traditions of Mexican Americans. By the 1860s, there were signs here and there across the Southwest that Mexican Americans were wrestling with questions of identity, gauging their position in that uneasy space that marked the intersection of the cultures of Mexico and the United States.

Mexican-American literature took shape in the context of a hybrid (Spanish, Mexican, Indian and Anglo[1]) frontier environment marked by episodes of intense cultural conflict. When a peculiar Mexican-American literary tradition began to emerge, it followed a course of development common among frontier or border cultures. Historical and personal narratives predominated: the first to preserve the memory of momentous and frequently heroic events, the second to locate one's participation within these experiences. Poetry, usually of the occasional and ephemeral variety, was also widely produced. Indeed the inundated editor of *La Aurora* in Santa Fe, one of dozens of Spanish-language newspapers in the Southwest that published literary items, in 1884 wrote a piece entitled "Remedies for Versemania" (Meyer 267). Clearly, Mexican Americans had much to say about their changing circumstances.

In the narratives and poems produced by Mexican Americans whose lives and fortunes had been directly diminished by growing Anglo domination, a note of bitterness and defiance is unmistakable. Mariano Vallejo, the patriarch of one of the great *californio* clans, composed his memoirs at monumental length to demonstrate that his people "were not indigents or a band of beasts." Vallejo's resentment of the *yanqui* conquest of California was virtually boundless, a disposition shared by his literary counterparts in New Mexico and Texas, the other regions where substantial Mexican-American communities were best established. Resentment was particularly high among those Mexican Americans who, like Vallejo, had at some point supported the Anglo presence in their homelands, only to be betrayed. For example, Juan Seguín related in his "Personal Memoirs" how he had participated in the movement for Texas independence, become mayor of San Antonio and then found himself cast into poverty and political oblivion by Anglo malefactors. In his "Memoirs" (completed in 1912 but not published until 1986), Rafael Chacón blamed Anglos for the corruption of New Mexican culture, a tragedy that unfolded before him as a young man in Santa Fe. In several of the key early Mexican-American narratives, we find a pattern that Frantz Fanon would have instantly recognized: the anger and humiliation of writers who had been duped into becoming agents of destruction within their own cultures, not understanding their complicity until their communities were degraded and all but powerless.

As for fiction, the first generations of Mexican Americans produced relatively little, especially in sustained forms such as the novel. Fictional sketches regularly appeared in the literary sections of newspapers, often as personalized versions of folktales and legends. Not surprisingly, the particular economic and cultural circumstances of the nineteenth-century Southwest were not conducive to the production of novels. Certainly, most residents lacked the luxury of time necessary for the writing of long fiction. Furthermore, the Mexican-American communities of the Southwest generally lacked both the resources necessary to print and distribute books as well as the audience base of a literate bourgeoisie. Consequently, at this early point in the investigation of nineteenth-century Mexican-American literary culture, only a handful of novels have come to light. From New Mexico, we know of several unpublished works written in the period 1880–1900 by Manuel Salazar and Manuel C. de Baca (Lomelí). In the same region, Eusebio Chacón, a prominent lawyer, community leader and essayist, actually brought out two novels in 1892: *El hijo de la tempestad* (The Son of the Storm) and *Tras la tormenta la calma* (The Calm After the Storm). What is most notable about these works is Chacón's self-consciousness in try-

El Hijo DE LA Tempestad

Tras la Tormenta la Calma.

DOS NOVELITAS ORIGINALES

Escritas por

Don Eusebio Chacon.

Edicion Limitada.

TIPOGRAFIA DE "EL BOLETIN POPULAR."

SANTA FÉ, N. M.

1892

Title page of *El Hijo de la Tempestad* by Eusebio Chacón (Special Collections, General Library, University of New Mexico).

ing to establish a distinctly Mexican-American mode of expression whose dominant characteristic would seem to be the rejection of Anglo influences. On the other hand, as Francisco Lomelí has pointed out, Chacón's novels are consistent with prevailing literary styles in Mexico and other parts of the Spanish-speaking world. Ultimately, Chacón achieved less than he had hoped for in terms of originality of theme and execution; what is perhaps most important about Chacón is his belief that distinctive Mexican-American experience required distinctive literary tools.

As the examples of "versemania" in Santa Fe and the novels of Eusebio Chacón indicate, New Mexico, of all the southwestern regions, seems to have had the most highly developed and active Mexican-American literary tradition in the nineteenth century. Unlike California and Texas, where Anglo fortune hunters and settlers quickly superseded the established Mexican-American populations, New Mexico was the site of stable and numerically-dominant Mexican-American communities. Landlocked, arid, mountainous and often brutally hot, New Mexico attracted far fewer Anglos than either California or Texas. In California, where the population surge caused by the gold rush virtually overwhelmed many Mexican-American communities, literary development was severely disrupted, leaving the field to the likes of Bret Harte, John Rollin Ridge, Helen Hunt Jackson and Gertrude Atherton to manufacture what Leonard Pitt has called the "fantasy heritage" of the state. In Texas, where enmity between Anglos and Mexican Americans was probably most intense, dating back to the Texas war for independence of 1835–1836 and the famous battles at the Alamo and San Jacinto, Mexican Americans developed a vigorous expressive tradition but not generally of a belletristic nature. The relatively late and gradual Anglo penetration of New Mexico allowed Mexican-American culture there to develop in a more measured, relatively less embattled manner.

The conventional American depictions of the Mexican-American Southwest in the nineteenth century invariably have emphasized its alleged backwardness and remoteness. American travelers of the period and American historians since have generally created an image of "sleepy," quaint villages both isolated from and indifferent to significant cultural activity. In fact, more recent scholarship has shown that Mexican-American communities were lively places, curious about the world around them and rather well connected to it. Several towns boasted literary clubs which sometimes issued an occasional journal of members' stories and poems. Traders, who moved actively to southwestern towns from cities in Mexico such as Durango and even Mexico City and from cities in the United States such as St. Louis and New Orleans, provided a steady stream of news about culture and politics. Theatre troupes and other cultural performers, again from both Mexico and the United States, traveled throughout the Southwest. Spanish-language newspapers reported not only on political events, locally and beyond, but provided information on culture and the arts. Through their newspapers, Mexican Americans sampled the romanticism of the Spaniard Gustavo Bécquer, the *modernismo* of the Mexican Manuel Gutiérrez Nájera and, in translation, the "local color" of the American Mark Twain.

Despite their frequent familiarity with contemporary belletristic trends, most early Mexican-American writers, including Eusebio Chacón, relied heavily on folkloric motifs and paradigms as the basic components of their work. Indeed, despite the abundance of conventional literary activity in Mexican-American communities during the last third of the nineteenth century, oral expression was still more significant. While the presence of the many Spanish-language newspapers in the region suggests that conventional estimates of literacy among Mexican Americans have been low, there is no doubt that both illiteracy and semi-literacy—often maintained through deliberate political and economic policy—were widespread; hence the preponderance of expression not in written but in oral forms such as the folktale, folk drama, legend and, most notably, the *corrido*.

A ballad form that evolved in Mexico, the *corrido* was widely embraced by Mexican Americans as the expressive instrument most suited to their particular circumstances. Like ballads from other countries, the *corrido*— in effect, a legend or a narrative poem set to music—flourished amid cultural conflict. As greater numbers of Anglos settled in the Southwest and antagonism between them and Mexican Americans increased, hundreds of *corridos* emerged in Mexican-American communities to constitute a literary/musical chronicle of their experiences.

By far the most fertile ground for *corridos* was the Rio Grande valley of south Texas. As early as the 1850s, *corridos* were composed, usually anonymously, to celebrate those border Mexicans from either side of the Rio Grande who resisted Anglo injustice. One of the classic Mexican-American *corridos* is "Gregorio Cortez," which treats a Mexican-born *vaquero* who kills a Texas sheriff for shooting his brother. The many variants of the Cortez *corrido*—still well known in Mexican-American communities eighty odd years after their initial appearance—represent a kind of epic that brings together many of the key themes of contemporary Mexican-American writing: ethnic pride, a forceful rejection of unflattering Anglo stereotypes and, through the celebration of Cortez's marvelous *vaquero* skills, an affirmation of the Mexican American's rootedness in the Southwest (A. Paredes). The Cortez and similar ballads remind their listeners that much that is admired in this country about the values of the cowboy and of the frontier is of Mexican origin. And because they are composed and sung in Spanish, a language with a longer history in North America than English, the ballads underscore the importance of Spanish in preserving a distinct Mexican-American identity.

Despite periods of relative decline, the *corrido* has endured as one of the key forms of Mexican-American expression. During World War II, Mexican-American soldiers composed *corridos* about MacArthur's campaign in the Pacific. In the 1960s, farm workers celebrated César Chávez and the farm workers' movement with a series of ballads. The *corrido* tradition still lives to commemorate important events and individuals. In the 1980s, for example, *corridos* lamenting the massacre of patrons (some of them Mexican American) at a McDonald's restaurant on the border near San Diego circulated in California. As an expressive tradition, *corridos* have assumed an importance in Mexican-American culture equivalent to that of the blues in African-American culture. And like the blues, *corridos* have influenced other art forms. A recent play by Luis Valdez consists of a series of dramatizations of popular ballads and is in fact entitled *Corridos*.[2]

By 1900 Mexican-American literature had emerged as a distinct part of the literary culture of the United States, especially in the Southwest where it has left an indelible imprint. Its origins were Mexican, its primary language was Spanish, and its religious sensibility was Roman Catholic. Despite its growing distinctiveness, Mexican-American writing remained largely within the orbit of Latin American letters. Given the proximity of Mexico, Mexican Americans could maintain ties to the homeland with relative ease, an advantage other ethnic minorities in the United States did not enjoy. People moved back and forth across the border frequently, invigorating both cultures. After 1910, when the Mexican Revolution and labor shortages in the United States intensified immigration, Mexican contributions to the development of Mexican-American literature increased. Julio Arce, a prominent newspaperman originally from Guadalajara, settled in San Francisco in 1915 and resumed his career as an editor and essayist. Ricardo Flores Magón, one of the leading Mexican intellectuals of the revolutionary period, fled first to San Antonio and then to Los Angeles, and in both cities became a major political and literary figure as well as the publisher of the newspaper *Regeneración*. Less prominent refugees also left their marks on the Mexican-American literary record, contributing tales of economic struggle, legends of the revolution, and *corridos* about the pain of immigration and acculturation. Once again, oral materials played a critical role in developing a literary sensibility that sought frequently to locate enduring values and nobility not in the bourgeoisie but among working people.

During the thirty years between the start of the Mexican Revolution and the coming of World War II, Mexican-American literature continued along established lines of development.[3] Historical and personal narratives, short fiction, poetry and folklore predominated, with New Mexico continuing as the center of activity. Among the most visible characteristics of New Mexican writing was a growing and exaggerated emphasis on its Spanish heritage. From 1598, when Juan de Oñate established a colony there, New Mexicans had done what they could to preserve and celebrate Spanish traditions; to a large extent, the early twentieth-century version of New Mexican Hispanicism clearly arose out of genuine ethnic and regional pride. But it also represented a calculated effort to blunt the effects of widespread Anglo resentment of Mexicans and Mexican Americans. In Anglo eyes, Spaniards were the least of Europeans, but they were considerably superior to the mongrelized, treacherous and shiftless Mexicans of American historical studies and popular fiction. Hoping to circumvent anti-Mexican sentiment, New Mexicans reinvented themselves and their history, creating their own "fantasy heritage" of virtually unadulterated Hispanicism.

At the forefront of New Mexican Hispanicism in the early twentieth century stood Aurelio M. Espinosa, a prolific folklorist who argued that New Mexican oral traditions were thoroughly Spanish, being virtually untouched by Indian, Mexican and Anglo influences. Espinosa's claims had vast implications for New Mexican culture in general, but they spoke with special force to writers struggling under the weight of anti-Mexican sentiment. Examples of New Mexican "Hispanic" literature include *Las primicias* (First Fruits), a collection of carefully wrought lyrical poems by Vicente J. Bernal published in 1916; *Obras* (Works), a collection of both poetry and fiction by Felipe Maximiliano Chacón issued in 1924; and *Old Spain in Our Southwest* (1936), by Nina Otero Warren. Probably the most talented champion of New Mexican Hispanicism has been Fray Angélico Chávez who, not surprisingly, has identified Spain's establishment of Catholicism as its greatest accomplishment in the state. Chávez's major works include *New Mexico Triptych* (1940), a collection of religious tales, and *Eleven Lady-Lyrics and Other Poems* (1945). In addition to promoting Hispanicism, the books by Otero Warren and Chávez signaled the appearance of a growing number of works by Mexican Americans in English, a trend of vast cultural implications.

Through World War II, Mexican-American literature generally retained several deeply romantic qualities: a love of nature and rural life; a celebration of common folk such as farmers and *vaqueros*; a nostalgic longing for an idealized past in which life was simple and unhurried and cultural traditions and values were unthreatened; and a frequently defensive dual patriotism both to the United States and to Mexico, especially during periods of political and economic turbulence. The supreme example of Mexican-American literary romanticism is Josephina Niggli's *Mexican Village* (1945), a beautifully written and immensely entertaining novel composed in ten closely

Fray Angélico Chávez (Special Collections, General Library, University of New Mexico).

related but virtually autonomous stories. *Mexican Village* focuses on the American-born Bob Webster, the illegitimate son of a Mexican mother and an Anglo father who rejects the boy because of his manifestly Mexican appearance. After a long period of wandering, Webster settles in Hidalgo, the home village in northern Mexico of the grandmother who had raised him, to satisfy a "nostalgia of the blood." Although he has never before lived in Mexico, Webster comes to feel comfortable there, connected to the culture and the people by his remembrance of his grandmother's recitation of local legends, folktales, proverbs and customs. In the end, he assumes his mother's family name, having discovered his essential and inescapable self.

Mexican Village was the first work of fiction by a Mexican American to reach a substantial Anglo audience. Recognizing the American public's meager understanding of Mexican experience, Niggli sought to convey an authentic sense of Mexican culture. An expert folklorist, she created fictional situations out of Mexican tales and legends and provided her characters with an abundance of folk wisdom. Through the extensive application of Spanish syntax and idioms, she managed to approximate the rhythms and flavor of Spanish and English. Furthermore, Niggli had a fine grasp of the ironies and contradictions of Mexican culture which she portrayed with a skill matched by only one other American writer, Katherine Anne Porter.

For all her vividness of language, her masterful appropriation of folklore and her insight on Mexican culture, Niggli's greatest accomplishment was her delineation of Bob Webster and his representative Mexican-American syncretism. On the one hand, although Webster claims Hidalgo as his home, he remains incompletely assimilated; his American qualities—his informality, egalitarianism and independence—prevent full integration. On the other hand, he is even less an American than a Mexican. His grandmother's influence and his memories of his father's bigotry have left him wary of American values and resentful of American feelings of superiority. Webster, quite simply, is an archetypal Mexican American who fashions his identity out of the materials of two cultures, intimately and sometimes painfully familiar with the defects of each. Like many contemporary fictional Mexican Americans, Webster is never totally at ease with himself and his identity, the memory of rejection in the United States and the difficult process of acceptance in Mexico remain quite vivid in his mind.

In effect, *Mexican Village* culminated a long era of Mexican-American literary romanticism that ended in the aftermath of World War II. The war thrust Mexican Americans into the national culture to an unprecedented extent. Tens of thousands of Mexican Americans either moved to large cities to take defense-related jobs or served in the armed forces. Both experiences, particularly the second, encouraged, if not assimilation, then certainly a more active presence in national affairs. Having made vital contributions to the war effort, Mexican Americans emerged from the war with heightened expectations in such areas as educational and economic opportunity. To a large extent, recent Mexican-American literature is the chronicle of a community, which despite its patriotic efforts, has continued to find itself marginalized, oppressed and ostracized. Only by turning inward, by focusing on Mexican-American communities as vigorous and self-sufficient, have Chicano writers generally found cause for celebration.[4]

A shift in the direction of Mexican-American literature was signaled in 1947 when a series of stories by Mario Suárez began to appear in the *Arizona Quarterly*. Suárez's "Chicanos"—a short way of saying *mexicanos* ([me]xicanos > shicanos > chicanos [Villanueva]), as the author himself explains—live in a Tucson barrio. At first glance, they seem to resemble the hapless *paisanos* of John Steinbeck's *Tortilla Flat*. But far from imitating Steinbeck, Suárez consciously repudiates him. His Chicanos are not at all childish and primitive stereotypes but authentic, intelligent fully-realized characters. Steinbeck's Mexicans are generally inept in the workings of American capitalism but Suárez presents a contrary view. In "Señor Garza," Suárez tells of a barber who surprisingly closes his shop on Saturdays when business is heaviest, preferring to spend time with his friends. Garza, living in American culture but not quite of it—it is significant that Garza often gets away from the barbershop by driving south across the border to Nogales—recognizes the dangers to his quality of life represented by unchecked capitalism and so determines to avoid them. Suárez ends his story with these lines: "Garza a philosopher. Owner of Garza's Barbershop. But the shop will never own Garza."

Like Josephina Niggli, Suárez used language to enormous effect. While Niggli captured the rhythms and certain idiomatic expressions of Spanish in English, Suárez, writing not about a Mexican village but a Chicano barrio, deftly employed *caló*, an argot combining Spanish and English popular among urban teenagers and which perfectly symbolizes the Chicanos' cultural position. In a story entitled "Kid Zopilote," Suárez writes of a young Chicano named Pepe García who mortifies his parents when he begins to wear zoot suits and use terms such as "watchar" and "styleacho." Pepe eventually comes to be considered a "zopilote" (buzzard) by the conservative residents of El Hoyo. Pepe, in a sense, is the urban, north-of-the-border equivalent of Niggli's Bob Webster, also neither quite Mexican nor American. What is notable about Pepe is his determination to forge his own particular identity out of the resources of two quite different and frequently conflicting cultures. In the mid-1940s, Suárez, like Niggli, understood that the Chicano was a group apart, now embarked on a bumpy road towards the delineation and articulation of a revised version of Mexican-American identity, this one urban, bilingual and profoundly influenced by American popular culture. For the likes of Pepe García, there is no "going back" to Mexico. In creating characters such as García and Garza, Suárez took up a position opposite to Niggli and across a watershed in Mexican-American literary history.

In the decade after the publication of Suárez's remarkable stories, Mexican-American literary production languished, as if to gather energy for the rapid growth just ahead. In 1959, however, another milestone was achieved with the publication of José Antonio Villarreal's *Pocho*, a work that not only stimulated a surge in Mexican-American literary activity but which helped to shape Chicano cultural debate. *Pocho* traces the experiences of a family from the time when its patriarch, Juan Rubio, quits the Mexican Revolution and settles in California to a time when he watches helplessly as American influences transform and nearly destroy his family. The focus of the novel eventually settles on Richard—Juan's only son—as he struggles to achieve an identity as an individual. Richard's development proves agonizing in part because his father wants him to remain uncompromisingly Mexican, and because American culture is so intolerant of ethnic loyalty.

Such events might seem merely trite were they not so paradigmatic. As the article-less title indicates ("pocho" refers, somewhat pejoratively, to an Americanized Mexican), Richard represents the often clumsy attempts of second-generation Mexican Americans at assimilation. His near obsession to win acceptance by the dominant culture is ultimately expressed in his decision to join the Navy at the beginning of World War II: what better proof, after all, of one's loyalty to a country than the demonstration of one's willingness to die for it. Richard's tragedy is that *Pocho* very conspicuously presents no evidence that his gesture will be regarded generously by the Anglo community.

Pocho is an assimilationist book not only in theme but in style and technique. Its language, so important a cultural indicator in Mexican-American writing, is, with scattered exceptions, standard English. Furthermore, in striking contrast, say, to the works of Chacón and Niggli, nothing about *Pocho's* structure or sensibility as a novel suggests a significant link to any literary tradition other than Anglo American.

To its Anglo readership, *Pocho* probably seemed a moving portrait of a necessary if painful process of assimilation. To a growing Mexican-American audience, however, awash in a rising tide of ethnic pride, *Pocho* was ideologically naive and tragic in a way Villarreal himself incompletely understood. More than the author intended, *Pocho* depicts a people victimized by insidious bourgeois institutions, most notably the educational system and that ostensible friend of Mexican Americans, the Catholic church. The political unsophistication of *Pocho* stimulated a widespread belief in the Chicano community of the 1960s that works of art should be instruments of political and cultural change; writers were not just artists but social activists and apostles of ethnic awareness. *Pocho*, achingly innocent about the coercive powers of American institutions, was precisely the kind of book a new generation of Mexican-American writers neither admired nor wanted to write.

Nothing exemplified the integration of literature into a program of Mexican-American cultural and political activism more than the Teatro Campesino, which was established in 1965 when Luis Valdez seized an opportunity to combine his theatrical ambitions with the goals of César Chávez's farm workers' union. Under Valdez's direction, the Teatro merged traditional Spanish and Mexican dramatic forms with contemporary agit-prop techniques to create powerful and entertaining skits in support of farm worker issues. Performed in open fields as well as university halls and theatres, the Teatro's *actos* attacked greedy farmers, dishonest labor contractors, brutal policemen and *vendidos*[5]—in short, all the enemies of the farm workers' union—with deadly wit. More than any other literary activity of the time, the Teatro Campesino demonstrated to Mexican Americans the power of art to provoke consideration of critical cultural and political issues.

Stimulated by the Teatro Campesino, Mexican-American literary activity expanded rapidly. In 1967 Quinto Sol Publications opened its doors in Berkeley for the express purpose of bringing out Mexican-American writing. Although diverse, the authors associated with Quinto Sol shared certain esthetic and ideological assumptions. They wanted to create a body of work that challenged Anglo-American stereotypes while remaining faithful to their Mexican folk and belletristic tradition; they wanted to find forms and techniques compatible with the social, political and cultural needs of their people; and they wanted, like their predecessors such as Niggli and Suárez, to depict their cultural experience in a distinctive idiom, in a vital Chicano language. In addition, they displayed a new-found pride in their Indian heritage by evoking Aztec thought and culture. The notion of *Aztlán*, the ancestral home of the Aztecs believed to be located in the American Southwest, became a controlling metaphor for many writers. *Aztlán* freed Chicanos from the onus of being recent, displaced immigrants and provided them a sense of place and continuity. With the concept of *Aztlán*, the Southwest became theirs again.

The Quinto Sol writers were experimenters, using multiple narrators, combining poetry and prose in single works, and obliterating boundaries between fiction and nonfiction. In poetry, the most interesting experimentation involved bilingualism or code-switching. The best Quinto Sol poets, such as José Montoya, blended English and Spanish, locating first in one language and then in the other the most appropriate phrase or image. Poems by Montoya such as "Pobre Viejo (Poor Old Man) Walt Whitman," "El Louie" and "La Jefita" (The Lady Boss) exemplify the leap in perceptual and esthetic power available to the bilingual poet.

Quinto Sol introduced three extraordinary writers of prose: Tomás Rivera, Rolando Hinojosa-Smith and Rudolfo Anaya. Like other writers associated with Quinto Sol, these three were animated by their ethnic sensibilities and their desire to depict vividly some essential part of Mexican-American culture. Rivera's major work is ... *y no se lo tragó la tierra* (... *And the Earth Did Not Part*), published in 1971. In a series of fourteen related stories and sketches, Rivera delineates the Mexican-American migrant farm worker's experience in a spare, detached manner reminiscent of the Mexican master Juan Rulfo. No recent Mexican-American writer has more effectively matched style and technique to subject matter. In vernacular Spanish that intentionally verges on artlessness, Rivera poignantly conveys the difficulties his characters experience in expressing themselves and in engaging ideas. His stories and sketches, shorn of explication, reflect the meagerness of the farm workers' lives. His major character is an unnamed boy who struggles through bigotry, violence and abject poverty. In some stories the boy is the narrator of the action, in others he is the subject of it. But throughout, his anonymity enhances his representativeness. Trapped, at least momentarily, at the bottom of the American social and economic hierarchy, he must learn not only self-respect and self-reliance but the larger lesson that every life is worth living well. By effacing his authorial presence as much as possible, Rivera gives his protagonist the run of his stories, allowing him a triumphant measure of free will and agency.

While Rivera's work seems rooted in the compact, harshly ironic narratives of Juan Rulfo, Rolando Hinojosa-Smith's stories draw on the *criollismo* movement of Latin America. They are steeped in the anecdotes, manners and oral traditions of a particular region; yet they are also attuned to human idiosyncrasies. They seem in fact to share an aim articulated by the Colombian master of *criollismo*, Tomás Carrasquilla: "to describe man in his milieu." Like Rivera, Hinojosa-Smith prefers to write in Spanish, to use Texas settings and to favor the sketch as a literary form. Both writers disdain authorial explication, and both eschew pronouncing moral judgment on their characters. But Hinojosa-Smith's work is distinctive from Rivera's in that its mood and language are much more buoyant and playful and it is populated by a broader range of characters, some rather well educated and others, within the context of their communities, economically secure.

Among the most prolific of contemporary Mexican-American writers, Hinojosa-Smith established the nature and trajectory of his most important fiction in his first two books: *Estampas del valle y otras obras* (Sketches of the Valley and Other Works, 1972) and *Generaciones y semblanzas* (Generations and Biographies, 1977). Although both works feature the same major characters (Rafa Buenrostro and Jehú Malacara), the true heroes in Hinojosa-Smith's fictions are the unremarkable Mexican Americans who endure hardships and transcend vicissitudes. In this way Hinojosa-Smith joins Rivera and other Chicano writers in identifying the common people as the primary guardians and bearers of culture, but without romanticizing or idealizing them. In Hinojosa-Smith's seemingly random collection of good-natured stories, the attentive reader discerns carefully-wrought depictions of cultural values, ethnic relations and economic issues of vital concern to Mexican Americans.

It is of signal importance that two of the finest Mexican-American writers to emerge in the 1970s selected Spanish as the language of their art. Although Rudolfo Anaya, the youngest of the distinguished Quinto Sol group, writes in English, he too has advanced Mexican-American literature. Of his various novels, short-story collections and plays, Anaya's best-known work remains his first novel, *Bless Me, Ultima* (1972). Set in a central New Mexico community at the end of World War II, the novel explores the transformation of rural Mexican-American culture subjected to both internal, conflicting forces and outside cultural pressures. One of the key symbolic events in *Bless Me, Ultima* is the testing of the atomic bomb in 1945 at White Sands. Without comprehending all its ramifications, Anaya's characters recognize the explosion as a sign of massive and irresistible change.

In *Bless Me, Ultima*, Anaya rejects the contrived Hispanicism of an earlier generation of New Mexico writers. Rather, he sees contemporary New Mexican culture as a complex of traditions—Spanish, Indian, Anglo— existing in a volatile confluence. For Antonio Márez, the young protagonist of the novel, the task is somehow to forge a personal identity from a bewildering array of cultural values. His tutor in this experience of self-realization is the magical Ultima, a *curandera* (healer) whose immense authority derives from her mastery of folk medicine and the oral traditions that have shaped the regional culture. Occupying a cultural position of true synthesis, she bequeaths to Antonio her store of knowledge and teaches him that possessing it fully, for him as for her, is the way of freedom. After the anxiety of Niggli's Bob Webster, Suárez's Pepe García, Villarreal's Richard Rubio and other archetypal literary Chicanos, Ultima and Antonio presented to Anaya's readers the lush possibility of moving beyond cultural schizophrenia to a condition of a fully integrated, functional and uplifting cultural identity. Anaya's achievement has been to open up the possibilities of a genuine cultural *mestizaje*.

By the mid-1970s, when the Quinto Sol house began to wane, its major objectives had been achieved. It had nurtured a group of writers who helped to determine the literary agenda for years to come. Whatever their differences of sensibility and perspective, Rivera and Hinojosa-Smith reaffirmed the importance of Spanish as a factor in cultural preservation and the need to retain, through literature or any other means, ties with Mexico and Latin America. Anaya, on the other hand, demonstrated the continuing relevance of oral traditions as a basis of sophisticated fiction. For Anaya's young readers, of whom there have been many, one of the major lessons of *Bless Me, Ultima* has been to listen carefully to the stories of their elders.

The emergence of Quinto Sol (and subsequent publishing houses devoted to Chicano and other Latino writers such as Arte Público Press and Bilingual Press) was indispensable for the development of Chicano literature because, until quite recently, most national commercial, trade and university presses have simply not been very interested in Chicano works. Regarded generally as a regional population, Mexican Americans hardly seemed to exist for major, mostly eastern publishers; on the rare occasions when they did bring out books on Chicano subjects by Chicano writers, they did so with little concern for appropriate editorial support and little understanding of effective marketing.[6] American publishing houses have been generally uninterested in Chicano works composed in Spanish and uneasy about books written bilingually and in Chicano idioms. More recently, large American publishing houses have opened their doors to Chicano and other Latino writers, largely because of two developments: the world-wide acclaim of Latin American writers such as Gabriel García Márquez and Carlos Fuentes; and the unprecedented critical and commercial success of *The Mambo Kings Play Songs of Love* (1989) by the Cuban-American writer, Oscar Hijuelos. For example, Sandra Cisneros brought out her latest collections of stories, *Woman Hollering Creek* (1991) with Random House while Guy García, author of *Skin Deep* (1988), has a novel upcoming from Simon and Schuster. Ana Castillo, a prize-winning poet, novelist and essayist, has a work in progress for W. W. Norton. On one level, these developments offer the hope that Chicano writers will be accessible to wider audiences. But the question arises regarding the sorts of compromises, linguistically, stylistically and thematically, that will be expected—or demanded—of Chicano writers. Will they be expected to write exclusively in English? Will they be asked to broaden their interests beyond Chicano issues to more "universal" topics? It will be some years before answers to these questions can be attempted but there is nothing about the recent history of the American publishing industry to suggest that there is any reason to be sanguine about the fate of Chicano literature in its hands.[7]

Whether through small presses or large, Chicano literature has grown and diversified since the Quinto Sol period. Two key works, one from the 1970s and another from the 1980s provide some measure of its political breadth. In 1973 Oscar Zeta Acosta's startling *The Revolt of the Cockroach People* appeared, only one year after his *Autobiography of a Brown Buffalo* had found a small but enthusiastic audience. Even more than the earlier work, "Cockroach People" is a novelized account of the author's experiences, this time focusing on his extraordinary adventures in Los Angeles during the heyday of Chicano militancy. Like his mentor, Hunter Thompson, Acosta was a reckless participant in the events he depicted, the more bizarre the better. Although he lived in Los Angeles only briefly, he transformed himself into the ultimate Angeleno. A former clarinetist in an Air Force band, Baptist missionary in Panama, copy editor for a San Francisco newspaper and undistinguished graduate of a night law school, Acosta arrived in the "most detestable city on earth" to leave his indelible mark. A self-styled cultural outlaw with scarcely a remnant of his Chicano heritage intact, Acosta locates the source of Los Angeles' vast squalor in its obliteration of its own Mexican heritage and its continuing oppression of Chicanos, the so-called "cockroach people." Acosta deems the city unsalvageable and punctuates his work with images of holocaust. Inevitably, Acosta abandons the city but only after participating, so he claimed, in the bombing of the Los Angeles Hall of Justice (Paredes 1984).

The absolute antithesis in every sense to *The Revolt of the Cockroach People* is Richard Rodriguez's *Hunger of Memory* (1981), probably the single work by a Chicano that has captured the greatest national attention. Rodriguez presents his autobiographical narrative as a "middle-class pastoral," erudite and self-consciously mannered, stylistically and ideologically worlds apart from the anti-intellectual, Gonzo-style polemic of Acosta. A Chicano variety of the conventional American conversion narrative, *Hunger of Memory* traces Rodriguez's growth from an unsophisticated child of working-class Mexicans to an educated, thoroughly-assimilated American bourgeoisie, more at home at a Bel Air cocktail party than at a family reunion in his parents' living room.[8] Just as Acosta acquires ethnic consciousness, Rodriguez discards his, contending that success in the United States, which he avidly pursues, requires a homogeneous public persona, in other words, totally assimilated. Along his way to this conclusion, Rodriguez attacks affirmative action and bilingual programs, two pillars of the Chicano ethnic activism he deplores.

Hunger of Memory is a milestone in Chicano writing for, whatever the merit of its ideological position, it represents a growing maturation in a literary tradition now extending across the entire political spectrum. The maturing of Chicano literature is evident as well in two other recent developments; the coming to prominence of writing by women, who often regard their feminist perspectives as closely aligned to those of other women of color; and the striking emergence of work with an explicitly homosexual stance and focus. Of course, women writers have long been prominent in Mexican-American literature—perhaps the most-broadly accomplished Mexican-American fictional work is Josephina Niggli's *Mexican Village*—but recently *Chicana* authors have had a more visible impact than ever before, often speaking directly to women about women's issues. Lorna Dee Cervantes' collection of poems, *Emplumada* (1981) is notable not only for esthetic excellence and thematic coherence but the courage to engage issues such as wife-beating and rape with brutal and eloquent authenticity. Sandra Cisneros' landmark *The House on Mango Street* (1984) treats the experiences of an adolescent Chicana with marvelous accessibility, ranging from the largely-unspoken devotion between father and daughter to the traumatic effects of an unwelcome kiss at a girl's first job.[9] A host of Chicana writers have lately zeroed in on various misogynistic institutions particularly conspicuous in—but not exclusive to—Mexican and Mexican-American cultures. Certainly, *machismo* seems all too alive and well and the patriarchal structure and practices of the Catholic Church (a favorite target of male writers as well) are also frequent sources of criticism. The plight of the Chicana laborer, often in sweatshop conditions, has been treated sensitively by Helena María Viramontes while other Chicana writers have focused on the traditionally taboo issue of female sexuality (Herrera-Sobek).

In many ways, the most powerful of contemporary Chicana writers is Cherríe Moraga, a self-described "Chicana feminist lesbian" whose poems, essays and plays have profoundly shaped Mexican-American feminism. In *Loving in the War Years* (1983), Moraga describes her troubled relationship with her remote, nervous and inarticulate father, wishing to recall him from his grave to answer for his incompetence as a parent. In "Lo que nunca pasó por sus labios" (What Never Passed Through His Lips), a wide-ranging essay that takes up nearly half the book, Moraga challenges the Mexican myth of the unreliability of women and the illusion of male superiority in both Mexican and Mexican-American cultures. Like other Chicana feminists, Moraga discredits the uncritical and naive cultural allegiance of many Mexicans and Mexican Americans; for her, there is much misogynistic cultural baggage to be discarded in a culture she broadly admires.

Perhaps because of the persistence of *machismo* and the particular pressures it brings to bear on Mexican-American men, male homosexuality, as a significant component of Chicano writing, has had a less visible impact than lesbianism. Significantly, the most prominent Mexican-American gay writer, John Rechy, has generally disassociated homosexual and Chicano themes in his work, primarily addressing the former in a series of well-known novels, especially *City Of Night* (1963), and the latter in magazine articles and essays.[10] The late Arturo Islas engaged homosexuality obliquely in *The Rain God* (1984) while Richard Rodriguez hints at the issue in *Hunger of Memory*. Michael Nava has created a gay Chicano lawyer, Henry Ríos, in his detective fiction, but in *Goldenboy* (1988), for example, Ríos inhabits the novel as a Chicano in name only; there is no significant presentation of Chicano culture and no supporting Chicano characters. Nava, it turns out, is concerned to solve a murder and to delineate the terrible impact of homophobia and the AIDS epidemic on the gay community. Male homosexuality is clearly an important component in contemporary Chicano writing but, unlike lesbianism, it awaits explicit and sustained engagement within the context of Mexican-American culture.[11]

In the last decade or so, much of the most satisfying work by Chicano writers has tended toward introspection within carefully-bounded environments rather than toward broad representational characterization and sweeping cultural perspectives. The poetry of Lorna Dee Cervantes, Omar Salinas and Gary Soto exemplify these qualities. Salinas' fierce talent is most visible in *Darkness Under the Trees/Walking Behind the Spanish* (1982), a collection of poetic responses to such varied experiences as walking in a park "to lecture sparrows" and contemplating the ghost of Emiliano Zapata. Much of Salinas' power derives from the courage and honesty with which he confronts his frail and flawed psyche. Soto is less wrenchingly intimate but in his poetry and, most recently, in his autobiographical sketches—*Living Up the Street* (1985); *Small Faces* (1986); *Lesser Evils: Ten Quartets* (1988)—he looks back to the Fresno *barrio* of his childhood to locate his formative experiences and values.

Soto's ethnic consciousness animates his work without circumscribing it (Olivares). His poetry moves easily across national boundaries, tracing lines of continuity between Mexicans and Chicanos. Although his most vivid characters are highly individualized, they identify strongly with their communities. Like Niggli, Suárez, Rivera and Hinojosa-Smith, Soto shapes his art out of ordinary materials and experiences; his best poems are often his most accessible. In the title poem from the collection, *Black Hair* (1985), Soto recalls going to a neighborhood playground to watch baseball. Though unathletic, the poet watches in admiration the exploits of one Hector Moreno until he comes to imagine himself circling the bases with Moreno, his face "flared," his hair "lifting / Beautifully, because we were coming home / to the arms of brown people." It is, of course, a fact of considerable importance that at the present moment in the development of Chicano writing, Soto writes in English and recalls growing up watching baseball.

As Soto and other contemporary Chicano writers fully appreciate, a major task—perhaps the major task—confronting them is how to maintain their cultural distinctiveness while reaching out to other communities, interacting and, inevitably, blending with one another on the basis of discovering common values and experiences among an array of differences.[12] For Chicano writers, the reasonable first step is toward the establishing of alliances with other Latino writers—Puerto Rican, Cuban American, Guatemalan American, etc.—whose own cultural backgrounds make the possibilities of cross-fertilization immensely attractive. Beyond lie other American ethnic communities, the larger national culture with a constantly-evolving mainstream and, ultimately, the rich cultures of Latin America and other parts of the world. Chicano literature has come a good distance away from the necessary stage of asserting, sometimes stridently, cultural identity and a community's right to retain it. But a defensive cultural nationalism seems less and less appropriate at this historical moment and Chicano writers, as *mestizos* themselves, are eager to participate in a program of authentic *mestizaje*, the intersection of cultures along many, evolving frontiers.

Notes

[1] The term "Anglo" is commonly used in the Southwest to refer to non-Latino Caucasians.

[2] José E. Limón, *Mexican Ballads, Chicano Poems*, makes the argument that the *corrido* is the precursor of much contemporary Mexican-American writing, especially poetry.

[3] A major event in shaping Mexican-American consciousness was the Spanish-American War of 1898. Spanish-language newspapers across the Southwest published essays, poems, even fictionalized depictions of the issues involved in the war. Many Mexican Americans regarded the war as an definitive test of their allegiances whether to a territory of similar heritage and culture circumstances or to the United States. Some writers denounced the bigotry and oppression of American society but a larger number recognized that Mexican-American linkages to the United States were by then more important, if not stronger, than ties to a besieged Spanish-American colony.

[4] From this point onward in this essay, the terms "Mexican American" and "Chicano" will be used interchangeably to reflect the growing currency the latter term acquired, especially among the young college-educated and politically active in the 1960s and 1970s.

[5] Literally "sell outs," Mexican Americans who serve Anglo-American cultural, political and economic interests rather than those of their own community, see: "Los Vendidos" in: Luis Valdez, *Luis Valdez—The Early Works*.

[6]Two notable examples of this are Richard Vasquez's *Chicano* (Garden City, NJ: Doubleday, 1970) and Edmund Villaseñor's *Macho* (New York: Bantam, 1973), both of which seemed to have been published—with similarly inane but presumably catchy titles—with no other purpose than to test the exploitability of the market for Chicano works.

[7]In noting the "recent history of American publishing," I am of course referring to its increasing takeover by multi-national and multi-industry corporations. In regard to the question of the growing influence of large publishing houses on Chicano writing, two examples are instinctive. Rolando Hinojosa-Smith, the author of the two excellent works in Spanish noted earlier in this essay, has more recently executed several projects in English and in popular genres, presumably to reach larger audiences. In neither case has Hinojosa-Smith approached the level of achievement manifested in his earlier work in Spanish. The second example is Victor Villaseñor (aka Edmond Villaseñor, the author of the lamentably-titled *Macho*) who withdrew his massive family history, *Rain of Gold*, from Putnam Berkeley Group over disagreements about the title (the publisher preferred *Rio Grande*), proposed cuts in the book's length and marketing strategy. In several conversations with me, Villaseñor complained that "The New York house didn't understand how to handle a Chicano book." *Rain of Gold* has since come out with an Arte Público Press imprint. See Martha Frase-Blunt, "A New Chapter," *Hispanic* (Sept. 1992): 30–38.

[8]I treat the issue of *Hunger of Memory* as a conversion narrative in "Autobiography and Ethnic Politics"; see also Rivera, "Richard Rodriguez's *Hunger of Memory* an Humanistic Antithesis."

[9]In a characteristic gesture, Sandra Cisneros dedicates this work "A las mujeres/To the Women."

[10]Rechy's best-known essay is the now classic treatment of the persistence of Mexican culture in the United States: "El Paso del Norte" *Evergreen Review* 2 (1958) 121–29. Rechy's fiction with homosexual themes contain Chicano characters but their ethnicity is rarely an important factor. Rechy's latest novel, *The Miraculous Day of Amalia Gomez* (1991) is the first to deal extensively with Chicano characters and themes.

[11]A recent example of a novel that treats lesbianism within Chicano culture is Terri de la Peña, *Margins* (Seattle: Seal 1992).

[12]An influential statement on cultural blending, although on a smaller scale than noted here, is Gloria Anzaldúa, *Borderlands: The New Mestiza* (San Francisco: Spinsters 1987). Anzaldúa argues for a new conception of "border" as a place where cultures converge, not where they are held apart.

Works Cited

Herrera-Sobek, María. "Introduction." *Chicana Creativity and Criticism: New Frontiers in American Literature.* Eds. María Herrera-Sobek and Helena María Viramontes. Houston: Arte Público, 1988. 9–39.

Limón, José E. *Mexican Ballads, Chicano Poems.* Berkeley: U of California P, 1992.

Lomelí, Francisco. "Eusebio Chacón: An Early Pioneer of the New Mexican Novel." *Pasó por Aquí.* Ed. Erlinda Gonzales-Berry. Albuquerque: U of New Mexico P, 1989. 149–66.

Meyer, Doris L. "Anonymous Poetry in Spanish-Language New Mexico Newspapers (1880–1900)." *Bilingual Review* 2 (1975): 259–75.

Olivares, Julián. "The Streets of Gary Soto." *Latin American Literary Review* 18 (1990): 32–49.

Paredes, Américo. *"With His Pistol in His Hand," A Border Ballad and Its Hero* [Gregorio Cortez]. Austin: U of Texas P, 1958.

Paredes, Raymund. "Autobiography and Ethnic Politics." *Multicultural Autobiography: American Lives.* Ed. James Robert Payne. Knoxville: U of Tennessee P, 1992. 280–96.

———. "Los Angeles From the Barrio." *Los Angeles in Fiction.* Ed. David Fine. Albuquerque: U of New Mexico P, 1984. 209–22.

Rivera, Tomás. "Richard Rodriguez's *Hunger of Memory* as Humanistic Antithesis." *Melus* 11.4 (1984): 5–13; rpt. *Tomás Rivera: The Complete Works.* Ed. Julián Olivares. Houston: Arte Público, 1992. 406–14.

Suárez, Mario. "Señor Garza." *Arizona Quarterly* 3 (1947): 116–21.

Villanueva, Tino, ed. "Sobre el término 'chicano.' " *Chicanos, Antología histórica y literaria.* México: Fondo de Cultura Económica, 1980. 7–34.

Puerto Rican Literature in the United States: Stages and Perspectives

Juan Flores

Can anyone name the great Puerto Rican novel? It is *La charca* by Manuel Zeno Gandía, published in 1894 and first available to American readers in English translation in 1984. The lapse, of course, is symptomatic. After nearly a century of intense economic and political association, endless official pledges of cultural kinship and the wholesale importation of nearly half the Puerto Rican people to the United States, Puerto Rican literature still draws a blank among American readers and students of literature. Major writers and authors are unknown and, with a handful of exceptions, untranslated; English-language and bilingual anthologies are few and unsystematic and there is still not a single introduction to the literature's history available in English. Even the writing of Puerto Ricans living in the Unites States, mostly in English and all expressive of life in this country, has remained marginal to any literary canon, mainstream or otherwise. Among the "ethnic" or "minority" literatures, it has probably drawn the least critical interest and the fewest readers.

Yet, as a young Puerto Rican friend once put it, "Puerto Rico is this country's 'jacket.' " In no other national history are twentieth-century American social values and priorities more visibly imprinted than in Puerto Rico's. Puerto Rico, in fact, or at least its treatment at the hands of the United States, is part of American history. Its occupation in 1898 after four centuries of Spanish colonialism, the decades of imposition of English, the unilateral decreeing of American citizenship in 1917, economic and social crisis during the Depression years, externally controlled industrialization, unprecedented migration of the work force and sterilization of the women, ecological depletion and contamination, relentless cultural saturation—all these events pertain not only to Puerto Rican historical reality but to the recent American past as well. And in no foreign national literature is this seamy, repressed side of the "American century" captured at closer range

53

than in the novels of Zeno Gandía and Enrique Laguerre, the stories of José Luis González and Pedro Juan Soto, the poetry of Luis Palés Matos and Julia de Burgos, or the plays of René Marqués and Jaime Carrero. Understandably, Puerto Rican literature in the twentieth century has been obsessed with the United States, whose presence not only lurks, allegorically, as the awesome colossus to the north but is manifest in every aspect of national life. Those intent on reworking literary curricula and boundaries would thus do well to heed this telling record of United States politics and culture as they bear on neighboring peoples and nationalities.

Closer still, of course, and more directly pertinent to a "new" American literary history, is the Puerto Rican literature produced in the United States. Not until the late 1960s, when distinctly Nuyorican voices emerged on the American literary landscape, did it occur to anyone to speak of a Puerto Rican literature emanating from life in this country. How, indeed, could such an uprooted and downtrodden community even be expected to produce a literature? Such relative newcomers, many lacking in basic literacy skills in either English or Spanish, were assumed to be still caught up in the immigrant syndrome, or worse, to be languishing in what Oscar Lewis termed the "culture of poverty." But in books like Piri Thomas' *Down These Mean Streets* and Pedro Pietri's *Puerto Rican Obituary*, there was suddenly a literature by Puerto Ricans, in English and decidedly in—and against—the American grain.

This initial impetus has since grown into a varied but coherent literary movement, and over the past decade the Nuyoricans have come to make up an identifiable current in North American literature. That this movement also retains its association to Puerto Rico's national literature and, by extension, to Latin American literary concerns is a crucial though more complex matter. In fact, it is Nuyorican literature's position straddling two national literatures and hemispheric perspectives that most significantly distinguishes it among the American minority literatures. In any case, those years of cultural and political awakening in the late 1960s generated an active literary practice among Puerto Ricans born and raised in the United States, who have managed to expound a distinctive problematic and language with a bare minimum of institutional or infrastructural support.

Critical and historical interest in this new literature has also grown. Journal articles and introductions to books and anthologies, although scattered, have helped provide some context and approaches. Along with critics like Edna Acosta-Belén, Efraín Barradas, Frances Aparicio and John Miller, Wolfgang Binder, professor of American studies at the University of Erlangen, deserves special mention. His substantial work on contemporary Puerto Rican literature is based on an ample knowledge of the material and close familiarity with many of the authors. Further study of this kind has ascertained with increasing clarity that Puerto Rican literature in the United States was not born, *sui generis*, in the late 1960s and that its scope, like that of other emerging literatures, cannot be properly accounted for if analysis is limited by the reigning norms of genre, fictionality, language or national demarcation.

In 1982 there appeared the first, and still the only, book on Puerto Rican literature in the United States, Eugene Mohr's *The Nuyorican Experience*. Mohr, professor of English at the University of Puerto Rico, offers a helpful overview of many of the works and authors and suggests some lines of historical periodization. I will therefore refer to Mohr's book, and especially to some of its omissions, in reviewing briefly the contours of Puerto Rican literature in the United States. How far back does it go, and what were the major stages leading to the present Nuyorican style and sensibility? To what extent does its very existence challenge the notion of literary and cultural canons, and how does this literature relate to other noncanonical and anti-canonical literatures in the United States?

*   *   *

The first Puerto Ricans to write about life in the United States were political exiles from the independence struggle against Spain who came to New York in the late decades of the nineteenth century to escape the clutches of the colonial authorities. Some of Puerto Rico's most prominent intellectual and revolutionary leaders, such as Eugenio María de Hostos, Ramón Emeterio Betances, Lola Rodríguez de Tío and Sotero Figueroa, spent more or less extended periods in New York, where, along with fellow exiles from Cuba, they charted further steps to free their countries from Spanish rule. The lofty ideals of "Antillean unity" found concrete expression in the establishment of the Cuban and Puerto Rican Revolutionary Party under the leadership of the eminent Cuban patriot Jose Martí. This early community was largely composed of the radical patriotic elite, but there was already a solid base of artisans and laborers who lent support to the many organizational activities. It should also be mentioned that one of these first settlers from Puerto Rico was Arturo Alfonso Schomburg, a founder of the Club Dos Antillas and, in later years, a scholar of the African experience.

The writings that give testimonial accounts and impressions of those years in New York are scattered in diaries, correspondences and the often short-lived revolutionary newspapers that still await compilation and perusal. Perhaps the most extended and revealing text to have been uncovered thus far is a personal article by the Puerto Rican poet and revolutionary

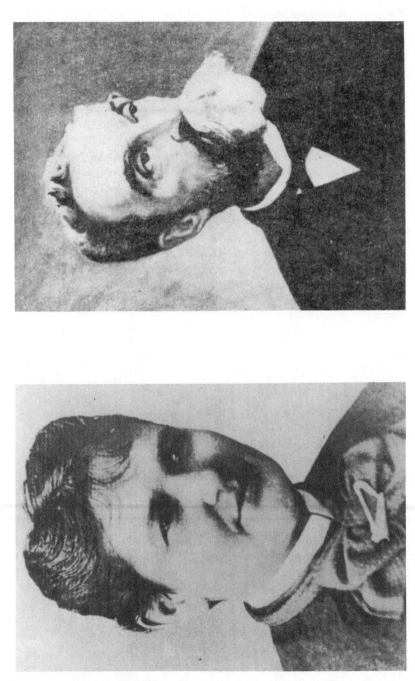

(Top) Eugenio María de Hostos. (Bottom) Lola Rodríguez de Tió.

martyr Francisco Gonzalo Marín. "Pachín" Marín, a typesetter by trade who died in combat in the mountains of Cuba, figures significantly in the history of Puerto Rican poetry because of his emphatic break with the stale, airy clichés of romantic verse and his introduction of an ironic, conversational tone and language. In "Nueva York por dentro: Una faz de su vida bohemia" (Inside New York: An Aspect of Its Bohemian Life), he offers a pointed critical reflection on New York City as experienced by the hopeful but destitute Puerto Rican immigrant.

In *The Nuyorican Experience*, Eugene Mohr makes no mention of "Pachín" Marín or of these first, nineteenth-century samples of Puerto Rican writing in New York, though the Cuban critic Emilio Jorge Rodríguez has drawn proper attention to them. The sources are of course still scarce, and that period of political exile was clearly distinct in character from the later stages, which were conditioned by the labor immigration under direct colonial supervision. Nevertheless, writings like that of "Pachín" Marín and some of the diary entries and letters of Hostos and others carry immense prognostic power in view of subsequent historical and literary developments. In a history of Puerto Rican literature in the United States they provide an invaluable antecedent perspective, a prelude of foreboding, even before the fateful events of 1898. When read along with the essays and sketches of José Martí on New York and the United States, these materials offer the earliest "inside" view of American society by Caribbean writers and intellectuals.

Mohr dates the origins of "the Nuyorican experience" from Bernardo Vega's arrival in New York in 1916, as recounted in the opening chapter of Vega's memoirs. While the *Memorias de Bernardo Vega* (Memoirs of Bernardo Vega) is a logical starting point, since it chronicles the Puerto Rican community from the earliest period, the book was actually written in the late 1940s and was not published until 1977 (an English translation appeared in 1984). Despite the book's belated appearance, though, Bernardo Vega was definitely one of the "pioneers." He and his work belong to and stand for that period from the First through the Second World War (1917–1945), which saw the growth and consolidation of the immigrant community following the Jones Act that decreed citizenship (1917), and preceding the mass migration after 1945. In contrast to the political exiles and other temporary or occasional sojourners to New York, Bernardo Vega was also, in Mohr's terms, a "proto-Nuyorican": although he eventually returned to Puerto Rico late in life (he lived there in the late 1950s and the 1960s), Vega was among the first Puerto Ricans to write about New York as one who was here to stay.

Puerto Rican literature of this first stage showed many of the signs of an immigrant literature, just as the community itself, still relatively modest

(Top) Bernardo Vega, 1948 (Courtesy of Center for Puerto Rican Studies, Hunter College, CUNY). (Bottom) Jesús Colón, ca. 1950s (Courtesy of Center for Puerto Rican Studies, Hunter College, CUNY).

in size, resembled that of earlier immigrant groups in social status, hopes for advancement and civic participation. The published writing was over-whelmingly of a journalistic and autobiographical kind: personal sketches and anecdotes, jokes and *relatos* printed in the scores of Spanish-language newspapers and magazines that cropped up and died out over the years. It is a first-person testimonial literature: the recent arrivals capturing, in the home language, the jarring changes and first adjustments as they undergo them.

Yet the analogy to the European immigrant experience was elusive even then, long before the momentous changes of mid-century made it clear that something other than upward mobility and eventual assimilation awaited Puerto Ricans on the mainland. The most important difference, which has conditioned the entire migration and settlement, is the abiding colonial re-lationship between Puerto Rico and the United States. Puerto Ricans came here as foreign nationals, a fact that American citizenship and accommoda-tionist ideology tend to obscure; but they also arrived as a subject people. The testimonial and journalistic literature of the early period illustrate that Puerto Ricans entering this country, even those most blinded by illusions of success and fortune, tended to be aware of this discrepant, disadvantageous status.

For that reason, concern for the home country and attachment to national cultural traditions remained highly active, as did the sense of particular social vulnerability in the United States. The discrimination met by the "newcomers" was compounded by racial and cultural prejudice, as the black Puerto Rican writer and political leader Jesús Colón portrays so poignantly in his book of autobiographical sketches set in those earlier decades, *A Puerto Rican in New York*. In both of these senses—the strong base in a distinct and maligned cultural heritage and the attentiveness and resistance to social inequality—Puerto Rican writing in the United States, even in this initial testimonial stage, needs to be read as a colonial literature. Its deeper problematic makes it more akin to the minority literatures of oppressed groups than to the literary practice and purposes of "ethnic" immigrants.

Another sign of this kinship, and of the direct colonial context, has to do with the boundaries of literary expression established by the norms of print culture. For in spite of the abundant periodical literature, with its wealth of narrative and poetic samples in that period and in subsequent periods of Puerto Rican immigrant life, surely the most widespread and influential form of verbal culture has been transmitted, not through publication, but through oral testimony and through the music. The work of oral historians in gathering the reminiscences of surviving "pioneers" will be indispensable in supplementing the study of printed texts. Also of foremost importance in this regard is the collection and analysis of the popular songs of the migration, the hundreds of *boleros*, *plenas*, and examples of *jíbaro* or peasant music dealing with Puerto Rican life in the United States, which enjoyed immense popularity throughout the emigrant community. Starting in the 1920s, when many folk musicians joined the migration from the Island to New York, the popular song has played a central role in the cultural life of Puerto Ricans in this country. It needs to be recognized as an integral part of the people's "literary" production. Only in recent years, and mainly in reference to the "salsa" style of the present generation, have there been any attempts to cull these sources for broader cultural and theoretical meanings (Duany). But it was in those earlier decades, when favorites like Rafael Hernández, Pedro Flores, Ramito, Mon Rivera, Cortijo, and Tito Rodríguez were in New York composing and performing songs about Puerto Rican life here, that this tradition of the popular song began.

* * *

A turning point in Puerto Rican literature, before the advent of the Nuyoricans in the late 1960s, came around 1950. This second stage covers the years 1945–65. Those two decades after World War II saw the rapid industrialization of Puerto Rico under Operation Bootstrap, and hundreds of thousands of Puerto Rican workers migrated to New York and other United States cities. This avalanche of newly arriving families, a significant part of the country's displaced agricultural proletariat, drastically changed the character of the Puerto Rican immigrant community, distancing it still further from the familiar immigrant experience. The "Puerto Rican problem" became more urgent than ever for official and mainstream America, as did the infusion of drugs, criminality and the forces of incrimination into the crowded Puerto Rican neighborhoods. It should be remembered that *West Side Story*, written and first performed in the mid-1950s, was intended to ease this explosive situation, though it actually has had the long-term effect of reinforcing some of the very stereotypes, so rampant in the dominant culture, that it sought to dispel. The same must be said of Oscar Lewis' book *La vida* and its infamous notion of the "culture of poverty."

It was in this period and because of these conditions that the migration and the emigrant community in the United States became major themes in Puerto Rican national literature. In prior decades some authors from the Island had of course shown an interest in their uprooted compatriots, setting their works in New York and choosing immigrants as their protagonists. Parts of *El negocio* (The Business) and *Los redentores* (The Redeemers), the later novels of Manuel Zeno Gandía, take place in the United States, and frequent bibliographical reference is made to still another unpublished novel by Zeno Gandía entitled *Hubo un escándalo* (There Was a Scandal) (or *En Nueva York*), though it has not yet been possible to study that manuscript. José de Diego Padró, an interesting but neglected writer active between 1910 and 1930, set much of his long bizarre novel *En Babia* (Lost in Thought) in New York, as did the dramatist Fernando Sierra Berdecía in his comedy *Esta noche juega el jóker* (Tonight the Joker Plays). But these are random and rare exceptions and still do not indicate any inclusion of the emigrant experience in the thematic preoccupations of the national literature.

By mid-century, though, accompanying the more general shift in the literature from a rural to an urban focus, the attention of Island authors turned decisively to the reality of mass migration and the emigrant barrio. Many writers, such as René Marqués, Enrique Laguerre, José Luis González, and Emilio Díaz Valcárcel, came here in those years to witness it directly, while a writer like Pedro Juan Soto, later identified more with the Island literature, actually lived through the emigration firsthand. The result was a flurry of narrative and theatrical works, all appearing in the 1950s and early 1960s, some of which still stand today as powerful fictional renditions of Puerto Rican life in the United States. In contrast to the primarily testimonial writings of the previous period, this was the first "literature," in the narrow sense, about the community here, in which imaginative invention, dramatic structure and stylistic technique are used to heighten the impact of historical and autobiographical experience.

Despite the undeniable artistic merit of some of this work—I would single out the stories of José Luis González, Soto's *Spiks*, and, for historical reasons, René Marqués' *La carreta* (The Cart)—it is also clearly a literature *about* Puerto Ricans in the United States rather than *of* that community. Mohr aptly entitles his second chapter "Views from an Island." That these are the "views" of visiting or temporary sojourners is evident in various ways but is not necessarily a detriment to their literary value. The tendency is to present the arrival and settlement experience in strict existential and instantaneous terms; instead of process and interaction, there is above all culture shock and intense personal dislocation. What these glimpses and miniatures gain in emotional intensity they often lose in their reduction of a complex, collective and unfolding reality to a snapshot of individual behavior. Another sign of the unfamiliarity and distance between the writer and the New York community is the language: though an occasional English or "Spanglish" usage appears for authenticating purposes, there is a general reliance on standard literary Spanish or, as in *La carreta*, a naturalistic transcription of Puerto Rican dialect. What is missing is any resonance of the community's own language practice, which even then, in the 1950s, was already tending toward the intricate mixing and code switching

(Top) José Luis González. (Bottom) *La carreta* playbill.

characteristic of Puerto Rican speech in the United States.

But despite such problems, these "views from an island" rightly remain some of the best-known works of Puerto Rican literature in the United States, their literary impact generally strengthened by the critical, anti-colonial standpoint of the authors. The pitiable condition of the authors' compatriots in United States cities is attributed and linked to the status of Puerto Rico as a direct colony. This perspective, and the constant focus on working-class characters, helps dispel the tone of naive optimism and accommodationism that had characterized the writings of such earlier middle-class observers of the emigrant community as Juan B. Huyke and Pedro Juan Labarthe. The writings of Soto, González and others, because of their quality and the authors' grounding in the national literature of the Island, form an important link to Latin American literature. A story like González's "La noche que volvimos a ser gente" (The Night We Became People Again) for example, is clearly a work of contemporary Latin American fiction, even though it is set in New York and its attention focuses on the subways and streets of the urban United States. The same is true of Díaz Valcárcel's novel *Harlem todos los días* (Everyday Harlem) and many more of these works.

It should be emphasized that during the 1950s there was also a "view from within" the Puerto Rican community, a far less-known literature by Puerto Ricans who had been here all along and who, lovingly or not, considered the barrio home. Here again Bernardo Vega and Jesús Colón come to mind, for although the *Memorias* and *A Puerto Rican in New York* chronicle the arrival and settlement over the decades, they were not written until the late 1940s and 1950s. There were also a number of Puerto Rican poets who had been living in New York for decades and who by the 1950s began to see themselves as a distinctive voice within the national poetry; among them were Juan Avilés, Emilio Delgado, Clemente Solo Vélez, Pedro Carrasquillo, Jorge Brandon and José Dávila Semprit. Back in the 1940s this group had included as well Puerto Rico's foremost woman poet, Julia de Burgos. What little is available of this material shows it to be largely conventional Spanish-language verse making little reference to the migration or to life in New York, much less anticipating in any way the complex bilingual situation of the generation to come. But much more of interest may still be found with further study, and it is important to refer to Pedro Carrasquillo for his popular *décimas* (ten-line stanzas) about a *jíbaro* (hillbilly) in New York, to Dávila Semprit for his forceful political poetry and to Solo Vélez and Brandon for the examples they set for many of the younger poets.

Perhaps the best example of literature from within the community at mid-century is the novel *Trópico en Manhattan* by Guillermo Cotto-Thorner. The contrast with the Island authors' treatment of the emigrant experience is striking: the shock of arrival and first transitions is extended and lent historical depth; individual traumas and tribulations are woven into a more elaborate interpersonal and social context. Most interesting of all as a sign of the author's proximity to and involvement in the community is, once again, the language. The Spanish of *Trópico en Manhattan*, especially in certain dialogue passages, is at times interspersed with bilingual neologisms of various kinds. And at the end of the book there is a lengthy glossary of what Cotto-Thorner calls "Neorkismos."

The contrast between the observers' and the participants' views in Puerto Rican literature of this period does not reflect so much the literary quality as the relation of the writers to the literature's historical development. A novel like *Trópico en Manhattan* may not surpass the stories of José Luis González and Pedro Juan Soto, but it does more extensively reveal the social contradictions internal to the community and give them a sense of epic duration and process. With regard to literary history, that relatively unknown and forgotten novel, with its early sensitivity to "Neorkismos," may more directly prefigure the voice and vantage point of the Nuyoricans than does *La carreta,* or even *Spiks*.

Another such transitional author of the period 1945–65 is Jaime Carrero, who also seeks to clarify that the "outsider-insider" contrast refers not only to place of residence but to cultural perspective. Carrero, whose bilingual poetry volume *Jet Neorriqueño: Neo-Rican Jet Liner* directly foreshadowed the onset of Nuyorican literature in New York, is from the Island, having been to New York for college and other visits. As Eugene Mohr points out, what distinguishes Carrero from those other Island-based writers is "the persistence of his interest in the *colonia* (neighborhood) and his sympathy with the Nuyorican viewpoint" (116). His attempts at bilingual verse and especially his plays, from *Pipo subway no sabe reír* (Subway Pipo Doesn't Know How to Laugh) to *El lucky seven*, give vivid literary expression to this internal, participants' perspective. Carrero has also written a novel *Raquelo tiene un mensaje* (Raquelo Has a Message) about the trauma of Nuyorican return migration to the Island, but Pedro Juan Soto's *Ardiente suelo, fría estación* (Burning Ground, Cold Season) is as yet unequaled in its treatment of that experience.

* * *

The third, Nuyorican stage in emigrant Puerto Rican literature arose with no direct reference to or evident knowledge of the writings of either earlier period. Yet despite this apparent disconnection, Nuyorican creative expression effectively draws together the firsthand testimonial stance of the "pioneer" stage and the fictional, imaginative approach of writers of the 1950s and 1960s. This combining of autobiographical and imaginative modes of community portrayal is clearest perhaps in the prose fiction: Piri Thomas' *Down These Mean Streets.* Nicholasa Mohr's *Nilda* and Edward Rivera's *Family Installments* are all closer to the testimonial novel than to any of the narrative "views from an Island."

This sense of culminating and synthesizing of the earlier phases indicates that, with the Nuyoricans, the Puerto Rican community in the United States has arrived at a modality of literary expression corresponding to its position as a non-assimilating colonial minority. The most obvious mark of this new literature emanating from the community is the language: the switch from Spanish to English and bilingual writing. This language transfer should not be mistaken for assimilation in a wide cultural sense. As the content of the literature indicates, using English is a sign of being here, not necessarily of liking it here or of belonging.

By now, the Nuyorican period of United States-based Puerto Rican literature is already unfolding a history of its own. The sensationalist tenor of the initial outburst has given way to a greater concern for the everyday lives of Puerto Rican working people. The growing diversity and sophistication of the movement is evident in the emergence of women writers, and female perspectives, as in such books as Sandra María Esteves' *Bluestown Mockingbird Mambo* and Nicholasa Mohr's *Rituals of Survival,* and in the appearance of writers in other parts of the United States. Also of key importance is the ongoing use of an actively bilingual literary field. For it becomes clear that, in the literature as in the community, the switch from Spanish to English is by no means complete or smooth, and it certainly is not a sign of cultural accommodation. For all the young writers, Spanish remains a key language-culture of reference even when not used, and some, like Tato Laviera, demonstrate full bilingual capacity in their writing. There also continues to be a Spanish-language literature by Puerto Ricans living here, some of which hovers between Nuyorican concerns and styles and those of contemporary Island literature. Such writers as Iván Silén and Victor Fragoso, like Jaime Carrero and Guillermo Cotto-Thorner before them, have served as important bridges between the two language poles of present-day Puerto Rican writing.

Thus, rather than abandoning one language in favor of another, contemporary Puerto Rican literature in the United States actually exhibits the full range of bilingual and interlingual use. Like Mexican American and other minority literatures, it cannot be understood and assessed on the basis of a strict English-language conceptualization of "American" literature, or of literary practice in general. Some of the best Nuyorican texts require knowledge of Spanish and English, which does not make them any less a part of

American, or Puerto Rican, literature. And the choice and inclusiveness of a literary language is but one aspect of a broader process of cultural interaction between Puerto Ricans and the various nationalities they encounter in the United States.

By its Nuyorican stage, Puerto Rican literature in the United States comes to share the features of "minority" or noncanonical literatures of the United States. Like them, it is a literature of recovery and collective affirmation, and it is a literature of "mingling and sharing," of interaction and exchange with neighboring, complementary cultures (Gelfant). What stronger source, after all, for the emergence of Nuyorican literature than Afro-American literature and political culture? What more comparable a context of literary expression than Chicano writing of the same period?

Perhaps most distinctly among these literatures, though, Puerto Rican writing today is a literature of straddling, a literature operative within and between two national literatures and marginal in both. In this respect Nuyorican writing may well come to serve as a model or paradigm for emerging literatures by other Caribbean groups in the United States, such as Dominicans, Haitians and Jamaicans. Despite the sharp disconnections between Island- and United States-based traditions, and between stages of the literary history here, it is still necessary to talk about modern Puerto Rican literature as a whole and of the emigrant literature—including the Nuyorican—as an extension or manifestation of that national literature. This inclusion within, or integral association with, a different and in some ways opposing national culture stretches the notion of a pluralist American canon to the limit. Ethnic, religious and racial diversity is one thing, but a plurality of nations and national languages within the American canon–that is a different and more serious issue. After all, if Tato Laviera and Nicholasa Mohr are eligible for canonical status, why not José Luis González or Julia de Burgos, or, for that matter, Manuel Zeno Gandía, the author of the great Puerto Rican novel *La charca*?

Yes, what about *La charca*? It's a fine novel; in fact, if it had been written by an author from a "big" country, say France or Russia, or even Argentina or Mexico, it would probably be more widely admired and even held up as an example of late nineteenth-century realism. It was published in 1894, before the United States acquired the Island, and its plot is set several decades earlier, long before any significant relations had developed between the two countries. And yet, though it does not mention or refer to the United States, *La charca* is still, somehow, about America, a literary pre-sentiment of what contact with North American society had in store for Puerto Rico. The isolated mountain coffee plantation issues into the wider world of commerce and international dealings, represented in Puerto

Rican history, and in Zeno Gandía's later novels, by the United States. Like Jose Martí, "Pachín" Marín and other Latin American intellectuals of the time, Zeno Gandía anticipated the coming of the Unites States' values and power. Even at such a remove, with America's presence still but a metaphor, *La charca* touches the American canon and contributes impressively to the larger task of American literature.

Works Cited

Binder, Wolfgang. *"Anglos are weird people for me": Interviews with Chicanos and Puerto Ricans.* Berlin: John F. Kennedy Institut für Nordamerikastudien at Freie Universität, 1979.

──────. *Puerto Ricaner in New York: Volk Zwischen Zwei Kulturen.* Erlangen: Städtische Galerie, 1978.

Carrero, Jaime. *Jet neorriqueño: Neo-Rican Jet Liner.* San Germán: Universidad Interamericana, 1964.

──────. *Pipo subway no sabe reír.* Río Piedras: Puerto, 1973.

──────. *Raquelo tiene un mensaje.* San Juan: Manuel Pareja, 1970.

Colón, Jesús. *A Puerto Rican in New York and Other Sketches.* New York: Mainstream, 1961.

Cotto-Thorner, Guillermo. *Trópico en Manhattan.* San Juan: Cordillera, 1960.

Díaz Valcárcel, Emilio. *Harlem todos los días.* México: Nueva Imagen, 1978.

Duany, Jorge. "Popular Music in Puerto Rico: Toward an Anthropology of Salsa." *Latin American Music Review* 5.2 (1984): 186–216.

Esteves, Sandra María. *Yerba Buena.* Greenfield: Greenfield Review, 1980.

Gelfant, Blanche H. "Mingling and Sharing in American Literature: Teaching Ethnic Fiction." *College English* 43 (1981): 763–72.

González, José Luis. "La noche que volvimos a ser gente." *Mambrú se fue a la guerra.* México: Joaquín Mortiz, 1972. 117–34.

Lewis, Oscar. *La vida: A Puerto Rican Family in the Culture of Poverty.* New York: Random, 1965.

Marín, Pachín. "Nueva York por dentro: Una faz de su vida bohemia." *La gaceta del pueblo* (1892).

Mohr, Eugene. *The Nuyorican Experience: Literature of the Puerto Rican Minority.* Westport: Greenwood, 1982.

Mohr, Nicholasa. *Nilda,* New York: Harper, 1973.

──────. *Rituals of Survival: A Woman's Portfolio.* Houston: Arte Público, 1985.

Padró, José de Diego. *En Babia.* México: El Manuscrito de un Braquicéfalo, 1961.

Pietri, Pedro. *Puerto Rican Obituary.* New York: Monthly Review, 1973.

Rivera, Edward. *Family Installments.* New York: Penguin, 1983.

Rodríguez, Emilio Jorge. "Apuntes sobre la visión del emigrante en la narrativa puertorriqueña." *Primer seminario sobre la situación de las comunidades negra, chicana, cubana, india y puertorriqueña en Estados Unidos.* Havana: Política, 1984. 445–85.

Sierra Berdecía, Fernando. *Esta noche juega el jóker.* San Juan: Biblioteca de Autores Puertorriqueños, 1939 and San Juan: Instituto de Cultura Puertorriqueña, 1960.

Thomas, Piri. *Down These Mean Streets*. New York: Knopf, 1967.

Vega, Bernardo. *Memoirs of Bernardo Vega*. Ed. César Andreu Iglesias. Trans. Juan Flores. New York: Monthly Review, 1984.

Zeno Gandía, Manuel. *La charca*. Trans. Kal Wagenheim. Maplewood: Waterfront, 1984.

_____ . *El negocio*. Río Piedras: Edil, 1973.

_____ . *Los redentores*. *Obras completas*. Vol. 2. Río Piedras: Instituto de Cultura Puertorriqueña, 1973.

Cuban Literature of the United States: 1824–1959

Rodolfo J. Cortina

I. Introduction

Cuban literature, Cuban exile literature, Cuban-American literature: where does one end and the other begin? It is in the midst of these thorny questions that the issue of definitions arises. In the case of other United States Hispanic literatures, such as that of Mexican, Mexican-American and Chicano literature, the demarcations are more clearly observed, although there were moments when these delineations became less precise. This is especially the case with regard to Mexican literature when, as Luis Leal notes in his periodization of Chicano literature (1973), it entered the United States as an exile literature. Traditionally, Cuban literature has been written both on the island and abroad. The cases of Heredia, Avellaneda, Casals, Merlín, Martí, Florit, Carpentier, Sarduy, Arenas are but a few examples of this phenomenon. So Cuban literature of the United States may appear as a contradiction in terms because Cuba, despite its many problems of sovereignty, is an island nation, and American literature has not traditionally included literature by and about Hispanics, especially when written in Spanish. But there have been Cuban refugees living in the United States since the late eighteenth century, their exile the result of many different immigrations due to political circumstances on the island—from the time that it was still a colony of Spain, aspiring to the independent status of nation-state, to this day when Cubans leave the island for the United States. The literature produced by these expatriated Cubans constitutes, therefore, a literary corpus that could be easily labelled Cuban exile literature. Likewise, when the political cause of the exiles finally triumphs or fails completely—as was the case of abolitionist literature in the former or annexationist literature in the latter—the literary corpus produced by this cause may end up as Cuban literature. The case of Villaverde's *Cecilia Valdés* for abolitionist literature in exile is interesting because it is a key novel of Cuban literature. Also

El laúd del desterrado (The Exile's Lute) makes the case for annexationist poetry which is mentioned by most, if not all, Cuban literary histories of the twentieth century (Souza). Then, if Cuban literature has often been written in exile, is there a difference between the two? The answer, of course, is no, as long as the writer is considered both as a national author and as an exile after his or her death.

Cuban-American literature, on the other hand, requires other considerations. For instance, the very nature of the context makes it difficult to make perfect analogies with other United States Hispanic literatures. Should Cuban-American authors be born in the United States? Should they write only in English or, at least, in alternating codes? Should they write only about their immigrant experience? To some degree, whereas the questions are legitimate, they are not so much irrelevant as they are impertinent. It seems to me that if José Martí lived in New York for fifteen years, he was to an extent a Cuban writer, an exile writer, but also a Cuban-American writer. There is no law that forbids literary historians from including the same figure in several categories, or even in distinct groupings that are based on nationalist definitions, when the author lives a transnational reality.

It is my preference to view Cuban-American authors as those who live and write in the United States, about whatever topics may interest them (home country, new country, other places, peoples or things), and to place them in generational cohorts for ease of classification. Hence, it would be better if we were to group authors in the following schema: a Neoclassic generation (roughly covering the years 1800–1825); a Romantic generation (1825–1850); a Realist-Naturalist generation (1850–1880); an Impressionist generation (corresponding to *Modernismo*: 1880–1910); an Avant-Garde generation (1910–1940); an Existentialist generation (1940–1960); a Revolutionary generation (1960–1985); and a Postmodern generation (1985–). These groupings correspond, roughly, with the nineteenth century for the first three, turn of the century for the next group, and the twentieth century for the final four groups. The purpose of this study is the organization of the following literary material according to these periods, not to impose any external demands on the texts mentioned below. This general classificatory schema also serves another very useful purpose: besides creating a mechanism for ordering the facts that we now know about the Cuban-American writers whose persons and works have received some attention, it prepares the way for other newly researched facts to fit into the outline, or to demand changes in it.

II. Theatre

The study of Cuban theatre raises problems of genre which demand

José Martí

our attention. Perhaps some of the best work on Cuban theatre history regarding the issue of genre has been in the major identification which has existed since Aristotle's *Poetics* distinguished tragedy from comedy. This has been done by Rine Leal in his books on Cuban theatre. The very nature of classifying across this gulf marked by laughter and tears is not in itself a problem; the notable exception is that theatre that is not funny becomes serious and, therefore, more important. This obviously has more to do with class prejudice than with anything else: the lords act tragically, the servants, comically.

From these considerations of dramatic genre definition, it is possible to classify Cuban theatre as follows: serious theatre, comedy, *teatro frívolo* (frivolous theatre), and *teatro bufo* (farce). But what appears logical in the deductive realm is contradicted by an investigation of historical experience. The origins of Cuban-American theatre are intimately tied to a tradition of theatre in Cuba which marked Cuban theatrical tastes, dramatic possibilities and artistic aspirations for actors, artists, playwrights, and entrepreneurs (R. Leal (1980). They are also inextricably connected to the dimension of exile literature which bring together the twin preoccupations with the homeland as a lost paradise and the new land as an alien place as has been observed by Maida Watson Espener. For Cuban-American theatre, therefore, the major themes will cluster around the political and the social lives of the exile and the immigrant communities respectively. But these are not the only divisions. Likely as not, Cuban-American theatre will tend to follow the dichotomy imposed by a similar dramatic schizophrenia in the late nineteenth and early twentieth centuries when Cuban theatre separated the popular slapstick from the elite dramaturgy. According to Rine Leal (1980), Spanish colonial censorship forbade the serious treatment of Cuban nationalist themes in the theatre. This led playwrights who preferred working the serious side of the stage to imitate Spanish drama. Thus, serious Cuban colonial theatre became a servile imitator of the Spanish stage. This took place not only in Havana but also in Tampa, Florida, the exile capital of Cuban independence patriots, where, according to Kanellos (1990) theatre flourished. The only authentic Cuban themes were left to the genres of comedy and farce.

With few exceptions in the 1920s and 1930s when labor and other social topics were introduced to the stage, this division has remained in place, practically to this day, as has been pointed out by Kanellos. The Cuban-American serious theatrical experience during the revolutionary period (1960–85) has been, for the first twenty-odd years, a struggle. Meanwhile, comic theatre has continued to blossom in Miami and in other areas of the United States as has been indicated by Kanellos (1987).

Another important circumstance that affected Cuban and Cuban-American theatre, as it has most theatres, was the advent and growth of the radio, film and television industries, according to Leal. These techno-logical innovations have made theatre an art of the masses in new ways, but have left traditional stagecraft as a more marginal enterprise. Entrepreneurs have, therefore, catered to the mass appeal of comedy, and to some extent to musical comedy. Such is the case today in Miami, New York and Tampa, where serious drama continues to lose ground to comedy.

Drama, of course, was published in various newspapers as well. Al-though the first Cuban newspaper published in the United States is José María Heredia's *El Habanero* (The Havanan, Philadelphia, 1824) (Poyo), printed some sixteen years after the first United States Hispanic periodical *El Misisipí* (New Orleans, 1808), it is during the latter part of the 1820s that New York boasted two Spanish-language newspapers, *El Mensajero Semanal* (The Weekly Messenger) and *El Mercurio de Nueva York* (The New York Mercury). These publications carried news as well as literary artifacts (Kanellos 1990). Editorial content consisted mainly of poetry and stories, but already in their pages there appeared actual dramatic literature from Spain. By the second half of the century, the Hispanic publishing in-dustry was including drama among its titles on all manner of subjects. Some books like Francisco Javier Balmaseda's novel *Los confinados a Fernando Poo* (The Prisoners of Fernando Poo), issued in 1869, are political tracts that took advantage of the venue for free expression, leaving their creative work for publication in their homeland. But others who had either fled per-manently or happened to have a passing connection with the United States did entrust their work to stateside publishers.

The play *El hermano generoso* (The Generous Brother) established a trend: The publication of politically committed literature, or protest litera-ture, abroad. Its author penned the play in the 1840s, under the pseudonym of Orman Tu-caes no doubt due to the unflattering allusions to the Spanish government (Kanellos 1990).

Beside obvious political works, there were others which dealt with non-subversive nationalist themes. But since this was sufficient, in and of itself, to be offensive to the Spanish colonial establishment, it made it easier for some writers to publish abroad, avoiding thereby the tortured language necessary to escape censorship if they published in the island. In this category we can place some of the Realist theatre of manners following the more political Romantic dramas. Among them Justo Eleboro's *El rico y el pobre* (The Rich Man and the Poor Man), a three-act play which appeared in New York in 1864. Among the important literary figures of the time, one of them had his plays published in New York: José María Heredia, whose *Abufar o la familia árabe* (Abufar or the Arabian Family) saw the light in 1854, though it had been written in 1826 and staged in 1833. Other Cuban-American plays of the time include José Jacinto Milanés' *Obras* (Works) reissued by Juan F. Trow y Cia. in one volume in New York in 1865; Luis García Pérez's *El grito de Yara* (The Cry of Yara) published in New York by Hallet & Breen in 1879; Diego Tejera's *La muerte de Plácido* (Placido's Death), a dramatic play on the death of the celebrated Cuban Romantic poet, appeared in New York under the imprint of Imp. Ponce de León in 1875; and Adolfo Pierra's *The Cuban Patriots: A Drama of the Struggle for Independence Actually Going On in the Gem of the Antilles, in Three Acts*, that appeared in Philadelphia in 1873 with a text which indicated that the piece was "written in English by a native Cuban." Meanwhile in Key West, Felix R. Zahonet saw his two-act *zarzuela* (operetta) printed by Imp. de la Revista Popular in 1890 with the title of *Los amores de Eloísa o Heroicidades de una madre* (Eloisa's Loves or the Heroic Deeds of a Mother). Two plays by Francisco Sellén also appeared in New York: *Hatuey*, a 147 page, five-act dramatic poem, was published by A. Da Costa Gómez in 1891. In 1892 G. Gómez y Arroyo had a one-act satirical, burlesque, comical, lyrical skit titled *Polilla regional* (Regional Moth) released by Conner in New York. Desiderio Fajardo Ortiz's *La fuga de Evangelina* (Evangelina's Escape), a one-act sketch in four scenes written to celebrate Evangelina Cossío's sensational escape from political Spanish imprisonment in Havana, was dated in 1898 by Howes upon publication in New York. With *Las apuestas de Zuleika* (Zuleika's Bets), a 33 page, one-act piece, offered by M. M. Hernández in 1901, we can bring the nineteenth century to a close. Most of these dramatic texts are available only in period newspapers and in Cuban archives in the island. They need to be recovered and reissued in scholarly format.

With Mario F. Sorondo's *Locura repentina* (Sudden Madness), published by The Speranto [sic] Student in Rutherford, NJ, in 1909, we may open the twentieth century. The history of twentieth century Cuban-American theatre is no less rich, but information is just as scanty and documentation is no less spotty. Thanks to José Luis Perrier and Nicolás Kanellos there is some sense of what may have taken place in the United States urban areas where Cubans and theatre intersected in the early part of the century; Matías Montes Huidobro, Maida Watson Espener and José Escarpenter have done much to document the last thirty years. In his *Bibliografía dramática cubana* (Cuban Dramatic Bibliography), Perrier provides an account of Cuban and Cuban-American dramatic publishing and production. (He also includes Puerto Rico and Santo Domingo in the book.) But Perrier's information is offered within a context of abundant periodical commentary by newspapers and magazines of the time in New York. Much of this material is lost or in recondite collections of difficult access. Kanellos (1990) painstakingly unearths some of that lost history. In two key chapters of his book (chapters 4 & 5, covering New York and Tampa respectively), he offers a careful reconstruction of the context of the times by utilizing old newspapers and magazines, looking for theatre chronicles, reviews, announcements and advertisements. This task is made more difficult for him because of a most peculiar characteristic. In Tampa and in New York, the Hispanic communities were that—Hispanic. They consisted of Spaniards and Cubans (in Tampa), plus Mexicans, Puerto Ricans, Argentines, Venezuelans, Dominicans, etc., in New York. It is sometimes difficult, if not impossible, to distinguish a particular writer's background. Here Perrier is invaluable, and Kanellos, relying on both Perrier and periodical materials, is able to detail some of that history.

The twentieth century may be segmented as follows for the purpose of establishing some order to available facts: from 1898–1925, from 1926–1940, from 1941–1960 and from 1961–1991. These dates correspond roughly with the aforementioned generational schema (Impressionist, Avant-Garde, Existentialist and Revolutionary). These labels are not meant to characterize (we know too little of actual content and style of much of the production of those earlier years), but to orient ourselves in terms of the broader categories of literary history. The first years, 1898–1925, are well set in Tampa where the institutions of the Hispanic (primarily Spanish and Cuban, though to some extent Italian) community were able to sustain a non-profit theatre activity which had two interesting characteristic notes. First, it left a legacy which continues to this day. In Tampa the children and grandchildren of the theatre crowd of that time have sustained, if in somewhat diminished form, a theatrical tradition. Second, it has had the distinct historical quirk of being the only Spanish-language Federal Theatre Project supported by the government during the Depression (Mardis). Tampa's tobacco workers and their families were able to group together into seven mutual-aid societies: the Centro Español, the Centro Asturiano, the Centro Español de West Tampa, the Círculo Cubano, the Unión Martí-Maceo, the Centro Obrero and L'Unione Italiana. Each of these societies had a show committee in charge of events, an amateur group and a theatre. The presentations ranged from light musical zarzuelas at the Centro Español, the most conservative society, to more liberal fare at the Centro Asturiano. The latter, without giving up zarzuelas, added the ever-present *bufos cubanos* (Cuban farcical plays), including the *negrito* and the *gallego* (literally, Blackie and the Galician, which referred to a traditional farcical couple: a picaresque Afro-Cuban and a dim-witted Spaniard), with the participation of directors like Manuel Aparicio and Rafael Arango, playwrights like Cristino R. Inclán, and actors

Centro Asturiano Theatre in Tampa, still functioning today.

and actresses like Bolito (Roberto Gutiérrez), Alicia Rico and Luís Guerra, all veterans of the Cuban and Cuban-American stage in Havana and in New York. At the Círculo Cubano and the Unión Martí-Maceo it was easier to find the *bufos*, while at the Centro Obrero more socially progressive protest plays and political satires could be enjoyed. Typical offerings in their various programs might include *La viuda alegre* (The Merry Widow) at the Español, *Bodas de Papá Montero* (Papa Montero's Wedding) at the Asturiano, the Círculo or the Unión; and *Justicia humana* (Human Justice) at the Obrero. Tampa-Ybor City audiences may have been working class, but they were not untutored. Through the institution of *lectores* or readers, cigar workers were able to listen to great literature while toiling in the factories. They also alternated amateur performances with those of professional traveling troupes which they invited to their theatres. According to Kanellos (1990) this made Tampa theatre better than could be otherwise reasonably expected at first glance. Cuban-American theatre, therefore, has always had a very good home there. The New York scene, much more complex because of the lack of clearly established Cuban or Hispanic theatrical centers throughout this period as is the case with Tampa, does acquire a firmer foothold in the later part of the Roaring Twenties.

During the 1926–1940 period, New York Cuban-American theatre history becomes a bit clearer. The first years of the century had seen some activity by groups like the Club Lírico Dramático Cubano (Cuban Lyrical-Dramatical Club) and later the Compañía de Bufos Cubanos (Cuban Company of Farcical Players and Singers). But until theatres like the Dalys, the Apollo, the San José (later Variedades), and the Campoamor (later Cervantes, and still later Hispano) provided solidity to the varied theatrical boom of the period, Cuban-American theatre could not take hold in New York City. In addition to the establishments themselves, there appeared an important group of playwrights and actors. Among the playwrights are several mentioned by Perrier including Alberto O'Farrill, editor of *El Gráfico* (The Graphic), a newspaper devoted to the theatre and entertainment world which went into publication in 1927. O'Farrill, a well-known blackface actor of Cuban farce, penned plays like *Los misterios de Changó* (Dr. Chango's Mysteries), *Un doctor accidental* (An Accidental Doctor), *Un negro en Andalucía* (A Black Man in Andalusia), *Kid Chocolate* and *La viuda como no hay dos* (A Widow Like No Other), all presented at the Apollo during 1926. Another dramatist, Juan C. Rivera, also an actor who played *gallego* roles opposite O'Farrill's *negritos*, authored *Terremoto en Harlem* (Earthquake in Harlem) and *Cosas que pasan* (Things That Happen), two *zarzuelas bufas* also presented at the Apollo in the same year. The most prolific of these playwrights was the famous Afro-Cuban singer Arquímides Pous who created over 200 *obras bufas cubanas*, among which one might mention *Pobre Papa Montero* (Poor Papa Montero) or *Las mulatas de Bombay* (Bombay's Mulatto Women). Other authors like Guillermo J. Moreno—*Bronca en España* (Wrangle in Spain), *De Cuba a Puerto Rico* (From Cuba to Puerto Rico), both of which premiered at the Apollo in 1927—had works produced at the Teatro Campoamor, such as *De la gloria al infierno* (From Heaven to Hell) as late as 1936. *The Cuba bella* (Beautiful Cuba) revue which was presented at the Teatro Hispano dates to 1937. But with few exceptions Cuban-American theatre appears to go from a strong river to a smaller stream into the next period.

The 1950s, which comprise the next period of Cuban-American stage, is the province of one very important playwright, María Irene Fornés, who, practically on her own, makes New York hospitable to Cuban-American theatre again. She spans the late 1950s to the 1970s and has served in different capacities as model playwright, perspicacious commentator, generous teacher and ardent advocate of Cuban-American, Hispanic and women's causes in the theatre. But María Irene Fornés has served it best by being the best. Maida Watson Espener points out that Fornés received critical acclaim in 1977 for her play *Fefu and Her Friends* in which eight women join each other for a weekend retreat during which they reveal their hopes, aspirations, frustrations, regrets and, most of all, their innermost selves. She has a varied repertoire among which we might mention *Promenade*, a light musical piece; *Mud*, an examination of dire poverty; *The Conduct of Life*, a consideration of the cruelties of a tyrannical dictator; and *Sarita*, set in the South Bronx from 1939–1947, in which she follows the life of her protagonist from age 13 to age 21 when she enters a mental hospital. Although her work has merited her six OBIE awards (literally O.B., Off-Broadway prizes for exceptional achievement), she has not attained popularity with mass audiences today as in the past. Nevertheless, Fornés stands alone in the United States during a critical period for the Cuban-American stage. The contemporary scene, varied and rich, located in other venues beside Tampa and New York, owes a great deal to her.

III. Novel

It is possible that the first Cuban novel published in the United States during the nineteenth century is the work of a philosopher writing about the conquest of Mexico by Hernán Cortés. The anonymous novel is *Jicoténcal* and the author, as proposed by Luís Leal (1960) with powerful arguments, is none other than Father Félix Varela, the Cuban patriot whose early advocacy for independence is predicated on his philosophical readings of the eighteenth-century liberal thinkers. Should Leal's case hold through the next thirty years as it has the last thirty, *Jicoténcal* will become not only the first Cuban-American novel, but also the first historical novel in the New World, as has been indicated by several other notable scholars.

Beyond speculations regarding Varela, the Cuban novel in the United States is represented in the nineteenth century by two writers whose subject, the abolition of slavery, was very popular both in Cuba and in the United States. For Cubans, as it was later for Puerto Ricans with regard to the United States, the identification of the slavery of Africans with the imperialistic hold of Spain over the colony had been the subject of Cirilo Villaverde's *Cecilia Valdés o La loma del ángel* (Cecilia Valdés or The Angel's Hill). The novel's first part appeared in 1839 in the Cuban periodical *La Siempreviva* (The Everlasting), but the book containing that first part together with a second part was not published until 1882, in New York. Villaverde himself was born in San Diego de Pinar del Río in 1812 and died in New York in 1894. He founded several newspapers in the United States, and he published another novel *El penitente* (The Penitent) in New York in 1889, a work like *Cecilia Valdés* rooted in the folkloric *costumbrismo* (literature of manners) so popular with prose writers of the Romantic period. In it he tells the story of a young woman's tragedy. She, an orphaned mulatto, falls in love with and has a girl by the young scion of a powerful slave-trading family. She accepts her social position and is prepared to be only his mistress, but when the young man decides to marry, she kills him after the wedding. The descriptions of people, places and customs are rich in detail and full of color. Dances, walks, festivals, ceremonies, plantations, sugar mills, plazas, temples and neighborhoods all enrich the texture of the narrative by serving as backdrops. According to Juan J. Remos, Villaverde moves with ease in rural as well as urban settings accumulating punctiliously every detail which he felt would be important. Also in the nineteenth century, Anselmo Suárez y Romero (1818–1878) had his novel, *Francisco*, which he had written in 1838, published posthumously in New York in 1880. Suárez y Romero is even more a romantic than Villaverde as he narrates the story of Dorotea and Francisco, two slaves whose love for each other makes them defy the master's prohibition for them to marry. They have a little girl and, with the consent of the master's mother, they do marry. But the master makes life impossible for Francisco, driving him to commit suicide by hanging. This happens because of and in spite of Dorotea's sexual surrender to her master. But Francisco's death is too much and she does not survive him for long. Again, the allegorical instrumentalization of slavery for political readings is evident in this novel. The human note lies in the novelist's use of romantic passion in the person of two slaves. The novelist follows the Rousseauian convention and thus attacks the depersonalization of slaves and their inhuman treatment, as has been noted by Remos and studied by Jorge and Isabel Castellanos. Little is known as to subsequent activities by novelists of Cuban background in the United States until 1959. Much research needs to be done in the early period. About this we have literally no documents. Some of the reasons may be that, indeed, there is no novel in the New World until the early nineteenth century. Also more research is needed on the nineteenth century, especially in the newspapers and on the printed books of the time, particularly in Philadelphia and New York. Finally, the first sixty years of the twentieth century, though dominated by activity in the island proper, appear as a block of time full of narrative ghosts awaiting to be embodied in hidden texts lost in libraries in New York, New Orleans and Tampa.

Recent activity in the novel comprises three distinct groups: the exile anti-Castro novelists with works such as Carlos Alberto Montaner's *Perromundo* (Dogworld) and Hilda Perera's *El sitio de nadie* (Nobody's Place), the Mariel writers, such as Reinaldo Arenas whose *El portero* (The Doorman) relates the experience of life in the United States, and the Cuban-American novelists such as Roberto Fernández's *Raining Backwards*, Oscar Hijuelos' *The Mambo Kings Play Songs of Love*, and Christina García's *Dreaming in Cuban*, whose works address the issues of culture and identity.

IV. Poetry

Cuban poetry in the United States established an island presence in continental letters dating from the early nineteenth century. The Neoclassical poet José María Heredia (1803–1839) fled the island to avoid imprisonment by Spanish colonial authorities who had accused him of being a separatist. In a tradition of dramatic escapes from the island, Heredia hid in the Galaxy, an American ship docked in Havana, and disembarked at Boston harbor in 1823 disguised as a sailor. By 1825 he published a book in New York titled *Poesías* (Poems), which included his famed "Oda al Niágara," a song written in praise of the falls. His "Himno del desterrado" (Hymn of the Exile), written in a different exile tradition of letters, tells of his love for home and the pain of separation from the homeland. He wrote this poem while at sea, traveling from New York to Mexico, after seeing in the distance Cuba's Pan de Matanzas mountain. His poetry praising the solitary star and the royal palm stimulated others to regard these symbols as nationalist triggers for their patriotic enthusiasm. Heredia's work, ironically, awakened a regard for independence which he himself was seeing from the disappointing perspective of Mexico's chaotic organization of its state. Heredia's brief return to Cuba, between late 1836 and early 1837, came at the price of renouncing his belligerence toward Spain.

The Romantic period yielded an important book *El laúd del desterrado* (New York, 1858), a collection of poems by a group of poets who felt a strong affinity for independence. Among them was, of course, the late poet Heredia, whose patriotic poems were included by the editors. The principal compiler was Miguel Teurbe Tolón (1820–1857), a highly educated professor whose energetic voice and great rancor toward Spain was evident in his "Himno de guerra cubano" (Cuban War Hymn); in "Mi propósito" (My Purpose); and in "El pobre desterrado" (The Poor Exile). Another voice from that group was that of Leopoldo Turla (1818–1877) whose fluidity of tone appears in "Perseverancia" (Perseverance), "Degradación" (Degradation), and in "A Narciso López" (To Narciso Lopez), a general of Venezuelan extraction who led a group of annexationists to Cuba. Pedro Angel Castellón (1820–1856) displayed his elegant, correct, yet spontaneous verse in "A Cuba" (To Cuba), and in "A los mártires de Trinidad y Camagüey" (To the Martyrs of Trinidad and Camagüey). Pedro Santacilia (1826–1910), who would also publish his *Lecciones sobre historia de Cuba* (Lessons on Cuban History, New York: Ateneo Democrático de Nueva York, 1859), cultivated verse and good taste as evidenced by his "A España" (To Spain) and his 1856 book of poems *El arpa del proscripto* (The Proscript's Harp). While in Mexico and the United States, Santacilia, Benito Juárez's secretary and son-in-law, worked tirelessly for Cuban independence. Another collaborator in the anthology was José Agustín Quintero (1829–1885) whose contributions "El banquete del destierro" (The Banishment Banquet), "¡Adelante!" (Forward!), "Poesía bajo la tiranía" (Poetry Under Tyranny), and his "A Miss Lydia Robbins" (To Miss Lydia Robbins) displayed the merit of his themes and his care for poetic forms. Another famous Cuban bard represented in the collection was Juan Clemente Zenea (1832–1871) with three compositions "El filibustero" (The Patriot), "El 16 de agosto de 1851" (August 16, 1851), and "En la muerte de Narciso López" (On Narciso López's Death). In 1860 he published a book in Cuba titled *Cantos de la tarde* (Afternoon Songs). He is known as Cuba's best poet of the elegiac tradition during the Romantic period. His importance, therefore, is somewhat ironic because his posthumous book *Diario de un mártir* (Diary of a Martyr) consists of sixteen poems published in New York's *El Mundo Nuevo* (The New World). The poems were delivered to the United States Consul on the eve of his execution in Havana. The book tells of his love for his wife and daughter, and of his love affair with Ada Menken, an American actress and poet.

Beyond *El laúd del desterrado* and its remarkable New York publication, there were other Romantic poets who lived and worked in the United States. Angel Turla (1813–1834) was, in fact, born in the United States. He did not publish any book of poems. Rather, his very tender poetry of delicate

artistry appeared in periodicals of the time. Nicolás Cárdenas y Rodríguez (1814–1868), a newspaperman and poet, had a book of poems titled
Ensayos poéticos por un cubano ausente de su patria (Poetic Essays by
a Cuban Absent from his Fatherland, New York, 1836). His brother, José
María, who also studied in the United States and was known in the island as a
famed *costumbrista*, was dubbed the Cuban Mesonero Romanos (a Spanish
folk-journalist known for his features on typical Spanish life) because of his
feature articles on Cuban manners and customs.

Another poet of the time, Issac Carrillo O'Farril (Havana 1844–New
York 1901) found himself incarcerated after writing a sonnet addressed to
Queen Isabel II of Spain in the New York weekly *La Revolución* (The Revolution). After his release, he moved to New York to practice law. There
he founded *La Revolución* in 1863. He wrote a novel, *María* (1863), a de-
scriptive poem, *Matilde*, several other poems, in addition to three plays, all
published in Havana: *Luchas del alma* (Struggles of the Soul), 1864; *El que
con libros anda* (He Who Fools with Books, 1867); and *Magdalena* (1868),
this last of which was written in prose. Two other poets of the Romantic
period were Rafael María Mendive (1821–1886), whose own translation of
Thomas Moore's *Melodías irlandesas* (Irish Melodies, New York, 1875)
reflects the softness and grace of the Irish bard, and José Jacinto Milanés
(1814–1863). This poet and playwright had his complete works *Obras de
José Jacinto Milanés* (Works by José Jacinto Milanés) published posthumously in New York by Juan F. Trow y Cia. in 1865, as a second edition of
his four volume set published earlier in Havana in 1846.

The post-Romantics are the Sellén brothers. Francisco Sellén (1838–
1907) had his *Poesías* issued in New York in 1890. He had published his
first poems in Havana, together with his brother Antonio's own verses in a
book *Estudios poéticos* (Poetic Studies, 1863). Francisco translated Heine
and Lord Byron. His brother Antonio (1839–1889), after his collaboration
on the *Estudios* with Francisco, published his own *Cuatro poemas* (Four
Poems, New York, 1877) which contained several translations of English
poets. Antonio also published other books including translations of poetry
from Danish, Swedish, German and French poets. He also included Polish
and English plays in his works. The Sellén brothers not only contributed
their poetry to Cuba and the United States, but they also made available in
Spanish the works of those European poets and playwrights whose influence
would be felt in the next Impressionist generation.

It is to the Impressionist aesthetic that we must include José Martí (1853–
1895), usually classified under the Spanish-American label of *Modernismo*
(Modernism; though not with the same meaning that is applied to American
literature). He is the poet who closes the nineteenth century in the United

States just as Heredia had opened it. Martí lived in New York from 1880 until 1895; in addition he traveled frequently to Key West, Tampa and Philadelphia in his quest for Cuban independence. Martí's famous book *Ismaelillo* (New York, 1882) was published the same year that Villaverde's novel appeared in New York. His book describes his love for his son in intimate poems delicately etched in diminutives and images of precious jewels. His *Versos sencillos* (Simple Verses, New York, 1891) pick up some of Heredia's poetic symbols of Cuba and sing his love for Cuba and of freedom. While in New York, Martí also published a book of essays *Cuba y los Estados Unidos* (Cuba and the United States) in 1889. But what memorializes his life in the United States are his two collections of articles (gathered each in one volume of his complete works) corresponding to people and events. The first one is titled "North Americans," where he portrays James Fenimore Cooper, Mark Twain, Washington Irving, Edgar Allan Poe, Henry David Thoreau, Walt Whitman, Generals Grant and Sheridan, Peter Cooper and many others. The second one is titled "North American Scenes." Here he depicts events such as the inauguration of the Statue of Liberty, the opening of the Brooklyn Bridge, a summer day on Coney Island, and his famous essay on the Charleston Earthquake. Martí's feature articles on the United States made many Latin Americans aware of people and events unknown to them. To the Cuban communities of the United States (Key West, Tampa, Philadelphia, New York), he was best known and loved for his oratory. His skill and passion put at the service of the cause of Cuban independence made him a draw at any political gathering. His final trek to Cuba in 1895 mythifies his person as a martyr and a hero. The significance of José Martí, like Heredia and Zenea, is that several key figures of Cuban poetry did, in fact, write most of their work in the United States in the context of a life of exile and adjustment to the new land.

The story of twentieth century poetry begins with Eugenio Florit y Sánchez de Fuentes (1903). Born in Madrid, Florit went to Cuba as a teenager and to the United States in 1940 as a diplomat. Florit taught from 1942 until 1969 at Columbia University's Barnard College when he was named Professor Emeritus at Columbia. During his tenure at Columbia he also taught from 1944 until 1964 at the Middlebury College's renowned Summer School. He is a member of the Hispanic Society of New York, the Modern Language Association and the American Association of Teachers of Spanish and Portuguese. In 1969 he received the Mitre Medal of the Hispanic Society. He also served as editor of the *Revista Hispánica Moderna* (Modern Hispanic Review) from 1960–69. Florit has been lawyer, diplomat, educator, critic, anthologist, but most importantly he has been a poet. He graduated from the Secondary Education Institute of Havana in 1918, and in 1926 he became a doctor of civil law at the University of Havana. Florit served in the Cuban diplomatic corps from 1927 until 1945. His books of poetry include *Hábito de esperanza: Poemas (1936–1964)* (Habit of Hope: Poems, Madrid: Insula, 1965); *De tiempo y agonía* (Of Time and Agony, Madrid: Ediciones de la Revista de Occidente, 1974); and *Castillo interior otros versos* (Interior Castle and Other Poems, Miami, 1987). As a young man in Havana he published other volumes of poetry; so by the time he arrived in the United States in 1940, he was an accomplished poet. Florit's merit as a poet lies in his lyrical qualities, his care of form and his controlled passion. In the realm of literary history, Eugenio Florit opens the twentieth century in the United States. He belongs to the *Vanguardia* (Avant-Garde) of the 1926 Cuban generation, which roughly corresponds to the sensibilities of the Spanish generation of 1927.

Clara Niggemann (1910–), whose books include *Canto al apóstol* (Song to the Apostle, Camagüey: El camagüeyano, 1953), her only Cuban publication; *En la puerta dorada* (At the Golden Door), prologue by Severo Sarduy (Valencia: Soler, 1973); *Como un ardiente rio* (Like a Burning River, Barcelona, 1985), and other unpublished books, is a member of this generation but does not belong to the *Orígenes* (Origins) group. She has had her poetry selected for many anthologies from all over Spain and Spanish America.

Most of the poets of this generation are associated with José Lezama Lima's *Orígenes* group. They comprise one of the most important pantheons of literary production in Cuba in particular and in Spanish America generally. Of the ten poets who published in the literary magazines *Verbum* (1937), *Espuela de plata* (Silver Spur, 1939), *Nadie parecía* (No One Appeared, 1942) and *Orígenes* (1944), which named the group, three went into exile after the Castro Revolution. Gastón Baquero (1916–) lives and works in Madrid, while Lorenzo García Vega (1926–) resides in Miami, and Justo Rodríguez Santos (1915–) in New York. The late Virgilio Piñera never left Cuba, but his work did. Some of his plays were published in the United States, several under the auspices of Luis González Cruz. During his exile, García Vega published three books: *Ritmos acribillados* (Riddled Rhythms, New York: Expúblico, 1972); *Rostros del reverso* (Reverse Faces, Caracas: Monte Avila, 1977); and *Los años de "Orígenes"* (The Years of "Orígenes," Caracas: Monte Avila, 1979). Rodríguez Santos also published three books: *El diapasón del ventisquero* (The Blizzard's Pitch, Madrid: Playor, 1976); *Los naipes conjurados* (The Plotting Cards, Madrid: Playor, 1979); and *Las óperas del sueño* (Dream Operas, Miami: Ediciones Orígenes, 1981).

The rest of the story remains unstudied and untold, primarily due to the lack of research resources. The contemporary scene has blossomed with the 1950s Generation which brought poets from the early days of the Cuban Revolution, and from the 1970s Generation, which includes the conservative group known as "El Puente," the Mariel group, and the Cuban-American "Atrevidos" group.

V. The Short Story

The Cuban short story in the United States begins with the publication of José María Heredia's *Cuentos Orientales* (Oriental Tales) in 1829. The setting of the stories speaks of the Romantic penchant for exoticism which occasionally took the form of an escape in time to the Middle Ages and at other times took the form of a geographical flight into other territories alien to the author's and the reader's homeland. Heredia (1803–1839), whose major literary achievements were in the field of poetry, spent several of his years of exile in the United States and in Mexico. In both countries he published important portions of his work. Cirilo Villaverde, in addition to his novelistic production, did engage the genre of the short story. Likewise José Martí (1853–1895), who is better known as a poet and as a patriot, wrote short stories for the children's magazine *La Edad de Oro* (The Golden Age). In 1883 he prologued the stories of one of his contemporaries, Rafael de Castro y Palomino who published his book of stories in New York entitled *Cuentos de hoy y de mañana* (Stories of Today and Tomorrow).

The short story, a rich genre in Cuba was also well represented in the United States in the many Cuban newspapers which were published in various American cities such as New York, Philadelphia, Tampa and Key West in the latter part of the nineteenth century and in the first half of the twentieth century. But the history of the short story of that period covering a little over a century, has yet to be written, because most of the material in those newspapers remains unknown to today's readers and unedited by our contemporary critical establishment. The material is more readily available during the course of the last thirty years coinciding with the revolutionary period.

VI. Research Guide

Finally, let me address the repositories of material for the actual research projects that may engage the interests of scholars and graduate students in search of dissertation opportunities. What follows is a list of places where one expects materials to be found for the preservation, research, and publication of literary artifacts belonging to the cultural heritage of Hispanics, including Spaniards and Cubans in Key West, Tampa, New York, Philadelphia, New Orleans and North Carolina communities of the late eighteenth, nineteenth and twentieth centuries:

1. The University of South Florida Archives contain the papers of the Sociedad Martí-Maceo (the Afro-Cuban association), those of the Sociedad Española de West Tampa, and of the Sociedad Española de Ybor City. Also there are the private papers of Tony Pizzo, which include complete runs of newspapers that contain unpublished works by José Martí, plus several Tampa writers with works also unpublished in book form. The archives also have the silver and gold anniversary celebration books published by each society with photographs and other memorabilia.

2. El Centro Asturiano Documents of the association, including literary documents, are to be found in the society's storage rooms in boxes in Tampa.

3. Asociación Cubana Social documents of the association in Tampa including some literary papers.

4. University of South Florida Tobacco Industry Special Collection contains documents of the industry which speak to the social and literary (*lector*) worlds of the worker.

5. University of Florida-Gainesville Microfilm of a trilingual newspaper published for 60 years in the Tampa area.

6. Spanish Little Theatre of Tampa Collection Twenty-six years of activity by the children of the theatrical actors and actresses of the twenties. Documents and props from that period.

7. Instituto San Carlos Archives-Key West contains three sets of documents: (a) the diplomatic papers of the Cuban Consulate; (b) the records of the school which was held there; and (c) social records and some literary documents from the cultural association which was established there. These materials have been microfilmed by the University of Texas-Austin with the support of the National Endowment for the Humanities.

8. Newspapers from Tampa, New York, Key West, Havana, Madrid, Long Island, Spanish Harlem, Los Angeles, San Antonio, Chicago, etc. These papers tended to carry cultural news and documents about their own communities as well as news from corresponding communities in the larger Hispanic context.

9. Dramatic texts, newspapers, and other literary documents from the United States, at several repositories in Cuba (University of Havana,

National Library, National Archives, etc.). These contain also most of the plays from the Tampa and New York theatre heydays.

Works Cited and Bibliography

A. General Reference

Castellanos, Isabel and Jorge Castellanos. *Cultura afrocubana. El negro en Cuba, 1492–1844.* Vol. 1. Miami: Universal, 1988.

————. *Cultura afrocubana. El negro en Cuba 1845–1959.* Vol. 2. Miami: Universal, 1990.

Cortina, Rodolfo J. and Alberto Moncada, eds. *Hispanos en los Estados Unidos.* Madrid: Cultura Hispánica (Colección Hispana), 1988.

Kanellos, Nicolas. *Biographical Dictionary of Hispanic Literature in the United States. The Literature of Puerto Ricans, Cuban Americans and other Hispanic Writers.* New York: Greenwood, 1989.

Lazo, Raimundo. *La teoría de las generaciones y su aplicación al estudio histórico de la literatura cubana.* Havana: Revista de la Universidad de La Habana, 1954.

————. *La literatura cubana.* México: Manuales Universitarios de la Universidad Nacional Autónoma de México, 1965.

Leal, Luis. "Mexican American Literature: A Historical Perspective." *Revista Chicano Riqueña* 1.1 (1973): 32–44, and in several reprints.

Mormino, Gary. *The Immigrant World of Ybor City.* New York: Statue of Liberty, Ellis Island Centennial Series, 1987.

Ortiz, Fernando. *Los negros brujos.* Miami: Universal, 1973.

————. *La música afrocubana.* Madrid: Júcar, 1975.

————. *Contrapunto cubano del tabaco y el azúcar.* Caracas: Ayacucho, 1978.

Poyo, Gerald E. *With All and for the Good of All: The Rise of Popular Nationalism in the Cuban Emigre Communities, 1848–1898.* Durham: Duke UP, 1989.

Remos, Juan J. *Proceso histórico de las letras cubanas.* Madrid: Guadarrama, S.L., 1958.

Ripoll, Carlos. *Cubanos en los Estados Unidos.* New York: Las Americas, 1987.

Souza, R. D. "Exile in the Cuban Literary Experience." *Cuban Exile Writers: A Bibliographic Handbook.* Eds. D. C. Maratos and M. D. Hill.

B. Theatre

Aguirre, Yolanda. *Apuntes sobre el teatro colonial.* Havana: Cuadernos Cubanos de la Universidad de La Habana, 1968.

Arrom, José Juan. *Historia de la literatura dramática cubana.* New Haven: Yale UP, 1944.

Castellanos, Isabel. "Lengua y sociedad en el teatro bufo cubano del siglo XIX." *Turia. Revista Cultural Instituto de Estudios Turolenses de la Diputación Provincial de Teruel* 13 (1990): 34–47.

Escarpenter, José and José A. Madrigal. "El teatro popular cubano hasta 1869." *Perro huevero aunque le quemen el hocico by Juan Francisco Valerio.* Boulder: Society of Spanish & Spanish American Studies, 1986. 9–46.

Greenbaum, Susan. *Afro-Cubans in Ybor City*. Tampa: University of Tampa and Sociedad Martí-Maceo, 1986.

Kanellos, Nicolás. *A History of Hispanic Theatre in the United States: Origins to 1940*. Austin: U of Texas P, 1990.

————. "Hispanic Theatre," which appeared in *Goodlife Magazine* in May 1985.

————, ed. *Hispanic Theatre in the United States*. Houston: Arte Público, 1984.

————. "Towards a History of Hispanic Literature in United States." *Images and Identities: The Puerto Rican in Literature*. Ed. Asela Rodríguez de Laguna. New Brunswick, NJ: Transaction, 1987.

Leal, Rine. *La selva oscura*. Havana: Arte y Literatura, 1975.

————. *Breve historia del teatro cubano*. Havana: Letras Cubanas, 1980.

Mardis, Robert. "Federal Theatre in Florida." Diss. U of Florida, 1972.

Perrier, José Luís. *Bibliografía dramática cubana*. New York: Phos, 1926.

Robreño, Eduardo. *Historia del teatro popular cubano*. Havana: Oficina del Historiador de la Ciudad de La Habana, 1961.

Watson Espener, Maida. *Cuban Exile Theatre* (forthcoming).

C. Novel

Kanellos, Nicolás. "La literatura hispana de los Estados Unidos y el género autobiográfico." Eds. R. J. Cortina and A. Moncada. *Hispanos en los Estados Unidos*. Madrid: Cultura Hispánica (Colección Hispana), 1988. 219–30.

Leal, Luis. "*Jicoténcal*, primera novela histórica en castellano." *Revista Iberoamericana* 25.49 (1960): 9–31.

Luis, William. *Literary Bondage: Slavery in Cuban Narrative*. Austin: U of Texas P, 1990.

Rice Cortina, Lynn. E. "The Perils of Evangelina: A Tale Thrice Told." *Cuban Heritage* 1.1 (1987): 42–47.

D. Poetry

Martínez, Julio A. "Fuentes bibliográficas para el estudio de la literatura cubana." *Revista Interamericana de Bibliografía* XXXVI (1986): 473–85.

Montes Huidobro, Matías y Yara González. *Bibliografía crítica de la poesía cubana*. New York: Plaza Mayor, 1972.

E. Short Story

Alzola, Concepción. *La más fermosa*. Miami: Universal, 1975.

Fernández-Marcané, Leonardo. *20 cuentistas cubanos*. Miami: Universal, 1978.

Hernández-Miyares, Julio E. "La cuentística cubana de la diáspora: recuento y posibilidades." *Escritores cubanos de la diáspora. Manual bibliográfico*. Eds. D.C. Maratos and M.D. Hill. Metuchen, NJ: Scarecrow, 1986.

————. "The Cuban Short Story in Exile: A Selected Bibliography." *Hispania*. 54.2 (May, 1971): 384.

Hernández, Gema. "La cuentística cubana." *Krisis 5* 2.1 (1977).

Izquierdo-Tejido, Pedro. *El cuento cubano. (Panorámica y antología)*. San José, C.R.: Lil, 1983.

Leal, Luís. *Historia del cuento hispanoamericano*. 2nd ed. Mexico: Andrea, 1971.

Valdés, Berardo José. *Panorama del cuento cubano*. Barcelona: Medinaceli, 1976.

PART II
Literary Forms and Regional Variations

Truth-Telling Tongues: Early Chicano Poetry

Luis Leal

On the second of February of 1848, the Republic of Mexico and the United States signed the Treaty of Guadalupe Hidalgo. One year later, according to Article VIII, the Mexican people who decided to remain in the ceded lands, a region today known as the Southwest, became American citizens, and were therefore threatened with the loss of their culture and their native language. That did not happen, however, as Spanish has survived as the spoken language of the people, due mainly to the constant influx of immigrants from Mexico and other Spanish-speaking countries of the Americas. Spanish also survived in their literature, which kept their language alive over the years, due to a desire to maintain a cultural tradition established when Mexico's northern provinces were colonized.

It is my purpose in this study to document the uninterrupted tradition that has existed in the writing of poetry in Spanish (the same could be done with other genres) by Americans of Mexican descent, and to examine the nature of that poetry, giving attention to the practice of using two languages in the same poetic construct, the presence of old and new popular forms, and thematic preferences. The emphasis of my study will fall upon the poetry produced between 1848 and 1910, although one immediate difficulty is that not all of this poetry is known, since most of it was published in Spanish-language newspapers, many of which have yet to be examined.[1] What has been collected by such literary historians as Aurelio M. Espinosa, Arthur L. Campa, Américo Paredes, Anselmo F. Arellano, Francisco Lomelí, Luis Torres and others, is sufficient, however, to make it possible to observe its influence. A second difficulty hindering the study of this poetry, and this applies to other genres as well, has been the problem of determining if the poems published were written by native composers or copied from Spanish or Latin American books or periodical publications. Although the appearance of poems by non-Chicanos demonstrates an interest in Hispanic literature in general on the part of the Spanish-speaking public residing in the Southwest, care must be taken to see that they are not included in studies or anthologies of the genre. Luis Torres for example, documents the anonymous publication of "Don Dinero" in *La Gaceta de Santa Bárbara* in 1881, which happens to be by the seventeenth-century Spanish writer Francisco de Quevedo; and in Reynaldo Ruiz's collection of poems published in the Spanish-language newspapers of Los Angeles between 1850 and 1900, there are some by such Latin American poets as José Joaquín Pesado, Luis Maneiro, Rosa Espino and others.

The preceding observations indicate that today no study about early Chicano literature can yet be called definitive. However, it is our belief that a study of what we already know could be useful in the understanding of what will be discovered in the future. Today we can already examine the nineteenth-century poetry of New Mexico in Arellano's book, *Los nuevomexicanos y su poesía, 1889–1950* (1976). New Mexican poetry not included in this work is being collected by Francisco Lomelí; and poetry produced in California is to be found in the unpublished collections of Luis Torres and Reynaldo Ruiz. I myself have an unpublished manuscript of the poetry found in the *Gaceta de Santa Bárbara* (California), published between 1879 and 1881. However, much more research must be undertaken in order to have a complete picture of nineteenth-century Chicano poetry.

The main formal characteristic of contemporary Chicano poetry is the artistic use of two languages in the same poetic construct. Although this rhetorical device acquired legitimacy only recently, especially with the poetry of Alurista, Ricardo Sánchez, Tino Villanueva and other contemporary poets, its practice has deep roots in the Chicano literary tradition, since as long ago as the sixteenth century, poets in Mexico were already using Spanish and Náhuatl in the same composition.[2] The best example of this practice, but not necessarily the first or only one, is the poetry of Mateo Rosas de Oquendo (1559?-1621?), who used native words in his Spanish poems to satirize the customs of the emerging society he found in Mexico. The poetic device he used in some of the verses of his "Sátira que hizo un galán a una dama criolla que le alababa mucho a México" (Satire Composed by a Young Man to a Criolla [woman of Spanish parents born in Mexico] Who Unduly Praised Mexico to Him) consists in closing the verse line with a native word, either in its original form or as modified by the Spaniards:

> Por la salsa tienen *chile*
> por velas queman *ocote*
> las damas mascan *copal*
> y es su fruta el *epasote*. (*Paz y Melia* 1906, 161)

> (For dressing they use chile
> instead of candles, ocote [torch-pine],
> the ladies chew copal

and their [favorite] fruit is the *epasote*.[3])

Or by enumerating the native products, as those used in the making of choco-late during the sixteenth century:

> El [chocolate] es hecho de *cacao*
> de *patastle* y de *achiote*,
> con *súchil, suchicatlastel*,
> con su *chipatleo* y *atole*. (*Paz y Melia* 1906, 161)

> (Chocolate is made with cocoa
> with patastle and achiote,
> with súchil and suchicatlaste,
> and with chipatleo and atole.)[4]

Oquendo's use of Náhuatl words related to food products, some of them still used in Mexico and by Chicanos today, has the function of demeaning the nature of Mexican cooking, unconscious of the fact that in Spain the process had been the same, with the introduction of Arabian words to designate certain foods and condiments. Although Oquendo used the two languages to satirize Mexican society in general, the most acerbic poems in which he employed this device were directed at the Indians.[5]

The use of the two languages continued in Mexico during the seven-teenth century in the work of Sor Juana Inés de la Cruz, especially in her *villancicos* (Christmas plays), where other languages and dialects appear, such as Latin by students or the language spoken by the blacks of Puerto Rico. In the "Villancicos" which she composed in 1677 in honor of San Pedro Nolasco there is a "Villancico de la ensaladilla," where the word "en-saladilla" (hodgepodge) refers to the use of assorted languages spoken by characters of different nationalities, a mixture that reflects the composition of the society for whom Sor Juana wrote her "villancicos." The Indian in the play sings and dances a "Tocotín mestizo" (mestizo song), in which we find not only isolated Náhuatl words, as used by Oquendo, but phrases and even complete sentences:

> *Huel ni machicahuac*
> no soy hablador
> *no teco qui mati,*
> que soy valentón. (*Obras* II, 42)

> (I may forget, [but]
> I'm not a liar,
> my master knows
> I'm a brave man.)

Unlike Oquendo, Sor Juana does not demean the indigenous culture; on the contrary, she presents an individual ready to fight to defend his rights.

The trend continued during the eighteenth century. In the "Entremés para las posadas" (short Christmas play), presented in Mexico City in 1790, there are several Indian characters who speak Spanish intercalating Náhuatl phrases. Even the Monigote (Lay Brother) who is perhaps a Criollo or a Mestizo, uses this type of discourse. It is assumed that the public still understood the Náhuatl language; otherwise, the rhetorical device would have had only a humorous function on the part of the Criollos and the Mestizos, since it made fun of the Indians.[6]

Even after Mexico obtained its political independence from Spain (1821), satirical poets continued to use Náhuatl in their compositions, not to denigrate the Indians but to ridicule those persons of Indian origin who had attained high positions in the government, especially those who sided with Maximilian when he was Emperor of Mexico from 1864 to 1867. Juan Nepomuseno Almonte, a general who had fought with Santa Anna at the Alamo and was made prisoner at San Jacinto (1836) and who was later instrumental in bringing Maximilian to Mexico, became the butt of many anonymous satirical poets. In "Glorias de Juan Pamuceno" (1862) the writer satirizes a fiesta Almonte gave for his powerful French friends, among them Generals Forey and Saligny. In this poem Almonte answers a question raised by his French friends, "los señores de rango" (the high ranking gentlemen): he calls Forey *Teutli*, the name given by the Aztecs to the Spaniards, whom they considered to be gods. The rhetorical device utilized by the anonymous poet is the same as that introduced by Oquendo:

> Estuvo el *Teuli* Forey
> con nosotros muy contento (. . .)
> comió pipián y *tamalli*,
> *tlemolito* con *xumiles*,
> y se hartó de *mextlapiles*
> en sus tacos de *tlaxcalli*.
> Saligny, no hay que decir,
> se bebió muchos *tzacoallis*
> de *neutli*, y en los *comallis*
> quiso su almuerzo engullir. (Campos 130–31)

> (*Teuli* Forey was there
> in our company very happy (. . .)
> he ate *pipián* and tamales,
> *tlemolito* with *xumiles*,
> and stuffed himself with *mextlapiles*
> in his tacos of *tlaxcalli*.
> Saligny, why say it,
> drank many *tzacoallis*
> of *neutli*; and from the *comallis*
> his lunch he gulped down.)[7]

The poets living in the Southwest after 1848 were familiar with this use of two languages for rhetorical purposes. The substitution of one language for the other (English instead of Náhuatl) was an easy matter, since the syntactical structure was not altered. This substitution occurred first in Mexico, during the years of the Mexican-American War (1846–1848), when English became popular due to the presence of the American soldiers, who did not know Spanish. As early as 1847 songs and corridos where English words appear became popular. In "De las Margaritas," the composer criticizes the Mexican girls who associated with the American invaders:

> Ya las Margaritas
> hablan el inglés,
> les dicen: —Me quieres?
> y responden: —*Yes.*
> *Mi* entiende de *monis*,
> mucho *güeno* está. (Mendoza 637)

> (The girls called Margaritas
> have learned to speak English,
> they are asked: "Do you like me?"
> and they answer: "Yes."
> Me know about money,
> which is very well.)

In the poetry appearing in the Spanish-language newspapers of the Southwest published after 1848, the use of interpolated English words and phrases was also common. The device was used in New Mexico by an anonymous poet to criticize the Mexican women who had become *agringadas* (had adapted Gringo culture) and refused to speak Spanish. In the *romance* "A una niña de este país" (To a young girl of this country), collected by professor Espinosa in New Mexico before the 1930s but not published until 1953, a dialogue is established between a Mexican with a limited knowledge of English and an *agringada*:

> A una niña de este pais [país]
> yo le hablaba una vez;
> yo le hablaba en español,
> y ella me hablaba en inglés.
> Le dije: —"Será mi amada
> y mi corazón también?
> Y me dijo la agringada:
> —*Me no like Mexican men.*
> Le empecé a hacer cariñitos
> en sus dientes de marfil,
> y me dijo con modito:
> —*I tell you, you keep still.*

Le escribí un papel por nota;
le dije: —Entérese de él.
Y me dijo la ingratota:
—*I tell you, you go to hell.*
—*I tell you*, te voy a decir,
I'll tell you, yo te diré,
si tú me quieres a mí,
es todo el inglés que sé. (*Romancero* 264)

(To a girl of this country
I was talking once;
I spoke to her in Spanish
and in English she would answer.
I said to her: "Will you be my beloved
and my sweetheart too?"
And the Americanized girl answered:
"Me no like Mexican men."
I began to praise her marble-like teeth,
and she said with affectation:
"I tell you, you keep still."
I wrote her a brief note;
I told her: "Please take notice."
And the ungrateful one said:
"I tell you, you go to hell."
"I tell you, *te voy a decir.*
I'll tell you, *yo te diré*,
Do you love me?
That's all the English I know".)

Similar compositions were collected by professor Américo Paredes in Southern Texas, one in the form of a song and the other as part of a *zarzuela* (operetta). In the first, "Los mexicanos que hablan inglés" (English-Speaking Mexicans), the *pochos*, the sons of Mexicans born in the United States, are criticized for refusing to speak Spanish:

En Texas es terrible
por la revoltura que hay,
no hay quien diga "hasta mañana,"
nomás puro *goodbye.*
Y *jau-didú mai fren,*
en ayl si yu tumora,
para decir "diez reales"
dicen *dola yene cuora.* (164)

(In Texas it is terrible
how things are all mixed up;
no one says "hasta mañana,"
it is nothing but "goodbye."

> And "howdy-dee-do, my friend,
> and "I'll see you tomorrow";
> when they want to say "diez reales"
> they say "dollar and a quarter.")
> (Translation by Paredes)

The formula was so popular that it was used on the stage for other purposes. In the fragment of a *zarzuela* reproduced by Paredes, English is used, not to ridicule but to produce a humorous effect:

> Como estamos en Texas
> el inglés hay que aprender,
> para que con nuestros primos [Americans]
> nos podamos entender.
> Y venderles charamuscas
> en la lengua del Tío Sam:
> —Mucho bueno palanquetas,
> piloncillo *very fine.*
> —*One cent the* merengues,
> *one cent the* pastel,
> *one cent the* turrones,
> *and* todo *one cent.*
> "What is it you want, Mister? (Paredes, 166)

> (Since we are in Texas,
> we must learn the English language,
> so that we can make ourselves
> understood to our cousins.
> So that we can sell them candy twists
> in the language of Uncle Sam:
> the honeyed popcorn is very good,
> the brown sugar loaves are very fine.
> "One cent the meringues,
> one cent the pie,
> one cent the nougats
> and everything one cent.
> "What is it that you want, Mister?)

In California some of the earliest Chicano poems appeared in *La Estrella* (1851), the Spanish-language supplement of the *Los Angeles Star*. About its director, Manuel Clemente Rojo, who published several poems, Antonio Blanco S. has said, "Rojo was not only editor and translator, but also a man of letters. We have collected a large number of the poems published under his name, which seem to us to be the product of a skillful poet. He deserves to be studied" (339). The second Spanish language newspaper in California, and one of the most important, was *El Clamor Público* (The Public Clamor; 1855–1859), edited by Francisco P. Ramírez, who also wrote poetry.[8]

Neither Rojo nor Ramírez used English in their poems. The earliest poem published in a California newspaper using the bilingual (in this case trilingual) device that has come to our attention is "El cura aprendiendo inglés" (The Priest Learning English), published in *El Nuevo Mundo* of San Francisco, the 29th of July, 1864, by a poet signing with the pseudonym "El Cura de Tamajona." The contents of this letrilla (festive poem of less than eight syllables) are ambiguous, since there are motifs belonging to two historical periods in the history of Mexico, the American invasion of 1846, and the French invasion of 1862, as well as the use of English and French words and phrases:

> *Reste sans cu*
> Abajo ... ... y dancen
> *Zi Yankee dul.* (Torres 58)

> (*Reste sans cu[llotes]*
> Down ... ... and dance
> The Yankee dul [doodle])[9]

This poem was probably published in Mexican newspapers first, and then reprinted in *El Nuevo Mundo*. By 1864 the stereotype of the American, as a man having a large frame, big feet, and being unable to speak Spanish correctly, was well established in Mexico; that is the way the Yankee appears in the poem, exaggeration making him even more grotesque:

> —Yo no te entende,
> dijo el atún
> (que era un Yankazo
> como un abedul,
> con cada pata
> como un almud) ...
> —Vieca [vieja] ... ˝no danzas
> *Zi Yankee dul?* (Torres 49)

> ("I don't understand you,"
> said the idiot.
> (He was a big Yankee,
> big as a birch-tree,
> with each foot
> like half an acre) ...
> (Torres' translation)

The purpose of this satirical poem,and others in which the American is presented as a grotesque individual was, of course, to instill pride in the Mexican people by demeaning the appearance of the invaders. The generalization about Americans having big feet was born during the invasion of 1846. As early as 1847, in the anonymous poem already cited, "De las Margaritas," they are referred to as "gringos patones" (Mendoza 637).

In California *El Clamor Público* was the first Spanish-language newspaper which accepted social protest poems, a theme that was to remain a constant in Chicano literature. As early as 1856 that newspaper published the anonymous poem "Justicia" (Justice), in which the Supreme Court is criticized for being biased against Chicanos ("el Tribunal / No nos considera igual" [this Tribunal / Does not consider us as equals]); for favoring the rich, and for other injustices.[10] The use of English and Spanish in social protest and political poems comes much later. It is not until the last decade of the nineteenth century that this literary device is utilized for such a purpose. One of the earliest examples of this type of bilingual composition, which was to become so popular with contemporary Chicano poets, is "Lo que dirá" (What He Will Say), a political poem published in *El Hispano Americano* of Las Vegas, New Mexico, October 15, 1892, and signed with the pseudonym "T. A. Tornillo" (Te atornillo, [I'll fix you]). In this type of truly bilingual construct the poet not only alternates the use of the two languages within the same sentence, but also between sentences. The poem is directed to the voters, telling them not to elect a certain candidate:

> Y que el pueblo vea
> That T.B. Catron don't get there.
>
> El 8 de noviembre lo dirá
> Si al pueblo, Catron, mancillará.
>
> El pueblo on that day will blare
> Que el panzón never got there.
>
> (And let the people see to it
> *That T.B. Catron don't get there.*
>
> November the 8th will tell
> If by Catron the people will be blemished.
>
> The people *on that day will blare*
> That the pot-bellied *never got there.*)

According to the poem, candidate Catron, apparently selected to run for office by the dominant Anglo politicians, should be rejected by the Hispanic voters because, as a banker, he has robbed the sheepherders. And no matter how much he will shout to the people in his political speeches, he will not be able to deceive them, nor silence the poet, who speaks the truth: For his bursting lungs / Can't silence truth telling tongues.

Although political subject matter proliferated during the last decade of the nineteenth century, some poets kept writing about traditional themes and in traditional forms. Representative of this so-called "learned" poetry are the poems of José Escobar, a Mexican expatriate living in New Mexico who edited several Spanish-language newspapers between 1891 and 1898. His style follows the trend established by the early *modernista* Mexican poets, whom he often imitated. Doris L. Meyer, who has collected and studied his poetry and that of others publishing in New Mexico during the last decades of the century, sees Escobar's contributions "as evidence of a 'learned' literature in New Mexico which, because it is less apparent than New Mexico's folk culture in Spanish, has been neglected by literary historians" (32).

Why have critics neglected the study of nineteenth century "learned" poetry? It is true that most studies have been dedicated to the popular aspects of early Chicano poetry. Lately, however, Arellano and Torres, in addition to Meyer, have been collecting and studying "learned" poetry. There is no question that this poetry is less representative of Chicano society than popular poetry. It is less representative because "learned" poets insisted on using standard Spanish to address a society that was rapidly becoming bilingual in writing about traditional subjects indistinguishable from those treated by most Latin American and Spanish authors and on rejecting the influence of popular forms, which have the greatest appeal for most newspaper readers, the medium in which the "learned" poems were published.

There is no question that early Chicano poetry was very close to the people, being generally influenced by traditional popular forms and popular themes, some of them having originated in Colonial Mexico, and others going further back to Medieval Spain. The oldest forms are found in New Mexico, the region which has the oldest poetic tradition, both popular and learned. The most common forms found there are the *trovo*, the *romance*, the *décima*, the *memoria*, and the *corrido*. Verse is also found in most of the popular religious forms, as the *pastorela*, the *auto*, the *villancico* and even in secular plays. As observed by Tomás Ybarra-Frausto, "these rhymed dramas have rarely been examined as popular poetry. As examples of people's verse, they document the process of oral transmission and collective improvisation" (6).

The *décima* and the *trovo* are two of the oldest forms used during the nineteenth century by Chicano folk poets, or *puetas*, as they were called by the people. The *décima* consists of four, ten-line stanzas introduced by a quatrain, which is glossed, a reason why the name *glosa* is often given to this form. Its origin was traced by professor Campa to sixteenth-century Spain, in the poetry of an obscure writer, Gregorio Silvestre. The form, which became very popular in New Mexico, was derived, however, directly from Mexico, where it was very common. In both regions it was used for political diatribes, as can be seen in those collected by Campos in Mexico and Campa in New Mexico.

The other form, the *trovo*, a dialogic poetic composition, was very popular in nineteenth-century Hispanic poetry, both popular and semi-popular. It is found in the *poesía gauchesca* of Uruguay and Argentina, as well as in Mexico, although not necessarily with the name *trovo*, a name derived from *trovar*. Its oral form consists in a contest between two *puetas*, who, accompanied by the guitar, challenge each other by asking difficult questions in octosyllabic verses grouped in stanzas of four, eight, or ten lines, that is, quatrains, *octavas* or *décimas*. The second *pueta* must answer the query beginning with the last rhyme of the previous strophe, that is, *debe trovar el verso* (must rhyme the verse). In Mexico this form was made popular by the folk poet José Vasconcelos, "El Negrito Poeta," a semi-mythical character to whom *trovos* were attributed. José Joaquín Fernández de Lizardi, in his novel *El Periquillo Sarniento* (1818), refers to him as being a contemporary of Sor Juana Inés de la Cruz, who was unable to rhyme a verse ending in the preposition *de*, a challenge that "El Negrito" had mastered (253).[11]

In New Mexico the most famous *pueta* composer of *trovos* was El Viejo Vilmas, whose compositions were studied by professor Espinosa (1914), in which he infers that, according to his New Mexican friends, Vilmas was a native *pueta*. However, he adds, "but there is no proof of it" (106). "El Negrito Poeta" appears in Vilmás' *trovos* as one of several *puetas* challenging him and, of course, losing the contest:

> Oy' [oye], afamado Negrito,
> ti [te] advierto que no soy pudiente;
> tú pensarás cai [caer] parado
> pero vas a cai de frente. (Espinosa 113)

> (Listen here, famous Negrito,
> I'm warning you I'm not powerful;
> you think you're going to land on your feet,
> but you're going to land flat on your face.)

The presence of these poetic forms, both popular and "learned," in early Chicano poetry indicates an adherence to a long established literary tradition, a tendency which often prevented poets from writing original compositions. This has been observed by professor Campa, who wrote, "As a rule, the metrical structure of the *décima* is too confining to allow much originality and spontaneity to the composer. The subordination of content to form makes the type of composition a bit stiff and unnatural. ... This lack of lyricism may be accounted for by the fact that *décimas* are no longer used as folksongs in New Mexico" (129).

Another reason for the abandonment of the *décima* and all other restrictive popular forms may be the popularity of the *corrido*, which has survived to the present. The *corrido*, as a narrative form, has a greater appeal than the *décima*, which was limited to expressing lyrical or philosophical themes. The desire to overcome the confining nature of the traditonal poetic structures led also to the creation of new forms, and eventually to free verse in all its ramifications, as observed in the multiform works of contemporary Chicano poets.

In conclusion it can be said that Chicano poetry has deep roots, that it is the product of a long uninterrupted literary tradition, and that its study can help the reader to better appreciate contemporary Chicano poetry, where some of the same characteristics may be found. From a historical perspective, it can be observed that some of the devices utilized by contemporary Chicano poets have their origin in the poetry of the nineteenth century, while others can be found in earlier periods of Mexican literature. The linguistic alternation of English and Spanish that the reader admires in the poetry of Alurista, José Montoya, Tino Villanueva and others, had been used by earlier poets, although they did it for purposes other than aesthetic, as is done today. Perhaps that is the greatest difference between early and contemporary Chicano poetry.

During the nineteenth century the use of both Spanish and English served mainly to provide social information, reveal cultural values, and expose the clash that had existed between the two cultures; it was also used to reflect the importance that interpersonal relationships have among the people of Mexican origin. In contemporary poetry, on the other hand, the extensive use of English and Spanish is not limited only to social purposes, but is used as well for the aesthetic values derived from the combination of the two languages, a procedure that has reached a distinctive equilibrium today.

The study of nineteenth century poetry also helps the critic and the linguist to trace other changes that have taken place in the use of the two languages by poets utilizing this literary device. Up to almost the end of the century, all poets used Spanish as the basic language, introducing English words only when referring to the culture of the *other*, or to ridicule those who had partially accepted the foreign culture, especially if they were women. In most contemporary poetry, on the other hand, English is the basic language, and Spanish is used most often to establish a relationship with the mother culture and for aesthetic purposes.

Although there are some studies (Keller, Valdés-Fallis) dedicated to the analysis of code-switching in contemporary Chicano literature, especially in poetry, there are hardly any studies examining its historical development.

The study of early Chicano poetry is in need of further development, not only in the collection of materials, but also in its analysis. We must establish the significance of the use of the two languages in the same poem and even in the same phrase, as well as the origins and uses of other changes throughout the history of this aspect of Chicano literary expression. This is important because poetry was the best means for the people to give vent to their thoughts and emotions, since poetry was easier to publish at that time in the newspapers available in their communities. Their poetry was first written in Spanish and then, as the change from Spanish to English took place, in both languages. The development of this process should be thoroughly documented as it will substantiate that there has existed a tradition which continues into the present. It will also lend testimony to the fact that the people of Mexican descent living in the United States have not been voiceless and expressionless, as portrayed until recently in sociological and historical studies.

Notes

[1]No complete listing exists of the newspapers published between 1848 and 1910. I have documented 138 newspapers. However, professor Lomelí informs me that in New Mexico alone more than 200 were published. Some of the earliest Spanish-language newspapers of the Southwest were *La Bandera* (Brownsville, TX, 1848); *El Museo Mexicano* (Santa Fe, NM, 1850); *La Verdad* (Santa Fe, NM, 1851); *La Estrella* (Los Angeles, CA, 1851); *La Crónica* (San Francisco, CA, 1854); *El Clamor Público* (Los Angeles, CA, 1855); and *El Bejareño* (San Antonio, TX, 1855). Although some of them lasted only a few months, in most of them poetry was published regularly. Only a small fraction of these poems has been documented.

[2]Code-switching by Chicanos in oral and written forms has been estudied by several critics, among them Gary D. Keller, Carol W. Pfaff, and Guadalupe Valdés-Fallis. It merits noting that the oldest manifestation of peninsular lyric poetry, the *jarchas*, of the ninth and tenth centuries, combine two or three languages: romance, Arabic and Hebrew.

[3]*zapote*, sapote or sapodilla. All translations from Spanish to English are ours, except as indicated.

[4]*patastle*, a kind of low-grade cocoa; *achiote*, annata; *súchil*, *suchicatastle*, *chipatleo*, aromatic flours used for flavoring; *atole*, corn-flour gruel.

[5]Oquendo's poetry has been studied by A. Paz y Melia and Alfonso Reyes.

[6]This "Entremés" has been reproduced in part by Rubén M. Campos.

[7]*pipián* is a stew of chicken and mutton with bacon and crushed almonds; *tamalli*, tamales; *xumilles*, insects eaten by the Indians of a tribe associated by Campos (131) to Almonte's ancestors; *mextlapiles*, tamales prepared with a certain kind of fish; *tacos de tlaxcalli*, snacks made with corn tortillas; *tzacoallis*, gourds used for drinking; *neutli*, pulque, a fermented drink made from the juice of the maguey; *comallis* (comales), griddles.

[8]Some of his poems have been collected by Luis Torres.

[9]Ending the verse with a truncated word was a common poetic device in Hispanic poetry. After writing this paper I discovered that the Mexican poet Guillermo Prieto (1818-1897), while in Monterrey, Nuevo León, published there in 1864 a weekly newspaper in verse entitled "El Cura de Tamajón." See Héctor González, *Siglo y medio de cultura nuevoleonesa*. Mexico City: Botas, 1946: 153, 188.

[10]This poem has been collected by Torres.

[11]The life and poetry of "El Negrito Poeta" has been studied by Nicolás León in Mexico and Espinosa in New Mexico.

Works Cited

Arellano, Anselmo F. *Los pobladores nuevomexicanos y su poesía*, 1889–1950. Albuquerque, NM: Pajarito, 1976.

Blanco S., Antonio. *La lengua española en la historia de California*. Madrid: Cultura Hispánica, 1971.

Campa, Arthur León. *Hispanic Folklore Studies of Arthur L. Campa*. Introduction by Carlos E. Cortés. New York: Arno, 1976. "The Décima," 127–31.

Campos, Rubén M. *El folklore literario de México; investigación acerca de la producción literaria popular (1525–1925)*. México: Publicaciones de la Secretaría de Educación Pública, 1929.

Cruz, Sor Juana Inés de la. *Obras completas*. Ed. Alfonso Méndez Plancarte. Vol. 2: *Villancicos y Letras Sacras*. México: Fondo de Cultura Económica, 1952.

"De las Margaritas." In Mendoza 636–38.

"Entremés para las posadas." In Campos 81–84.

Espinosa, Aurelio M. *Romancero de Nuevo Méjico*. Madrid: Consejo Superior de Investigaciones Científicas, 1953.

———. "Los trovos del Viejo Vilmas." *Journal of American Folklore* 27 (1914): 105–18.

Gaceta de Santa Bárbara. Santa Barbara, CA, 1879–1881. Photocopy in my files.

"Glorias de Juan Pamuceno." In Campos 130–32.

Jacobson, Rodolfo. "The Social Implications of Intra-Sentential Code-Switching." *New Directions in Chicano Scholarship*. Santa Barbara, CA: Center for Chicano Studies, University of California, 1984. 227–50.

Keller, Gary D. "How Chicano Authors Use Bilingual Techniques for Literary Effect." *Chicano Studies: A Multidisciplinary Approach*. Ed. Eugene E. García *et al*. New York: Teachers College, 1984. 171–90.

Leal, Luis. "F. N. Gutiérrez, poeta barbareño del siglo XIX." *Xalmán* 5.1–2 (1983–1984): 23–26.

León, Nicolás. *El negrito poeta mexicano y sus populares versos; contribución para el folklore nacional*. México: Imprenta del Museo Nacional, 1912.

Lomelí, Francisco A. *Eusebio Chacón: A Literary Portrait of 19th-Century New Mexico*. Albuquerque: Southwest Hispanic Research Institute, U of New Mexico, 1987. "Working Papers" No. 113.

———. Unpublished collection of early New Mexican poetry.

Mendoza, Vicente T. *El romance español y el corrido mexicano; estudio comparativo*. México: Imprenta de la Universidad de México, 1939.

Meyer, Doris L. "Anonymous Poetry in Spanish-Language New Mexico Newspapers, 1880–1900." *The Bilingual Review/La Revista Bilingüe* 2 (1975): 259–75.

————. "The Poetry of José Escobar, Mexican Emigré in New Mexico." *Hispania* 61 (1978): 24–34.

Paredes, Américo. *A Texas-Mexican "Cancionero"; Folksongs of the Lower Border.* Urbana: U of Illinois P, 1976.

Paz y Melia, A. "Cartapacio de diferentes versos a diferentes asuntos, compuestos o recogidos por Mateo Rosas de Oquendo." *Bulletin Hispanique* 8 (1906): 154–62, 257–78; 9 (1907): 154–85.

Pfaff, Carol W., and Laura Chávez. "Spanish/English Code-Switching: Literary Reflection of Natural Discourse." *Missions in Conflict; Essays on U. S.-Mexican Relations and Chicano Culture.* Ed. Renate von Bardeleben et al. Tübingen: Gunter Narr Verlag, 1986. 229–54.

Reyes, Alfonso. "Sobre Mateo Rosas de Oquendo, poeta del siglo XVI." *Revista de Filología Española* 4 (1917): 343–70.

Torres, Luis. "Poemas chicanos de California, 1855–1881." Unpublished ms., 1986. Copy in my files.

Valdés-Fallis, Guadalupe. "The Sociolinguistics of Chicano Literature: Towards an Analysis of the Role and Function of Language Alternation in Contemporary Bilingual Poetry." *Point of Contact/Punto de Contacto* 1.4 (1977): 30–39.

Ybarra-Frausto, Tomás. "Chicano Poetry: The Furrow and the Seed." Unpublished ms., n.d. copy in my files.

A Socio-Historic Study of Hispanic Newspapers in the United States

Nicolás Kanellos

The Nineteenth Century

Throughout the last two centuries Hispanic communities from coast to coast have supported newspapers of varying sizes and missions, running the gamut from the eight-page weekly written in Spanish or bilingually to the highly entrepreneurial large-city daily written exclusively in Spanish. Since the founding in New Orleans in 1808 of *El Misisipí*, probably the first Spanish-language newspaper in the United States, the Hispanic press has had to serve functions hardly ever envisioned in Mexico City, Madrid or Havana. Besides supplying basic news of the homeland and of the Hispanic world in general, advertising local businesses and informing the community about relevant current affairs and politics of the United States (often through unauthorized translations of the English-language press and/or news agencies), Hispanic periodicals additionally have had to offer alternative information services that present their own communities' views of news and events. At times this information has had to take on a contestatory and challenging posture vis-à-vis the English-language news organizations and U. S. official government and cultural institutions. Furthermore, the newspapers have had to take the lead in the effort to preserve Hispanic language and cultural identity in the face of the threat of annihilation by Anglo-Saxon culture and the English language. Most of the Hispanic press, whether a small weekly or a large city daily, has had to assume a leadership role in cultural (if not political) resistance and, beyond that, in the battle to protect the very real economic and political interests of the local Hispanic community, whether envisioned as a community, an internal colony or a racial-minority ghetto.

In many cases during the last two centuries, the local Hispanic press has often provided leadership—quite frequently with churches and mutualist societies—solidifying the community, protecting it and furthering its cultural survival. Not always as a means of furthering its own commercial interests and financial profit, the newspaper has assumed roles that have been associated with patriotic and mutualist societies, such as sponsoring patriotic and cultural celebrations and organizing the community for social and political action for such altruistic goals as founding Spanish-language schools and community clinics, fighting segregation and discrimination, and collecting funds for relief of flood victims, refugees and other needy and displaced persons. The pages of these newspapers have offered editorials and letters to the editor in support of community needs; the newspapers in general have had to take political stands regarding the homeland and the United States. They have offered their pages to the playing out of the dramas that envelope their special communities.

Finally, historically and to the present, the newspapers have functioned as purveyors of education, high culture and entertainment. During the nineteenth century and the first half of the twentieth, they became the principal publishers of literature by including poetry, literary prose and even serialized novels in their pages. As a function of cultural preservation and elevating the level of education of the community, the newspapers provided this fare, which often was drawn from local writers as well as reprinted from works by writers in the homeland and from throughout the Hispanic world. And as an extension of the latter interest, many newspapers founded publishing houses and some even bookstores to further distribute Hispanic intellectual and artistic thought.

The impact of this publishing movement in the early twentieth century should not by minimized, given the considerable economic resources concentrated in this effort; the large-scale involvement and cooperation of hundreds of intellectuals, creative writers, political figures and businessmen; and the production and distribution of writings by distinguished and important political and literary figures.[1]

The Southwest

Even before the Mexican American War in 1846, Hispanic newspapers in what became the Southwest of the United States were already carrying on and promoting political activities, as has been pointed out by scholar Luis Leal in "The Spanish Language Press: Function and Use." For instance, Santa Fe's *El Crepúsculo de la Libertad* (The Dawn of Liberty) headed up a campaign in 1834 for the election of representatives to their Mexican Congress, and it also served as a forum for Antonio Martínez's defense of the civil rights and land ownership rights of the Taos Indians. And after the Mexican American War, as Leal has pointed out, the Spanish-language press defended the rights of the Mexican inhabitants in what had become the new territories of the United States.

On the foundation laid by such newspapers as *El Crepúsculo de la Libertad*, *La Gaceta de Texas* (The Texas Gazette) and *El Mexicano* (The Mexican), all founded in 1813, numerous Spanish-language newspapers were founded and began to offer an alternative to the flow of information from Anglo-American sources during the period of transition from Mexican government to United States rule following the Mexican American War (1846–1848). This was only logical, for it was their specific business mission to serve the interests of the Mexican (-American) and Hispanic communities. The important commercial centers of Los Angeles and San Francisco supported dozens of periodicals at this time, including *La Estrella de Los Angeles* (The Los Angeles Star) and *El Clamor Público* (The Public Clamor) during the 1850s and Los Angeles' *La Crónica* (The Chronicle) from the '70s to the '90s; San Francisco's *La Voz de México* (The Voice of Mexico) from the 1860s to the 1890s, *La República* (The Republic) from the '70s to the '90s and *La Voz del Nuevo Mundo* (The Voice of the New World) in the '70s and '80s. Of course, the port cities were not the only populations that supported Spanish-language newspapers; Hispanic journalism also flourished in the inland towns and villages, especially in New Mexico, where virtually every sizable town had its own weekly, including Bernalillo, Las Cruces, Mora, Santa Fe, Socorro and Las Vegas.

While the newspapers published various types of creative literature, it is noteworthy that one of the expressions of this period was a serialized novel which illustrated the clash of Mexican and Anglo-American economic and cultural interests. "Las Aventuras de Joaquín Murieta" (The Adventures of Joaquín Murieta), based on the life of the legendary social bandit, was one such serialized novel published in Santa Barbara's *La Gaceta* (The Gazette) in 1881. Murieta's pursuit of vengeance on the Anglo-American newcomers surely coincided with popular resentment among the Californios who were losing their lands and their rights wholesale.

New York

Although in the Southwest the Spanish-language newspapers often took up the defense of their communities, this was not as pressing an issue as Hispanic American independence movements were for the newspapers serving Hispanic immigrants in New York during the same time period. In New York, the Spaniards, Cubans, Mexicans and other Hispanic immigrants founded periodicals that provided more for the typical interests of immigrants: news from the homeland, coverage of local Hispanic affairs and business, and also the preservation and enrichment of the Spanish language and Hispanic culture in the alien environment. The earliest newspapers on record were *El*

Mensajero Semanal, 1828–1831 (The Weekly Messenger), *El Mercurio de Nueva York*, 1828–1833 (The New York Mercury), *La Crónica*, 1850 (The Chronicle) and *La Voz de América* (The Voice of America) in the 1860s.

It was not until the end of the nineteenth century that the periodicals began to multiply in New York, undoubtedly responding to increased Hispanic immigration and the political fervor that developed in the Cuban, Dominican and Puerto Rican communities that were promoting independence from Spain for their homelands. In this regard, the most noteworthy institution was the Cuban newspaper *La Patria*, 1892–1898 (The Homeland), in whose pages can be found essays by the leading Cuban and Puerto Rican patriots. The newspapers like *La Patria* served not only as forums for revolutionary ideas, but were actually tools of organization and propaganda around which many of the expatriate conspirators rallied.

The most widely circulated Hispanic weekly in New York was *Las Novedades*, 1893–1918 (The News), whose theatre, music and literary critic was the famed Dominican writer Pedro Henríquez Ureña. Other periodicals publishing at this time were *El Porvenir* (The Future) and *Revista Popular* (The People's Magazine).[2] Just how many other periodicals existed at the end of the nineteenth century is not known, but probably there were not many more, judging from the size of the population.

The Twentieth Century

At the beginning of the twentieth century, a record number of immigrants from Mexico, from Cuba and Puerto Rico, and from Spain entered the United States, seeking refuge from political violence in their home countries. Spanish-language periodical literature immediately flourished throughout the Southwest, Midwest, New York and Tampa to service the needs of these immigrants and refugees.

The Southwest

In the U. S. Southwest, educated political refugees of the Mexican Revolution played a key role in publishing. From their upper class, expatriate perspectives, these intellectuals and entrepreneurs created and promoted—and here the newspaper was essential—the idea of a Mexican community in exile, or a "México de afuera" (Mexico on the outside), in which the culture and politics of Mexico could be duplicated until Mexico's internal politics allowed for their return. The "México de afuera" campaign was markedly nationalistic and militated to preserve Mexican identity in the United States. We see some of the movement's ideology in Clemente Idar's editorial in his Laredo newspaper, *La Crónica* (The Chronicle) on November 26, 1910:

> We do not preach the antagonism of the races ["race" in Spanish also
> means "culture"], as we are only interested in the preservation and
> education of our own so that it will no longer be looked down upon
> for not improving its physical and intellectual abilities. In the United
> States of North America, the problem of race is a question of color,
> and we who belong to a multicolor Latinized race, upon immigrating
> to this country with all of our ignorance, find ourselves in a decidedly
> and traditionally hostile environment. ... With rare exceptions, the
> Americans do not believe that those of us who are citizens of their
> country are capable of being good, responsible and loyal citizens, and
> the result is that, because of that belief, Mexicans are practically with-
> out a nationality. Well, those being the facts, let all of us Mexicans
> pull together with the holy ties of blood, and as Latins let us be as
> united as the Anglo-Saxons, fighting with valiant ardor for the glory of
> our Mexican heritage in the areas of culture, intellectual pursuits and
> morality. (Trans., mine)

Among the most powerful of the political, business and intellectual figures in expressing the "México de afuera" ideology was Ignacio E. Lozano,
founder and operator of the two most powerful and well distributed daily
newspapers: *La Prensa* (The Press) and *La Opinión* (The Opinion). Lozano
settled in San Antonio in 1908, founded *La Prensa* in 1913, and in 1926
established *La Opinión* in Los Angeles. He brought to Hispanic journalism
in the United States a professionalism and business acumen that resulted
in longevity for his two newspapers. Indeed, *La Opinión* is still published.
His sound journalistic policies and emphasis on professionalism were reflected in his hiring of well-trained journalists, starting at the top with his
appointment to editor of *La Prensa* of Teodoro Torres, the "Father of Mexican Journalism."[3] The ideas of men like Torres reached thousands not only in
San Antonio but throughout the Southwest and Midwest—as well as interior
Mexico—through a vast distribution system that included newsstand sales,
home delivery and mail. *La Prensa* also set up a network of correspondents
throughout the United States who were able to regularly issue reports on
current events and cultural activities of the Mexican community in exile and
other Hispanics in such far away places as Detroit, Chicago and even New
York.

Lozano and many of his prominent political writers became leaders of
the diverse Mexican/Mexican-American communities they served in the
United States, precisely because they were able to dominate print media.
Businessmen such as Lozano captured an isolated and specialized market.
They shaped and cultivated their market for cultural products and print media
as efficiently as they did for material goods, Mexican foods and specialized
immigrant services. The Mexican community truly benefitted in that the
entrepreneurs and businessmen did provide needed goods, information and

services that were often denied by the larger society through official and open segregation. And, of course, the writers, artists and intellectuals provided the high culture and entertainment in the native language for the Mexican community that was not offered by Anglo-American society. As for the creation of Spanish-language theatre by many of the journalists, it should be remembered that many theatres and movie houses were also segregated and off limits to Mexicans at this time.

In the editorial offices of *La Prensa* in San Antonio and Los Angeles' *La Opinión* and *El Heraldo de México* (The Mexican Herald), some of the most talented writers from Mexico, Spain and Latin America earned their living as reporters, columnists and critics, including such writers as Miguel Arce, Esteban Escalante, Gabriel Navarro and Daniel Venegas. These and many others used the newspapers as a stable source of employment and as a base from which they launched their literary publications in book form or wrote plays and revues for the flourishing dramatic stages. Various newspaper companies themselves established publishing houses and marketed the books of these authors and others. The Casa Editorial Lozano, an outgrowth of San Antonio's *La Prensa*, not only advertised the books in the family's two newspapers to be sold via direct mail, but also operated a bookstore in San Antonio, as did *El Heraldo de México* in Los Angeles. In addition to the publishing houses owned by the large dailies, in the same cities and in smaller population centers there were many other smaller companies operating, such as Laredo Publishing Company, Los Angeles' Spanish American Printing and San Diego's Imprenta Bolaños Cacho Hnos.

The largest and most productive publishing houses resided in San Antonio. Leading the list was the Casa Editorial Lozano, owned by Ignacio E. Lozano. Issuing and distributing hundreds of titles per year, it was the largest publishing establishment ever owned by an Hispanic in the United States. Another was the Viola Novelty Company, owned by P. Viola and associated with his two satirical newspapers, *El Vacilón* (The Joker) and *El Fandango* (The Fandango), active from 1916 through at least 1927. The Whitt Company, run by the descendants of an English officer who had remained in Mexico after his tour of duty under Maximilian's reign, still exists today, but only as a printing establishment. And another was the Librería Española, which today survives only as a bookstore. These houses produced everything from religious books to political propaganda, from how-to books (such as Ignacio E. Lozano's *El Secretario Perfecto*) to novels and books of poetry. Many of the novels produced by these houses were part of the genre known as "novels of the Mexican Revolution"; the stories were set within the context of the Revolution and often commented on historical events and personalities, especially from a conservative or reactionary perspective. In

Daniel Venegas

this perspective, many of them may also be considered exile literature.

Typical of these polemical works that often attacked the Revolution and particular political leaders were Miguel Bolaños Cacho's *Sembradores de viento*, 1928 (Sowers of the Wind), Brígido Caro's *Plutarco Elías Calles: Dictador Bolchevique de México*, 1924 (Plutarco Elías Calles: Bolshevik Dictator of Mexico) and Lázaro Gutiérrez de Lara's *Los bribones rebeldes*, 1932 (The Rebel Rogues). Many were the authors of this very popular genre—including Miguel Arce, Conrado Espinosa, Alfredo González, Esteban Maqueos Castellanos, Manuel Mateos, Ramón Puente and Teodoro Torres—but the most famous has become Mariano Azuela, author of the masterpiece that has become one of the foundations of modern Mexican literature, *Los de abajo* (The Underdogs), which was first published in 1915 in a serialized format in El Paso's newspaper *El Paso del Norte* (The Northern Pass) and was issued later by the same newspaper in book form.

Although most of the novels published during these years gravitated toward the political and counter-revolutionary, there were others of a more sentimental nature. Other titles, however, can be considered forerunners of the Chicano novel of the 1960s in their identification with the working-class Mexicans of the Southwest, their use of popular dialects, and their political stance as regards the government and society of the United States. The prime example of this new sensibility was issued from the pen of another Los Angeles newspaperman, Daniel Venegas. His novel *Las aventuras de Don Chipote o Cuando los pericos mamen*, 1928 (The Adventures of Don Chipote or When Parakeets May Suckle Their Young) is a humorous picaresque account of a fictional Mexican, country-bumpkin immigrant who travels through the Southwest, working here and there at menial tasks and hard labor and encountering one misadventure after the other. He becomes the victim of rogues, con men, the authorities and his foremen during his search for the mythic streets lined with gold that the United States is supposed to offer immigrants. Don Chipote is at once a novel of immigration, a picaresque novel and a novel of protest; furthermore it is an historical document which records the language and customs of Mexican workers in the 1920s. In the autobiographical passages of the book, Daniel Venegas shows himself to be proud of having been a laborer, as he recounts his own experiences in crossing the border, working on the railroad and chafing at the customs and attitudes of his Mexican-American brothers.

Besides being a novelist, Venegas also edited (he wrote each entire issue himself) the satirical weekly newspaper *El Malcriado* (The Brat) in Los Angeles during the 1920s. It was a chatty periodical which employed worker's dialect and openly identified with Chicanos, the term used both in the newspaper and in his novel. In addition, Venegas wrote plays and headed up a

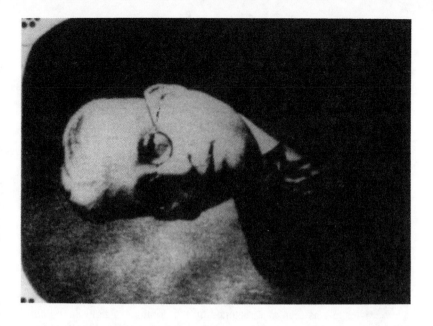

(Top) Julio G. Arce, who, under the pen name of Jorge Ulica, publishes his "Crónicas diabólicas." (Detail of the cover photo of his 1982 reprint collection, courtesy of Maize Press). (Bottom) Front page of *El Malcríado*.

vaudeville company that performed to working class audiences in Los Angeles, which revealed once again his class stand as departing significantly from his elite brethren among the writers and newspaper publishers.

While the novels were an important expression of the ideology of exile and of nationalism, there was another genre that was more traditionally identified with and central to Hispanic newspapers that became essential in forming and maintaining community attitudes. It was the *crónica*, or chronicle, a short, weekly column that humorously and satirically commented on current topics and social habits. It owed its origins to Addison and Steel in England and to José Mariano de Larra in Spain, but it was cultivated extensively throughout Mexico and Spanish America. In the Southwest, it came to function and serve purposes never imagined in Mexico or Spain. From Los Angeles to San Antonio and up to Chicago, Mexican moralists assumed pseudonyms and, from this masked perspective, commented satirically in the first person as witnesses to the customs and behavior of the colony whose very existence was seen as threatened by the dominant Anglo-Saxon culture. In writing their columns they were heavily influenced by popular jokes, anecdotes and popular speech, and in general they became a real mirror of the social environment in which they lived. It was the *cronista*'s job to fan the flames of nationalism and to enforce the ideology of "México de afuera." He had to battle the influence of Anglo-Saxon immorality and Protestantism and protect against the erosion of the Spanish language with equally religious fervor. Using such pseudonyms as El Malcriado (The Brat—Daniel Venegas), Kaskabel (Rattle Snake—Benjamín Padilla), Az.T.K. (The Aztec) and Chicote (The Whip), the *cronistas* were literally whipping and stinging the community into conformity, for example commenting on or simply poking fun at the common folks' mixing of Spanish and English and becoming overly impressed with Yankee ingenuity and technology.

Women, in particular were a target for these chroniclers, apparently because the men were worried that their wives, daughters and girlfriends would take the example of Anglo women in assuming some of the leadership and responsibility heretofore reserved for men in Hispanic culture—this was symbolized by the more masculine haircuts of flappers, their smoking in public and their higher hemlines during the liberalizing, roaring twenties. But more subtly, women were in short supply in the Mexican immigrant communities, and their assimilation to Anglo culture would lead the way to their inter-marriage with Anglos; and this posed a very real threat to the genetic and cultural survival of the Mexican community. The most hostile of the satirists of women was without a doubt Julio G. Arce (1870–1926), who used the pen name of Jorge Ulica in his syndicated "Crónicas Diabólicas" (Diabolical Chronicles). He satirized such apparently normal and insignificant practices as their adopting the American customs of giving surprise parties and celebrating Thanksgiving, but most of all he attacked their supposedly dominant husbands, their entrance into the workplace as secretaries and their appropriation of what to Ulica were masculine prerogatives, all of which were supposedly learned from American women "wearing the pants" in the family. In one of his *crónicas* he even went to the absurd extreme of writing a court scene in which a wife is exonerated for killing her husband by pushing him out a window because she is embarrassed by his backward Mexican ways.

Despite the campaign against women's liberation waged by various journalists, there is an extensive record of feminist writings in Southwestern newspapers. Among the first manifestations of this are the editorials and publications of teachers such as Sara Estela Ramírez (1881–1910) and Leonor Villegas de Magnón (1876–1955) in Laredo's *La Crónica*, and in Ramírez's own periodicals, *Aurora* and *La Corregidora*. There was also El Paso's short lived newspaper, *La voz de la mujer* (1907) and newspapers founded by revolutionaries, the Andrea and Carlota Bermúdez sisters, in San Antonio. An important woman *cronista*, poet and novelist was San Antonio's María Luisa Garza, who used the pen name of Loreley in her columns in *La Prensa*. But one of the most interesting women in this literary tradition was Lucía Eldine Gonzales (1853–1942), who was married to social journalist, Albert Parsons. Under the name of Lucy Parsons, she authored numerous poems, articles and editorials in support of labor, socialist and anarchist organizations and causes. She became one of the most prominent reformers and labor organizers in the late nineteenth and early twentieth centuries and one of the original founders of the Industrial Workers of the World (IWW). Although she was a Texas native, having been born in Johnson County, she moved with her husband to Chicago in 1873, and most of her writings and activities were undertaken there.

Much of this journalistic and literary activity in the Southwest came to an abrupt end with the Great Depression and the repatriation, both forced and voluntary, of Mexican immigrants. A large segment of the society Mexicans had created in the Southwest disappeared over a period of some ten years, beginning in 1930. With the economic distress brought on by the Depression and the depopulated Mexican communities, numerous periodicals and publishing ventures failed. It was not until the 1960s that small weeklies would begin to flourish again in Mexican-American communities.

New York

In New York, the period from 1880 to 1930 was one of increased Hispanic immigration and of intense interaction among various Hispanic national groups. While Spaniards and Cubans made up the majority of New York's Hispanic community, this period saw increased migration of Puerto Ricans facilitated by the Jones Act of 1917, which declared Puerto Ricans to be U. S. citizens. From the 1930s to the 1950s, Puerto Rican migration to New York assumed the proportions of a diaspora, as economic conditions worsened on the island and the United States suffered labor shortages in manufacturing during World War II. Also in the 1930s, a new wave of refugees from the Spanish Civil War was drawn to New York's Hispanic community.

At the turn of the century, Spanish and Cuban journalists dominated the print media environment in New York. The first decade of the century saw the founding of *La Prensa* (The Press), a daily whose heritage continues today in *El Diario-La Prensa* (The Daily-The Press) born of the fusion of *La Prensa* with *El Diario de Nueva York* (The New York Daily) in 1963. Also publishing during this decade were *Sangre Latina* (Latin Blood) at Columbia University, *Revista Pan-Americana* (Pan American Review) and *La Paz y el Trabajo-Revista Mensual de Comercio, Literature, Ciencias, Artes* (Peace and Work-Monthly Review of Commerce, Literature, Sciences and Arts). Even as far north as Buffalo there were journalistic enterprises, such as *La Hacienda* (The State), founded in 1906.

Among the various specialized weeklies that appeared in New York between 1910 and 1930, one merits special attention: *Gráfico* (The Graphic). What was notable about the newspaper, aside from its intent to live up to its title by including numerous photos and illustrations, was that in its early years it was an openly declared "amateur" enterprise written and directed by writers and artists, many of whom were involved in the Hispanic professional stage in Manhattan and Brooklyn. The founders of *Gráfico* felt that they could better defend community interests, especially those of Spanish Harlem, as amateurs, because the professional Spanish-language newspapers, which depended greatly on advertising, could not deal with controversial social and political issues. *Gráfico* was founded in 1927 under the editorship of Alberto O'Farrill, an important playwright and comic actor of the *teatro bufo cubano* (Cuban black face, musical farces). As such, *Gráfico* was replete with theatre and entertainment news, as well as poems, short stories, essays and *crónicas* by the leading Hispanic writers in the city.

Gráfico published some of the most notable *cronistas* in New York under such pseudonyms as Maquiavelo (Machiavelli) and O'Fa (O'Farrill himself). As in the Southwest, these *cronistas* labored to unify the Hispanic community; a difficult task because of the various Hispanic national and racial groups there. While in the Southwest the immigrant writers and entrepreneurs promoted "México de afuera," in New York they often articulated a "Trópico en Manhattan" (a Tropics or Caribbean culture in Manhattan).

In the pages of *Gráfico* one finds expressions of an intense Hispanic nationalism. The need to defend the civil rights and culture of the Hispanic community living in Anglo and Jewish areas of Spanish Harlem was continually voiced. In an editorial published bilingually in English (this was the only portion of the paper written in English) and Spanish on July 31, 1927, one reads:

> We want to make this weekly publication an efficient instrument dedicated to the defense of the Spanish speaking population of Harlem and a vehicle for mutual understanding and compensation between the two main racial groups living in this section.
>
> We do not expect financial compensation. The cooperation given to GRAFICO will not be used for individual aggrandizement. Ours is amateur and disinterested journalism.
>
> We feel the immediate necessity of taking up important issues pertaining to our common defense instead of leaving them to be defended by any individual that may betray us as it happened oftentimes. We stanchely [sic] believe that, whoever wants something well done, must do it himself.
>
> With our numerical strength, with our prestige as civilized human beings, with our unity in aspirations and our efforts for the common good, we shall reach as good moral, social and economic standards as any other racial group living in this community.

On the same editorial page appeared the following plea to Harlem's Jewish merchants:

> Hath not a Jew eyes? Hath not a Jew hands?" The Jewish merchants and business men of the Harlem section should not antagonize and create friction with our racial group. The fact that we are mostly working men and women victims of industrial slavery does not justify any attack, abuse or humiliation from anybody.
>
> The bulk of the Spanish-American population in this city lives in Harlem. It is a matter of a few years more and Harlem will be known as the Spanish centre in New York.
>
> As a natural outcome of the concentration of our racial group, the commercial, professional and social activities of the Spanish element are becoming wider and wider. ... We are ready to condemn any unjustified or uncalled for action on the part of our conationals, but will come forward to defend our rights, our lives and homes whenever they will be at stake. "For sufferance is (not) the badge of our tribe. ... "

The Hispanic community in New York saw itself at this point as the most recent of immigrant groups bent on establishing a permanent place for itself

(Top) Front page of *El Gráfico*. (Bottom) Alberto O'Farrill (*El Gráfico* newspaper, June 11, 1927).

on the ladder of economic opportunity. Hispanics in New York were there to stay; they were not just awaiting the end of the Mexican Revolution before returning home, as was the case with expatriate Mexicans in the Southwest. The plea for the protection of their civil rights in an English-language editorial is understandable in this light.

There are also notable differences in the Spanish and English language versions of these two editorials. Notably absent from the English language version is the attack on "todos los periódicos hispanos que han venido aquí con el estribillo de defender los intereses de la Colonia (all of the Hispanic newspapers that have come here with the refrain of defending the interests of the community), probably because of the desire not to air dirty laundry outside of the community. More importantly, in Spanish the first editorial ends with these words: "ya que estamos condenados a prolongar nuestra residencia aquí" (being that we are condemned to prolong our residence here). It seems that the writer or writers elaborated in English the immigrant's theme of searching for a better life in the United States, but in Spanish made somewhat of an about-face, touching upon the ideology of exile or at least indicating an unwilling sojourn in the United States. The stance, therefore, when one takes both English and Spanish language versions into account, is ambivalent, and while not as militantly separatist as the ideology expressed in the Southwest, it is not quite that of the European immigrant either, who has immigrated to stay, to become an American citizen, to trade the old culture and language for the new in order to succeed in America.

Attitudes towards the use of English in Spanish-language newspapers seem to have varied enormously. In O'Fa's *crónica* "Pegas Suaves" (Soft Blows/Jabs) of February 27, 1927, and elsewhere, he uses Anglicisms in his Spanish to reflect daily usage in the community; except for the word "express," referring to the express subway train, he does not set the English terms apart in quotation marks or italics, nor does he satirize their use. Some examples follow:

> Son las tres de la mañana; a esta hora como de costumbre abandono el suave y delicado alambre de mi caucho ... (It's three in the morning; and as is my custom I abandon the soft and delicate wire of my couch ...)
>
> ... me meto las manos en los bolsillos, saco los cinco pennies que tengo de ciñuelo y entre la vacilación de que si convierto en metálico el nickel o no ... (... I put my hands into my pockets and pull out my last five pennies and not deciding whether to exchange the pennies for a nickel ...)
>
> Atravieso el hall chiflando mi valsesito ... (I cross the hall whistling a little waltz ...)

Daniel Venegas in *El Malcriado* and in *Las aventuras de Don Chipote* made use of working class Chicano speech in his writings. Like most of his elite colleagues, he did make an issue of mixing English and Spanish and went to pains to italicize Anglicisms. Julio G. Arce, on the other hand, attacked such impure Spanish with biting satire. It represented the beginnings of assimilation and loss of identity, as well as low class behavior. O'Fa, assuming the persona of a common penniless worker, was not sensitive to these linguistic rules; neither were many of the other *cronistas* in New York where competition between Anglos and Mexicans and Hispanic-Anglo culture conflict did not have a long and bloody history on soil that was once part of the Mexican homeland, as was true in the Southwest. The cultural nationalism expressed in New York was just not as acrid and widespread as it was in the Southwest at this juncture in history. Then, too, the stigma against speaking Spanish and being an immigrant was not as strong in New York as it was among Anglos in the Southwest. As far as the Spanish language was concerned, when evoked as a topic in the newspapers in New York as well as in the Southwest, it was always a motive for pride and nationalism.

New York was a veritable Tower of Babel, which had drawn peoples from the far corners of the earth and where many languages could be heard every day. There was not this sense in New York of two major groups, the Anglos and the Mexicans, confronting each other, locked in mortal embrace over time and existing at the expense of each other as was the case in the Southwest.

Nevertheless, the Hispanics in New York were aware of racial and cultural prejudice, and they did not hesitate to fight back. Newspaper editorials often expressed community sentiments, as can be read in *Gráfico* on August 7, 1927:

> The great majority of our detractors forget that the citizens residing in the Harlem vicinity enjoy the prerogatives and privileges that American citizenship brings. We are almost all originally from Puerto Rico and the rest of us are naturalized citizens. Whosoever has identified himself with the history of this country knows that when we speak of foreigners we are talking about ourselves, because that is what the inhabitants of this young nation are. The United States is a young nation and we believe that the melting pot of peoples that it constitutes clearly indicates that its components belong to all of the cultures and all of the nations of the world. Thus, we are making fools of ourselves when we try to categorize anyone here as a foreigner.
>
> Many of the individuals who attempt to knock down our co-citizens in this locale were no better than them before learning the customs and ways of this country. One has to be blind not to see in any of those individuals who call themselves complete citizens the fringes of their old country and their old customs. . . .
>
> We, of course, do not participate in this intransigent hate and we

are not going to wave the battle flag of animosities and prejudices that
would further feed hate and serve no other purpose. . . .
    The recent clashes between inhabitants of the barrio and some au-
thorities who have also lowered themselves to the common and ignorant judgment about our colony have obligated us to take up the forum
ready to brave the consequences implied in our just and reasonable
defense.

The above editorial also points to another major difference, of course,
between the Puerto Rican and Mexican communities in the United States.
Here, the editorial writer was claiming his community's rights of citizenship,
and from that basis was appealing to the melting pot theory. The ideology
of exile among Mexicans in the Southwest left no room for citizenship nor
was it interested in promoting a Mexican addition to the American stew;
instead it promoted a return to Mexico, the American experience posited as
temporary. But citizenship and pluralism did not translate to assimilation
for the Puerto Ricans; once they were automatically citizens, the pressure
to assimilate was lessened. With the advent of the Depression, New York
did not experience the massive repatriation of Hispanics that occurred in the
Southwest. Instead, the opposite was true. Hard economic times brought
even more Puerto Ricans to the city, a trend that would intensify during World
War II as northeastern manufacturing and service industries experienced
labor shortages.

    The 1930s and 1940s saw an increase of immigration from Spain as the
refugees of the Spanish Civil War streamed into Hispanic population centers,
such as New York, Tampa and Puerto Rico. In New York newspapers were
founded to serve the new migrants and immigrants. They also reflected a renewed interest in working-class culture, labor organizing and socialism. In
the pages of *Vida obrera* (Worker Life, 1930), *Alma Boricua* (Puerto Rican
Soul, 1934), *España Libre* (Free Spain, 1943) and *Cultura Proletaria* (Pro-
letarian Culture, 1943) one finds a literature that reflected the life interests
of the common working person, their battles against labor exploitation and
their struggles in an alien society. These newspapers contain autobiographical sketches, anecdotes and stories, quite often in a homey, straight-forward
language that was replete with pathos and artistic sensibility.

    The first truly significant writings in English by a Puerto Rican began
to appear in newspapers in the late 1930s. The columns of Jesús Colón are
considered landmarks in the development of Puerto Rican literature in the
continental United States because they foreshadowed a racialized working-
class identity that characterized much of New York Puerto Rican (Nuyorican)
writing that appeared in the 1960s and that prevails today. Colón was born
in 1901 into a working-class family in Cayey, Puerto Rico. At the age of

sixteen, Colón stowed away on a ship that bound for Brooklyn. In New York, he worked at a series of jobs that exposed him to the exploitation and abuse of lower-class and unskilled laborers. He became involved in literary and journalistic endeavors while working as a laborer, trying to establish a newspaper and writing translations of English-language poetry. As he strove to develop his literary and journalistic career, he encountered racial prejudice, mainly because of his skin color, for Colón was of Afro-Puerto Rican heritage. Despite discrimination, Colón became active in community and political activities. He became a columnist for *The Worker*, the publication of the national office of the Communist Party. Colón also founded and operated a small publishing house, Hispanic Publishers (Editorial Hispánica), which published history, literature and political pamphlets in Spanish.

A selection of Jesús Colón's newspaper columns and essays was published in 1961 under the title of *A Puerto Rican in New York and Other Sketches*. In this selection, Colón's major themes are: the creation and development of a political consciousness; his own literary development and worth; advocacy for the working-class poor; and the injustices of capitalist society in which racial and class discrimination are all too frequent and individual worth does not seem to exist. The whole collection is richly expressive of a socially conscious and humanistic point of view. With the exception of the socialist and working-class Spanish-language newspapers mentioned above, many of Colón's writings would not have been welcomed for their political content in other community-based Spanish-language newspapers that were typically operated by an immigrant of the entrepreneurial class. But his stance and writings are totally consistent with the points of view expressed in *Vida Obrera*, *Cultura Proletaria* and the early years of *Gráfico*.

Tampa

The history of Spanish-language newspapers in Tampa diverges somewhat from that of the periodicals in Hispanic communities in other parts of the United States. At the end of the nineteenth century, the Tampa area became home to a large segment of Cuba's cigar manufacturing industry. Various cigar companies engineered this move to avoid the hostilities of the Cuban wars for independence from Spain, to relocate closer to their principal market in the United States, to avoid excise taxes and to skirt labor unions. In 1886, factories were built in the mosquito-infested swamps just east of Tampa in what became Ybor City, which was named after the principal cigar manufacturer, Rafael Ybor. The owners were not able to escape the labor unrest that characterized the industry in Cuba, and only partially escaped the repercussions of the wars of independence, which were followed upon by the Spanish American War.

The Tampa-Ybor City Hispanic community was divided by ethnicity, nationality and class. The owners and managers of the cigar industry were mostly conservative Spaniards, who sympathized with European colonial power. The cigar workers were mostly Cuban, Asturian and other working-class Spaniards. Ethnic and racial divisions in this group were reflected in the establishment of various mutualist societies: the Centro Español (Spanish Center), the Centro Asturiano (Asturian Center), the Círculo Cubano (Cuban Circle) and the Sociedad Martí-Maceo (Martí-Maceo Society), the latter being a center for Afro-Cubans who were not welcome in the other clubs and who experienced discrimination from Anglos and Hispanics in the Jim Crow South.

These class, race and ethnic divisions were reflected in periodical literature. Among the periodicals that served the interests of the owners of the cigar factories, was *La Revista* (The Magazine), directed by Rafael M. Ybor, the son of the owner of the largest and most important factory. Several periodicals served the interests of the workers and unions: *Federación* (Federation), *Federal* (Federal), *El Internacional* (The International) and *Boletín Obrero* (Worker Bulletin). Some of the ethnic societies also issued periodicals, such as the bi-weekly review of the Círculo Cubano: *El Cubano* (The Cuban). The Afro-Cubans were given very little coverage in any of the Tampa newspapers. There were other periodicals that promoted ethnic unity in the Hispanic community. Out of these efforts came such publications as *Tampa Ilustrado* (Tampa Illustrated) and *La Gaceta* (The Gazette), whose unifying effort was "Latin," rather than Hispanic, by even including Tampa's Italian community. To this day *La Gaceta* is published trilingually: English, Spanish and Italian.

Summary

Before World War II there existed two large categories of Spanish-language newspapers in Hispanic communities in the United States: (1) the dailies and (2) the weeklies and bi-weeklies. Dailies were large business enterprises that only existed in major urban centers: San Antonio's *La Prensa*, Los Angeles' *La Opinión* and *El Heraldo de México*, New York's *La Prensa* and *El Diario de Nueva York*. They distributed their papers widely in other towns, cities and states, and maintained a corps of correspondents in the major Hispanic communities in the country. Before the Second World War, as now, these enterprises counted on a clientele made up largely of immigrants and recent arrivals, as opposed to Americans of Hispanic descent.

They depended on a population whose principal mode of obtaining information was the Spanish language. These dailies clustered at ports of entry where Hispanics settled in "colonies," barrios or ghettoes and, thus, made up a more or less homogeneous market—something that these newspapers' ideologies of exile and ethnic solidarity incidentally or subtly promoted. A few of these newspaper dailies expanded into the publication and distribution of books, some of which were written by their own journalists, editors and owners, and this easily extended their intellectual leadership and influence. Of course, such genres as the "novel of the Mexican Revolution"—a clear forerunner of the Cuban exile novel of the last thirty years—and the political tracts that were published in book form also promoted the ideology of exile maintained by the elites.

From the mid-nineteenth century on, there existed literally hundreds of small weekly newspapers in the Southwest, and numerous others in New York and Tampa from the latter part of the nineteenth century. The small weekly was the most representative type of Hispanic periodical because its modest staff and equipment made publication possible even in the smallest of communities. They provided the most important local, regional, national and home-country news, and printed literature, entertainment and political and cultural commentary. To this day weeklies are the most popular and frequently published Hispanic periodicals, maintaining a flexibility that mirrors the evolution of their communities. They are the most likely to serve the interests of a particular segment of a heterogeneous Hispanic community in a large city—in Houston today, for instance, various ethnic communities subscribe to their own papers: the Mexican Americans to *El Sol* (The Sun) and *El Mexica* (The Aztec), the Cubans to *Información* (Information), the general Hispanics to *La Voz* (The Voice); in Chicago, the Mexicans to *La Raza* (The Race), the Puerto Ricans to *El Puertorriqueño* (The Puerto Rican), etc.

After World War II some of these weeklies began publishing in bilingual format while others published just in English. Today, local and national monthly magazines in English are an outgrowth of this tradition. *Hispanic*, *Vista* and *Nuestro* (Ours) specifically promote a national Hispanic identity and market. Before 1940 weeklies were the most vocal instruments of cultural and linguistic resistance to assimilation.[4]

Spanish-language newspapers have been published in the United States since the beginning of the nineteenth century. But it was not until the 1920s and 1930s that they actually flourished, especially in California, Texas, Florida and New York. During these prosperous years, there seems to have existed a national Hispanic consciousness that coincided with a sense of resistance to acculturation and assimilation. In the elite society of publishing, there was an integration of writers, publishers and cultural workers from throughout the Spanish-speaking world. Of course, in the Southwest and the Midwest the personnel, context and culture of Mexico predominated, while in New York and Tampa the culture and references of Spain and Cuba prevailed. During the 1920s and 1940s, the Puerto Rican influence in New York was felt more and more, but it should be remembered that New York always maintained a cosmopolitan and international Hispanism, regardless of the population size of one group compared to another.

Much of Hispanic periodical production was influenced by the great political movements in Hispanic countries of origin. Indeed, various Hispanic newspapers in the United States were founded to promote or were themselves products of these political movements: wars of independence, revolutions, civil wars. While in the Southwest the Great Depression and the repatriation of Mexicans were catastrophic for Hispanic newspapers, in New York and Tampa the Depression and the Second World War interrupted and retarded their development, but did not bring about their demise.

Notes

[1]Included among the latter were the Mexican novelist Mariano Azuela, the Dominican writer and journalist Pedro Henríquez Ureña, the Puerto Rican patriot of independence and writer Pachín Marín, the Cuban patriot and writer José Martí, the Mexican philosopher and educator José Vasconcelos and scores of others who in the past were active and known in U. S. Hispanic communities, but unknown in their respective fatherlands.

[2]See *La Patria* 3 February 1984.

[3]Lozano's publishing house also issued two of Torres' novels, one of which was a biting satire of the Revolution: *Como perros y gatos* (Like Cats and Dogs), and various other novels of the Mexican Revolution.

[4]However, by the end of the nineteenth century in New Mexico, the larger Hispanic population figures and greater political and economic power of Hispanics was reflected in newspapers publishing bilingually and even Hispanic and Anglo clientele subscribing to the same bilingual periodicals.

Works Cited
and Additional References

Arce, Julio G. *Crónicas diabólicas de "Jorge Ulica."* Ed. Juan Rodríguez. San Diego: Maize, 1982.

García, Richard A. "Class, Consciousness and Ideology—The Mexican Community of San Antonio, Texas 1930–1940." *Aztlán* 8 (1977): 23–69.

Gutiérrez, Félix. "Spanish Language Media in America: Background, Resources, History." *Journalism History* 4.2 (1977): 34–41.

Kanellos, Nicolás. "Daniel Venegas." *Chicano Writers* in *The Dictionary of Literary Biography* 82 (1989): 271–74.

Two Texts for a New Canon:
Vicente Bernal's *Las Primicias* and
Felipe Maximiliano Chacón's *Poesía y prosa*

Erlinda Gonzales-Berry

This long over-due project, Recovering the U. S. Hispanic Literary Heritage, by its very nature places us in the rather uncomfortable position of creating a literary canon, that is to say, in the position not only of codifying an ethnic literary identity, but also of assigning a standard of value to a corpus of texts. We must begin by recognizing that we are engaging in an act of political interpretation, and that interpretive acts, as Elizabeth Meese reminds us, "inevitably install us in a matrix of difference and differential relations, an (ex)tended field of tensions which are reduced to or contained only with limited success as pure 'identity' " (33).[1] Fifteen or twenty years ago the task might have been easier. At that time many of us here would have agreed that it was possible to create a monolithic Chicano identity. We were perhaps mistaken but more certain then, than we are now, of what configurations that identity might assume. Today we hear Chicano scholars like Ramón Gutiérrez admitting that Chicano scholarship of the early years "defined the Chicano community as more homogeneous and unified that it really was." Gutiérrez adds that "emerging paradigms have forced Chicanos to explore the way factors like race, class, gender, sexual preference and geographic location alter Chicano identity" (1990). I believe that these factors obtain not only for the present but also for past centuries and that they cannot be ignored when assessing literary texts of earlier epochs.

If the development of this recovery project is indeed governed by an awareness of a "matrix of difference," my apprehension diminishes somewhat, for I can then envision the creation of what Meese calls a canon of abundance rather than one of scarcity (31). There is still the problem, however, of value. How do we assign value to the texts we recommend? Do we approach them with the notion that they possess some "intrinsic" or "universal" value? If so, how do we arrive at a consensus regarding what exactly constitutes such elusive qualities? Is it our objective to select texts that show life as it "really was," that is, are we seeking historical accuracy and authenticity? If so, how do we, from our present position, judge how life really was in the past? Are we committed to publishing works with a specific ideology?

We must base our judgments on the understanding "that the value of the text is contingent on how well it may perform certain desired/able functions for one set of subjects" (Hernstein Smith 30). We must understand, of course, that we are merely one set of subjects with specific desires. And even then, we may not all be motivated by the same desires nor by shared responses to the corpus of texts under consideration. The best that I can do at this moment is attempt to clarify my own subject position—expose my own criteria for assigning contingent value.

To begin with, I part from the position assumed by Genaro Padilla, that "what interests me is not so much to [affix] a degree of historical truth-value to [these] testimonies or [to argue] the merits of their representativeness of Hispano Mexicano culture . . . [but rather] to recover the voices and stories of these ghosts" (93). However, since I am certain that limited funds will force us to be selective with regard to the actual number of ghostly voices we can resurrect, a guideline for me in the selection of pre-twentieth century texts, would reside in the response to the following question: "To what extent does the text stand as a discourse of contestation?"[2] This criteria would allow me to privilege all texts that were written in Spanish regardless of the author's class interest. The very use of Spanish by authors who were literate in English (e.g. Felipe M. Chacón, Miguel C. de Baca) was an act of contestation to the mainstream canon. I would not, however, exclude texts written in English merely because they were written in the dominant language, so long as they clearly demonstrate an attempt to contest texts that privileged hegemonic practices. I think specifically of María Amparo Ruiz Burton's *The Squatter and the Don*, a novel riddled with ambivalence that clearly points toward the desirability of assimilation for the *rico* class, yet protests loudly against the machinations and chicanery by which this class was stripped of its landholdings in California. Her posture toward *las clases populares* is offensive, to be sure, yet therein lies her position in the matrix of "difference."

In keeping with my criteria of contestation, I recommend the publication of as many texts written/or narrated by women as possible, for these narratives lead us to conclude that voices uttered from a male subject position, tainted by the biases of patriarchal phallocentric discourse, can be either limited in scope or misdirected in their interpretations of the *mexicana* experience. The narratives of María Inocenta Pico, Eulelia Pérez, Dorotea

Valdez and Felipa Osuna de Marrón in the Bancroft Library chronicle the coming of the *americanos* and the reactions of the *mexicanos* in California to their dispossession and marginalization. These narratives also call attention, in a most compelling way, to the responses of Californio women to historical change. The publication of as many of these texts as possible would go a long way in eschewing a canon of scarcity, openly recognizing gender difference as an important and inexorable component of the broader hispano/mexicano experience.

A nineteenth century text to which I assign a high level of contingent value is the anonymously penned drama *Los tejanos* (The Texans). This well-documented play lies hidden away in the pages of a 1944 issue of the journal *Hispania* (Espinosa and Espinosa). *Los tejanos* is a historically important text that stands out like a beacon in an era of literary scarcity. That the author of this play may well have been the Spaniard who appears as Capitán Ramírez playing one of the two main roles in the play should not discourage its inclusion in our project. Regardless of whom the writer may have been he explicitly supported self-determination for *el pueblo Nuevomexicano* (New Mexican people).

Los tejanos should be printed along with various versions of another inaccessible New Mexican drama, *Los Comanches* (A. Espinosa 1907). This late eighteenth century text is important but because it demonstrates that, despite the geographical isolation of the New Mexican colony, there was a sense of belonging to a broader culture, of affiliation with a literary tradition whose threads can be traced back to the epic verses of Pérez de Villagrá, *La Historia de la Nueva México* (1610), and Ercilla de Zúñiga's *La Araucana* (1569)—an epic on the attempted conquest of the Araucanos (Chile)—, and to the Iberian medieval dramatic tradition.

This tradition had a colonial agenda about which we must be very honest. It is important that we attempt to clarify if there are links which allow us to understand how the colonial subject was transformed into the colonized subject of Chicano literature. How do we bind together into a single tradition works whose authors must be situated in two very distinct positions: those bearing testimony to a Spanish colonial project and those writing from a position of colonized "otherness." While it is not my intent to resolve this aporia here, I will point out some possible links.

The soldiers who wrote about northern New Spain, some of them barely literate, attempted to justify a project which, failing to deliver the new Tenochtitlan, was suspect at best, illegitimate at worst.[3] It was their duty to convince their superiors that their labor was not in vain. The inscription of self as agents of a precarious enterprise was as often riddled with exaggeration as with disillusion. Much of the literature written by the *me-*

xicano population of the Southwest after the Mexican American War bears testimony to a similar disillusion. Those who hoped the new regime would bring the progress promised but unrealized by Mexican rule, inscribed their disillusion in their own chronicles of despair. Mariano Vallejo, for example, registered the following: "What a difference between the present time and those that preceded the usurpation by the Americans. If the Californians could all gather together to breathe a lament, it would reach Heaven as a moving sigh which would cause fear and consternation to the Universe. What misery!" (Paredes 48).

The distance of Spain's colonial soldiers from their cultural and political centers also produced in their writing a sense of rupture and discontinuity. Their dependence on those centers led them to produce chronicles that communicated their experiences in unknown territories. An examination of the literature produced by *mexicanos* after 1848 in the occupied American Southwest likewise reveals a strong sense of rupture and discontinuity. These writers, faced with the traumatic separation which the annexation of Mexican territory to the United States brought them, attempted through the written word to bridge this political rupture and to remain linked to a cultural tradition by recording their experiences in the unknown cultural territories imposed upon them.

Nuevomexicano literature of the nineteenth century offers some interesting examples of works that bear a strong sense of grief and disillusion of the sort than can be found in colonial texts. The prolonged battle for statehood and the accompanying defamation campaign, which was nurtured by a flagrant discourse of domination, placed the Nuevomexicano population in a defensive position, the very position held by the frustrated seekers of the New Tenochtitlan. This position accounts in part for the sometimes ambivalent tone of the literature of this period. The need to sustain and to remain identified with a cultural tradition whose future was threatened by political rupture inspired a bounteous corpus of Spanish-language texts in all genres. As I stated elsewhere, "One senses from a reading of the extant material that the motivating force was to affirm cultural identity by a positing of the Spanish-language word as an amulet against imminent displacement" (5). We must also acknowledge that the desire to validate the image of Nuevomexicanos vis-à-vis Anglo Americans, who would issue judgment regarding their fitness for statehood, lent itself to an exaggerated rhetoric of patriotism not unlike the exaggerated rhetoric of Fray Marcos de Niza who attempted to convince the viceroy of the worthiness of his enterprise.[4] Despite this ambivalence, the majority of the texts produced during the territorial period by Nuevomexicano writers bear witness, some in a veiled manner, others blatantly, to a spirit of resistance to forces of assimilation that threatened cultural survival and continuity.

Returning to the selection of texts for this historical recovery project, I would urge strongly the publication of the two novellas of Eusebio Chacón, *Hijo de la tempestad* (Son of the Storm) and *Tras la tormenta la calma* (After the Storm the Calm). These brief texts were produced by a journalist and newspaper editor who rallied with force against the displacement of Nuevomexicanos. Although published in 1893 in Las Vegas, New Mexico, they have long been ignored. When Francisco Lomelí and Donald Urioste found the slim volume that contains both novellas ensconced in the special collections section of the University of New Mexico Library in the early 1970s, they rejoiced at having found the "first Chicano novel." Since then, earlier works have been discovered. Nonetheless these two novellas continue to be important testimonies to the awareness by Nuevomexicanos of the aesthetic and literary currents of the rest of the Spanish-speaking world and of their desire to form a part of its literary tradition despite the reality of political rupture and of pressures to abandon *that* cultural identity in favor of "Americanization." *Hijo de la tempestad* is perhaps the quintessential example of *sturm und drang* Romanticism in the literature of Aztlán. As such, it makes for interesting analysis at the aesthetic level. My agreement with Lomeli's response to the work as an allegory of protest and resistance would lead me also to assign this text a high value on the scale of contestation.

A text of special interest to me is Manuel Salazar's *Aurora y Gervasio, o sea, la historia de un caminante* (Aurora y Gervasio, or rather, the Traveler's Story). One of the first novels of Aztlán, it remains an obscure unpublished text. The original, dated 1881 and beautifully penned on the pages of a business ledger, is currently in the hands of Anselmo Arellano who was given the text by Salazar's family. The story bears the marks of the French neoclassical, neopastoral genre. It also contains resonances of Peninsular neopastoral narratives of the period. Despite what to a modern reader might seem to be a mere treatment of frivolous love triangles, this text stands in competition with the dime novels of the period penned by writers of the dominant culture which contributed creation of the Mexican-as-barbarian stereotype. The main characters in *Aurora y Gervasio* are a far cry from the greasers that populated the discourses of the dominant culture of that period and of Hollywood films in the twentieth century. The males in Salazar's novel are well-bred gentlemen, though not all of them landed gentry—Gervasio is, in fact, the son of peasants—motivated by idealized love and an equally idealized code of honor. The women are coquettes upon whose individual virtue depends the intricacies of the Hispanic code of honor. And though honor and female virtue may appear trivial to us today, we must recognize that it was an important code that for centuries, as

Ramón Gutiérrez affirms, governed social relations in the Spanish/Mexican borderlands. Salazar's text sheds light on an important cultural phenomenon that has received little attention beyond Gutiérrez's seminal study.

Two texts written by Miguel C. de Baca also merit republication. *Vicente Silva y sus cuarenta bandidos* (Vicente Silva and His Forty Bandits, 1896), is fairly well known and accessible through translations. The other, a serialized narrative about Los Gorras Blancas (The White Caps), which appeared in an 1892 newspaper, *El Sol de Mayo* (The May Sun), owned by C. de Baca, is more obscure. This latter text, apocaliptically titled *Noches tenebrosas en el Condado de San Miguel* (Spooky Nights in San Miguel County), will not elicit a favorable response from a contemporary Chicano reading audience who has come to view Los Gorras Blancas as folk heroes for their acts of guerilla resistance in late nineteenth-century New Mexico. C. de Baca, from his position as a member of the conservative elite, treats Los Gorras Blancas with the same scorn he reserved for the bandido Vicente Silva. Their leader, *El Gran Capitán*, is portrayed as an opportunist who dupes the *obreros* (workers) *"ignorantes"* and leads them on rampages, which include fence cutting, barn burnings, the beating of non-collaborative widows, and the rape of their young daughters. Its value, and thus its relationship to Ruiz Burton's novel, lies in what it can teach us about the attitudes of New Mexico's *rico* class toward accommodation with the dominant Anglo political order.

Two Texts for a Canon

The remainder of this essay focuses on the work of two Nuevomexicano writers whose lives spanned the territorial and early statehood periods in New Mexico and the nineteenth and twentieth centuries: Vicente Bernal and Felipe Maximiliano Chacón. Bernal's poetry of exile is perhaps more interesting for what it does not express than for what it does. His apparently neutral stance toward the political events of his time does not necessarily reflect acquiescence. But neither does his work fall explicitly within a discourse of resistance that was gradually being written by those who found themselves marginalized from mainstream society. Perhaps his ambivalent stance was the only one afforded Nuevomexicanos at a time when they were trying to prove their worth as bona fide American citizens, yet were not completely oblivious to the machinations that denied them legitimacy. Chacón also grapples with this issue as he extolled the patriotic virtues of his fellow Nuevomexicanos, urging them to be model citizens. There is, nonetheless, an awareness in his work of the damaging effects of the discourse of domination. Contrary to more blatant countertexts, Chacón makes much of the fact that having endured and survived that discourse is precisely what, in

Vicente J. Bernal (Courtesy of the Archives of the University of Dubuque).

the long run, will make Nuevomexicanos more worthy of a place in the new order afforded by statehood.

The contingent value of these texts for me lies in the fact that both of these writers continued to inscribe in their work the Spanish language literary tradition introduced to the region in the sixteenth century, despite the fact that they were products of an English language education, and that they did not view assimilation with a jaundiced eye. My desire is to create a space for these authors in our new canon lest they be forgotten forever.

Vicente Bernal, 1888–1915

Born in 1888 and spending the early part of his life with his grandparents in Costilla, New Mexico, Vicente Bernal, like many New Mexicans of his generation, worked tending sheep and farming. His education began at the Presbyterian Mission School in Costilla and in 1907 he transferred to the Menaul Presbyterian School in Albuquerque. In 1910 he was admitted to Dubuque College in Iowa and would have attended Dubuque Seminary had he not died on April 28, 1915, of a brain hemorrhage. His single collection of poetry and ten brief pieces of prose and oratory were published posthumously by the Telegraph-Herald of Dubuque in 1916. This work demonstrates mastery of a classic American education and of the language of that culture. He does not, however, ignore his mother tongue as half of his collection is written in Spanish. Those who commented on his life and work praised young Bernal for "his diligent and conscientious spirit of getting the best from his tasks." Robert McLean who with Vicente's brother, Luis Bernal, gathered and edited *Las Primicias* (First Fruits), comments further in his brief prologue to the text that Bernal "was quiet and unassuming but with a beauty of character that remains to this day strong in the memories of his classmates and teachers" (7). W. O. Rouston, Dean of the College, in an introduction to the text, adds to the minimal sketch we have of Bernal that "in his association with men, the boy showed ready wit, which made him an acceptable companion. ... Indeed humor was one of his chief intellectual qualities and enabled him always to keep a cheerful outlook" (10).

Las Primicias: The Fruits of Assimilation or Sublimation?

Bernal's early experiences in rural New Mexico left a deeply imprinted love and appreciation of nature that surfaced again and again in his poetry. In fact, nature is often a source of comfort and revelation, a mediator between the secular poetic voice and the divine:

Two birds I spied on [a] verdant hill;

> Their heads were near, their breasts more near;
> I heard no warbling, heard no trill,
> But was inflamed by God's own love.
> ("To Miss Self and Jimmy," 24)

In addition to religiously inspired verse of this nature, there are examples in *Las Primicias* of metaphysical musings. A poem bearing the noncommital title "To———," reveals a contemplative posture and a highly lyrical sense of the precarious nature of human existence:

> But why should I desire to scan
> More thorny hills, if life's a breath
> Which seeks an ampler sphere!
> A flickering flame, the life of man
> Extinguished by the breath of death
> Which lurks forever near. (28)

This is but one of several poems with allusions or direct references to death and one wonders if Bernal had a premonition of his own premature death. If, in fact, he did, he does not pine away but, rather, exalts in his love of life: "Oh let me kiss thy brow and locks, / And draw thee to my side, my life" (28).

There are a number of occasional poems, some expressing admiration for unnamed young women, others dedicated to classmates. Three of the twenty-four English language poems are songs dedicated to the college, one of which was set to music and accepted as the alma mater of Dubuque College. Bernal's sense of humor is apparent in his poetry, though it is not always goodwilled. It occasionally takes on a biting edge, thus allowing him to satirize behavior that he finds objectionable. The following lines from a poem called "A Teacher," clearly demonstrate this side of Bernal's wit:

> But years brought greater needs
> and greater needs more money.
> Till mother lived on weeds,
> while he was saying "Honey." (25)

Humor quickly turns to satire in this poem, as Bernal chastises selfish young men who live the good life while their parents sacrifice.

An intriguing question regarding this pioneer New Mexican poet is one upon which we can only speculate for there are no answers in his creative production. Given the times in which Bernal lived, given his ethnic and class background, given the spiritual rootedness, the *querencia* of Nuevomexicanos for their land, one wonders whether Vicente Bernal felt alienated during his tenure at Dubuque. Bernal lived in a period in which Hispanics were feeling the increasing pressure of displacement. Beyond their social and economic marginalization, New Mexican mexicanos were severely maligned during the statehood battle. The unflattering portraits initiated as a result of early contacts by Josiah Gregg, William W. Davis, Susan Shelby Magoffin, Lewis Garrard, Phillip St. George Cook, and others, became in the 1880s and 1890s full-fledged caricatures in Eastern newspapers.[5]

Surely Bernal's teachers and classmates were not ignorant of the political fracas between Washington D.C. and New Mexico nor of the stigmatized images of Nuevomexicanos produced by the conflict. But if Bernal indeed felt like a foreigner upon his arrival in Iowa in the fall of 1910, or during any part of his six-year tenure at Dubuque College, his English language texts leave no clues regarding social alienation. Dubuque was a mission school dedicated to the education of foreigners. Its primary objective was to teach "so many of strange tongue the syllables of liberty and brotherhood, guiding their first steps to higher planes of usefullness" (editor's dedicatory note of *Las Primicias* to Dubuque College). This attitude may well have discouraged explicit expression of feelings of culture shock or of ethnic and cultural differences.

Instead of giving vent to feelings of alienation, Bernal's poetry demonstrates a high level of assimilation to the new cultural experiences offered by Dubuque College. The fruits of his immersion in his secular studies are apparent in his frequent intertextual dialogs with poets and writers of the English Language. "Rubyat," "To Tennyson," "To Byron," "Elvira by the Stream," "To Miss Self and Jimmy," are examples of the homage he paid to those who inspired his own muses. Bernal's response to the historical reality of his times, with a serious commitment to education, was not out of context. Doris Meyer in her investigation of New Mexican newspapers of the territorial period observes: The newspapers reveal a three-part reaction by Mexican Americans to negative stereotyping—first, an awareness of being rejected on the grounds of inferiority and unfitness, especially regarding the agonizing quest for statehood; second, a strong defensive reaction critical of unfounded negative stereotyping; and third, a campaign to transform the image of Mexican Americans through education" (77).

Did Bernal indeed write this poetry to prove his worth as an American citizen? We will never know, yet early readers of his poetry must have been convinced that this young man "from the hills of New Mexico" (*Las Primicias* 7), unequivocally had mastered the rules of the game and thus had become a fit candidate for acceptance to the club.

Putting aside the political issues, we turn now to examine a more personal question. Bernal was immersed in a foreign milieu far removed from his home. Judging from his poetry, Bernal's exile was not of the sort that sharpens the vision of the homeland or engenders nostalgia for the familiar. It was rather an exile that appears to have obliterated his past. The allusions to the landscapes of New Mexico are few. One lone dark-haired girl, a poem to his mother, a short poem prompted "by a postal received from home bearing a picture of a house and the word *Bonita*" (Editor's note 18), scant generic references to the mountain and desert landscapes of the West exhaust the inventory. There is one short story that suggests Hispanic trappings. In "The Wedding Feast," the names of the characters are Estrella, Porfirio, and Bernardo. And though a specific setting is not indicated, the description of the wedding feast and mysterious apparitions conjure the voices of New Mexico villagers spinning folk yarns of *brujería* (witchcraft) and the like. Beyond this short sketch, however, we find no other traces of New Mexican custom or tradition in Bernal's English-language prose or poetry.

There remains one very clear indication that Bernal did not totally negate his Hispanic ancestry, though he indeed seems to gloss over his cultural roots. About half of the poems included in the collection are written in Spanish. It is in these poems that we find some, though not persistent, expression of longing for home. The frequent mention of letters is perhaps a projection of his *tristeza*. In one poem called "Parte de una carta," (Part of a Letter) nostalgia forms the central motif of the poem. In the following lines he focuses on the strangeness of a typical Midwestern repast:

> ¡O! de papas no te decía
> Pues esas nunca faltan.
> Las tengo tres veces al día
> Si supieras, ya me hartan (69)

> (O! Had I mentioned potatoes
> Well there are plenty of those.
> I eat them three times daily
> If only you knew how fed up I am)

The final expression of being "fed up" might just be figurative as well as literal, in which case a sense of alienation may lie between the lines. The fact that the theme is handled humorously is perhaps an indication of a need to sublimate explicit negative evaluations regarding his experiences in the Midwest and his status at Dubuque College.

The inclusion of Greenleaf Whitter's poem "The Barefoot Boy," in translation, is an interesting choice. In this poem the simple education of a barefoot youth under the tutelage of nature suggests Bernal's own upbringing. In fact, explicit identification of the poetic voice with the addressee of the poem occurs in the final line of the first verse: "Parabienes jovencito / Yo también fui descalcito" (Best wishes barefoot boy / For I too was one of you, 55).

This poem together with one in which Bernal calls attention to his duties as a dishwasher and with the poem in which he chastises his spendthrift class-mates suggest that Bernal was not unaware of his underprivileged position at Dubuque College. Rouston, upon calling attention to the fact that Bernal spent his vacations working in local establishments, suggests that Bernal's situation did not represent the norm for Dubuque students. As such, we might conclude that the young poet experienced a double dose of marginal-ization. Yet he was apparently more willing to call attention to his class status than to his ethnicity. In fact, the latter would have been lost to future readers had he not written some verse in his mother tongue.

Bernal's Spanish language poems do not equal, neither in rich intertextu-ality nor in the treatment of universal themes, those written in English. And though Rouston assures us that Bernal studied both English and Spanish literatures, his Spanish language poetry tends to be uninspired and charac-terized by facile rhyme. Nonetheless, these poems stand as testimony to Bernal's pride in being bilingual and to his willingness to call attention to the very aspect that for so long marked his people as unfit for citizenship in the United States.

Vicente Bernal intended to return to New Mexico as an ordained minister. He hoped also to write a history of the region based on his grandfather's recollections. Unfortunately, this was not to be, for he lived only twenty-eight years. "Written on notebooks, and upon odd-sized pieces of papers" (Las Primicias 14), his poetry left notice of his life and of a gift which, in the words of Dean Rouston, was "finely literary" (14). His "first fruits" moreover stand as one more link in New Mexico's long and rich Hispanic literary tradition.

Felipe Maximiliano Chacón, 1873–1948

The work of Felipe Maximiliano Chacón virtually has gone unrecog-nized. The poetry and short prose pieces collected under the title *Obras de Felipe Maximiliano Chacón, "El Cantor Neomexicano": Poesía y Prosa, 1924* (The Works of Felipe Maximiliano Chacón, "The New Mexican Singer: Poetry and Prose), come from the pen of a man with a sharp sense of the past and its relation to his time, and a profoundly reflective and poetic sen-sibility. The little that we know of Chacón's life is included in the prologue of the collection written by historian and statesman Benjamin Read. Read is generous in his praise of "the New Mexican Bard" and impressed that he wrote in a language for which there were few opportunities for formal training. Read's praise of Chacón as the first "to call attention to his country in the beautiful language of Cervantes" (5), demonstrates that the literary achievements of earlier Nuevomexicano writers (Eusebio Chacón, Manuel C. de Baca, Vicente Bernal) were either ignored or embedded in oblivion. Whether or not Chacón's published collection received attention or acclaim in its time is not known. We do know that the collection was not mentioned in any of the early Southwestern or New Mexican literary bibliographies.[6] Yet Chacón was somewhat of a public figure. Like his father Urbano Chacón, who served as the public school superintendent for Santa Fe County in the 1880s, Felipe was involved in journalism. He edited such varied Spanish language newspapers as *La Voz del Pueblo* (The People's Voice), *La Bandera Americana* (The American Flag), *El Eco del Norte* (North Echo), and *El Faro del Río Grande* (The Lighthouse of the Río Grande).

Given Chacón's work in the newspaper industry, he very likely used this medium as an outlet for his poetry prior to publication of *Poesía y Prosa*.[7] Read affirms that Chacón's verse, which he began to write at the age of fourteen, was celebrated extensively in New Mexico, but he does not indicate the medium through which it reached the public. Further research may divulge that some of the anonymous satirical ditties printed in the late 1880s in *La Aurora*, a newspaper edited by Don Urbano, belong to Felipe. These bear a distinct similarity to the "Saeta política" and the "Nocturno a . . . " included in the 1924 collection. However, Anselmo Arellano's collection of New Mexican Spanish-language periodical poetry includes only samples from Chacón's published collection. If Chacón did indeed print some of his poetry anonymously, this gives all the more reason to believe Read's opinion regarding Chacón's modesty: "Another characteristic of Chacón is his aversion to publicity, his dislike for appearing important . . . . Chacón is a genius, and like all geniuses, he does not know how to esteem himself" (10–11, translations mine).

Read mentions that Chacón attended public primary schools and later studied at St. Michael's College, which at that time provided only secondary training. He dropped out in order to help support the family when his father died, but he continued to educate himself on his own. That his education went beyond what he might have achieved in high school is apparent in the frequent and extensive classical and historical references in his poetry. Likewise, seven translations of poets such as Byron, Longfellow, and Dresden, included in the prologue of *Poesía y prosa*, as well as references to Latin American poets, demonstrates the breadth of his exposure, in two languages, to the humanities. That he may have flaunted his knowledge is suggested by the fact that Casimiro Varela maliciously refers to Chacón as "el catedrático" (the professor; see note 6).

Matters of the Heart, the Soul and the Body Politic

A reader familiar with Latin American literature will be struck by occasional resonances of Spanish-American Modernism in Chacón's work.[8] Especially in his more abstract poems, Chacón, in true Modernist style, avoids commonplace vocabulary and prosaic expression, deliberately stringing his lines in such a way as to capture the musicality of Modernist verse. Though he is not as adept as a Leopoldo Lugones or Rubén Darío, he does create original, well-wrought strophes such as the following:[9]

> Y continuando ufana su carrera
> Vino la noche y la metió en desvelo
> Y ya en casa, en su ambición y celo
> Tomó el candil por flor en primavera ("La vida" 46)

> (As she pursued her haughty flight
> Night arrived and cast its spell
> And once at home in greed and zeal
> For a flower she mistook the flame)

Chacón parts ways with the Modernist aesthetic in that he does not cultivate the "ivory tower" pose of the majority of Modernists. In fact, he proves himself to be solidly grounded in the concrete events of his time and not above imitating folk humor through the exploitation of oral verse forms. His stylistic eclecticism is observed in the neoclassical trappings of his heroic odes and the romantic embellishments of his novella, "Eustacio y Carlota," and of a poem called "Nocturno a . . . ." In this poem Chacón demonstrates that he was familiar with at least one Latin American poet, the Mexican Manuel Acuña, whose famous romantic verse he imitates to ridicule a political figure whom obviously he disdained. The disparity between his topic and the form and language chosen to express his sentiments renders an acerbic yet humorous attack. The subject of the poem is identified as one Oñate, though a footnote clarified that the name is fictitious. Further probing in historical annals may reveal that the object of his barb is territorial governor Miguel Otero. What is impressive about this poem is Chacón's fidelity in syllabication and rhyme—on occasion he copies lines verbatim from Acuña's poem only to add an unexpected humorous twist—to the original model. This sort of discipline, demonstrated throughout his verse making, tells us that Chacón took poetry seriously and was indeed a master of his craft.

Chacón's *Poesía y prosa* is divided into three sections: "Cantos patrios y miscelánea" (Patriotic Verse and Miscellaneous), "Cantos del Hogar y traducciones" (Family Verse and Translations), "Saetas políticas y prosa" (Political Barbs and Prose). The first part is the most extensive and also the most interesting because of its variety. The forty-five Spanish-language poems in this section of the book can be placed in six broad categories: love, personal misfortune, philosophical musings, patriotism and homage, commemoration of special occasions and humor. The poems of personal misfortune, together with those of philosophical bent and his domestic poems, demonstrate his Modernist tendencies. In his poems of misfortune, the specific sources of the vicissitudes endured remain unnamed, though the poems of death, unrequited love and betrayal by friends certainly must be taken as evidence of misfortune. We know, for example, that Chacón's family was touched by death on several occasions. In addition to the death of two children mentioned in the domestic poems, the nostalgic poem entitled "Santa Fe" alludes to the death of his mother and some brothers. In the poem "Al enviudar mi madre" (Upon the Widowing of my Mother), he takes the death of his father—according to Read, Chacón was thirteen years old at the time—as the point of departure. But, rather than focusing on the father's attributes or on his own sentiments on the death of Don Urbano, Chacón calls attention to the mother's pain, as the poetic voice assumes the mother's persona:

> Sola, sola lloré,
> Y al tenderme la noche sus crespones,
> Mi llanto con un suspiro agoté. (89)

> (Alone, alone I cried,
> and as night cast her darkness upon me,
> I spent my tears with sighs.)

A poem of equal lyrical quality is the sonnet "Devoción." Here the poet speaks of a lost love to whom he remains devoted and whose resting place he frequently visits. As in all the poems dedicated to his children, the garden is the key metaphor:

> ¡Oh, cielo!, qué tesoro me ha costado
> Ese albergue de un polvo tan querido
> Ese sitio de flores nacarado
> Su cadaver precioso está dormido
> Bajo esa bóveda que yo he regado
> Con lágrimas del alma que he vertido (74)

> (Oh! Heaven, how dear has been the price
> paid for that niche of dust I so deeply love
> For that nectar bed of flowers
> The precious cadaver sleeps
> Under that dome that I have showered
> With tears wrenched from my soul)

There is no indication whatsoever who this loved one might be. It is tempting to speculate that it is a wife. Of the ten poems dedicated to family members, not a single one mentions a mate as the object of love. Two poems speak in passing of a mother and a father, and the first person plural verbs allude to both parents, but never by name or by epithet is the wife referred to here or elsewhere. Could it be that the absence is deliberate and perhaps linked to the personal tribulations alluded to, not only in several poems but also in a conversation attributed to Chacón by Read: "I have suffered great strokes of bad luck on various occasions in my life . . . but I have not known a pain that I have not been able to conquer. I have faced my fortune, acerbic tribulations, reminding myself that they could be worse, and in that manner triumphed vis-à-vis adversity" (10). The poetry itself reveals only passing allusions to misfortune, and the tenor is one of acceptance rather than of self-pity. Related to the poems of this category are those whose theme is unrequited love. Once again the tone is not one of intense emotion but rather one of resignation. Of course, it is possible that the poems of this ilk were written in adolescence and not linked in any way to misfortune in his adult life.

Chacón's sense of acceptance in the face of adversity tends to be expressed in a number of poems in which he stirs the ashes of the most ancient and perplexing of riddles. It is not, however, twentieth-century horror of the abyss that Chacón expresses but rather tempered sorrow in view of the ephemeral nature of life. These pale sentiments of angst are further overcome by the conviction that it is through action that humans give meaning to life and inscribe themselves in immortality:

> Porque sólo el hombre que lucha cada hora
> Transmite su nombre perene a la Historia
> ¡Jamás su memoria se aleja y se va!

> (For only he who acts each hour
> Transmits forever his name to History
> And never his memory will time devour!)

This conviction is the motivating force behind his many poems dedicated to persons whom he admired and events he held in awe. "A La Señora Adelina Otero Warren" (To Mrs. Adelina Otero Warren), "Al explorador del Oeste" (To the Explorer of the West), "A los legisladores" (To the Lawmakers), and a poem in honor of Octaviano Larrazolo, reveal a poet who admired men and women of action.[10] Together with his patriotic poems, these homages are particularly interesting for what they reveal of Chacón's attitudes toward the sociopolitical events of his time. They also allow us to glimpse the beginning of an ideology that allowed middle class Nuevomexicanos to balance their precarious position in a rapidly changing society and to maintain a foothold in the political arena.

Taken as a lot these poems reveal the tenor of Chacón's thought in two directions. The first is a didactic appeal to Hispanic New Mexicans to take pride in their ancestral culture. The lesson is replete with examples of the deeds of honorable and heroic fellow Nuevomexicanos and with warnings against the evils inherent in being mislead by "others."[11] Additional incentives are offered when he calls attention to the racial prejudice and injustices suffered by Nuevomexicanos particularly in the long battle for statehood. And while he speaks of burying the past and creating a new slate filled with honorable acts, in "A Nuevo Mexico" he nonetheless feels compelled to inscribe past injustices, thereby calling attention to his people's mettle. Despite decades of ignominious acts by outsiders, they have endured and survived with their integrity intact, prepared to be outstanding citizens. They must not, however, forsake their origins is his message in "A los legisladores."

The second tendency in these poems is an insistence on bearing witness to personal and collective patriotism. As proof of loyalty to the United States, Chacón recalls the participation of Nuevomexicanos in the Civil and Spanish American Wars. In a long panegyric dedicated to Nuevomexicanos who fought in World War I, Chacón attempts to set the record straight once and for all. It is not enough, however, to state merely that they fought bravely; it is the *Americanness* of their acts that ennobles the soldiers and completes the encomium. How burdened Hispanics of this period must have been with the suspicion of disloyalty!

The high point of Chacón's patriotic rhetoric is reached with a poem written in 1918, commemorating the Declaration of Independence of the United States. Six years have passed since New Mexico joined the Union and citizen Chacón has weathered the storm of change. Gone are all allusions to injustice and gone the insecurity embedded in the defensive testimonies of collective loyalty of other poems. Instead, we hear in "A la patria" (To My Country) a self-assured poet claim filial ties to his forefathers Washington, Adams and Jefferson as he unabashedly appropriates for himself the myths of their (now his) country:

> Mas al pensar bendigo yo la estrella
> Que dirije en la tierra mi destino [sic]
> Y que guía mis pasos con su huella
> de cívica igualdad por el camino
> Bajo el pendón augusto que descuella
> Sobre tu altar cual símbolo divino
> Do Wáshington trazó con letras de oro
> "La Libertad", el sin igual tesoro. (24)

(Reason leads me to bless the star
That leads my destiny upon the earth
And in its wake with civic equality
It guides my steps upon that path
'Neath the august banner wrapped
As a divine symbol round your altar
Where Washington wrote with golden letters
"Liberty," the unequalled treasure)

In exchange for the privilege of filiation, the poet offers his unyielding patriotism: "Recibe por tanto, Patria mía / Las notas de mi ardiente patiotismo" (Receive therefore sweet land of mine / the notes of my fervent patriotism).[12]

At first glance Chacón's patriotic discourse would seem to indicate that he was under extreme pressure to demonstrate, display, or otherwise prove his loyalty and that he seizes the pen to do so. Nonetheless, we cannot ignore the fact that his verse is written in Spanish and therefore intended for a Spanish rather than an English reading public. Did his public need be reminded of its own loyalty and patriotism? Probably not. How then can we reconcile Chacón's ambivalent rhetoric which, on the one hand, calls for loyalty to and pride in ancestral culture and, on the other, pledges uncompromising patriotism to the "new way" in a language that bears testimony to his commitment to the former? It is unlikely that Chacón was openly advocating official cultural pluralism. The struggle for statehood had proven, in a most profound manner, that cultural difference was not viewed favorably by the dominant culture. Thus, to assume a position of advocacy when the events were still within the reach of memory might have been dangerous. Perhaps herein lies a clue to Chacón's use of Spanish. He could do, in that language, what he dared not do in English. And, yet, there remains a blatant contradiction. If Chacón's demonstration of patriotism deflates somehow what appears to be a radical and potentially dangerous call to cultural preservation, as I believe it does, why did he bother with this push-me-pull-me pose in the first place? Is it possible that his rhetoric on the importance of cultural identity was more symbolic than radical?[13] The appeal to ethnic identity has long been a universal ploy of the ethnic middle class to consolidate power within boundaries of dominant sociopolitical networks. Since this has been and continues to be a political *modus operandi* in New Mexico, what we have in Chacón's creative work is evidence of the early stages of this strategy. When Chacón exclaims in his homage to Larrázolo that it is not only the Democratic party that stood behind him, but *the people*, we can almost detect the message implicit in his verse: "Together we elect one of our own; / divided [into two parties] we loose out to the bulls of the world" (To the Lawmakers).[14] Save face but maintain (political) space is what Chacón's ambivalent rhetoric advises. The achievement of the task he laid out before himself involved a certain amount of skill and a good dosage of veiled manipulation. There is no doubt that Chacón the editor (the political persona) hid behind Chacón the poet to inspire poetry that covertly testifies to a deeply entrenched Nuevomexicano political ploy that for decades has nurtured cultural survival and simultaneously ensured participation in the political machine of the dominant society.

F. M. Chacón's three narrative pieces complement, each in its own way, the poetry. The first piece, "Un baile de caretas" ("A Masked Ball") is a humorous sketch that tells the story of the deception of a fatuous young man by his buddies who set him up to fall for a mysterious stranger at a masquerade ball. Upon unmasking herself, Carmen Hinojosa turns out to be José Olivas. The smitten lover takes the next train out of town and does not return for many years. The highbrow style of what turns out to be a rather mundane tale places the story squarely in the Modernist vein, recalling the narrative of Rubén Darío.

"Don Julio Berengara" tells the sad tale of a sheepherder who splurges his money on a saloon girl with whom he falls in love. Crushed when he discovers that she has abandoned him for an americano, he takes solace in the memory of the night he met her, the night that "he was king." The final note expressed in this sketch is very much in keeping with Chacón's attitude of accepting one's lot as doled out by destiny.

The modern reader of the third prose piece entitled simply "Eustacio y Carlota" might be tempted to read it as a parody, inasmuch as Chacón resuscitates the trappings of the by then worn-out Byzantine novel that has as its theme separation, mistaken identity, and subsequent recognition of two loved ones. However, since no motive for parody is apparent, the second choice is to dismiss the piece as a product of Chacón's romantic temperament. There are some interesting details in the story which suggest an allegorical reading. The two Quintanilla orphans, after the death of their mother in a tenement in New York City, are adopted by Anglo parents and given Anglo names. The young boy makes a name for himself in the Rough Riders batallion during the Spanish American War. The sister is educated by a wealthy family in Colorado. As fate would have it, they meet in California, fall in love, and marry, only to discover as they undress on their wedding night, the identical medals given to them by their dying mother. And just to make sure, the young girl bears the proverbial identifying birthmark. The marriage is annulled and Amanda marries her brother's childhood friend, Orlando. The two children born of this union are given the original names of the orphan siblings: Carlota and Eustacio. Despite the melodramatic tone of this romance, might it be possible to read it as a parable for the *rico* class of New Mexico? Such a reading is suggested by the loss of natural parents (Mexico); "legal" adoption by Anglo parents (United States) and subsequent assimilation; discovery and acceptance of true identities; affirmation and reappropriation of ancestral roots by restoring original names and bequeathing them to the new generation. There is, furthermore, a character named Melitón Gonzales, a native New Mexican who like Henry fought bravely in the Spanish American War. His popular speech sets him apart, identifies him as a member of the non-elite group. He is not fond of women (symbol of marriage, the machinery that most rapidly sets the assimilation process in motion). In the end Melitón succumbs to the inexorable hand of destiny. He marries a distinguished woman from San Bernardino, ever acting with "nobility of heart, sanity, common sense," and fidelity to duty. Is that duty the duty of husband to wife, or the duty of citizen to country? (The same patriotic duty displayed by Melitón's participation in the Spanish American War?) Patriotic duty oils the wheels of assimilation. If this reading is considered, the message of Chacón's ideology, hidden beneath an ambivalent rhetoric of assimilation and of ethnic preservation, draws to a neat closure.

The lives of Felipe Maximiliano Chacón and Vicente Bernal spanned two centuries and two cultures. Like their fellow Nuevomexicanos they had begun to assimilate those aspects of the dominant culture that would ensure them participation in the mainstream social order. They did not, however, deem it necessary to abandon their own cultural values and traditions but rather struggled to achieve a state of biculturalism whereby they could remain faithful to the ways of their ancestors, yet enjoy the promise offered by their new political status. Their work reveals, in one case overtly and in the other more subtly, an ambivalent double-edged discourse of resistance and assimilation from which we can glean some insight into the process of inscribing colonial subjectivity.

Notes

[1]The second part of this paper appeared in *Pasó por aquí: Critical Essays on the New Mexican Literary Tradition, 1542–1989.*

[2]Padilla's " 'Yo sola aprendí': Contra-Patriarchal Containment in Women's Nineteenth-Century California Personal Narratives" likewise makes contestation an important consideration in his study of early texts.

[3]With the conquest of central Mexico complete in 1921, the Spanish crown shortly began to send exploration parties to its northern frontiers with hopes that these ventures would prove to be as lucrative as those which led to the discovery, conquest and colonization of the Aztec Empire. The existence of sedentary tribes who occupied highly organized communities in what is today Arizona and New Mexico continued to lure exploration and colonization forays well into the eighteenth century.

[4]Though New Mexico became a territory of the United States in 1850, it was not admitted into the Union until 1912. This long road to statehood was riddled with struggle and disappointment. A translation of Fray Marcos' text *Descubrimiento de las siete Ciudades de Cibola* can be found in Hammond and Rey.

[5]See, for example, Josiah Gregg, *Commerce of the Prairies: The Journal of a Santa Fe Trader*, who in one of the earliest *americano* texts sets the tone for subsequent evaluations of New Mexico and her people, stating: "The New Mexicans appear to have inherited much of the cruelty and intolerence of their ancestors, and no small portion of their bigotry and fanaticism. Being of a high imaginative temperament and of rather accommodating moral principles—cunning, loquacious, quick of perception and psychopathic, their conversation frequently exhibits a high degree of tact—a false glue of talent eminently calculated to mislead and impose. They have no stability except in artifice; no profundity except in intrigue; qualities for which they have acquired an unenviable celebrity. Systematically cringing and subservient while out of power, as soon as the august mantle of authority falls on their shoulders, there are but little bounds of their arrogance and vindictiveness of spirit" (143).

[6]See Mabel Major, Rebecca W. Smith and T. M. Pearce, *Southwest Heritage: A Literary History with Bibliography*; and Lester Rains, *Writers and Writings of New Mexico*. Doris Meyer's article, "Felipe Maximiliano Chacón: A Forgotten Mexican-American Author," is the first critical attention called to Chacón's work.

[7]Chacón's political views were certainly aired in journal print. A letter, called to my attention by Francisco Lomelí, written by Colorado statesman Casimiro Varela in response to an article published by Chacón in *La Voz del Pueblo*, appears in *El Independiente*, 30 January, 1913. Varela accuses Chacón of betrayal, resorts to a good deal of name calling, and attributes Chacón's ill-mannered behavior to the fact that he is fatherless. Might Chacón's response to Varela be contained in a short poem called "Ingrato" (Ungrateful One), in which he lambasts a friend who turns his back in time of need?

[8]Modernism was an artistic movement (1888–1910). It is characterized by a new and fresh language, a search for the ideal in both expression and concept, exoticism embodied in oriental and classical themes, symbolism and musicality. Modernism allowed Latin American artists to forge an identity independent from European models and, at the same time, prompted a hearty welcome to the modern aesthetic mainstream.

[9]Lugones was an Argentine Modernist and Darío, a Nicaraguan, is considered the father of Latin American Modernism. I disagree with one critic who sees Chacón's poetry as typical of the sort of "florid verse popular in his time." I believe Chacón was much more conscious of his craft and, on the whole, his poetry surpasses that of other poets of the period.

[10]Octaviano Larrazolo, originally from Zacatecas, Mexico, is the first Hispanic to have served as governor of the State of New Mexico.

[11]The "others" are alluded to in this poem as tyrants of yesteryear. In the homage to Larrazolo, they are more explicitly identified as members of the Santa Fe Ring.

[12]The significance of the placement of this poem within the collection must not be overlooked. It appears in the number two slot, immediately after "A los Heroes" (To the Heroes). The first poem bears proof of loyalty. The second demonstrates that loyalty has borne its just desserts, that is, Nuevomexicanos have earned the right to consider themselves bona fide citizens of the United States.

[13]Had Chacón's or any other Hispanic's call to cultural preservation been of a politically radical nature, the Spanish language would not have disappeared from public education and the official public domain (i.e., the courts) as early and as easily as it did. Despite the fact that the framers of the state constitution set forth stipulations for the maintenance of Spanish in public education, the Hispanic community was apparently not very active in demanding adherance to the law until the late 1960s.

[14]Beyond alluding to the "bullish" nature of Lazarrolo's opponents, the poet refers to a concrete person, Richard "Bull" Andrews, who apparently was one of Chacón's least favorite politicians. The poem entitled "Saeta Política" (Political Barb) has as its theme Andrews' political chicanery.

Works Cited

Arellano, Anselmo. *Los pobladores neomexicanos.* Albuquerque: Pajarito Publications, 1976.

Chacón, Eusebio. *Hijo de la tempestad* [and] *Tras la tormenta la calma.* Santa Fe, NM: Tipografía "El Boletín Popular," 1982.

Chacón, Felipe Maximiliano. *Obras de Felipe Maximiliano Chacón, el "Cantor neomexicano": Poesía y Prosa.* Published by the author. Albuquerque, 1924.

Espinosa, Aurelio M., ed. "Los Comanches." *U of New Mexico Bulletin* 45 (1907).

———. and José M. Espinosa. "Los tejanos: A New Mexican Spanish Popular Dramatic Composition of the Middle of the Nineteenth Century." *Hispania* 27 (1944): 289–314.

Gonzales-Berry, Erlinda, ed. *Pasó por aquí: Critical Essays on the New Mexican Literary Tradition, 1542–1989.* Albuquerque: U of New Mexico P, 1988.

Gutiérrez, Ramón. *When Jesus Came, The Corn Mothers Went Away.* Stanford: Stanford UP, 1991.

Gregg, Josiah. *Commerce of the Prairies: The Journal of a Santa Fe Trader.* New York: Henry G. Langley, 1844; rpt. Dallas: Southwest, 1933.

Hernstein Smith, Barbara. "Contingencies of Value." *Canons.* Ed. Robert von Hallberg. Chicago: U of Chicago P, 1984. 5–39.

Lomelí, Francisco. "Eusebio Chacón: An Early Pioneer of the New Mexican Novel." *Pasó por Aquí*: 149–66.

Major, Mabel, Rebecca W. Smith & T. M. Pearce. *Southwest Heritage: A Literary History With Bibliography.* 3rd ed. Albuquerque: U of New Mexico P, 1972.

Meese, Elizabeth. *(Ex)tensions: Re-figuring Feminist Criticism.* Chicago: U of Chicago P, 1984.

Meyer, Doris. "Early Mexican-American Response to Negative Stereotyping." *The New Mexico Historical Review* 53.1 (1978): 75–79.

———. "Felipe Maximiliano Chacón: A Forgotten Mexican-American Author." *New Directions in Chicano Scholarship.* San Diego: Chicano Studies, U of California-San Diego. 111–26.

Niza, Fray Marcos de. *Descubrimiento de las siete Ciudades de Cíbola. Narratives of the Coronado Expedition, 1540–1542.* Eds. George P. Hammond and Agapito Rey. Albuquerque: U of New Mexico, 1940. 66–79.

Padilla, Genaro. "'Yo sola aprendí': Contra-Patriarchal Containment in Women's Nineteenth-Century California Personal Narratives." *The Americas Review* 16.3–4 (1988): 91–110.

Paredes, Raymund A. "The Evolution of Chicano Literature." *Three American Literatures: Essays in Chicano, Native American, and Asian American Literature.* Ed. Houston A. Baker. New York: MLA, 1982. 33–79.

Rains, Lester. *Writers and Writings of New Mexico.* New Mexico Highlands U, 1934; bound Ms. Special Collections, Zimmerman Library, U of New Mexico.

Winkler, Karen. "Ramón Gutiérrez." *Chronicle of Higher Education* (Sept. 26, 1990): A4.

Memorias de la Beata (Memories of the Pious Woman, 1878), to the fully-sustained autobiography of Cleofas Jaramillo, *Romance of a Little Village Girl* (1955). Unfortunately, these autobiographical narratives remain generally unpublished and unread. Vallejo's *Recuerdos históricos y personales*, like Lorenzana's *Memorias de la Beata* and scores of other California narratives, remain in manuscript within the vast holdings of the Bancroft Library at the University of California at Berkeley; and, even though published, both Rodriguez's *The Old Guide* (ca. 1900) and Jaramillo's *Romance of a Little Village Girl* have been out of print for decades and are nearly impossible to find. Scores of autobiographical narratives from throughout the West and Southwest therefore remain silent.

Discovering, identifying, reading, and categorizing autobiographical narrative is a major undertaking, especially when such work has little and often no precedent. Recent scholarship in Mexican-American literary history, carried out almost exclusively by Chicano scholars, is recovering what will amount to a huge inventory of literary material which must, and shall, overturn the ethnocentric assumption that Mexican-American culture has a meagre literary tradition. Without such a collective and critical undertaking, one would think that there had been no autobiographical voice within a culture that has had a vital literary tradition for hundreds of years. Yet only recently has even contemporary autobiography begun to receive serious attention as a distinct genre (Padilla, Márquez, Saldívar 1984). In 1988 *The Americas Review* published a special issue on *U.S. Hispanic Autobiography* in which essays on Oscar Zeta Acosta, Ernesto Galarza, Richard Rodriguez, Gary Soto, Anthony Quinn and personal narratives of nineteenth-century Mexican California women appear with essays posing theoretical questions about autobiographical ideology, cultural subjectivity in autobiographical narrative, and the autobiographics of recent verse chronicles. In his *Chicano Narrative: The Dialectics of Difference*, Ramón Saldívar has written saliently on "the rhetoric of autobiographical discourse ... [and] the ideologies that surround" Richard Rodriguez's *Hunger of Memory: The Education of Richard Rodriguez* (1982) and Ernesto Galarza's *Barrio Boy: The Story of a Boy's Acculturation* (1971). In fact, the socio-ideological problematics of autobiographical self-fashioning in contemporary Chicano writing, imbricated as it is with questions about Chicano literary production as a major articulation of resistance to American social and cultural hegemony, appears in nearly all of the current thinking on Chicano autobiography as a genre in which individual experience and collective historical identity are inextricably bound. However, almost all of the scholarship has focused on issues operating in contemporary Chicano autobiography, as though autobiographical consciousness and narrative production—with all of the problems of identitarian inconsistency, ideological contradiction, rhetorical maneuvering—had developed only in the last two or three decades. This fixation on the contemporary period has had the effect, in my estimation, of reaffirming the perception that Chicano literature is a recent phenomenon and, more problematically for our own work, has largely ignored prior personal narrative formations in which ideological complications—historical repression as well as contestatory articulation—comprise the originary preoccupation autobiographical expression in Mexican-American culture.

The intention of my work here, therefore, is to show that the formation of autobiographical consciousness—with all of the ideological and rhetorical stresses it now evinces—originated in prior narrative concern about marking individual and collective experience. Encouraged by the archival recovery and the critical re-examination of early African-American and Native-American literary production, I wish to help win back a Mexican-American literary tradition that has been, not lost, but ignored and suppressed. Like that work undertaken by black scholars in reconstructing the African-American literary heritage,[3] my work aims not only to resuscitate dormant autobiographical material, but to refigure the complex system of cultural coding, aesthetic desire, oppositional purpose, which since 1848 has produced autobiographical discourse within a dangerous social space. Likewise, my thinking has been influenced by the rigorous and provocative critical attention Native-American autobiography is receiving from innovative scholars like Arnold Krupat, who reads the complex power relations at work in "bicultural composite composition" of Native-American autobiography as a contestory "textual equivalent of the frontier" (33) and Hertha Wong, who reads Native-American "pictography as autobiography." Rather than regarding Native-American autobiography as the textual equivalent of the museum in which the noble but vanished Indian is represented as a cultural relic, Krupat argues that it is in the textual "presentation of an Indian voice not as vanished and silent, but as still living and able to be heard that the oppositional potential of Indian autobiography resides" (34). Krupat's assiduous reconstruction of the social, historical, and ideological conditions under which Native-American autobiography was (and is) produced provides an exemplary model of analysis, one which has forced us to rethink the naive expectations for cultural representation that have too often been brought to the reading of ethnic autobiography. And although she agrees that most Native-American autobiography is the product of narrative collaborations with white anthropologists and historians, Hertha Wong has rather audaciously challenged the common assumption that Native Americans did not engage in "autobiographical activity" before contact with Europeans. Wong's revisionist work argues that "long before ethnographers came along,

Native Americans were telling, performing, and painting their personal histories. One potential preliterate model of autobiography, at least among Plains Indian males, is the pictographic personal narrative. The symbolic language of pictographs allowed preliterate Plains Indians to "read" about each other from painted robes, tipis, and shields (295). Reading scores of self-representing pictographic narratives, Wong details the rich tradition of storytelling in which self and communal identity share the same comfortable space of tribal life. Her project reminds us that the forms of "autobiographical activity" are various, that the very category of the "self" is in many cultures bound up with the idea of community, and, most importantly, that autobiographical consciousness itself is culturally divergent, complex and variable in its articulation.

While there are obviously vast differences between post-1848 Mexican-American personal narrative, the formation of African-American autobiography as it evolved from the slave narrative and the recording of Native America autobiography, there are significant similarities in the extra-cultural representational function incribed in each for registering opposition to racial and ethnocentric assumptions. Perhaps the most compelling socio-literary associations between the three traditions is what Henry Louis Gates, Jr. in describing the collective function of slave narrative practice, refers to as "a communal utterance, a collective tale, rather than merely an individual's autobiography." Given the physical and spiritual demoralizations to which African Americans as a group had been subjected by slavery, individual autobiographers understood that the "character, integrity, intelligence, manners and morals" of the entire community was staked on "published evidence provided by one of their number" (x). For Native Americans, as Krupat points out, while the nineteenth-century collaborative production of Native-American autobiographies generally served as "an acknowledgement of Indian defeat," the Indian prisoner whose life story was recorded opened space for narrating the expansionist brutality visited not only upon the speaker but upon all of his people. The Native-American speaker, often a tribal leader, recognized the collective function of the autobiographical occasion and, rather than focusing only upon himself, articulated identity within the context of a culture that was being systematically destroyed. Likewise, after 1848, Mexican Americans were conscious of the historical consequences of such "communal utterance." As Mariano Vallejo wrote to his son, his *Recuerdos históricos y personales* (1875) would oppose negative representations of Mexican Californians pervasive in both pre- and post-1848: "I shall not stop moistening my pen in the blood of our unfounded detractors ... you know I am not vindictive but I am and was born hispano. To contradict those who slander is not vengeance, it is to regain a loss" (Brown Emparán 86). Vallejo's *Recuerdos históricos y personales* tends toward a strategy of historiographic refutation against "our unfounded detractors" rather than focusing on his own rather remarkable personal and public accomplishments.

The heavy burden of collective representation, however, created a problem for Mexican-American autobiography as it had for slave narrative. As William Andrews points out, nineteenth-century whites produced and read slave narrative "more to get a first hand look at the institution of slavery than to become acquainted with an individual slave" (5). Indeed, as John Blassingame, Thomas Couser, Robert Stepto and Houston Baker have all shown, the struggle for narrative autonomy by African Americans was waged against scores of white abolitionist editors, amanuenses, publishers who not only sponsored slave narratives but, through the complex authenticating apparatus which framed the narrative, "addressed white readers over the invisible bodies of black narrators" (Couser 120). I would likewise argue that, after 1848, Anglo Americans in general were not interested in encouraging the production of, much less in reading, personal narrative which would acquaint them with the perceptions and feelings of Mexicans who had presumably just been granted all the rights of American citizenship. Whereas slave narratives were indeed published and often widely distributed to promote the abolitionist cause, Mexican-American personal narratives—for example, the more than 100 personal narratives of nineteenth-century Mexican Californians—were meant to function only as supplemental material for American historians and were, therefore, quite intentionally not published. Hence, scores, perhaps hundreds, of Mexican-American personal narratives remain in small state and regional historical society libraries, university special collections, as well as in major archival repositories like the Huntington and Bancroft libraries. Only when we undertake the difficult work of recovering our autobiographical literature from such archival incarceration will the "collective utterance" of our autobiographical tradition disclose its origins, evolution, and cultural significance. Only by activating Houston Baker's "anthropology of art" (xv–xvii) for Mexican-American autobiography can we, as William Andrews advises, begin to reconstruct the "full context in which a genre originated, evolved and took on cultural significance" (4). Like Baker, I believe that "an imaginative reconstruction of a cultural context is mandatory" (xvii) if we are to understand the complex, interrelated codes which constitute the "cultural sign" of autobiographical narrative which emerges from social trauma, dislocation, and suppression.

II

The contradictory positions Mexican Americans have occupied in American society since the U. S.-Mexican War of 1846–48 develop as narrative obsession in much autobiographical expression throughout the nineteenth and much of the twentieth century. The earliest post-American narratives record, in their different forms and in different registers, the effects of the military takeover on the Mexican community in general and on individuals specifically. And although I agree that class divisions, regional differences and gender distinctions must be carefully calculated into our understanding of how people responded variously to the American annexation, I believe that the life histories of Mexican-American women and men tend, as a group, to express a wide sense of individual and communal disjuncture. Whether embittered, confounded, acquiescent, resistant, self-denying or assertively defiant, the personal narratives I have read display a set of responses that mediate the nascent national and existential realities imposed upon the daily lives of Mexican (American)s by a regime that mouthed a rhetoric of demo-cratic ideals but practiced unrelenting hostility in its relations with them. This historical situation has for over a century sustained a rhetorical site upon which Chicano literary production has had as one of its generative principles the reconciliation of vexing contradictions. In autobiographical literature, we see again and again a narrative ground (often a battleground) upon which an individual is contending with social, cultural and ideological forces that simultaneously so disrupt identity as to unfix it, yet, paradoxically, in disrupting identity establish identity as a destablized condition.

Since autobiographic narrative produced after 1848 was marked by a need to meditate upon the upheaval that traumatized the entire spectrum of Mexican-American life, the narrative retrieval of the past may be seen as the direct product of socio-cultural stress, often of outright dread of impending personal harm, of a sense that the world was coming to an end—which in many respects it was. The post-1848 personal narratives, as a group, exhibit an obsessive nostalgic tendency to recreate "los dias pasados" (the days of yore) as a means of divesting the second half of the nineteenth century of its absurdity. However idealized the pre-American cultural community may ap-pear in these narratives, the autobiographical reconstitution of life before the occupation was less a self-deluding compensation or naive wish-fulfillment fantasy than what I consider a strategic narrative activity—conscious of its general social implications—for restoring order, sanity, social purpose in the face of political, social and economic dispossession. Dispossession often articulated itself in an autobiographical sigh of deep sadness and longing for another socio-cultural life, but there is always a barely suppressed rage run-ning within the same narrative. Throughout the Southwest, nostalgia mixed with anger functioned to mediate the manifold social forces which infringed upon the spirit of those people who resided in the vast territory that became the Western United States in 1848, but which geo-spiritually became a kind of floating island upon which Mexican (American)s were left to work out their historic destiny.

But, of course, our history begins well before 1848. So does our literary culture. So does autobiographical impulse. Before drawing the line at 1848, I wish to suggest that more work on Indigenous and Spanish colonial autobiographical articulation which pre-figures later formations must be undertaken by succeeding scholars who, I hope, will extend the terrain of autobiographical scholarship beyond my work here.

On the indigenous side of the Chicano cultural heritage one might argue, as many scholars indeed have, that the pre-Columbian literature of Mexico comprises a cherished part of the Chicano's literary estate.[4] Suggestive of the kind of "anthropology of art" open to further development, therefore, I encourage further study of "autobiographical activity" that may be measureable in indigenous Mexican literature. As a project in and of itself, I invite succeeding scholars to engage in a "anthropology of art" which will rigorously document the autobiographical activity of pre-Columbian Mexico, as well as succeeding autobiographical writing, and then calculate the influence of an indigenous autobiographical poetics on the contemporary Chicano literary production. On the European side of the *mestizo* cultural face, one can indeed trace a continuous Spanish colonial discourse of conquest, exploration and settlement between 1492 and the beginning of the nineteenth century which charts the formation of a new subjectivity in the Americas. Alvar Núñez Cabeza de Vaca's *Relación* (1542), one may say, represents the first autobiographical account of life in the New World, which together with Pedro Castañeda's narrative *Relación de la jornada a Cíbola* (Report on the Expedition to Cíbola, 1582) of Francisco Vásquez de Coronado's expedition of 1540–42, Juan de Oñate's *Proclamación* (1598), Fray Alonso de Benavides' *Memoria* (1630), Fray Eusebio Kino's *Favores Celestiales* (Celestial Favors), and scores of other military and missionary *relaciones, diarios, memorias and viajes* (travels) constitute an enormous field of narrative that may be considered in part autobiographical. After all, American literary historians have identified British travel narratives, journals, diaries, histories as the first literary productions of the nation; likewise, autobiography scholars have been quick to identify William Bradford's *Of Plymouth Plantation*, John Winthrop's *Journal*, Mary Rowlandson's *Captivity Narrative*, Samuel Sewall's *Diary* and numerous other histories and personal narratives as part of the nation's autobiographic tradition. Both the Spanish and the British narratives, as well as the full range of the indigenous literary production of the Americas, all constitute the beginnings of American literature since they produce a textual domain shaped by the experience of the Americas.

The project to recover the pre-Columbian, indigenous and Spanish colonial literary tradition must commence, but I would like to suggest, along with literary historians Luis Leal and Raymund Paredes, that such prior traditions be considered not as separate, but separately from that literary production that followed the U. S.-Mexican War of 1846–48.[5] Like Leal and Paredes, therefore, I wish to argue that a Mexican-American literary formation begins with the American violence that ripped the Mexican map in Tejas in 1836, and then completely blanched the geography of northern Mexico in 1846–48. For it is the literature written after the invasion by the United States which begins to name us as a people living upon a distinct, startling and confounding plane of history. As Juan Bruce-Novoa argued in an influential essay, the space between the social signifiers—Mexican American—opened at this historical juncture: "we are the space (not the hyphen) between the two ... the intercultural possibilities of that space. We continually expand the space, pushing the two influences out and apart as we claim more area for our reality ... "[6]

As Raymund Paredes points out in a significant essay on "The Evolution of Chicano Literature":

> The great divide in Chicano history is the year 1848 when the Treaty of Guadalupe Hidalgo ended twenty-one months of warfare between Mexico and the United States. ... Although a distinctive Mexican-American literary sensibility was not to emerge for several generations, the signing of the [Treaty], more than any other event, required southwestern Mexicans to reassess their relationships to the old country and the United States. (36)

Among the many modes of reassessment, an autobiographic narrative formation opened at this break, a narrative formation that emerged from rupture itself, from the necessity of restoring and sustaining the past in everyday life while reconstituting life within the rupture, transforming rupture into the expanding, and expansive, space of intercultural possibility. A Mexican-American literary formation which would "expand the space" and "claim more area for our reality" arose from that traumatic historical moment when the United States violently appropriated northern Mexico in the mid-nineteenth century (see McWilliams, Acuña, Pitt). The war itself and the rapid Americanization of the West set off a social, political, economic, linguistic and cultural shockwave which generated a rhetorical situation in which Mexicans inscribed themselves upon history as a warrant against oblivion. The violent transformation of a well-established society forced a systemic shift in the modes of cultural self-recognition which would eventually develop into a cultural production steeped in resistance to American society, even as people accommodated themselves to socio-political reality.

After 1848 a crushed social economy led to radical transformation in the cultural epistemology: the disorientation of defeat and the profound rupture in everyday life produced a situation in which subordination constituted a new grid of subjectivity. In other words, even though most people retained the daily self-identificatory practices of language, social customs and communal relations, the rupture produced a situation in which Mexican people were forced to adapt to an alien social economy while increasingly struggling to remember themselves with a culture and a history of their own.

III

Among the earliest autobiographic narratives in the Southwest are José Antonio Menchaca's "Reminiscences" (c. 1850) and Juan Seguín's *Personal Memoirs* (1858), both of which are ambivalent and often bitter defenses of complicity in the Anglo-Texas rebellion of 1836. Seguín's brief personal narrative, for example, is an anguished attempt to come to terms with a string of events that, within the space of a few years, saw him transformed from a member of the landed Tejano elite who fought for Texas independence from Mexico (because, as he says, he believed in American democratic ideals) to an outcast who suffered political and economic dispossession. Ironically, Seguín was forced to retreat to Mexico when his life was threatened by Americans and then, absurd as it may sound, he fought on the side of the Mexican army when it recaptured San Antonio, where he had just served as American Mayor. Seguín's *Personal Memoirs* is in many of its details the prefigurative narrative of the forms of personal and cultural schizophrenia witnessed in succeeding Mexican-American autobiographical narratives.

In Texas alone there are other narratives that exhibit the transformation of the cultural subject discovered in the Seguín memoirs. Santiago Tafolla's unpublished *Nearing the End of the Trail* (c.1890) is the life history of a man who ran away from home when he was twelve, spent his youth traveling in the eastern United States with an Anglo benefactor, settled in Texas, and then fought on the side of the South during the Civil War, only to be forced to desert when he and fellow Mexicano Confederate troopers learned they were about to be lynched by white soldiers because they were "greasers." José Policarpio Rodríguez's narrative *"The Old Guide:" His Life in His Own Words* (1897) describes his life as a "Surveyor, Scout, Indian Fighter, [and] Ranchman," and ends as a conversion narrative much in the Augustinian tradition. As it turns, out, Tafolla and Rodríguez were cousins who both became Protestant ministers late in life, and who remember each other in their respective narratives. Another duo who met on and off the pages of their memoirs were Jesse Pérez, Texas lawman, and Catarino E.

Garza, journalist, union organizer, and revolutionary. Garza's *La lógica de mis hechos* (The Reasoning of My Activities) is a 280-page handwritten manuscript that describes the social conditions of Mexican Americans in South Texas and St. Louis, Missouri, between 1877 and 1889, and details his own efforts to help establish the *sociedades mutualistas* (mutual aid societies) before he returned to Mexico to participate in the Revolution of 1910. And Jesse Pérez, strangely enough, was a member of the Texas Rangers in the 1890s when that group was terrorizing the Mexican-American communities of South Texas. In the early 1920s, Pérez struggled with a typewriter to compose his *Memoirs*, part of which recount those occasions when he chased Garza along the border as Garza and other revolutionaries ran guns from Texas into Mexico. However, unlike other Rangers, Pérez never saw his *Memoirs* published, perhaps because the very notion of a Mexican Texas Ranger was a contradiction in terms.[7]

In New Mexico, Padre Antonio José Martínez wrote and published his autobiographical brief, *Relación de méritos* (Report on Merits), on his own (and the first) printing press in New Mexico in 1838. Martínez's "Relación de méritos" describes his birth in Taos, New Mexico, in 1793, his boyhood in a land-owning family, his marriage to María de la Luz Martín, who bore him a daughter but soon thereafter died leaving him a young widower who decided to become a priest at twenty-four. Not only did Martínez become a priest, he became the politically influential and widely revered prelate who was excommunicated from the Church in 1861 by Archbishop Jean-Baptiste Lamy because he resisted the liturgical Americanization in New Mexico which denigrated the Mexican clergy and robbed the people of locally established religious practices. Citing the library of doctrinal texts which constituted his intellectual personality, the *Relación de méritos* describes Martínez's socio-intellectual formation and the theological knowledge which would eventually put him at doctrinal odds with a bishop who had been sent to New Mexico with the express purpose of Americanizing the Mexican Catholic populace. Although Padre Martínez was a member of the constitutional convention and the territorial legislature, when he defended the religious cultural practices of his people he was vilified by Lamy and his assistant, Reverend Joseph Machebeuf, and driven ignomiously from his pulpit in Taos. In 1927, Willa Cather's *Death Comes for the Archbishop* perpetuated and perhaps forever hardened the image of Padre Martínez as a brutal, self-aggrandizing and ugly man who dictated the lives of his Mexican parishioners and stood in the way of American progress. Although recent biographical scholarship is restoring Padre Martínez's historical and cultural significance, his own extant writings, scores of letters and essays, as well as his *Relación,* have yet to be collected and published.

Miguel Antonio Otero (Miguel A. Otero Collection, Special Collections, General Library, University of New Mexico, Neg. No. 000-021-0004).

In addition to Padre Martínez's, there are also other journals and narratives by New Mexican political and military figures that require further examination. In 1833, five years before Martínez published the *Relación de méritos,* Rafael Chacón was born outside of Santa Fe to a family with deep roots in *Nuevo Mexico* and who, like most other *Nuevomexicanos,* lost their homelands after the American conquest. Chacón was a thirteen-year-old cadet in the Mexican militia when the Americans invaded New Mexico; after 1848 he mustered in as a soldier in the American army, fighting in the only Civil War engagement in New Mexico territory and campaigning against the Navajo and Apache. After his retirement from the military in the 1860s, he struggled to build a home for his family under difficult economic and social conditions. Chacón, who wrote his *Memorias* between 1906–1912, remembers the terror instilled by the invading Americans as well as his service in the American army where he and his fellow Nuevomexicanos were treated disrespectfully. However, what I found most appealing about Chacón's *Memorias* are not the military exploits Jacqueline Meketa, his translator and editor, finds remarkable, but rather the sense of cultural and familial devotion which motivates the composition of a personal document he hopes will textually sustain the family name in a time of social uncertainty.

After the turn of the century, there are a group of New Mexicans whose lives spanned the last quarter of the nineteenth century and whose autobiographies chart the transformation of the social and political life of the territory. Miguel Antonio Otero, Jr. (1859–1944), the son of a prominent Santa Fe *político,* went to school in St. Louis and went on to become territorial governor of New Mexico from 1897–1903. Although not produced until the 1930s, Miguel Antonio Otero's autobiographical trilogy charts his experience from 1859, when he was born in St. Louis, Missouri, to his years as territorial governor of New Mexico at the turn of the century. *My Life on the Frontier, 1864–1882* (1935), provides a fascinating account of Otero's boyhood on the Missouri and New Mexico frontier where he met such legends as Wild Bill Hickock, Buffalo Bill Cody and Billy the Kid. *My Life on the Frontier, 1882–1897* (1939), relates his experiences as a young man rising to affluence and political power in New Mexico, and ending with notice of his appointment as territorial governor by President McKinley. Otero's *My Nine Years as Governor of the Territory of New Mexico, 1897–1905* (1940) records in detail his years in office as the first Hispano governor of the state since the American conquest, his futile attempts to gain statehood for New Mexico, his help in organizing Theodore Roosevelt's Rough Riders (among them many Nuevomexicanos whose loyalty to the U. S. was still in question) and his rise to national prominence during the late territorial period in New Mexico.

From the 1920's through about 1950, a group of women in New Mexico wrote books in which cultural traditions, family and community customs and social history are combined with personal narrative. Their versions of personal life history and culture are mostly a form of narrative pageantry in which the Spanish colonial past is imagined as a vital element of New Mexican Hispano identity with, like many of the men's, little reference to Indian and Mexican heritage. Nina Otero Warren's *Old Spain in Our Southwest* (1936); Cleofas Jaramillo's *The Genuine New Mexico Tasty Recipes: Old and Quaint Formulas for the Preparation of Seventy-five Delicious Spanish Dishes* (1939); *Sombras del Pasado/Shadows of the Past* (1941) and *Romance of a Little Village Girl* (1955); Aurora Lucero White-Lea's *Literary Folklore of the Hispanic Southwest* (1953), and Fabiola Cabeza de Baca's *The Good Life: New Mexico Traditions and Food* (1949) and *We Fed Them Cactus* (1954) are all books that may generally be characterized as a hybrid of personal narrative, folkloristic transcription, recipe book, family, community and general socio-cultural history. Cultural traditions and daily customs are not only transcribed but given personal, familial and historical context in *Old Spain in Our Southwest, Sombras del Pasado/Shadows of the Past* and *The Good Life*. Recipes for traditional foods are contextualized by personal and familial *recuerdos* (memoirs) to such a degree that culinary and cultural knowledge are inextricably bound. And, as Tey Diana Rebolledo points out, such knowledge tends to be topographically distinct and gendered: "Recipes are integrated with accounts of folk life, as if the female sense of rootedness and place is passed down through the distinctive foods nature offers" (102). The personal reminiscences of *We Fed Them Cactus* and *Romance of a Little Village Girl* are likewise tied to such traditional narrative practices as relating *cuentos* (folktales), *romances* (narrative ballads), religious drama like the *pastorelas* (pastoral plays), and *recuerdos* (memoirs) in which the personal life is matrixed within a family genealogy of *tías* and *tíos* (uncles and aunts) *abuelas y abuelitos* (grandparents), *primas hermanas* (first cousins), *padrinos* (godparents) and *compadres* (co-parents and close family friends). In fact, community, family and personal history are usually so integrated that, while cookbooks such as Jaramillo's *The Genuine New Mexico Tasty Recipes* and Cabeza de Baca's *The Good Life* are ethnographic texts, they are also what Anne Goldman calls "culinary autobiographies." Goldman describes such narrative as a complex form of cultural and self representation: "reproducing a recipe, like retelling a story, may be at once cultural practice *and* autobiographical assertion. If it provides an apt metaphor for the reproduction of culture from generation to generation, the act of passing down recipes from mother to daughter works as well to figure a familial space within which self-articulation can begin to take place." Intergenerational exchange of cultural knowledge thus constitutes a form of cultural subjectivity rooted in an enduring sense of place, in a sense not only of rootedness but ownership of cultural terrain.

These narratives, however, tend to read the past nostalgically, evoking a harmonious and happy cultural domain while occluding the social fragmentations of the present. Indeed one discovers a tendency to dismiss this body of writing for what Raymund Paredes rightly refers to as its "hacienda mentality." Yet, I also agree with Tey Diana Rebolledo who reframes our thinking about such narrative production by reminding us that during this period (1930s to 1950s) most "women had no education and even those who did had little leisure to write. Nor were they encouraged to write; they were confined to fairly rigid gender roles, carefully watched and cared for. It is a wonder they wrote at all" (99). More recently, Rebolledo has gone a step further to argue that this group of women were neither "naive" nor "innocent" in their writing, that in fact they established a set of "narrative strategies of resistance" that are "constantly subverting the 'official' text" of Anglo-American writing about *Nuevomexicanos* which offered little more than a romanticized representation of a people whose 'quaint' customs and culture were ostensibly disappearing in the modern Anglo world. Rebolledo agrees with my contention elsewhere that this group of women writers constructs a sentimental and nostalgic view of the past which is a form of embryonic resistance, yet convincingly argues that women's strategies of resistance were not merely " 'sparks' of dissent" but complex and powerful narrative articulations of self and culture that consciously operate to subvert Anglo-American hegemony (1990: 135).[8]

In California the largest single group of personal narratives was collected in the 1870s by Hubert Howe Bancroft, bookdealer, document collector and professional historian, who solicited scores of oral dictations from the *Californios,* as the California Mexicans called themselves. These narratives undergird his massive *History of California* published in seven volumes between 1884 and 1889, as well as *Pastoral California* (1888),[9] an often ethnocentric and romanticized history of pre-American California society. As Bancroft himself wrote of the project in *Literary Industries* (1890), he and his field assistants collected some "two hundred volumes of original narrative from memory by as many early Californians, native and pioneers, written by themselves or taken down from their lips . . . , the vivid narratives of their experiences" (282). Most are personal narratives collected as oral dictations by Bancroft's field researchers Enrique Cerruti and Thomas Savage, who during a period of some six years travelled a wide circuit from San Francisco to San Diego transcribing the lives of the *Californios.*[10] There are, from my count, over one hundred Californio personal narratives of lengths varying from ten pages to a fair number that are hundred of pages long. I must confess not only my sense of wonder, but my sense of resurrective power at discovering scores of disembodied voices, textualized lives stored away in Bancroft's manuscript storehouse of California lives during the 1870s: María Inocente Avila, *Cosas de California* (Things about California); Juan Bernal, *Memoria de un Californio*; Josefa Carillo de Fitch, *Narración de una Californiana*; Rafael González, *Experiencias de un soldado* (Experiences of a Soldier); Apolinaria Lorenzana, *Memorias de la Beata*; José del Cármen Lugo, *Vida de un Ranchero* (A Rancher's Life); Eulalia Pérez, *Una vieja y sus recuerdos*; Pío Pico, *Narración histórica*; Vincente Sánchez, *Cartas de un Angelino* (Letters of an Angelino); Felipa Osuna de Marrón, *Recuerdos del pasado* (Memories of the Past); Pablo Véjar, *Recuerdos de un viejo* (An Old Man's Recollections) (Mss. Bancroft Library). These and scores of other personal narratives still await the kind of exhaustive recovery, editing, translation and publication which will rescue them from archival obscurity.

This Californio manuscript collection constitutes a major narrative formation, solicited by Bancroft, but composed in collaboration or alone by individuals who wished to relate the history of their community in their own language and from their own cultural perspective in a manner that, as it turned out, often contested popular and historiographic representations of Mexican Californians, which by the 1870s were highly derogatory at worst or condescending at best. Mariano G. Vallejo, Juan Alvarado, Juan Bandini, Pío Pico and Antonio María Osío were some of the men of power and influence in pre-American California who composed sustained collaborative narratives in which the "self" figures prominently in the social transformation that was displacing them even as they wrote. Mariano Vallejo's *Recuerdos históricos y personales tocante a la alta California* (1875) occupies some five volumes of nearly one thousand pages of historical and personal impressions of California society before and after the American occupation.

Vallejo's *Recuerdos* confirms Georges Gusdorf's proposition that "memoirs are always ... a revenge on history" (36). For Vallejo, the *Recuerdos* was a form of discursive revenge upon negative representations of Mexicans undergoing constructing during his own lifetime, as well as a form of prior "revenge" upon the negative history he had reason to believe would be written about his people after him. I have no doubt that Vallejo collaborated on the *Recuerdos* to gratify his own ego; after all, he claimed that Bancroft's projected *History of California* could not be written without the name *Vallejo* at its center. Vallejo was indeed among that class identified by Gusdorf as "the minister of state, the politician, the military man [who] write in order to celebrate their deeds (always more or less misunderstood), providing a sort of posthumous propaganda for posterity that otherwise is in danger of forgetting them or of failing to esteem them properly" (Gusdorf 36). Nevertheless, Vallejo also recognized the stakes involved for all of his people when he wrote the *Recuerdos* and encouraged other Californios to relate their narratives; in a letter to a friend, he wrote that unless they did so they would "disappear, ignored by the whole world." Vallejo's work indeed operates as "a sort of posthumous propaganda for posterity," except that, as a keen response to the historiography of his own moment, the *Recuerdos* was preemptive narrative intended not so much to forestall as to master-script Bancroft's history. Rather than strictly self-aggrandizing, therefore, his writing and document gathering constituted a forceful act of opposition to contemporary as well as future historiographic erasure. As he wrote to his son, Platón, when he was nearly finished with the huge five-volume undertaking, "the history will come out and it will be as you've heard me say many times, the truth impartially written so it can serve posterity as a guide."

The Bancroft collection also contains about fifteen narratives by women that describe events before and during the Americanization of the territory from a gendered perspective which both criticizes patriarchal constraint in Mexican society and yet refutes common assumptions that Mexican women were not bothered by the conquest. Indeed, one of the reasons there are not more narratives is because many women were so angry with the Americans that they simply refused to collaborate in giving their personal narratives; as Leonard Pitt writes in his classic study on *The Decline of the Californios*: "The widows of the Carrillo brothers stiffly refused any recollections, and Señora José Castro bristled at the merest suggestion that she should contribute information to clear her husband's clouded reputation" (281). And although Rosalía Vallejo de Leese did speak, she was so incensed that she speaks through clenched teeth about the American conquest; "those hated men inspired me with such a large dose of hate against their race," she recalls, "that though twenty eight years have elapsed since that time, I have not forgotten the insults heaped upon me, and not being desirous of coming in contact with them I have abstained from learning their language" (1876, Ms. Bancroft Library). Notwithstanding their ambivalence, other women like María Inocente Avila, Catarina Avila de Ríos, Apolinaria Lorenzana, María Angustias de la Guerra and my favorite, Eulalia Pérez, a woman said to be 139 years old when her life story was recorded, are among some dozen women who offer revealing views on gender relations in Californio society and disclose their own strategies of self-empowerment.

As Sidonie Smith argues in *The Poetics of Women's Autobiography*, "since the ideology of gender makes of woman's life script a nonstory, a silent space, a gap in patriarchal culture, the ideal woman is self-effacing rather than self-promoting, and her 'natural' story shapes itself not around the public, heroic life but around the fluid, circumstantial, contingent responsives to others that according to patriarchal ideology, characterizes the life of woman. ... From that point of view, woman has no 'autobiographical self' in the same sense that man does. From that point of view, she has no 'public' story to tell" (50). However, as Smith suggests, women have long resisted such voicelessness and have likewise reconstructed themselves as figures possessed of a will to power in the world. Rather than subordinate themselves to domestic memory, that is, to a version of the "women's sphere" which would make of their "life script a nonstory, a silent space, a gap in patriarchal culture," Mexican-American women—speaking their lives to Bancroft—invariably voiced resistance to the patriarchal domination which characterized social relations in Mexican California and figured themselves as working actively in the social world they inhabited along with—not at the side of—men. At the behest of Bancroft's assistants, Eulalia Pérez's and Apolinaria Lorenzana's personal narratives may begin with descriptions about their domestic work in early California missions, but voice quickly opens toward recollection of their tough-minded independence and will toward self-sufficiency in a male dominated society. From Angustias de la Guerra, Bancroft's interlocutor Thomas Savage wished to solicit information on "government matters" and political events because of her affiliations with powerful public men—her father, her brothers, and her first husband. What one witnesses in the women's narratives, however, is that women like de la Guerra remember themselves as agents in political events rather than as domestically passive witnesses to men's activities in the public realm. In fact, de la Guerra figures herself and other women as socio-politically perspicuous and courageous, whereas the political patriarchs of the country were, she charges, more often than not blind to the threat of American encroachment, enfeebled by political corruption and embarrassingly cowardly when "it came time to defend the country."

As with nearly all nineteenth and early twentieth century autobiographic narratives by Mexican Americans, the archaeological recovery of the Californio narratives requires lifting these life histories from their lower case status, chipping away the Bancroft text which encases them, brushing the dust off their covers and, by publishing and reading them, restoring their voices. Felipe Fierro, Vallejo's contemporary and the editor of the San Francisco newspaper *La Voz del Nuevo Mundo* (The Voice of the New World), recognized the gravity of recording life histories when he pleaded with his readers to participate in the Bancroft project, not for Bancroft's benefit but in anticipation of the day their stories would be given a public life of their own. Fierro's editorial comments to the Californios in *La Voz* on March 7, 1876, echoed in other parts of the West: "De ese modo llegará el día en que los sucesos, lo mismo que los servicios de los buenos ciudadanos sean dados a la luz de una manera digna de ellos" [In such manner the day will arrive when the events, as well as the contributions of these good citizens will be given public light in a manner deserving of them].

IV

Among the issues that come into question when thinking about the Californio personal narratives is the *auto*biographical integrity of the narratives. The degree to which these dictated narratives direct, distort or otherwise decentralize the autobiographical subject is, I believe, an important issue. I argue that, whereas for Bancroft the collection of these personal narratives was foundational research for his *History of California* project, for the narrators themselves it was the critical and perhaps only occasion for recreating the life of the self, together with the world inhabited by that self. Yet, precisely because some of the narratives to which I refer were neither self-composed nor meant, strictly, to function as autobiography, claiming autobiographical status for certain texts once again raises the proprietary issue of genre which must be clarified. To echo one of the questions Arnold Krupat asks about Native-American autobiography: "to what extent is it responsible to treat works presented as contributions to history and ethnography as works of literature?" (31–2). Such an issue is of immediate concern for anyone intent upon explaining the socio-cultural, ideological and the discursive conditions that underlie the formation of autobiographical consciousness in Mexican-American society. The dilemma confronted by Krupat, H. David Brumble and other scholars of Native-American autobiography who have had to consider the autobiographical fashioning of native people by Anglo-American amanuenses, whether historians, anthropologists, poets, journalists serves as both warning and instruction for my work. As Krupat saliently points out: "Indian autobiographies are collaborative efforts, jointly produced by some White—who translates, transcribes, compiles, edits, interprets, polishes, and ultimately determines the form of the text in writing—and by an Indian who is its subject and whose life becomes the content of the 'autobiography' whose title may bear his name" (30).

One can no longer naively read collaboratively produced narrative without thinking about editorial construction with all of its customary manipulations, performative stagings, transcriptional excisions, translations (not to mention mistranslations), additions and refashionings. Certainly, the problematics of Hubert Bancroft's collection of scores of California personal narratives from oral dictations with all of the editorial mechanics of formulaic questioning (masked in most narratives but noticeable when comparing statement clusters on certain crucial historical events), the selecting out of many informants whose memories were considered faulty, the hurried pace of collection mentioned in the prefatory statements of the field collectors and evinced by numerous transcriptional truncations requires recognition and analysis of the power differential inscribed within the very formation of autobiographical articulation. Although we must of course recognize and assess the interpolations of editorial construction, we must also recognize that, as Krupat suggests, bi-cultural collaboration is a site of contention for authority over narrative self-representation (at the ground level of speech), as well as the site of socially symbolic contestations over the Mexican American's political, cultural and social status in the U. S. The disclosure of individual experience and the overlay of individual personality upon the description of external socio-political events mark the Californio narratives with distinct autobiographic authority, just as the signature of the "I" identifies authorial status in various autobiographical enunciations, markings, and representations throughout the narratives. Autobiographical authority, I would therefore argue, needs not be thought of as issuing only from the hand which scribes personal experience, but rather from what I believe is a deep human desire to shape and control narrative, to modulate its articulation by that small stubbornness of voice that insists on its own story and that reconstructs the past in a register which claims ownership of the past, especially when ownership of the present is endangered.

Central to this reclaiming of the past was the narrative habit of remembering oneself within a community of the past. It is no surprise, therefore, to see that many of the nineteenth- and early twentieth-century narratives which comprise the beginnings of Chicano autobiography construct a culturally matrixed subjectivity in which the "I" is subsumed within a narrative of regional or cultural history. This displacement of a self-absorbed "I"-centered narrative by narrative in which the cultural "We" is reconstituted may be regarded as a filial act. The historicizing "I" indeed sustains itself by narratively restoring the cultural ecology in which it lives: the history of the cultural community constitutes the history of the "I" or, to put it another way, the "I" is but an empty cipher, a floating signifier without content until it is grounded by a collective identitarian utterance, by an act of cultural recuperation of the kind Cleofas Jaramillo (in the opening epigraph) refers to as describing a "current invisible to the stranger and understood only by their inhabitants" or, as in the case of Mariano Vallejo, reading himself into the Spanish colonial and Mexican social and political history of California. Indeed, such narratives reside outside the formal boundaries scholars have traditionally reserved for a singularly, self-disclosing text, "a retrospective prose narrative produced by a real person concerning his own existence, focusing on his individual life, in particular on the development of his personality."[11] However, as more and more autobiography scholars, especially feminist and third world practicioners, are arguing, traditional genre constraints have been exclusionary and must be renegotiated, wedged open to alternate forms of self-representation—historiography, cultural ethnography, folkloristic narratives—which do not focus exclusively upon the development of individual personality so much as upon the formation, and transformation, of the individual within a community transformation. Hence, narratives that some scholars would consider more properly within the domain of social history or cultural ethnography, but which I believe a culturally historicized and contextually reaccentuated reading will discover to be a kind of communitarian autobiography, must not be categorically dismissed as non-autobiographical. This is not to argue that Mexican-American autobiographical expression is devoid of ego (Mariano Vallejo telling Bancroft's scribe, "I will not be hurried or dictated to. It is my history and not yours I propose to tell."), but rather that in the years after 1848 the entire community underwent such a global assault that even powerfully, self-assertive individuals like Vallejo were put in a position of reading their own lives against the ruins of their social world. Therefore we must read for autobiographical content within a complex narrative matrix in which the individuals who composed or related their communal histories were simultaneously composing the history of the self and its shaping, twisting, reconfigurating response to social transformation in a voice (voices, really) which appropriated the exogenous historiographic and ethnographic discourses through which they were licensed speak.

Mariano Vallejo, like Juan Seguín before and Cleofas Jaramillo after, knew that claiming ownership of the past (however that past was fashioned) must fill a space emptied of presence by American social domination and, its adjunct, a historiography of the American conquest which discursively decimated Mexican people. Fully cognizant that they must write their own history or, as he wrote to Anastacio Carrillo, "disappear, ignored of the whole world" (Pitt 278), Vallejo wrote 900 pages of personal memoirs in the 1860s only to have the manuscript burn in a fire which destroyed his home in 1867. Then, while he was traveling throughout California in the 1870s, writing his own memoirs once again and encouraging men and women of his generation to dictate their personal narratives as well as to archive their papers, Vallejo beseeched people to remember and restore the past against misrepresentation and betrayal. As Leonard Pitt writes, because they "perceived themselves not merely as the victims of annexation or assimilation, but of deliberate betrayal and bone-crushing repression" Mexican Californians like Vallejo emphasized "injustice, violence and broken promises in their memoirs" (Pitt 278, 283). Indeed nostalgia appeared in their memoirs, but memory was politicized by loss and anger. Rather than uncritical celebration of an idyllic and unobtainable past, therefore, nostalgia may be seen to function as ideological opposition to having one's world destroyed. The autobiographical formation in Mexican-American culture may indeed figure the past as utopian, but this is because post-1848 life was a nightmare; so, if the social economy of pre-American life was fashioned as coherent and sane, it was because the present of the American regime was culturally incoherent and socially insane. Nostalgia for an earlier world emerges from grief for a world lost, which, because it tends to suffuse the past with a glow of the ideal and idyllic, masks the anger underlying dislocation that produces nostalgia in the first place. In other words, nostalgia is a realization that there are future stakes involved in the re-construction(s) of the past. To remember is not only the act of not forgetting but an act of not being forgotten, just as remembering the past as utopian cultural terrain reveals the very condition of cultural dislocation which makes a necessity of such retrospective communitarian idealization. Figured as a studied response to displacement and erasure, a narrative of nostalgia may be read as a consciously produced strategy of opposition rather than an unmediated and non-critical reflex to displacement. Anger, therefore, finds its outlet in this controlled strategy of revisiting the past as idyllic—at least in comparison to the ruins and hostility of the post-1848 present.

Unless we wish to think of our *antepasados* (forebears) as either blind or stupid, therefore, I believe we must recontextualize our reading of their narrative production in order to understand their social and discursive situations. We must recognize that colonized Mexicans were often speaking out of both sides of their mouths with visionary social purpose. What may at first appear as ideologically subordinate speech actually constitutes multi-addressed utterance in which pragmatic appeasement reads at one surface of language while anger and opposition read at other, and often upon the same surfaces. Such strategic utterance, I maintain, constitutes a form of rhetorical camouflage which first appropriates a public "voice" for an individual from an otherwise "silenced" group and then turns that voice to duplicitous purpose. Discursive duplicity functions to communicate different stories to different audiences, with an implicit understanding that one's own people will, to invoke Fierro's comment, someday read them "de una manera digna de ellos" (in a manner deserving of them). We must read early literary discourse, and autobiography specifically, in a manner that restores the difficult conditions under which they were produced and through which they must speak to us—that future audience to which Fierro referred and for which Vallejo hoped. The narrative reconstitution of an idealized prior world may indeed be tainted by utopian imagination, but both the original trauma of displacement (American conquest of 1846–48) and an unrelenting assault upon the cultural habitat established a form of autobiographical consciousness in which Seguín, for example, understood that his posterity's future was staked in establishing a version of the past, a historical text, which had to stand against erasure at worst, or negative historical representation at best. Post-1848 Mexican-American autobiographical narrative projects a future condition, therefore, in which a Chicano reader in the late twentieth century reads personal narrative "de una manera digna de ellos." That is, as an expression of our collective historical desire to sustain presence in the face of a still unrelenting assault upon our history, culture, and literary production.

Notes

[1]Leonard Pitt records one such example of correspondence between brothers Antonio María and Pablo de la Guerra, member of an affluent and politically influential California family: "As he set out for the 'new world' of the north [northern California], Antonio vowed to his brother to 'write something of my compañeros that will entertain you.' He did so in a series of lively letters which illuminate the Californio's sense of alienation outside his home precincts." *The Decline of the Californios*: 141–47.

[2]Pitt, for example, devotes an entire chapter to the work of Francisco P. Ramirez, who edited and published *El Clamor Publico*, a Los Angeles newspaper which, in addition to carrying general news about Latin America, argued forcefully on behalf of Mexican Americans" (184, 181–89).

[3]See John Blassingame, *Slave Testimony: Two Centuries of Letters, Speeches, Interviews, and Autobiographies*; Gilbert Osofsky, ed. *Puttin' on Ole Massa: The Slave Narratives of Henry Bibb, William Wells Brown, and Soloman Northrup*; Arna Bontempts, ed. *Great Slave Narratives*; Robert Stepto, *From Behind the Veil: A Study of Afro-American Narrative*; Joanne Braxton, *Black Women Writing Autobiography: A Tradition within a Tradition*.

[4]There have been scores of essays by Chicano scholars which seek to recover the connections to pre-Columbian literature and culture. For the most complete collection of essays on appropriation of pre-Columbian myth, metaphor, and culture see *Azltan: Essays on the Chicano Homeland* (Albuquerue, New Mexico: Academia/El Norte Publications, 1989), Rudolfo A. Anaya and Francisco Lomelí, eds.

[5]As Leal says, "We shall consider works, especially dating before 1821, written by the inhabitants of this region with a Spanish background, to belong to an early stage of Chicano literature," "Mexican American Literature: A Historical Perspective," 22.

[6]Here I accept Bruce-Novoa's recent "compromise" in "The Space of Chicano Literature Update: 1978," of his original proposition that the space signified "the intercultural *nothingness*."

[7]Menchaca's "Reminiscences" (Manuscript), Seguín's *Personal Memoirs"* and Pérez's "Memoirs" (Manuscript), Barker Texas History Center, University of Texas, Austin; Tafolla's "Nearing the End of the Trail" (Manuscript), and Garza's "La lógica de los hechos" (Manuscript), Benson Latin American Collection, Mexican American

Archives, University of Texas, Austin; Rodriguez, *"The Old Guide": His Life in His Own Words* (Dallas: The Methodist Episcopal Church, 1897).

[8]Rebolledo's essay, "Narrative Strategies of Resistance in Hispana Writing," provides a provocative and thoughtful exchange with views I had expressed in a 1987 conference paper published as "Imprisoned Narrative? Or Lies, Secrets and Silence in New Mexico Women's Autobiography."

[9]*History of California*, Vols. 1–7, and *Pastoral California*, like all of Bancroft's historical work, were published by his own San Francisco publishing house, The History Company.

[10]Both Cerruti and Savage left manuscript reports of their ethnographic expeditions that contain valuable insight into their collection methods.

[11]Lejeune, "The Autobiographical Contract," additionally insists that such forms as the memoir, diary and autobiographical poem do not properly satisfy the "conditions" of autobiography. There is, of course, a rather large body of critical literature that has moved well beyond a rigid definition of autobiography as a singularly self-disclosing text that reads something like St. Augustine's or Rousseau's *Confessions*. To follow Francis R. Hart, "Notes for an Anatomy of Modern Autobiography," autobiography proper is no longer restricted to the construction of "a personal history that seeks to communicate or express the essential nature, the truth, of the self."

Works Cited

Acuña, Rodolfo. *Occupied America: A History of Chicanos*. 2nd ed. New York: Harper, 1981.

Amador, José María. "Memorias sobre la historia de California," ms. Bancroft Library, U of California, Berkeley.

Andrews, William. *To Tell a Free Story: The First Century of Afro-American Autobiography, 1760–1865*. Chicago: Chicago UP, 1988.

Angustias de la Guerra, María. "Ocurrencias en California," 1878, ms. Bancroft Library, UC Berkeley.

Augustus, Jennings Napoleon. *A Texas Ranger*. Dallas: Turner, 1930.

Ávila, María Inocente. "Cosas de California," ms. Bancroft Library, UC Berkeley.

Baker, Houston. *The Journey Back: Issues in Black Literature and Criticism*. Chicago: Chicago UP, 1980.

Bancroft, Hubert Howe. *History of California*. 7 vols. San Francisco: History Company, 1884–1889.

———. *Pastoral California*. San Francisco: History Company, 1888.

———. *Literary Industries*. San Francisco: History Company, 1890.

Bernal, Juan. "Memoria de un Californio," ms. Bancroft Library, UC Berkeley.

Blassingame, John. *Slave Testimony: Two Centuries of Letters, Speeches, Interviews, and Autobiographies*. Baton Rouge: Louisiana State UP, 1977.

Bontemps, Arna, ed. *Great Slave Narratives*. Boston: Beacon, 1948.

Bruce-Novoa, Juan. *RetroSpace: Collected Essays on Chicano Literature*. Houston: Arte Público, 1990.

Cabeza de Baca, Fabiola. *The Good Life: New Mexico Traditions and Food*. Santa Fe. 1949. Santa Fe: Museum of New Mexico, 1982.

———. *We Fed Them Cactus*. Albuquerque: U of New Mexico, 1954.

Carillo de Fitch, Josefa. "Narración de una Californiana," ms. Bancroft Library, UC Berkeley.

Cather, Willa. *Death Comes for the Archbishop*. New York: Knopf, 1927.

Cerruti, Enrique. "Ramblings in California," ms. Bancroft Library, UC Berkeley.

Chávez, John R. *The Lost Land: The Chicano Image of the Southwest*. Albuquerque: New Mexico UP, 1984.

Chacón, Rafael. "Memorias." 1912. (Chapters 1-3) U of Colorado Library, Boulder.

Columbus, Christopher. *The Journal*. Trans. Cecil Jane. New York: C. N. Potter, 1960.

Couser, Thomas G. *Altered Egos: Authority in American Autobiography*. Oxford: Oxford UP, 1989.

Douglass, Claude L. *The Gentlemen in the White Hats: Dramatic Episodes in the History of the Texas Rangers*. Dallas: Turner Co., 1934.

Emparán, Madie Brown. *The Vallejos of California*. San Francisco: San Francisco UP, 1968.

Fierro, Felipe. Editorial. *La Voz del Nuevo Mundo* [San Francisco] 7 Mar. 1876.

Garza, Catarino E. "La lógica de mis hechos," 1877–1889, ms. Benson Latin American Collection, Mexican American Archives, U of Texas, Austin.

Gates, Henry Louis. "Introduction." *The Classic Slave Narratives*. New York: New American, 1987.

Gillet, James B. *Six Years with the Texas Rangers, 1875–81*. New Haven: Yale UP, 1925.

Goldman, Anne. " 'I yam what I yam': Cooking, Culture and Colonialism." *De/Colonizing the Subject: Politics and Gender in Women's Autobiographical Practice*. Eds. Sidonie Smith and Julia Watson. Minneapolis: U of Minnesota P, 1992. 169–95.

González, Rafael. "Experiencias de un soldado," ms. Bancroft Library, UC Berkeley.

Gusdorf, Georges. "Conditions and Limits of Autobiography." Rpt. in *Autobiography: Essays Theoretical and Critical*. Ed. James Olney. Princeton: Princeton UP, 1980. 28–48.

Hart, Francis R. "Notes for an Anatomy of Modern Autobiography." *New Literary History* 1 (1969–70): 485-512.

Jaramillo, Cleofas. *Romance of a Little Village Girl*. San Antonio: Naylor, 1955.

————. *The Genuine New Mexico Tasty Recipes: Old and Quaint Formulas for the Preparation of Seventy-five Delicious Spanish Dishes*. 1939. Santa Fe: Seton Village, 1942.

————. *Sombras del Pasado/Shadows of the Past*. Santa Fe: Ancient City, 1941.

————. *Cuentos del Hogar*. El Campo, Texas: Citizen, 1939.

Krupat, Arnold. *For Those Who Come After: A Study of Native American Autobiography*. Berkeley: California UP, 1985.

Leal, Luis. "Mexican American Literature: A Historical Perspective." *Revista Chicano-Riquena* 1 (1973): 32–44. Rpt. *Modern Chicano Writers: A Collection of Critical Essays*. Eds. Joseph Sommer and Tomas Ybarra-Frausto. New York: Prentice-Hall, 1979. 18–30.

Lejeune, Phillippe. "The Autobiographical Contract." *French Literary Theory Today*. Ed. Tzvetan Todorov. New York, 1982.

————. *On Autobiography*. Minnesota UP, 1989. 3–30.

Leon-Portilla, Miguel. *Pre-Columbian Literatures of Mexico*. Norman: U of Oklahoma P, 1969.

————. *The Broken Spears: Aztec Accounts of the Conquest of Mexico*. Boston: Beacon, 1961.

————. *Los Antiguos Mexicanos através de sus Crónicas y Cantares*. Mexico City: Fondo de Cultura Economica, 1961.

Lorenzana, Apolinaria. "Memorias de la Beata," 1878, ms. Bancroft Library, UC Berkeley.

Martinez, Padre Antonio Jose. "Relacion de meritos," 1838. New Mexico State Records Library.

McWilliams, Carey. *North from Mexico: The Spanish-Speaking People of the United States*. Philadelphia: Lipincott, 1948. rpt. New York: Greenwood, 1968.

Meketa, Jacqueline Dorgan. *Legacy of Honor: The Life of Rafael Chacón, A Nineteenth-Century New Mexican*. Albuquerque: New Mexico UP, 1986.

Menchaca, José Antonio. "Reminiscences," ca. 1850, ms., ts. Barker Texas History Center, U of Texas, Austin.

Osuña de Marron, Felipa. "Recuerdos del pasado," ms. Bancroft Library, UC Berkeley.

Otero, Miguel Antonio, *My Life on the Frontier, 1864–1882*. New York: Pioneers, 1935.

————. *My Life on the Frontier, 1882–1897*. Albuquerque: New Mexico UP, 1939.

————. *My Nine Years as Governor of the Territory of New Mexico, 1897–1905*. Albuquerque: New Mexico UP, 1940.

Padilla, Genaro M. "Self as Cultural Metaphor in Acosta's *The Autobiography of a Brown Buffalo*." *Journal of General Education* 35 (1984): 242–58.

————. "Imprisoned Narrative? Or Lies, Secrets and Silence in New Mexico Women's Autobiography." *Criticism in the Borderlands: Studies in Chicano Literature, Culture, and Ideology*. Eds. Hector Calderon and Jose David Saldivar. Durham, NC: Duke UP, 1991. 43–61.

————. " 'Yo sola aprendí': Mexican Women's Personal Narratives from Nineteenth-Century California." *Revealing Lives: Autobiography, Biography, and Gender*. Eds. Susan Groag Bell and Marilyn Yalom. New York: State UP of New York, 1990.

Paredes, Raymund. "The Evolution of Chicano Literature." *Three American Literatures*. Ed. Houston A. Baker, Jr. New York, 1982. 33–79.

Pérez, Eulalia. "Una Vieja y sus Recuerdos," 1877, ms. Bancroft Library, UC Berkeley.

Pérez, Jesse. "Memoirs," ts. Barker Texas History Center, U of Texas, Austin.

Pico, Pío. "Narración historico," ms. Bancroft Library, UC Berkeley.

Pitt, Leonard. *The Decline of the Californios: A Social History of the Spanish-Speaking Californios, 1846–1890*. Berkeley: California UP, 1971.

Rebolledo, Tey Diana. "Tradition and Mythology: Signatures of Landscape in Chicana Literature." *The Desert is No Lady: Southwest Landscapes in Women's Writing and Art*. Eds. Vera Norwood and Janice Monk. New Haven: Yale UP, 1987. 96–124.

————. "Narrative Strategies of Resistance in Hispana Writing." *The Journal of Narrative Technique* 20 (Spring 1990): 2:134–146.

Rodríguez, José Policarpio. *"The Old Guide": His Life in His Own Words*. Dallas: The Methodist Episcopal Church, ca. 1897.

Saldívar, Ramón. *Chicano Narrative: The Dialectics of Difference*. Madison: Wisconsin UP, 1990.

———. "Ideologies of the Self: Chicano Autobiography." *Diacritics* (Fall 1985): 25–34.

Sánchez, Vicente. "Cartas de un Angelino," ms. Bancroft Library, UC Berkeley.

Savage, Thomas. "Report on Labors on Archives and Procuring Material for the History of California," 1874, ms. Bancroft Library, UC Berkeley.

Seguín, John N. *Personal Memoirs: From the Year 1834 to the Retreat of General Woll from the City of San Antonio, 1842*. San Antonio: Ledger Book and Job Office, 1858.

———. Personal Memoirs, 1858, ts. Barker Texas History Center, U of Texas, Austin.

Stepto, Robert. *From Behind the Veil: A Study of Afro-American Narrative*. Urbana: Illinois UP, 1979.

Tafolla, Santiago. "Nearing the End of the Trail," ca. 1890, ms. Benson Latin American Collection, Mexican American Archives, U of Texas, Austin.

Vallejo, Mariano Guadalupe. "Recuerdos históricos y personales tocante a la alta California." 5 vols. 1875, ms. Bancroft Library, UC Berkeley.

———. "Historical and Personal Memoirs Relating to Alta California." Trans. Earl R. Hewitt, ts. Bancroft Library, UC Berkeley.

Vallejo, Salvador. "Notas historicas sobre California," ms. Bancroft Library, UC Berkeley.

Vallejo de Leese, Rosalía. "History of the 'Osos,'" 1876, ms. Bancroft Library, UC Berkeley.

Véjar, Pablo. "Recuerdos de un Viejo," ms. Bancroft Library, UC Berkeley.

Vigil, José María. *Nezahualcoyotl, el rey poeta*. Mexico: Andrea, 1957.

Warren, Nina Otero. *Old Spain in Our Southwest*. New York: Harcourt, 1936.

Weber, David J. *Foreigners in their Native Land: Historical Roots of the Mexican Americans*. Albuquerque: New Mexico UP, 1973.

White Lea, Aurora Lucero. *Literary Folklore of the Hispanic Southwest*. San Antonio: Naylor, 1953.

Wong, Hertha. "Pictography as Autobiography: Plains Indian Sketchbooks of the Late Nineteenth and Early Twentieth Centuries." *American Literary History* 1 (Summer 1989): 295–316.

The Building of a Community:
Puerto Rican Writers and Activists
in New York City (1890s–1960s)

Edna Acosta-Belén

Until recent years, most major studies about the New York City Puerto Rican community suffered from serious limitations. Rarely were the initial stages in the evolution of this community chronicled, nor was much attention given to the establishment of Puerto Rican communities in other U. S. cities. The historiography on the development of early Puerto Rican *colonias* has been scarce, making it more difficult to fully comprehend the meaning and complex dynamics of Puerto Rican migration as an essential feature of the Island's century-long colonial relationship with the United States. Less than three decades ago, for example, Nathan Glazer and Daniel P. Moynihan emphasized the "the relative weakness of community organization and community leadership among them" (101) and the absence of "spontaneous grass-roots organizations" (107) among Puerto Ricans in New York. They also deplored what they considered to be the deficiencies and thinness of Puerto Rican traditions, and framed their analyses of the Puerto Rican experience within a problem-oriented discourse and deficiency models that focused primarily on issues of poverty, unemployment, crime and dropout rates. Oscar Lewis used Puerto Ricans to illustrate his catchy but misleading "culture of poverty" concept, and Julius Horwitz saw them as trapped in "the culture of public welfare." Many of these conceptualizations have been repeated *ad nauseum* by subsequent scholars as objective statements of fact.

With the publication of Virginia Sánchez Korrol's *From Colonia to Community: The History of Puerto Ricans in New York City, 1917–1948*, many of the critical failures of previous scholarship have been pointed out and corrected. Sánchez Korrol documented the multiple factors that pushed Puerto Ricans from their native land and those that pulled them into the United

179

States. She described their settlement patterns; the kinds of organizations they developed after their arrival; the fundamental role of women in sustaining the community; the extent to which Puerto Rican emigrants participated in city politics; and the critical importance of the settlements established during the last decades of the nineteenth century and early decades of this century in providing essential support systems that defined and reinforced a sense of community for Puerto Ricans during subsequent migratory waves.[1]

This essay attempts to define a research agenda for expanding the continuing process of reconstruction of the Puerto Rican historical and literary legacy in the United States. I stress the need to focus on parallel developments in the various stages of the migratory process between the island and U. S. contexts and to examine the links and interconnections shared by the versatile cast of participants introduced herein.

The dates Sánchez Korrol used to delimit her pathbreaking study mark two crucial events in Puerto Rican history: the passage of the Jones Act by the U. S. Congress in 1917, which made Puerto Ricans U. S. citizens, and the election of Luis Muñoz Marín in 1948 as the first Puerto Rican governor, thus ending a half century of federally appointed officials running the Island's government first imposed by the United States in 1898. U. S. citizenship allowed Puerto Ricans to move back and force between the Island and the colonial metropolis without restrictions. The policies and programs of the Muñoz Marín populist government, particularly its *Operation Bootstrap* industrialization program of the 1950s, provoked a massive displacement of rural workers and intensified the level of migration to the United States.

Understanding how Puerto Rico became a nation of perennial migrants, with a continuing circular migration pattern between the Island and the colonial metropolis, entails a more elaborate historical and structural analysis of the interplay of international economic realities that give impulse to these population movements, and, in the particular case of Puerto Ricans, of the diverse implications and ramifications of their colonial experience, first, under the Spanish and, subsequently, under U. S. metropolitan power. Such an historical analysis of national and transnational economic development and of Puerto Rico's colonial condition demonstrates that the pervasive displacement of workers that the Puerto Rican population has experienced so intensely for more than a century is a constitutive aspect of capitalist expansion and the relations and changes it engenders. These forces are determining factors in shaping migration patterns and in creating the parallel conditions faced by Puerto Rican workers at home and in the United States (see Bonilla and Campos). Although such detailed discussion is beyond the scope of this essay, it points to the importance of reaching back over a period of more than a hundred years and tracing the origins of the Puerto Rican presence in U. S.

society in order to shed new light on many of the mistaken but commonly held assumptions and prevailing myths about the quality of life Puerto Ricans were able to forge for themselves as members of the underprivileged U. S. working class.

In contrast to previous groups of immigrants, Puerto Ricans are colonial migrants since Puerto Rico is not a sovereign nation and has remained under U. S. control and jurisdiction since 1898. The mass migration of the 1950s did not signal, as some scholars mistakenly concluded, the conspicuous presence of Puerto Ricans in New York City as "newcomers."[2] On the contrary, this postwar massive migratory wave was just a continuation of an ongoing process that had begun more than half a century before.

By 1960, the Puerto Rican population in the United States was almost a million; twelve and a half times higher than what it had been in 1940 (see Table 1 below). In 1910 the Puerto Rican population amounted to less than 2,000 individuals, but, as Table 1 illustrates, it is during this period that Puerto Ricans began to migrate in significant numbers. The peaking of this migratory process is found in the 1950s and early 1960s. Since then migration has continued as a predictable aspect of Puerto Rican life, reaching, as Clara Rodríguez has noted, the fluctuating pattern of net migration of recent decades and greater dispersion of the population to other parts of the United States (4).

Table 1: Growth of Puerto Rican Population in the United States 1910–1990*

Year	Total Population	Percent of Increase
1910	1,513	_____
1920	11,811	680.6
1930	52,774	346.8
1940	69,967	32.6
1950	301,375	330.7
1960	887,662	194.5
1970	1,429,396	61.0
1980	1,983,000	17.5
1989	2,330,000	_____

*Sources: U. S. Department of Commerce, Bureau of the Census, *The Hispanic Population in the United States, March 1989* (Washington, D.C.: Government Printing Office, 1990); Frank L. Schick and Renee Schick, eds. *Statistical Handbook on U. S. Hispanics* (Phoenix, AZ: Oryx, 1991); Kal Wagenheim, *A Survey of Puerto Ricans on the U. S. Mainland in the 1970s* (New York: Praeger, 1975).

This contemporary phase, described by Meléndez, Rodríguez and Barry-Figueroa as a "revolving-door" or "commuter" migration, produces a bidirectional flow of exchanges and interactions between the homeland and the metropolitan center. According to Sutton (17–20), these interactions have created a "transnational socio-cultural system" that allows migrants to reconstitute their lives in New York City, and to affirm a separate cultural identity, while maintaining close ties with their countries of origin. This process, which Sutton generalizes to Puerto Ricans and other Caribbean migrants, further creolizes Caribbean cultures and identities in both New York City and the countries of origin, challenging antiquated notions of immigrant assimilation and acculturation, and marking new possibilities in their struggles for political and cultural empowerment. In my essay "Beyond Island Boundaries: Ethnicity, Gender, and Cultural Revitalization in Nuyorican Literature," I provide a detailed analysis of the contact process from which new syncretic forms of cultural convergence are emerging, and of the effort toward the reconstruction and reappropriation of a cultural tradition being made by those groups generally excluded from the U. S. cultural mainstream.

The process of recovering and reconstructing community history involves more than "an exercise in documentation," notes Rina Benmayor. She affirms that "What underlies this effort is the political and social commitment to understand the past in order to better confront the problems faced now and in the future" (69). She further argues that "understanding how people perceive themselves and interpret their lives, what struggles they waged and how they have survived helps us move the struggle forward and leave for younger generations a foundation from which they can derive clarity and strength" (69–70). The increasing attention given to scholarship on the Puerto Rican experience in recent decades is partly due to the emergence of Puerto Rican studies programs at several U. S. higher education institutions during the early 1970s and the establishment in New York City, in 1973, of the Centro de Estudios Puertorriqueños as a major research and documentation center.[3] These institutionalized efforts allowed for the concentration of cadres of Puerto Rican studies specialists at teaching colleges and major research universities and favored the training of a new generation of scholars now engaged in the process of examining neglected areas, uncovering new information that dispels many of the prevailing myths and conceptualizing alternative paradigms for the study of people of color that are no longer based on traditional ethnocentric assumptions. Research universities are also generating important projects, enhancing their library collections, and developing database sources.[4]

According to a 1989 census population report, Puerto Ricans constitute about 2.5 million of the total U. S. population with a little over a million of this total residing in the state of New York. The population of the island of Puerto Rico stands at 3.5 million, which highlights the fact that more than forty percent of all Puerto Ricans now reside in the United States. From a historical point of view, these demographic realities testify to the pressing need to continue searching for scattered, neglected or lost materials that will enhance our knowledge base and further document the history of the various Puerto Rican communities throughout the United States, not only in New York City, but also in cities with established population concentration patterns such as Chicago, Newark, Patterson, Philadelphia, Milwaukee, Hartford, Miami, New Orleans, Los Angeles, Lorain and in the state of Hawaii— to name only a few areas where there has been a palpable Puerto Rican presence during different historical periods. Although considerable changes in the geographic distribution of the U. S. Puerto Rican population have occurred throughout this century, sizeable communities are found in eight states including New York, where, according to recent population reports, the Puerto Rican population is still over one million; New Jersey, with over a quarter of a million; Illinois with over 100,000, and Florida, California, Pennsylvania, Connecticut and Massachusetts with figures of at least 75,000 each (U. S. Department of Commerce). A detailed analysis of census data for this century should give us an idea of the point in time at which the various Puerto Rican communities began to grow, although this effort might require more elaborate data searches based on place of birth due to the fact that it was not until 1980 that the Census of Population form included a self-identification category for Puerto Ricans that separated them from other Latino groups.[5]

Regarding the evolution of the New York City Puerto Rican community, there are two significant works that bear testimony to the struggles and contributions of early settlers: *Memorias de Bernardo Vega* (Memoirs of Bernardo Vega, written in the 1940s, first published in 1977) and Jesús Colón's, *A Puerto Rican in New York and Other Sketches* (1961). Besides the compelling autobiographical and testimonial nature of these works, they both represent invaluable historical sources. From the narratives and other writings of these two enlightened *tabaqueros* (cigar workers) who emigrated to New York City at a young age from the countryside town of Cayey, Puerto Rico, and stayed for a significant portion of their lives, we have first hand insights into an urban world of shared interethnic solidarities and working class strifes.[6] Both Bernardo Vega (1885–1965) and Jesús Colón (1901–1974) describe the formation of an emigré Latino community (primarily Cuban and Puerto Rican) that began to flourish in the latter part of the nineteenth and early part of this century.[7] It was a community where intellectual pursuits and sociopolitical activism often came hand in hand, and where prominent members of the Hispanic Caribbean islands' intellectual elites stood side by side with enlightened members of the working class, educated within the walls of the cigar factories, in their struggles for the independence of their respective countries from Spanish colonial rule and in their pursuit for social justice.[8] This was a period in which social class and racial distinctions frequently were put aside for the common goals of Antillean unity and independence, or to improve the living standards and combat the detrimental socioeconomic conditions and discrimination faced by Puerto Ricans and other Latino workers in the city.

The significance of Vega's and Colón's testimonial accounts, and of the more recent studies by Sánchez Korrol and the Centro de Estudios Puertorriqueños' volume *Extended Roots: From Hawaii to New York. Migraciones puertorriqueñas a los Estados Unidos* (1986), cannot be underestimated. These works laid substantial groundwork for researching the formative years of the community, and the revolutionary fervor and shared solidarities within the Puerto Rican working class. Moreover, they promoted the further examination of different kinds of documentation, drawing attention to a mixture of traditional and unconventional sources such as oral histories, diaries, letters, reports, official documents from municipal, state, and federal archives, and popular music;[9] encouraging further scrutiny of the wealth of Hispanic newspapers, magazines, and newsletters of the many community organizations. These periodicals often provide heartfelt glimpses into the every day life within the diverse Latino communities.[10]

In one of the sketches included in *A Puerto Rican in New York* ("The Library Looks at the Puerto Ricans," 138–140), Jesús Colón refers to a list of books on Puerto Ricans disseminated by the New York Public Library and regrets that even though ninety five percent of the population in the city was working class, the bibliography had no entries on trade unions or on Puerto Rican labor in general; a world that both Vega and Colón had experienced first hand through their active involvement in socialist and labor movements, and through their journalistic activities. Colón points to the many articles that had appeared in newspapers and other types of periodicals. In his *Memorias*, Vega, as if trying to forge a historical record himself, provides meticulous accounts of the many publications that flourished during those years such as his own weekly newspaper *Gráfico*, published between 1927–1931 (see Appendix). Juan Flores notes in his "Foreword" (xiii) to the second edition of Colón's *A Puerto Rican in New York*, that both men contributed frequently to progressive publications in New York City, as did many other Puerto Rican men and women labor activists.

Colón's book includes several of the weekly columns that he published in *The Daily Worker*, an organ of revolutionary working class expression. He was also a frequent contributor to *El Machete Criollo* (The Creole Machete), *El Nuevo Mundo*, *Gráfico*, *Pueblos Hispanos* (Hispanic Communities), *The Worker*, *Mainstream*, and *Liberación*. His weekly column "As I See It From Here" was published in *The Daily Worker* from 1955 to 1957, and in *The Worker* from 1958 to 1968. His columns "Puerto Rican Notes" and "Lo que el pueblo me dice" (What the People Tell Me) appeared respectively in *The Daily World* from 1968 to 1971 and *Pueblos Hispanos* in 1943. Overall more than four hundred pieces of Colón's writing have been identified already from these periodicals.[11]

The Centro de Estudios Puertorriqueños at Hunter College is the repository of Colón's papers and writings, including a copy of his unpublished and unfinished manuscript *The Way It Was*. This manuscript, just as his previous *A Puerto Rican in New York and Other Sketches*, provides engaging insights into the expanding world of Puerto Ricans in the metropolis from the perspective of a socially committed man who did more than record anecdotes of his own experiences and community life. Colón can be considered a visionary of sorts, in the sense that he recognized during his time the need to forge a historical record for posterity of the building of a community by the labor, energy, and endurance of common people. The publication of this manuscript represents one of the most pressing priorities in the restoration of the Puerto Rican cultural legacy in the United States.[12]

To chronicle this cultural past many existing Hispanic periodicals must be examined. In many cases immediate microfilming will be required for preservation purposes, since these publications represent a major primary source in the systematic study of the history of our communities. Deserving particular attention are those writings scattered in labor and community newspapers, magazines and in correspondence among its most active leaders. Some of these materials could be published in anthologies using specific themes as a selection criteria (e.g. Puerto Rico's political status; the beginnings and expansion of the New York community; worker struggles; women's condition; leading figures; community organizations, etc.). Undoubtedly, making these writings available would further enhance our understanding of Puerto Rican and Latino life in New York City during the first half of this century.

Both Vega and Colón are two of the most obvious major figures whose scattered writings should continue to be examined, collected and published. The same can be said about the writings of Arturo Alfonso Schomburg, whose contributions were considerably acknowledged in the writings of both Colón and Vega, particularly those writings that refer to Latin American and Caribbean topics or to life in the early community.[13] Schomburg, a black Puerto Rican, arrived in New York City in 1891 at the age of seventeen.

He joined other Puerto Rican and Cuban exiles in the struggle for Antillean independence and later developed profound affinities with members of the African-American community, eventually becoming a tireless and consummate bibliophile who collected documents about the Black experience from all over the world. The thousands of publications he ultimately accumulated are now part of the Schomburg Center for Research on Black Culture of the New York City Library. Schomburg already stands as a recognized figure within the African-American community, but most Latinos are still unaware of his contributions to the Latino community nor are they cognizant of the fact that he was born and raised in Puerto Rico.

In stark contrast to the writings of Vega and Colón is the novel *Son of Two Nations: The Private Life of a Columbia Student* (1931) by Pedro Juan Labarthe, a work that follows the model immigrant success story that Americanization makes possible and which reflects the world view of more privileged Puerto Ricans. Likewise, Juan B. Huyke's *Estímulos* (1922) glorifies the relationship between Puerto Rico and the United States and views migration as a trip to the land of opportunity. Huyke was Commissioner of Education in Puerto Rico during the controversial governorship of E. Mont. Reily (Emmett Montgomery Reily, but he never used his full name prefering the abbreviated version), and editor of *El país*, a newspaper that defended the ideals of the pro-statehood movement on the island.[14]

Nicolás Kanellos in his *History of Hispanic Theatre in the United States* (1990), maintains that most New York Latino playwrights "did not write their plays for publication but for production on the commercial stage" (136). Through his exhaustive research, Kanellos was able to identify several published and unpublished plays. For example, he located a copy of *Los hipócritas* (1937), a dramatic comedy, authored by feminist labor leader Franca de Armiño. A figure brought to light by the contemporary women's movement, what is known to date about Franca de Armiño's writings and activities is rather limited to her involvement with the *Federación Libre de los Trabajadores de Puerto Rico* (FLT Free Workers Federation of Puerto Rico) and the *Liga de la Mujer Obrera* (League of Women Workers), her 1919 participation in the *First Congress of Women Workers*, and her role as leader of the *Asociación Feminista Popular* founded in 1920 to defend the working conditions of Puerto Rican women and universal suffrage.[15] Little is known about her activities and writings during the period she lived in New York City in the 1930s, except that she was working on three other publications: the dramatic comedy *Tragedia puertorriqueña*, the essay collection *Aspectos de la vida* and the book of poems, *Luz en las tinieblas* (Light in Darkness), which have not yet been found. We must, therefore, intensify our efforts to locate Franca de Armiño's lost works. As a leading feminist

Julia de Burgos (Photo by Gil and courtesy of Olmo and the Center for Puerto Rican Studies Library, Hunter College, CUNY).

of her time, her writings are of major consequence in the ongoing historical reconstruction of the Puerto Rican feminist movement.

Other feminist labor activists, Luisa Capetillo, among them, were part of a long list of sojourners to the United States with prolonged periods of residence during which they collaborated on many worker publications. Capetillo, for instance, came to New York City in 1912 and wrote articles dealing with women's emancipation that were published in the newspaper *Cultura Obrera* (Work Culture). She also spent a year working in the tobacco factories of Ybor City, Florida, where there was an established Cuban and Puerto Rican presence, and where she published the second edition of her book *Mi opinión* (1913) and wrote several of the pieces later included in her *Influencia de las ideas modernas* (1916).

Among Puerto Rican women writers, poet Julia de Burgos (1914–1953) has received most of the scholarly attention, particularly from feminist literary critics. Her journalistic contributions to the magazine *Pueblos Hispanos*, during her resident years in New York (1946–1953), still awaits further attention.[16] Publications such as *Revista de Artes y Letras*, edited by Josefina Silva de Cintrón from 1933–1945, also should be carefully examined from the perspective of women's concerns and struggles.

Kanellos' critical study of U. S. Hispanic theatre also documents a rich theatre tradition, particularly among workers that, in the case of Puerto Ricans, ran parallel to the *teatro obrero* that was such an integral part of the labor movement back on the Island during the 1920s and 1930s.[17] In this respect, his study is a vital source in capturing the spirit of the times and the major social and political concerns of a primarily working-class community. Playwrights such as Gonzalo O'Neill or Frank Martínez, whose unpublished play *De Puerto Rico a Nueva York* (1939) appears to be an important antecedent to René Marqués' classic work *La carreta* (1955), a dramatization of the Puerto Rican migratory experience, also deserve further attention.[18]

In my own searches at the Colección Puertorriqueña of the University of Puerto Rico, I examined O'Neill's *La indiana borinqueña* (published in 1922), a patriotic dialogue in verse affirming Puerto Rico's right to self-determination, and the comedy, *Moncho Reyes* (1923), which ironically criticizes the arbitrary Americanization policies of the island colonial government under U. S. governor E. Mont. Reily. All of these works are now out of print. Some of these out of print or unpublished works help us appreciate the writers' commitment to the workers and Puerto Rican liberation struggles, and illustrate the spirit of survival and prevailing national consciousness among Puerto Rican migrants in New York City.

Several times in his weeekly column "As I See It From Here," Jesús

Colón expresses his indignation about the way in which many U. S. news-papers portrayed Puerto Ricans in the worst light possible. Being the man of historical vision that he was, Colón continuously emphasized the importance for Puerto Ricans to recognize their progressive leaders and writers, to note their affinities with other oppressed groups and to learn from the spirit of solidarity and enduring experiences of the early pioneers. Thus the path is now wide-open and we must follow the trails left to us by these energetic pi-oneers and continue the process of searching, expanding, appropriating and reconstructing a tradition for ours and for the future generations of Puerto Ricans/Latinos whose lives become intertwined by the challenges and perils of the immigrant experience.

In his sketch entitled "Name in Latin," Colón tells the story of a Latin American printer and poet who in the 1920s wanted to start a weekly to combat the abuses and discrimination against the Latino community. He invited a group of friends, Colón among them, to decide on a name for the publication. After much discussion they could not agree on a name and the publisher-to-be suggested the Latin name *Vae Victis*, meaning *El ay de los vencidos* in Spanish (The Cry of the Defeated). Although he was able to eloquently persuade his friends of the desirability of the name, after the first issue of *Vae Victis* was printed hardly anyone bought it. The first issue turned out to be the last. As Colón tells us, "The Greeks though it was a publication for the Italians, the Italians though it was a magazine for the Romanians, the Romanians thought it was a paper for the French" (54). With his characteristic sense of humor and vision, Colón remembers what in restrospect seemed a foolish idea, and laments that he did not keep a copy of the only issue, which would now be considered "a rare collector's item for the unborn researcher who will be writing the history of the Puerto Ricans in New York fifty years from now" (55).

It has not yet been fifty years since Colón recorded this anecdote. None-theless, we are now engaged in a search for that which has been forgotten, ignored or remains hidden in some dark, dusty library room waiting for someone to bring it back to life, and just like Vega and Colón did, unveil another hidden chapter in the history of the Puerto Rican community that will continue to enrich and enhance its knowledge of itself, as well as its sense of building and reclaiming its own cultural and historical tradition in the United States.

Notes

[1]Besides Sánchez Korrol's pioneering work, most of the attempts to record the unwritten history of the Puerto Rican working class community in New York City have been made by the Centro de Estudios Puertorriqueños History and Oral History

Task Forces. See Centro History Task Force, *Labor Migration Under Capitalism: The Puerto Rican Experience* (New York: Monthly Review, 1979); *Sources for the Study of Puerto Rican Migration, 1879–1930* (New York: Centro, 1992); Oral History Task Force, *Extended Roots: From Hawaii to New York. Migraciones Puertorriqueñas a los Estados Unidos* (New York: Centro, 1986); *Stories to Live By: Continuity and Change in Three Generations of Puerto Rican Women* (New York: Centro, 1987), eds. Rina Benmayor et al.

[2]The titles of Oscar Handlin's *The Newcomers: Negroes and Puerto Ricans in a Changing Metropolis* (New York: Doubleday, 1959) and C. Wright Mills, Clarence Senior and Rose Golden's *The Puerto Rican Journey: New York's Newest Migrants* (New York: Harper, 1950) give the mistaken impression that Puerto Ricans did not have a historical presence in New York City prior to the "great migration" (1946–1964).

[3]During the early 1970s, Puerto Rican Studies programs were established at Hunter College, Queens College, Brooklyn College, City College and a few other units of the City University of New York (CUNY) system. There were two programs initiated within the State University of New York (SUNY) system, located at the university centers in Albany and Buffalo. In the state of New Jersey, a few programs were established within the Rutgers University system. The same occurred in several Midwestern universities, such as Northeastern Illinois University, Wayne State and Indiana. Most of these programmatic initiatives took place in higher education institutions in the Northeast and Midwest regions of the United States, areas with an established Puerto Rican population concentration pattern.

[4]A recent example is the *Albany PR-WOMENET Database*, a major bibliographic source on Puerto Rican women established at the University at Albany, SUNY in 1991. See Edna Acosta-Belén, Christine E. Bose, and Anne Roschelle, *Albany PR-WOMENET Database: An Interdisciplinary Bibliography on Puerto Rican Women* (Albany: CELAC/IROW, 1991). The Centro de Estudios Puertorriqueños' Evelina López Antonetty Puerto Rican Research Collection at Hunter College holds the most extensive collection of materials on the Puerto Rican experience in the United States.

[5]Puerto Ricans in the United States can be identified in the census by birthplace using data for 1900 through 1980 and/or by parental birthplace, which is available from 1900 through 1970 only. Because most Puerto Ricans in the United States are first or second generation migrants, they are more easily found through census data than are Mexican-origin persons. Separate published information on Puerto Ricans does not appear until the 1950 census, making access to such information prior to 1950 available only through census data tapes. While mother tongue (1960 and 1970) and home language other than English (1980) also have been used to identify Puerto Ricans, in 1970 the census moved from these objective measures to more subjective ones for identifying the Hispanic-origin population. The new questions are closer to sociological definitions of ethnic group identity. The Spanish-origin question was tested with only a five percent sample in 1970, while they relied on a complicated composite concept of Spanish heritage, which was based on parentage, surname and language for many published items. The latter was dropped in 1980 and the Spanish-origin question was revised and used for all respondents. This is a self-identification question asking if the respondent is Mexican/Mexican American/Chicano or Puerto Rican or Cuban or of other Spanish/Hispanic origin. In 1980, the census also replaced the old question on parents' place of birth with a more general one on a person's ancestry—this means less continuity with earlier definitions, but tends to have little

effect on counting Puerto Ricans. In 1990 a Central and South American category was added. For further detail on these changes, see Frank D. Bean and Marta Tienda, *The Hispanic Population of the United States* (New York: Russell Foundation, 1987).

[6]Regardless of their differences in age (Vega was fifteen years older than Colón), these two cigar makers had in many ways parallel lives. They were from the same mountain town of Cayey and came to New York around the same period, 1916 and 1918, respectively, where they endured the hardships and discrimination shared by most Puerto Ricans. They were both self-educated men, tireless community activists, strong defenders of Puerto Rican independence, and committed socialists with a strong affinity for journalistic writing. For more information on their lives see Juan Flores' "Translator's Preface" and César Andreu Iglesias' "Introduction" to *Memoirs of Bernardo Vega*, ix-xix; Juan Flores' "Foreword" to *A Puerto Rican in New York and Other Sketches* by Jesús Colón, ix-xvii; and *The Jesús Colón's Papers Finding Aid* (New York: Centro de Estudios Puertorriqueños, 1992). In his sketch, "A Voice Through the Window" in *A Puerto Rican in New York and Other Sketches*, 11–13, Colón describes the importance of the factory readers, generally connected with the socialist movement, for the instruction of workers who barely could read or write, but in this way became familiar with the works and ideas of famous writers and thinkers.

[7]Among the Puerto Rican intellectual and political leaders that came to New York during this period are Ramón Emeterio Betances, Eugenio María de Hostos, Lola Rodríguez de Tío, Francisco "Pachín" Marín and Sotero Figueroa. They wrote for several newspapers of this period, among them, *El Pastillón, Patria* (1892–1898), *El Porvenir, La gaceta del pueblo* and *Revolución*.

[8]Gerald E. Poyo has researched this period from the perspective of the Cuban community. See his "Cuban Communities in the United States: Toward an Overview of the 19th Century Experience," in *Cubans in the United States*, eds. Mirien Uriarte-Gastón and Jorge Cañas Martínez (Boston: Center for the Study of the Cuban Community, 1984): 44–64.

[9]Certain forms of Puerto Rican popular music, such as the *plena* and the *décima*, represent valuable sources to researchers as expressions of the world view of the Puerto Rican working class and its responses to specific events or social conditions at a given historical moment. See the documentary film *Plena is Song, Plena is Work* (1989) prepared by the Centro de Estudios Puertorriqueños and the essay "Cortijo's Revenge" by Juan Flores, *Centro* 3.2 (1991): 8–21.

[10]Nélida Pérez and Amílcar Tirado of the Centro de Estudios Puertorriqueños at Hunter College in "Boricuas en el Norte," *Revista de Historia* 2.3 (1986): 128–166, provide extensive bibliographic information about the literature of Puerto Rican migration and suggest new perspectives for its interpretation. They stress the need to identify and gather many key primary sources. Also see "Notes Towards a History of Puerto Rican Community Organizations in New York City" by Carlos Rodríguez-Fraticelli and Amílcar Tirado, *Centro* 2.6 (1989): 35–47. The importance of Hispanic periodicals is also emphasized by Nicolás Kanellos in "A Socio-Historic Study of Hispanic Newspapers in the United States," and Clara Lomas in "Periodical Literature: 19th and 20th Centuries." These two papers were presented at the conference *Restoring the Hispanic Literary Legacy of the United States*, Triangle Park, National Humanities Center, November 9–10, 1990. The former is collected among the present essays.

[11]In addition to his regular columns in the newspapers *The Daily Worker, The*

Worker, and *The Daily World*, Colón published the column "En Neoyorquino" in *Gráfico* during 1927–1928 using the pseudonym Miquis Tiquis, and wrote other articles under other pseudonyms. In the process of collecting Jesús Colón's scattered journalistic writings, I was assisted by Andrew P. Tishman, who used some of these materials for his Master's thesis project, *The World of Jesús Colón: Puerto Ricans in New York City, 1850–1930*, University at Albany, State University of New York, Department of Latin American and Caribbean Studies, 1991.

[12]An edition of *The Way it Was* is being prepared by Edna Acosta-Belén and Virginia Sánchez Korrol for publication by Arte Público.

[13]In his *Memorias* (Río Piedras, P.R.: Huracán, 1977; trans. New York: Monthly Review, 1984), Bernardo Vega pays tribute to Schomburg's contributions: "He came here as an emigrant and bequeathed a wealth of accomplishments to our countrymen and to North American Blacks. What a magnificent example of solidarity among all oppressed people!" (1984: 196). Schomburg remained an unknown figure for the Island and U. S. Puerto Rican communities until recent years. A few major studies have been published in the United States and Puerto Rico giving due recognition to his remarkable accomplishments. Among them, Victoria Ortiz, "Arthur Schomburg: A Biographic Essay/Arturo Schomburg: un ensayo biográfico" in *The Legacy of Arthur Alfonso Schomburg: A Celebration of the Past, A Vision for the Future* (New York: Schomburg Center for Research on Black Culture, 1986): 18–117; Flor Piñeiro de Rivera, *Arturo Schomburg: Un puertorriqueño descubre el legado histórico del negro* (San Juan, P.R.: Centro de Estudios Avanzados de Puerto Rico y el Caribe, 1989) and the video documentary *El legado de Arturo Schomburg*, with a script written by Jack Delano. Also see Jesús Colón's, "Arthur Schomburgh [sic] and Negro History," *The Worker*, February 11, 1962: 9.

[14]For more information about Huyke's works see *Divided Arrival: Narratives of the Puerto Rican Migration 1920-1950*, Juan Flores, ed. (New York: Centro, n.d.). For information on Labarthe, see Eugene V. Mohr, *The Nuyorican Experience: Literature of the Puerto Rican Minority* (Wesport, CT: Greenwood, 1982).

[15]The *Asociación Feminista Popular* was founded by women workers who were active in the ranks of the Puerto Rican Socialist Party. It was led by Franca de Armiño and Carmen Gaetán, who were also presidents of two tobacco strippers unions. Some of Franca de Armiño's contributions to the FLT official newspaper, *Justicia*, include: "¿Por qué la mujer puertorriqueña debe interferir en el gobierno de su país?," *Justicia*, n.d.: 5; "A la mujer obrera puertorriqueña," in *Justicia*, 1924. Also see Yamila Azize, *La mujer en la lucha* (Río Piedras, P.R.: Cultural, 1985), Norma Valle Ferrer, *Luisa Capetillo: Historia de una mujer proscrita* (Río Piedras: Cultural, 1990), and Alice Colón, Margarita Mergal and Nilsa Torres, *Participación de la mujer en la historia de Puerto Rico* (Río Piedras, P.R.: Centro de Investigaciones Sociales/CERES and Rutgers University, 1986).

[16]It is known that Julia de Burgos delivered the speech "La mujer ante el dolor de la patria" at the assembly of the Frente Unido Pro Convención Constituyente in 1936, but the text is not available in any of the major anthologies of her works. According to María Solá in her edited volume *Julia de Burgos: Yo misma fui mi ruta* (Río Piedras, P.R.: Huracán, 1986), the poet also wrote the article "Ser o no ser es la divisa," which received the journalism prize in a contest sponsored by the Institute for Puerto Rican Culture in 1946. She also wrote regularly for the *Pueblos Hispanos* (1943–1944).

[17]Two major scholarly studies have expanded the historical analysis of Puerto

Rican labor: Angel Quintero Rivera's *Worker's Struggle in Puerto Rico: A Documentary History* (New York: Monthly Review, 1976), first published in Spanish under the title *Lucha obrera en Puerto Rico* (Río Piedras, P.R.: CEREP, 1971) and which documents the development of the labor movement in Puerto Rico between 1904 and 1973 and includes some writings by its leading figures; and *Labor Migration Under Capitalism: The Puerto Rican Experience* (New York: Monthly Review, 1979) by the Centro de Estudios Puertorriqueños, History Task Force. The latter focuses on the economic and political factors that led to Puerto Rican mass migration and the consequences of such displacement both for the Island and the United States. The incursions of workers in the field of dramatic writing are exemplified in Rubén Dávila's *Antología del teatro obrero en Puerto Rico* (Río Piedras, P.R.: CEREP, 1984).

[18]The symbol of *La carreta* (the oxcart), taken from René Marqués play (Río Piedras, P.R.: Editorial Cultural, 1955) has come to embody the Puerto Rican migratory cycle, as it takes a peasant family to the slums of San Juan and the tenements of New York City, facing economic hardships, family disintegration and tragedy before they decide to return to the island. The mythical return to the native land found in Marqués play was the inspiration for the collection of poems, *La Carreta Made a U-turn* (Gary, IN: Arte Público, 1979) by Nuyorican writer Tato Laviera. This particular work is written from the perspective of those generations of Puerto Ricans born or raised in the United States. For an insightful discussion of these perspectives see Juan Flores, John Attinasi and Pedro Pedraza, "La Carreta Made A U-Turn: Puerto Rican Language and Culture in the United States," *Daedalus* 10.2 (1982): 196–203.

Works Cited

Acosta-Belén, Edna. "Etnicidad, género y revitalización cultural en la literatura nuyorriqueña," *Homines* (1992).

————. "Beyond Island Boundaries: Ethnicity, Gender, and Cultural Revitalization in Nuyorican Literature," *Callaloo* 15.4 (1992).

Andreu Iglesias, César, ed. *Memorias de Bernardo Vega*. Río Piedras, P.R.: Huracán, 1977.

Armiño, Franca de. *Los hipócritas*. New York: Modernistic Editorial, 1937.

Arroyo, William. "Lorain, Ohio: The Puerto Rican Experiment—A History Unexplored" in *Extended Roots*. New York: Centro de Estudios Puertorriqueños, 1986. 27–34.

Benmayor, Rina. "Doing Community History: The Oral History and Community History Workshop Notes" in *Extended Roots*, 69–78.

Berry-Cabán, Cristóbal. *Hispanics in Wisconsin*. Madison: The State Historical Society of Wisconsin, 1980.

Bonilla, Frank and Ricardo Campos. *Industry and Idleness*. New York: Centro, 1986.

Camacho Souza, Blase. *Boricua Hawaiiana: Puerto Ricans of Hawaii: Reflections of the Past and Mirrors of the Future. A Catalog*. Honolulu: Puerto Rican Heritage Society of Hawaii, 1982.

————. "Boricuas Hawaiianos" in *Extended Roots*, 7–18.

Capetillo, Luisa. *Mi opinión*. San Juan: Biblioteca Roja, 1911. Second edition, 1913. Ybor City: J. Mascuñana.

Capetillo, Luisa. *Influencia de las ideas modernas*. San Juan: Tipografía Negrón Flores, 1916.

Colón, Jesús. *A Puerto Rican in New York and Other Sketches*. New York: International, 1982. First edition, 1961.

Flores, Juan. "Foreword" in *A Puerto Rican in New York and Other Sketches* by Jesús Colón. New York: International, 1982. ix-xvii.

————. "Translator's Preface" in *Memoirs of Bernardo Vega*. Ed. César Andreu Iglesias. New York: Monthly Review, 1984. ix-xii.

Glazer, Nathan and Daniel P. Moynihan. *Beyond the Melting Pot: The Negroes, Puerto Ricans, Jews, Italians, and Irish of New York City*. Cambridge, MA: Harvard UP, 1963.

Horwitz, Julius. *The Inhabitants*. Cleveland, OH: World, 1960.

Huyke, Juan B. *Estímulos: Libro de inspiración y optimismo para la juventud*. New York: Rand McNally, 1922.

Kanellos, Nicolás. *A History of Hispanic Theatre in the United States: Origins to 1940*. Austin: U of Texas P, 1990.

Labarthe, Pedro Juan. *Son of Two Nations: The Life of a Columbia Student*. New York: Carranza, 1931.

Lewis, Oscar. *La vida: A Puerto Rican Family in the Culture of Poverty—San Juan and New York*. New York: Random House, 1966.

Meléndez, Edwin, Clara Rodríguez and Janis Barry-Figueroa, eds. *Hispanics in the Northeast and the Changing Economy*. Cambridge, MA: Plenum, 1990.

Ojeda, Félix. "Early Puerto Rican Communities in New York" in *Extended Roots*, 41–54.

O'Neill, Gonzalo. *La Indiana Borinqueña*. New York: n.p., 1922.

————. *Moncho Reyes*. New York: Spanish-American, 1923.

Padilla, Félix. "A Brief History of Puerto Ricans in Chicago, 1950-1970" in *Extended Roots*, 55–68.

————. *Latino Ethnic Consciousness: The Case of Mexican Americans and Puerto Ricans in Chicago*. Notre Dame, IN: U of Notre Dame P, 1985.

Pérez, Martín. "Living History: Vineland, New Jersey" in *Extended Roots*, 19–26.

Pérez, Nélida and Amílcar Tirado. "Boricuas en el Norte," *Revista de Historia* 2.3 (1986): 128–66.

Piñeiro, Jorge. "Extended Roots: Puerto Ricans of San José, California" in *Extended Roots*, 35–40.

Rodríguez, Clara. *Puerto Ricans: Born in the U.S.A.* Boston: Unwin, 1989.

Rosario Natal, Carmelo. *Éxodo puertorriqueño (Las emigraciones al Caribe y Hawaii: 1900-1915)*. San Juan, P.R.: S.E., 1983.

Sánchez Korrol, Virginia. *From Colonia to Community: The History of Puerto Ricans in New York City, 1917–1948*. Westport, CT: Greenwood, 1983.

Sutton, Constance R. "The Caribbeanization of New York City and the Emergence of a Transnational Socio-Cultural System." *Caribbean Life in New York City: Sociocultural Dimensions*. Ed. Constance R. Sutton and Elsa M. Chaney. Staten Island: Center for Migration Studies, 1987. 15–30.

Torre, C. A., H. Rodríguez, and W. Burgos, eds. *The Commuter Nation: Perspectives on Puerto Rican Migration*. Río Piedras, P.R.: U of Puerto Rico, in press.

U. S. Department of Commerce, Bureau of the Census. *The Hispanic Population in the United States, March 1989*. Washington, D.C.: Government Printing Office, 1990.

Appendix

Hispanic periodicals in New York City mentioned in the works of Bernardo Vega and Jesús Colón, and from Other Sources.[1]

Mensajero Semanal (founded in 1828)
El Mercurio de Nueva York (1828)
Revolución (1869)
La Voz de Puerto Rico (1874)
La Gaceta del Pueblo
El Separatista (1883)
Las Novedades (1887)
El Porvenir (1888)
Palenque de la Juventud
Patria (1892–1898)
Cultura Proletaria
Borinquen (1898)
Puerto Rico Herald (1901–1904)
El Norteamericano (1919)
El Comercio
El Corsario
Puerto Rico (1923)
Hispano (1924)
El Machete Criollo (1926)
Metrópolis (1926)
Gaceta Popular (1926)
Bolívar (1927)
El Portavoz (1927)
Frivolidades (1927)
Nuevo Mundo (1928–1930)
Gráfico (1927–1931, weekly)
Liberación (1946–1949)
Pueblos Hispanos (1943–1944)
La Prensa (1913-present; first weekly, daily after 1918)
Vida Obrera (1930-1932)
Alma Boricua (1934–1935)
Justicia (1914–1926)
La Voz (1938–1939)
Revista de Artes y Letras (1933–1939, monthly)

---

[1] Dates were provided when available. In most cases only the beginning publication date is listed.

PART III
Literary Canons

Some Considerations on Genres and Chronology for Nineteenth-Century Hispanic Literature

Charles Tatum

The collective project of Recovering the United States Hispanic Literary Heritage is to establish the parameters for this recovery, at once an exciting and daunting scholarly enterprise. It is exciting because it affords us the opportunity to help in shaping an intellectual enterprise of great magnitude. Isn't this, after all, what scholars are trained for and long to do at some point in their careers? The project, however, is daunting for essentially the same reason: we are assigning ourselves the task of defining and delimiting what authors and works will be included in a canon that during the past twenty-five years has only begun to emerge as a literary tradition of immense variety and richness.

While as individuals we have participated to different degrees through our research, writing and professional involvement in proposing and establishing categories, chronologies, genres, hierarchies of works and writers, the wide dissemination of our collective deliberations has the potential to shape the future of U. S.-Hispanic literatures in very profound and permanent ways. We can serve to bring order and to encourage research in vital areas of creative expression, but at the same we may also, albeit unintentionally, contribute in a negative way to discourage original and imaginative scholarship if our project is conceived too narrowly.

If the last decade of canon wars in the academy and in professional associations have taught us any one lesson, it is that scholars such as ourselves, who are in the enviable position to proscribe and define an entire body of literature, can wield tremendous power over future doctoral dissertations, the nature of curricula and programs from elementary through graduate school, and even what publications are accessible to the general reading public. As individuals who are all too familiar with how U.S-Hispanic literatures have historically been excluded from the canon of American literary studies, we should approach our project already sensitized to the dangers implicit in significantly expanding and redefining this present canon we have identified as U. S.-Hispanic literature.

Rosaura Sánchez's provocative theoretical study, "The History of Chicanas: Proposal for a Materialist Perspective," provides some general guidelines that I have found helpful in formulating my task to propose genres and a chronology to contextualize nineteenth-century Hispanic literature. Sánchez reminds us that the historian, in selecting historical material, "is objectively conditioned by social factors and discursive practices which are always multiple" (14). In our roles as literary historians and canonizers, we too face in our task a social network of interacting, signifying or discursive practices which conceptualize and reconceptualize social differences according to changes in the society of the writers whose works we will, through our deliberations, elevate to a new position of authority. Like the historical text on which Sánchez comments, the literary texts we consider necessarily will be intertextual by token of reflecting a multiplicity of discourses, some of which are as contradictory as the society from which the writers come.

We may also find Rosa Linda Fregoso and Angie Chambram's analysis of the word "Chicano," useful in approaching our project. They are critical of the tendency among Chicano intellectuals, especially those formed during the Chicano student movement, to fix Chicano cultural identity as "a static, fixed and one-dimensional formulation" which "failed to acknowledge our historical differences in addition to the multiplicity of our cultural identities as a people" (205). In their view, such a mimetic notion of representation led to equating the naming of cultural identity with cultural identity itself, a notion that ignored critical points of difference and the experience of rupture and discontinuity that also shape Chicano identities in decisive ways. Fregoso and Chambram highlight the "heterogeneous experiences of migration, conquest and regional variation" (206), which historically may determine differences among various Spanish-speaking populations in the Southwest and California.

Referring specifically to the nineteenth century, embedded in each literary text are the heterogeneous conditions prevalent within Spanish-speaking communities in terms of generation, immigrant status, rural/urban origin, language dominance, literacy, employment status, age, occupation, civil and family status, income, place of residence, church affiliation and so on. We would be prudent to remember Sánchez's words of advice for historians. Any consideration of nineteenth-century literary works must take into account the fact that while the writers may be of Mexican origin, "this population is as diverse as any other living group of people. There can be no simple labeling which can encompass the diversity represented by this population, despite the fact that there are certain general social changes which have affected the entire population" (15).

Chicano historians have now solidly established that it is foolhardy to gloss over the significant sociohistorical experiences of Spanish and Mexican populations in the Southwest. The vast regional differences that can be perceived during the nineteenth century among these populations in Texas' Lower Rio Grande Valley, New Mexico and southern Colorado's Upper Rio Grande Valley, Arizona's Pimería Alta and the California's southern and central coast are due to a wide range of demographic, geographic, cultural and political factors that affected these groups during, first, Spain's exploration and colonization of the Southwest and, later, during Mexico's political policies towards its northern territories. To cite a specific example, Spanish settlements in the mountainous regions of northern New Mexico and southern Colorado and along the fertile Rio Grande River Valley from Mesilla in the south to San Luis Valley in the north contributed heavily to the founding of enclaves that culturally survived Anglo-American expansion in the mid to late nineteenth century. While it cannot be denied that the sociopolitical and economic foundations of many of this area's Spanish/Mexican communities were altered between 1848 and the early part of twentieth century, Spanish cultural traditions and practices as well as the Spanish language itself continued to thrive in forms such as *penitente* groups, the performance of religious and folk dramas of Spanish and Mexican origin, and the oral tradition of *cuentos, adivinanzas,* and *corridos.*

The tenacity and continuity of cultural forms in New Mexico and southern Colorado is very different from other areas such as northern California where, due to the region's relative vulnerability to the incursion of Anglo culture and values, traditions and practices of the original Hispanic population evolved more rapidly toward hybrid forms. An obvious manifestation of such change is the lack of a strong Spanish-language oral tradition in northern California. It is thus no surprise that the Mexican expatriate journalist Julio G. Arce—known better by his pseudonym Jorge Ulica—would frequently poke fun at his fellow Mexicans and Mexican Americans in the San Francisco Bay Area for their loss of language facility and their eagerness to adopt American ways. For example, two of his *crónicas diabólicas*, "Por no hablar inglés" (By Not Speaking English) and "No hay que hablar en pocho," (It's Not Necessary to Speak in Pocho [Spanglish]), satirize the failure of Mexican and Mexican Americans to maintain facility in their native language. As a citizen of Mexico with a strong nationalist identity, Arce often chooses to distance himself from the resident Spanish-speaking population that, although it might be able to trace its origins to the Spanish *californios*, is rapidly losing touch with its past, linguistically and culturally.

To return to Rosaura Sánchez's observations about differences among nineteenth-century Hispanic communities, the contrast between New Mexico and California illustrates how two factors, language dominance and immigrant status, are embedded in the literary texts from each region. The diversity of experience among the various Chicano communities throughout the Southwest and California should therefore guide us in establishing genres, chronologies and other delimiting elements for nineteenth-century literature. To ignore such diversity is to risk making generalizations that can only undercut our task of recovering a rich literary heritage.

Gayle Greene and Coppelia Kahn have observed that the social construction of categories such as gender—other categories such as literary aesthetics, genres and periodization could also be included, although Greene and Kahn do not deal specifically with them—takes place through the workings of ideology, that is, "the system of beliefs and assumptions—unconscious, unexamined, invisible—which represents in Althusser's words, 'the imaginary relationships of individuals to their real conditions of existence' " (2–3). Ideology is also a system of practices that informs every aspect of daily life such as the creation of literature and literary categories. Although ideology originates in particular cultural conditions, it authorizes its beliefs and practices "universal" and "natural," for example, presenting what constitutes "good literature" not as a cultural construct, but as eternally and everywhere the same.

Together with heterogeneous conditions listed by Rosaura Sánchez—generation, language dominance, civil and family status, income, place of birth—, considerations of gender should also play a vital role in setting forth genres and in establishing periods for nineteenth-century Hispanic literature. As we do so, it is important to be guided by Chicana feminist literary critics, particularly those like Yvonne Yarbro-Bejarano and Tey Diana Rebolledo, who approach the issue of gender in relation to other categories of social determination such as race, class, culture and ethnicity. Yarbro-Bejarano, for example, believes that perhaps the most important principle of Chicana feminist criticism "is the realization that the Chicana's experience as a woman is inextricable from her experience as a member of an oppressed working-class racial minority and a culture that is not the dominant culture. Her task is to show how in works by Chicanas, elements of gender, race, culture and class coalesce" (140). Both Yarbro-Bejarano and Rebolledo include as an essential part of a Chicana literary feminist agenda the recuperation and construction of a women's literary tradition that goes back at least as far as the nineteenth century. Yarbro-Bejarano rightly observes that the early Chicana writer "derives literary authority from the oral tradition of her community, which in turn empowers her to commit her stories to writing" (141). Both critics recognize that the specific experience of women has been traditionally excluded from literary representation due, in large part, to a prevalent tendency among critics to categorize their works as "non-literary."

Rebolledo includes among the problems that Chicana critics face the need to recognize that contemporary women writers have not "arisen from a complete void" (133) but in fact have evolved out of both a written and oral tradition in which women's images and concerns are similar to those being expressed today. Rebolledo has been at the forefront in raising these concerns and in resurrecting women authors of the past from obscurity. Such a project necessarily involves examining Hispanic women's texts and orally transmitted material from a new literary/aesthetic perspective, one that privileges such texts and materials rather than marginalizing them. An example of such a revised reading strategy is Rebolledo's study on signatures of landscape in early twentieth-century Hispanic as well as in contemporary Chicana women's writing.

Just as Chicana feminist scholars have effectively challenged the assumptions underlying "the way things are, the natural order of things," we as high priestesses and priests of a new canon in the making must challenge the way things are as we go about the recovery of U. S.-Hispanic literature. In terms of nineteenth-century Hispanic literature, we should not avoid viewing sacrosanct categories such as literary genres as social constructs defined and perpetuated by a largely male literary establishment under which most of us were educated and trained. We should question the rigidity of such categories and be willing to bend, reshape, and even create new ones in order to accommodate the broadest spectrum of literary/creative expression, especially, but not limited to, that of women. Rather than proscribing nineteenth-century genres as those passed down through the academic winnowing process, we should err on the side of openness by being willing to consider, for example, a document such as a recipe as a form of creative expression. Given the severe material conditions under which the vast majority of Hispanic women lived during the nineteenth century, it is conceivable that seemingly simple and practical jottings might yield a rich source of imaginative expression. In any case, such documents should not be rejected out of hand simply because they do not fit our preconceived notions of literary aesthetics or fit comfortably within a specific list of pre-determined genres.

A cursory examination of most studies of nineteenth-century Hispanic literature—including my own—reveal a narrow rather than an expansive list of "acceptable" genres: novel, short story, poetry, theatre, memoirs, correspondence, creative essay, and missionary and military expeditionary descriptions and reports. While this seems like a generous list—and one that would appear to challenge an accepted view of genre categories—the writers of such works have in common a self-consciousness that they were writing to be read. With a potential audience in mind, the authors reveal an interest in their readers' response, whether those readers were military or ecclesiastical superiors or members of a general public.

In addition to the above genres, we also need to deal with other literary forms and discourses. For example, self-reflective writing not destined for any audience except the writer herself. We might include diaries—writing clearly associated more with women than with men—as such a form of expression. By privileging diaries as a legitimate category or genre, we immediately open up to literary critics, archivists and historians a gender-dominant form of writing that might otherwise be overlooked or at least undervalued. To my knowledge, invesigators have not yet discovered self-reflective documents such as diaries, but it is not unreasonable to speculate that, except for a small group of Chicana feminist literary critics, to date there has not been much interest expressed in them. In any case, we would be prudent to include diaries and other gender-inflected forms of creative expression in our list of nineteenth-century genres.

Greene and Kahn observe that "writers call upon the same signifying codes that pervade social interactions, re-presenting in fiction the rituals and symbols that make up social practice." Drawing upon Terry Eagleton and Michele Foucault, they observe that "literature [...] is a 'discursive practice' whose conventions encode social conventions that are ideologically complicit. Moreover, since each invocation of a code is also its reinforcement or reinscription, literature does more than transmit ideology: it actually creates it—it is a mediating, moulding force in society that structures our sense of the world" (4–5). Extrapolating from these general observations to nineteenth-century Hispanic literature, we should be careful, as Rebolledo and Yarbro-Bejarano admonish us, not to privilege written expression that might tend to reflect a world view of a literate, educated class. We should also keep in mind that orality performs an important function in every class' preservation and transmission of its culture. That is, both rich and poor, literate and illiterate, Hispanics in the nineteenth century had an oral poetics. Oral forms of expression were probably just as dominant among those who could write as among those who could not. Such a mix of written and oral poetics gave rise to hybrid literary forms. Folk poetry and folk drama are probably the two forms that have been most carefully documented. We should not, however, discount the possibility of discovering others still buried or of revalorizing those forms that perhaps have not been given sufficient importance. To adequately reflect creative expression of all segments of the population—from the most highly educated to the semi-literate and illiterate—means grappling with the knotty problem of the relationship of writing and orality.

Folk and oral expression must then be privileged if we are to begin to construct a complete picture of nineteenth-century Hispanic expressive culture. Two examples of secular folk drama that might be included are *Los comanches* and *Los tejanos.* The first was written in the last quarter of the eighteenth century, the second between 1841 and 1846. These plays were performed throughout the nineteenth century, especially in central and northern New Mexico during local celebrations. The performance of *Los tejanos,* which dealt with General Manuel Armijo's defeat of the Texan expedition to New Mexico in 1841, must be viewed as an act of cultural resistance against foreign invaders.

Some examples of religious folk drama are *Moros y cristianos* (Moors and Christians), *Los reyes magos* (The Wise Kings), *Los pastores* (The Shepherds), *El niño perdido* (The Lost Child), a variety of *autos sacramentales* (miracle plays), and *Las posadas* (Searching for an Inn). All of these plays probably were variants of or at least were based on Spanish folk religious dramas used throughout Latin America and in the Southwest to reinforce the beliefs of the Catholic church. Their periodic performance in the isolated communities of New Mexico and Colorado was particularly important in keeping alive a spirit of religious fervor.

Several excellent collections of folktales, including those by Juan B. Rael, Aurora Lucero-White Lea, Elaine Miller and Aurelio Espinosa, Sr., could serve as a rich source of material for recovery and interpretation. These Spanish and (later) Mexican tales were passed on orally from generation to generation from the sixteenth century forward. Even today, some Hispanic communities in New Mexico and Colorado continue to have a strong story-telling tradition thus providing opportunities for future oral historians and scholars of literature.

Among the traditional Spanish folk poetry and folksong forms that survived into the nineteenth century and beyond are the *romance,* the *canción,* and the *décima.* The *romance* still exists today throughout the Southwest as a ballad form, and its offspring the Mexican *corrido* proliferates throughout the Southwest and California, especially along the U. S.-Mexican border. María Herrera-Sobek's recent study of the Mexican *corrido* from a feminist perspective would well serve as a model to analyze and interpret other folk poetry and folksong forms. The ballad form with its several thematic and content categories—novelesque ballads, unrequited love ballads, religious ballads, and burlesque ballads—particularly lend themselves to further study. Other oral and folk genres that could be considered in nineteenth-century literature include *adivinanzas, dichos,* hymns, *oraciones,* and *mila-*

gros.[1]

Establishing a chronology of nineteenth-century Hispanic literature is every bit as problematic as a conceptualization of genres. I would agree with Luis Leal (see his article included in this volume) that doing so would be difficult until we have a definitive inventory of the development of nineteenth-century Hispanic literature. Although we will not know for certain what is "out there" to be discovered and classified until we are well into our project of recovery, we can be reasonably sure that there is probably a wealth of material in both personal and public archives, public records, private collections, etc. Moreover, we have not yet given much serious scholarly attention to the works and authors we do know.

Luis Leal has been in the forefront among scholars of U. S.-Hispanic literature in proposing a chronology—albeit a tentative one—for Hispanic literature in general. In this volume and elsewhere, he proposes using historical dates when significant events took place: 1803, the Louisiana Purchase; 1819, the year Spain sold Florida to the U. S.; 1836, the year Texas declared its independence, and so on. I would agree with Leal that the periods within these dates, while they may reflect sociopolitical change for different Hispanic populations, do not necessarily coincide with literary history. I would, however, question the usefulness of relying on, even on a temporary basis, fixed dates and the periods they encompass.

Once again, Rosaura Sánchez's words serve to caution us about accepting uncritically such seeming verities as fixed historical dates. She warns us that we must not overlook social structural conditions "which have encouraged historians to concentrate on dominant white male figures within the superstructure (government, military, political, religious and educational institutions) ignoring the vast majority of men and women" (2–3). For our purposes, "dominant Spanish and Mexican male figures" could just as well be substituted for "white male figures" as we critically examine the periodization of colonial and nineteenth-century Spanish and Mexican history. We need to ask ourselves to what extent pre-defined historical periods such as those referred to above have resulted from historians concentrating on dominant male figures to the exclusion of others, such as women, rural populations and the working class, who are sometimes given lesser importance when the historical record is constructed. We also need to explore to what extent dates we associate with historical events of importance (e.g., 1836, Texas independence from Mexico) represent significant changes in the material conditions of Hispanic groups and possibly related cultural shifts, shifts that frequently manifest themselves in creative expression.

In addition to what I consider an inherent danger of using important dates on which to key a literary chronology, I would add a second cautionary note about relying too heavily on literary history itself, at least as an enterprise shaped by a literary elite whose exclusionary practices narrowly define literature and place it within certain predetermined cultural contexts. Like other historians, literary historians bring to their intellectual task racial, cultural, class and gender biases that, unless they are acutely aware of and take care to monitor, will inevitably affect the product of their studies. For examples of such biases, we can draw amply on the lessons learned from male literary historians who have historically excluded the works of women from their histories, or from Anglo-American literary historians who have not considered valid works from ethnic and cultural literary traditions not their own. Why else has it taken so long for Chicano authors, for example, to be included in the pages of the Norton anthology?

Those of us involved in recovering the literary heritage of U. S. Hispanic literature would do well to remind ourselves that, despite our good will and best intentions, we, too, are capable of letting biases and baggage creep into our noble project. As we establish a chronology for nineteenth-century Hispanic literature, we need to keep in the foreground the notion that subtle patterns will begin to reveal themselves to us as we weave the complex tapestry from discovered and recovered strands of creative expression. We should take extreme care not to superimpose upon nineteenth-century literature preconceived ideas of either what elements constitute valid literary forms or of how to arrange such forms into seemingly neat but useless categories. There is, then, an intimate interrelationship between genre and chronology. The more expansive we are towards defining the former, the less difficult and more fruitful it will be to discern and begin to fix the latter into usable categories.

Our collective work of recovering the U. S. Hispanic literary heritage is too important not to approach it cautiously in terms of preconceived cultural/literary notions, and openly in terms of developing new ways of defining, evaluating, and categorizing creative works and how they fit together chronologically. Students and scholars for the foreseeable future will refer for guidance to our framing of the project. We owe our gratitude to past generations of authors and researchers of U. S.-Hispanic literature and at the same time we have an obligation to those who will cover this ground in the future.

Notes

[1]Sandra Cisneros, in her recently published *Woman Hollering Creek* (New York: Randon House, 1991), very effectively uses *milagros* to convey the deeply felt sentiments of men, women, and children. It is thus reasonable to include *milagros* and

other religious and non-religious forms of nineteenth-century creative expression not traditionally considered to be valid genres worthy of scholarly study.

Works Cited

Fregoso, Linda and Angie Chabram. "Chicana/o cultural representations: reframing alternative critical discourses." *Cultural Studies* 4.8 (October 1990): 203–12.

Greene, Gayle and Coppélia Kahn, eds. *Making a Difference. Feminist Literary Criticism.* London and New York: Methuen, 1985.

Herrera-Sobek, María. *The Mexican Corrido. A Feminist Analysis.* Bloomington: Indiana UP, 1990.

Leal, Luis. "The Rewriting of American Literary History." *Criticism in the Borderlands. Studies in Chicano Literature, Culture and Ideology.* Eds. Héctor Calderón and José David Saldívar. Durham: Duke UP, 1991: 21–27

Rebolledo, Tey Diana. "The Politics of Poetics: Or, What Am I, A Critic, Doing in this Text Anyway." *Chicana Creativity and Criticism: Charting New Frontiers in American Literature.* Eds. María Herrera-Sobek and Helena María Viramontes. Houston: Arte Público, 1988. 129–138.

―――――. "Tradition and Mythology. Signatures of Landscape in Chicana Literature." *The Desert Is No Lady. Southwestern Landscapes in Women's Writing and Art.* Eds. Vera Norwood and Janice Monk. New Haven: Yale UP, 1987. 96–124.

Sánchez, Rosaura. "The History of Chicanas: Proposal for a Materialist Perspective." *Between Borders: Essays on Mexicana/Chicana History.* Ed. Adelaida del Castillo. Encino, CA: Floricanto, 1989. 1–29.

Yarbro-Bejarano, Yvonne. "Chicana Literature from a Chicana Feminist Perspective." *Chicana Creativity and Criticism: Charting New Frontiers in American Literature,* 139–46.

Canon Formation and Chicano Literature

María Herrera-Sobek

That was when he began writing on the walls
in his own handwriting
on fences and buildings
and on the giant billboards.
The change was no small thing
quite the contrary
in the beginning
he fell into a deep creative slump.

It's just that sonnets don't look good on walls
and phrases he was mad about before, like
"Oh abysmal sandalwood, honey of moss"
looked like a big joke on peeling walls.
                    (Roque Dalton, "A History of a Poetic")

Monsieur Dupont calls you uneducated
because you don't know which was
the favorite grandchild of Victor Hugo.

Herr Muller has started shouting
because you don't know the day
(the exact one) when Bismarck died.

Your friend Mr. Smith
English or Yankee, I don't know,
becomes incensed when you write *Shell*
(It seems that you hold back an "l"
and that besides you pronounce it *chel*)

O.K. So what?
When it's your turn,
have them say cacarajicara
and where is the Aconcagua
and who was Sucre
and where on this planet

did Martí die.

And please
make them always talk to you in Spanish.
(Nicolás Guillén, "Problems of Underdevelopment")

The above poems by two Latin American poets, Roque Dalton and Nicolás Guillén, underscore a fundamental concern with canonicity and the necessity for a radical transformation of the Western European canon whether
this change be undertaken in poetic structures, orthographic correctness or
language itself. The poems question basic assumptions of European (French,
German, English and American) canonical authority and the relevance of
nineteenth century romantic conceptions of "literarily correct" poetic structures as opposed to politically engaged discursive strategies. They challenge
imperialist conceptualizations of what native Third World peoples should
learn and attack the "white is right" notions of poetics. The European power
drive to transform the "natives" into their own image by disempowering and
alienating them from their autochthonous literary discourses and, indeed,
their languages, is forcefully criticized and underlined. The subversion of
the European and American canon and the supplanting of this with indigenous literary discourses are explicitly and actively advocated within the
stanzas of the poems.

The above two poems and their message are significant for contemporary
Chicanos/as involved in the Academy or publishing enterprises because we
too are seriously concerned with the problems of inclusion or exclusion of
literary works in our teaching as well as our growing number of publications.
It is my position that in our re-examination of the canon we should be as
inclusive as possible and keep an open policy with respect to the publication
of materials from the colonial period to the present. Our primary task in
the initial stages of our project of recovery should be that of identifying and
making available to critics and the public the works which for too long have
been unavailable. I propose that recovery and recuperation of documents
should be our highest priority. We are keenly aware that Chicano/a literature
is undergoing a reassessment; it is being reevaluated with respect to origins,
legitimacy in the Academy, its national ties and so forth. For example, it was
not too long ago that Chicano/a literature, was thought to have entered the
literary stage in the 1960s. As this ethnic literature continued to flower in
the last three decades and literary historians began to carefully scrutinize its
origins, a new date—1848—was bandied about as the birth of this literature,
since that was the date Mexico's northern territories were severed from the
motherland and incorporated into the United States. However, since it is
quite obvious that literary production does not bloom out of nowhere, the

date had to be moved to a colonial past which, although imperialist and Spanish, nevertheless had been rich in literary production and was written by the ancestors of contemporary Chicanos/as who colonized and settled the Southwest (Herrera-Sobek).

The task of reconstructing the Chicanos/as' literary heritage and the establishment of an inclusive as opposed to an exclusive canon is important because the literary history (and indeed social and political status) of Mexican Americans in the United States has been one of marginalization and outright exclusion. The colonial literature of this ethnic group has been excluded because of its supposed foreign character, that is, the Hispanic literary production was viewed as belonging to Spain or Mexico. The fact that it was written in Spanish made it doubly difficult for the hegemonic Anglosaxon English-speaking population to accept literary writings from the Southwest produced during the 1540–1848 period. Even writings from latter periods, after the Southwestern territories were officially annexed to the United States, were, for all practical purposes, ignored, since they too were perceived as "quaint" or exotic.

Of course during the eighteenth and nineteenth century, canon formation was barely taking place in Europe itself. It is instructive to learn that the English literary canon or the formation of the Great Tradition in literary studies in England is, comparatively speaking, a fairly recent development. The English canon is a social construct that developed in the past two centuries as a result of political expediency. During these past two centuries, the English themselves did not have a concise concept of literature and were grappling with its definition. Terry Eagleton notes:

> In eighteenth-century England, the concept of literature was not confined as it sometimes is today to 'creative' or 'imaginative' writing. It meant the whole body of valued writing in society: philosophy, history, essays and letters as well as poems. What made a text 'literary' was not whether it was fictional—the eighteenth century was in grave doubt about whether the new upstart form of the novel was literature at all—but whether it conformed to certain standards of 'polite letters.' The criteria of what counted as literature, in other words, were frankly ideological: writing which embodied the values and 'tastes' of a particular social class qualified as literature, whereas a street ballad, a popular romance and perhaps even the drama did not. (17)

And the rationale for the above notion of what was literature was directly tied to the political and social climate in which eighteenth-century England found itself. Basically, the country was striving for a sense of national cohesiveness; it was weaving a fabric of national unity and those in power perceived literature as one powerful thread that could aid in the binding of a national consciousness. Literature was needed, Eagleton states, "to incorporate the increasingly powerful but spiritually rather raw middle classes into unity with the ruling aristocracy, to diffuse polite social manners, habits of 'correct' taste and common cultural standards" (17).

Bernard Bergonzi reiterates the nationalist project permeating the formation of the English canon.

> To British-born English-speakers the study of the literature of their own language might seem the most natural thing in the world. But the process whereby the classical texts of English literature replaced, or at least complemented, the classics of Greece and Rome as a major constituent of humanistic education was argued warmly and at length. It was part of a major change in the landscape of European culture from the eighteenth century onwards, when vernacular literature became a powerful instrument in forming national consciousness. (29)

Bergonzi argues that the same nationalist projects were transpiring on the European continent (29). For England he cites the English Government publication *The Teaching of English in England* published in 1921 as a *prima facie* case of that country's power elites promoting cultural nationalism. It is obvious that the institutionality of English literature was a product of the late nineteenth-century nationalist movement. As a matter of fact, the Oxford Honours School of English Language and Literature was not established until the late nineteenth century, and the King Edward VII Chair of English Literature did not come into being until 1912 (40–43).

Needless to say, at this particular juncture in English letters, American literature was completely excluded. In fact, the Oxford English canon excluded its own twentieth-century literature altogether. Up until the 1950s, the literature that was taught in that prestigious university stopped at the 1830s since it was widely believed that "living authors were not to be studied" (80).

For the English, therefore, canon formation coincided with the education of the masses for nationalistic unification and the perceived need to instill in them a spirit of "Englishness" during the industrial revolution and the subsequent creation of the proletariat. Eagleton points to the failure of religion and the increased alienation of the proletariat as a stimulus for the introduction of English literary studies. Literature was viewed as a new weapon against the continued loss of religious beliefs. As Eagleton states:

> By the mid-Victorian period, this traditionally reliable, immensely powerful ideological form [i.e. religion] was in deep trouble. It was no longer winning the hearts and minds of the masses, and under the twin impacts of scientific discovery and social change its previous unquestioned dominance was in danger of evaporating. This was particularly

> worrying for the Victorian ruling class, because religion is for all kinds
> of reasons an extremely effective form of ideological control. (22–23)

A new discourse that could supplant religion was needed and this new discourse was found in the nation's literary production. As George Gordon, a professor of English Literature at Oxford pointed out: "England is sick, and ... English literature must save it. The Churches (as I understand) having failed, and social remedies being slow, English literature has a triple function: still, I suppose, to delight and instruct us, but also, and above all, to save our souls and heal the state" (23).

Gordon's literary evangelism clearly demonstrates how the rise of English studies in England was directly and inextricably linked to nationalistic concerns; it was tied to the explicit purpose of building "solidarity between the social classes, the cultivation of 'larger sympathies', the instillation of national pride and the transmission of 'moral' values" (Eagleton 27). This is in accordance with Benedict Anderson's thesis expounded in his book *Imagined Communities*: "Nationalism has to be understood, by aligning it, not with self-consciously held political ideologies, but with large cultural systems that preceded it, out of which—as well as against which—it came into being (19). Homi Bhabha concurs with the above notion, and in his "Introduction" to the anthology *Nation and Narration* expands:

> Nations, like narratives, lose their origins in the myths of time and
> only fully realize their horizon's in the mind's eye. Such an image of
> the nation—or narration—might seem impossibly romantic and exces-
> sively metaphorical, but it is from those traditions of political thought
> and literary language that the nation emerges as a powerful historical
> idea in the west. (1)

For the English, literature was linked to their expansionist policies of the nineteenth and twentieth century and served as a powerful tool in the "civilizing" mission of its empire building ideology.

The Great Tradition discussed above and gradually instituted for political purposes over the past two centuries has become difficult to dislodge. Eagleton underscores the power of the Great Tradition as T. S. Eliot, an influential conservative critic of the 1920s defined it:

> Eliot's [ordering of the Tradition] is in fact a highly selective affair:
> indeed its governing principle seems to be not so much which works of
> the past are eternally valuable, as which will help T. S. Eliot to write his
> own poetry. This arbitrary construct, however, is then paradoxically
> imbued with the force of an absolute authority. The major works of
> literature form between them an ideal order, occasionally redefined
> by the entry of a new masterpiece. The existing classics within the

cramped space of the Tradition politely reshuffle their positions to
make room for a newcomer, and look different in the light of it; but
since this newcomer must somehow have been in principle included in
the Tradition all along to have gained admission at all, its entry serves
to confirm that Tradition's central values. (39)

However, in the last three decades, women, minorities and influential
mainstream critics have begun to challenge the canon. Herbert Lindenberger
facetiously defines "canon" as: "A term the [Academy] ignores when its
referent remains in stable condition but that which the Academy invokes
incessantly whenever it is threatened with change" (xiii). Lindenberger
continues in a more serious vein: "Canons take the form of banners by
means of which particular movements, nations and regional constructs such
as the so-called West establish pedigrees, define an identity, and present
themselves to the world" (xiii). In tracing the salient points in the history of
canon formation, for example, Lindenberger, points out how canonicity for
the Greeks surfaced around the third century B.C. and second century A.D.
At this time a Greek edition of twenty-four Greek tragedies was published.
Upon reading the works selected for inclusion, certain biases can be detected
for the "tragic" view of life since most of the plays end in catastrophe (136–
137). Some theorists view this as a specific social engineering process in
the privileging of the tragic world view. This may have been a means by
which the ruling elites tried to wean "the readers away from what they saw
as the vulgar melodramatic actions endemic to popular Hellenistic romance
in their time" (137).

Lindenberger points to the formation of the German canon as another
example of how extra-literary concerns influenced inclusion or exclusion of
literary works and indeed the very formation of their literary canon. The
German literary canon, like the English canon, is a fairly recent phenomenon.
It was constructed and stabilized in the mid-nineteenth century. According
to Peter Hohendahl, the canon was designed to meet the cultural needs of the
moment, which demanded the creation of a German national identity defined
by writers who could radiate a classical status comparable to that of the
Elizabethan writers in England or the French writers of the Age of Louis XIV.
Lindenberger adds that the German canon stabilized at precisely the time
that the unified German state came into existence. The creation of university
chairs for the practice and dissemination of this academic field consolidated
and added legitimacy and prestige to it. Furthermore, the German academy
introduced methodologies designed to support those works within the canon
and discouraged those outside the canon. The result of these supposedly
scientific methodologies was to inhibit the expansion of German literature
since the system that prevented the evaluative process to take place was

artificially restrained and stunted.

Lindenberger stresses how canon making is "rooted in its own time and place" and how this canon formation "manifests certain biases characteristic of this particular time and place" (137). And he adds "It is when readers during these later times perceive this loss of relevance that it becomes possible to initiate canon change or, at best, to reinterpret canonical figures in the hope of endowing them with a new and hopefully more timely significance" (137–38).

Commenting on this need for change in canonical dictums, Barbara Harlow, author of *Resistance Literature*, writes:

> The poetry written in the context of national liberation organizations and resistance movements, remain singularly unavailable to the literary institutions of the West. Nor do they conform to the conventional and canonical criteria of poetic inspiration and composition applied by the Western critics and practitioners of poetry. Neither concerned with the contemporary theories of the "pleasure of the text" nor invoking the Romantic tradition of "recollection in tranquility," the poems of resistance, often composed on the battlefield or commemorating its casualties, the losses to the community, challenge instead the bourgeois institutions of power which often limit such luxuries to the economically privileged and leisured classes of the world readership. (35–36)

Since Chicanos/as are engaged in the process of canon formation and definition, it is instructive for us to examine closely other cases of canon construction and the ideology informing these canons in order for us not to repeat the same mistakes made by other national literature projects. It may come as an unpleasant surprise to conservative mainstream canon defenders to know that the canon is a human construct and not formulated by a Divine Entity in heaven. It is, as a matter of fact, subject to the vagaries of all human idiosyncrasies, such as prejudice, political expediency, personal taste, ideological concerns and so forth. Furthermore, what a particular century or generation values or privileges may not be privileged by subsequent generations. For example, Leavisian criticism which came into the fore in England during the 1920s and 1930s valued the vague notion of "essential Englishness" and thus devalued such poets as Milton and Shelley whom they perceived as not English enough while exalting the virtues of a Donne and a Hopkins (Eagleton 37). Eagleton underscores that "there was no question of seeing such re-mapping of the literary terrain as simply one arguable *construction* of a tradition, informed by definite ideological preconceptions: such authors, it was felt, just did manifest the essence of Englishness" (37). Thus a canon is formed not on the specific intrinsic merit of the work per se, but on attributed values from *outside* the work, especially as they are perceived to conform to a certain ideological aim.

Just as the English were at the crossroads of canon formation as recently as the 1920s and 1930s, so too Chicano/a scholars and publishers are presently engaged in setting forth a canon for Chicano/a literature. Because of our historical, political and social specificity, much of our literature, although not all, falls within the parameters of resistance literature, of cultural conflict, as Américo Paredes postulated several decades ago in *"With a Pistol in His Hand": A Border Ballad and Its Hero* (1958). Ramón Saldivar has discussed the vectors of resistance informing Chicano/a literature and Paredes' role in pinpointing in the 1950s the *corridos'* (Mexican ballads) function as a paradigmatic model for Chicano/a literature (3–45). In *Chicano Narrative: The Dialectics of Difference*, Saldivar states: "[I] ... have argued that the corrido can be construed as a residual cultural form that continues to underwrite contemporary Chicano narrative. Decisive in this relationship of prefiguration between ballad and narrative is Américo Paredes' *With His Pistol in His Hand* in its presentation of literary and historical paradigms for the production of a shared narrative community" (47).

Although I believe other forms of literary structures have informed Chicano literature, such as the folktale, the legend, the *retablo*, the *canción* and so forth, I concur with his statement that Chicano literature poses a "serious challenge to the established ways of defining the canons of both the theory and the practice of literature and its criticism as these have developed in the Anglo-American world" (3). Saldivar and other Chicano/a critics, such as Tey Diana Rebolledo, question the validity of using European and American critical theories for the analysis and interpretation of Chicano literature, since this literary production has been from its very inception an "oppositional" and "differentiating" construct to mainstream Anglosaxon literature. As a subaltern group claiming a large corpus of cultural productions, Chicanos/as speak with their own voice and define themselves differently from the mainstream. Thus, the Chicanos/as' literary voice will be different from and value a different set of aesthetic parameters than that of the hegemonic voice.

It has been well established by both Chicano/a scholars and others in various fields of investigation that Chicanos/as have not been historical subjects in dominant discourses. It has been up to us and through our forebears' efforts to insert ourselves in historical and literary discourses. We have been forced to invent a counter discourse which introduces new discursive subjectivities. Our strategy has been to insist on the specificity and socio-historical context of our literary discourses. Chicanos/as have been extremely successful in carrying out this project in the last three decades. They have been successful in challenging the mainstream canon, if this success is measured in terms of Chicano/a literature courses being taught in

English and Spanish Departments throughout the United States and in terms of the number of publications in recent years. However, a new canon which will properly valorize our literary output needs to be created. The vectors and parameters of minority literatures must of necessity be judged differently because they arise out of a different socio-cultural context, just as English literature emerged out of a particular socio-political context. Therefore, if the English had the right to formulate a canon for their own literature, Third World peoples have the right to formulate their own canon.

Chicana Literature and The Canon

If Chicano literature in general was deemed outside academic canonical strictures and suffered as a result of this snobbery, the Chicana's artistic endeavors received even greater negative reception from two sources: exclusion has come from mainstream publication outlets and within the Chicano canon itself. It has been viewed in the past in a negative light or, worse yet, totally ignored. Part of our task, therefore, is to rescue those texts written by women which have languished unnoticed in dusty archives. New norms and aesthetic criteria need to be applied to these texts too. As Rosaura Sánchez has observed, feminist historians "reject masculine categories in determining what is of social significance" (1). And so too in feminist literary studies. Thus, in the amplification of the mainstream canon, Anglo-American feminists have reinscribed traditional tales, diaries, letters, prayers, etc., and in this manner have amplified and redefined the concept of what a literary work of art is. In adhering to this feminist canon, Chicanas are also reevaluating previous literary texts which had been devalued by traditional scholars. Tey Diana Rebolledo and Eliana Rivero's *Infinite Divisions: An Anthology of Chicana Literature* includes material dating from the nineteenth and twentieth centuries. Because of unequal educational opportunities accorded to women, scant material has been found that was written by Mexican-American women in the colonial period. Furthermore, the harshness of the environment in the newly settled territories of the Southwest implied women were busy at their household chores and did not have the leisure time to involve themselves in literary endeavors. Nevertheless, Rebolledo found Mexican-American women did posses a rich repertoire of oral literature: folktales, legends, riddles, folksongs, proverbs, folk remedies, recipes and so forth. And a few women did manage to write romantic novels and stories.

Rebolledo found in the Federal Writers' Project, a program instituted by the Federal Government during the years of the Great Depression, an important source of Mexican-American women's oral literary production.

During the 1930s, field workers in New Mexico from the Federal Writers' Project interviewed Mexican-American women and recorded these interviews. Rebolledo has identified an important source of literary texts which can be of significant use for recuperating the Chicanos/as literary heritage. The recordings yield important information regarding women's role in the colonization of the Southwest as well as their role as carriers of culture and tradition. Their many *cuentos* and folksongs detail their involvement in the settlement of the Southwest. Rebolledo adds that "Many contemporary Chicana writers are 'first generation' writers who are telling the *cuentos* of their mothers and grandmothers, thus preserving this oral tradition" (*Infinite Divisions*). She provides four examples of literary texts emanating from oral tradition:

1. "Eufemia's Sopapillas." Told by Catalina Gurulé and Patricia Gallegos. Compiled by Lou Sage Batchen. New Mexico Federal Writers' Project. Sept. 17, 1938.

2. "An Old Native Custom: La Curandera." New Mexico Federal Writers' Project. 5-5-49 #45.

3. "Quiteria Outwits the Witch Nurse." Told by Rumaldita Gurulé. Compiled by Lou Sage Batchen. New Mexico Federal Writers' Project, Sept. 17, 1938.

4. "Las Tres Gangozas (The Three Snuffy Sisters)." Told by Guadalupe Gallegos. Compiled by Bright Lynn. New Mexico Federal Writers' Project. 5-57-4 (Infinite Divisions).

Publication of forgotten and or neglected material is important in the current endeavor to rescue and reconstruct a Chicano/a literary heritage. If Spain has been able to publish the series *Biblioteca de Autores Españoles*, which includes much of Spanish colonial literature, we should be able to do the same. However, we should keep clearly in mind our goals for the project. I believe one of these goals is that of cultural recovery. We need to rescue those texts that have been marginalized, neglected or disdained by previous literary canons. In doing this we should be aware of the history of canon formation in other nations so that we may learn from their success as well as from their errors. Once we have accomplished this, it will be up to future generations to evaluate and revise. The rescue and recovery of forgotten texts can be our legacy to future generations.

Works Cited

Anderson, Benedict. *Imagined Communities*. New York: Verso, 1991.
Bhabha, Homi K., ed. *Nation and Narration*. New York: Routlege, 1990.

Bergonzi, Bernard. *Exploding English: Criticism, Theory, Culture.* Oxford: Clarendon, 1991.

Dalton, Roque. "A History of a Poetic," in Barbara Harlow, *Resistance Literature,* 1.

Eagleton, Terry. *Literary Theory: An Introduction.* Minneapolis: U of Minnesota P, 1989.

Guillén, Nicolás. "Problems of Underdevelopment," in *Resistance Literature,* 31.

Harlow, Barbara, ed. *Resistance Literature.* New York: Methuen, 1987.

Herrera, Sobek, ed. *Reconstructing a Chicano/a Literary Heritage: Hispanic Colonial Literature in the Southwest.* Tucson: U of Arizona P, (forthcoming).

Hohendahl, Peter. *Building a National Literature: The Case of Germany 1830–1870.* Ithaca: Cornell UP, 1989.

Lindenberger, Herbert. *The History in Literature: On Value, Genre, Institutions.* New York: Columbia UP, 1990.

Paredes, Américo. *"With a Pistol in His Hand": A Border Ballad and Its Hero.* Austin: U of Texas P, 1958.

Rebolledo, Tey Diana and Eliana Rivero. *Infinite Divisions: An Anthology of Chicana Literature.* Tucson: U of Arizona P, (forthcoming).

———. "The Politics of Poetics: Or, What Am I, A Critic, Doing in This Text Anyhow? In *Chicana Creativity and Criticism: Charting new Frontiers in American Literature.* Houston: Arte Público, 1987. 129–38.

Saldivar, Ramón. *Chicano Narrative: The Dialectics of Difference.* Madison: U of Wisconsin P, 1990.

Sánchez, Rosaura. "A History of Chicanas: Proposal for a Materialist Perspective." *Between Borders: Essays in Mexicana/Chicana History.* Ed. Adelaida del Castillo. Encino, California: Floricanto 1990. 1–29.

Po(l)etics of Reconstructing and/or Appropriating a Literary Past: The Regional Case Model

Francisco A. Lomelí

> ... cuando en un futuro lejano se haga la historia sobre la vida cultural de Las Vegas (New Mexico), se tendrá que afirmar que 1892 es el año de las sociedades literarias y de ayuda mutua.
>
> *La Voz del Pueblo* (4/9/1892)

> ... Whenever in the far future a history is done of the cultural life of Las Vegas (New Mexico), one will have to affirm that 1892 is the year of literary and mutual aid societies.

I. Prolegomenon: From the Establishment of Identity to the Exploration of a Literary Legacy

Until the 1970s it was not altogether clear whether Chicanos could trace their literary tradition much before the contemporary period. A definite void or fissure seemed to exist between the present and the past. Understandably, literature created by Chicanos was perceived by most as a recent by-product of the Civil Rights movements in the 1960s and the radical experiments of the 1970s, that is, as pamphleeterism or engagée expression. The ultimate goal at the time was to address the political urgency of the times, for example, by focusing on identity, an image warfare against pernicious stereotypes and the reconstruction of ethnicity. Viewed as intrinsically contemporary or young by many, the literature possessed qualities that encased an expression

221

of renewed vitality and originality relative only to recent social phenomena. Although uplifting in vindicating past social ills, its combative spirit systemically targeted the American socialization process, as well as its institutions, that had denied our Mexicanness. It was an effort to recapture and refocus our imagination as a viable form of liberation. As a result, the notion of an historiographical black hole before 1965 emerged as if to imply that only Mexico could be identified as a referent point of our being. The idea was that of a quantum leap from limbo to centerstage in order to reclaim a rightful place in modernity by bringing into question our longstanding invisibility and second-class status.

This was the case for most of Aztlán, with the exception of New Mexico in which Mexico was nothing more than a distant memory. New Mexico as a remote region within *el vasto norte* (the vast north) shared a sense of a distinct past and a history—almost as a cultural island—, easily pointing to the chain of pueblo settlings along the Río Grande in the form of a continuous civilization dating back to the previous millenium. Contrary to Californians, for example, New Mexicans were not a product of cultural hydroponics, but rather descendants of a long tradition dating back to the turn of the sixteenth century and longer with the inclusion of Native-American bloodlines. Also, contrary to Texans and Arizonians, New Mexicans were not overrun by Anglo Americans, but instead, maintained a semblance of themselves through time by retaining part of the power base in economics, politics and the means of production. New Mexico's remoteness, at first a liability—for it inhibited growth and made frontier life harder—later became an asset culturally in the preservation of a regionally unique ethnos. The Hispanic literary production of the aforementioned regions bears this out. In fact, it can be stated that by the end of the nineteenth century, New Mexico experienced an early literary renaissance and autonomy like no other region, judging from the massive amount of works produced within its boundaries (Lomelí 1990).

New Mexico, more than any other region in what became the American Southwest, knew empirically and intuitively that it had a past. Although its Hispanic peoples had lost many of their original holdings from Spanish landgrants, they were not all reduced to a mere laborer status (Camarillo) or urban pariahs. Memories of past glories were commonplace in conjunction with an acute historical consciousness about a change in their status. Besides, these New Mexicans did not feel like recent immigrants, nor could they be described as such, because they could trace their background to eight, ten or more generations. We are dealing here with a resilient, deeply-rooted, and proud people who created a regional culture through gumption and ingenuity while having a number of characteristics proper to their area. New Mexico's isolation and remoteness contributed to producing a hardy stock of people who were initially motivated to colonize by their Spanish zeal and culturally conditioned by indigenous and Mexican experiences. Fray Angélico Chávez views the process in these terms:

> From the start, the Hispanic colony of New Mexico, for reasons of geography and the circumstances of the times, had little connection with New Spain, which was much later to evolve into present Mexico. Nor had she anything to do with the later thrust into Texas, Arizona and California. This New Mexican enclave developed, or degenerated in some ways, if you will, in almost complete isolation from Spain and the rest of Spanish America, yet proudly (if rather pathetically) 'Spanish' in its self-identification. This was due to the people who established the culture, the pastoral character of the region, the almost complete lack of education as well as cultural separation from the rest of the civilized world for over two centuries. (245)

The result is a syncretism of forms, tastes, values and outlooks, strongly influenced by a distinct cuisine, a linguistic reservoir of sixteenth-century Spanish and Native-American dialects, a religious iconography and styles of worhip, plus an architecture, sometimes called Santa Fe-Pueblo, "which accentuates Spanish building techniques and Native-American pragmatism to offer harmonious spatial representations between nature and humankind" (Lomelí 1988, 84).

II. Between Paradigms and Finding Models for Reconstructing a Literary Past

Concerted efforts in documenting early Chicano literary history either went unnoticed or initially stirred little interest. Some of the first attempts lacked scientific backbone in their quest to satisfy an insatiable thirst for folklorism and quaint depictions of romanticized settings and characters. Aurelio M. Espinosa in 1915 was the first to offer a working model in "Romancero nuevomexicano" (New Mexican Ballads) by proposing the residual Spanish framework, suggesting that lore from the region derived directly from Spain. His hispanophile slant led to a discussion and analysis of traditional poetic forms, as if they were principally 'uncontaminated' vestiges imported from Spain. Espinosa's model did not involve literary history per se, but other followers, such as Nina Otero-Warren in *Old Spain in Our Southwest* (1936), Arturo L. Campa in *Spanish Folk Poetry in New Mexico* (1946), and Juan Rael *Cuentos españoles de Colorado y Nuevo México* (Spanish Tales of Colorado and New Mexico, 1957), perhaps more compilers than critics, certainly contributed to the promulgation of a folksy portrait couched in purely Hispanic terms. Such an emphasis later motivated Carey McWilliams in

North of Mexico (1949) to label much of this trend as part of a "fantasy heritage," that is, a convenient self-invention in order to appease the dominant culture while making Hispanic cultural modes more palatable.

A significant deviation from the above occurred in 1959 when José Timoteo López, Edgardo Núñez and Roberto Lara Vialpando, in *Breve reseña de la literatura hispana de Nuevo México y Colorado* (A Brief Survey of Hispanic Literature of New Mexico and Colorado), had as their primary objective the categorization of extant writings. Another important difference lies in that they do not strictly concentrate on poetry or short fiction, including remarkably scintillating assessments on the novel and theatre. In addition, the focus is not to render folkloric popular expression, but rather to approach the subject with sensitivity and a critical eye, particularly by intimating the cultural conflict paradigm without fully developing it. Although rudimentary in nature and methodology, they nonetheless offer some semblance of a literary history for New Mexico, offering such pithy evaluations as: "Las novelas en Nuevo México [están] escritas en un español sencillo y casi dialectal lleno de modismos y giros propios del Suroeste" (17) (The novels in New Mexico are written in simple and almost dialectical Spanish, full of idioms and registers proper to the Southwest). Unfortunately, their efforts remained completely obscured or forgotten until the middle 1970s when New Mexico once again became a focus of attention for its abundant collections of writings. Nonetheless, they established a key paradigm in a modest but comprehensive attempt at commenting on all genres while providing early examples of the variety and scope of New Mexican literature. Their efforts, however, would not be in vain.

In 1971 two independent events were to take place: Philip D. Ortego's completion of his dissertation titled "Backgrounds of Mexican-American Literature" and the publication of *Bibliografía de Aztlán: An Annotated Bibliography*, edited by Ernie Barrios. The former studies at length the origins, place and dilemmas surrounding this newly discovered body of 'American' literature by showing its trajectory and range. Ortego expands its conceptualization as a well-entrenched literary tradition, thus dismissing the notion of being a recent phenomenon. In many ways, his work modernized and established links with the past as described by the authors of *Breve reseña*. On the other hand, *Bibliografía de Aztlán* represents the first critical annotated bibliography, which served as a starting point for Francisco A. Lomelí's and Donaldo W. Urioste's augmented version in *Chicano Perspectives in Literature: A Critical and Annotated Bibliography* (1976). Barrio's *Bibliografía de Aztlán* coalesced entries into a brief listing, causing one to wonder if that was all Chicanos had produced up to that time. Furthermore, the inclusion of various works by Mexicans and Anglos implicitly questioned the literature's definition and intrinsic nature. The unresolved question left for a curious reader is as follows: Is there more and how far back can we go? Ironically, *Pocho* by José Antonio Villarreal was uncovered or rediscovered at the same time the bibliography was in press, too late to be included.

Luis Leal shortly thereafter in 1973 made some startling assertions in documenting Chicano literary historiography in his famous essay "Mexican American Literature: A Historical Perspective." First of all, he proposes a functional definition for the literature that is neither limited nor dogmatic, but, most of all, he situates Chicano creativity within a larger diachronic context between American and Mexican relations, particularly as an extension of Mexico while retaining a distinctiveness in its literary constructs. Therefore, he clarifies and qualifies much of what was previously considered a void, meticulously demonstrating that contemporary writings do indeed have antecedents and a background. His groundbreaking interdisciplinary work uncovers evidence and gives historical validity to what others had intuited yet had not been able to prove. Leal expounds on an "inter-literary historical" framework (Lomelí "Interhistoria literaria") and especially on a didactic periodization to better appreciate the development and evolution of the literature. The result is the first most comprehensive description and analysis of the various components comprising Chicano expression from the beginnings to its most recent manifestations. For the first time, this literature gained cohesion, an identity, a face and a *raison d'être* as a unique entity but not apart from both Mexican and American historical developments. Chicano literature, as the bridge between the two, stood apart but also inextricably tied to both.

Luis Leal's inter-literary historical model later served as the framework with which to subsequently speak of regionalism or Aztlán as a unifying concept, not only in a mythical sense but also in nationalistic literary terms, supporting what Guillermo Rojas in 1973 has called "literatura aztlanense" (literature of Aztlán). Others like Francisco A. Lomelí, in "An Overview of Chicano Letters: From Origins to Resurgence" (1983), have expanded this model as a working paradigm with which to fill in gaps and insert newly discovered texts. Still others like Raymond Paredes in "The Evolution of Chicano Literature" (1982) and Alejandro Morales in "Visión panorámica de la literatura mexicoamericana hasta el boom de 1966" (1976) have concentrated on either the American and the Latin American aspects, respectively. In addition, other referentially specific approaches include María Herrera-Sobek's Chicana feminist overview in *Beyond Stereotypes* (1985), Chuck Tatum's general summary in *Chicano Literature* (1982), Luis Leal *et al.* (1982) focus on a given time frame in *A Decade of Chicano Literature (1970–1979)*, Cordelia Candelaria's in-depth examination of a single genre in *Chicano Poetry: A Critical Introduction* (1986), as well as Nicolás Kanellos' treatment of theatre in *A History of Hispanic Theatre in the United States: Origins to 1940* (1990), and Ramón Saldívar's theoretical focus on narratology in *Chicano Narrative: Dialectics of Difference* (1990).

In other words, there currently exists a proliferation of critical approaches in dealing with the vast variety and sheer volume of both contemporary and early works of Chicano letters. But most of all, the literary vacuum notion of a disinherited past has waned considerably, because dealing with an historical backdrop is no longer an oddity; it is now a requirement in doing serious scholarship in the field. The 1980s definitely marked an upsurge in this area of study, whereas previously only a few isolated cases could be identified. Chicano literary historiography has reached a peak for various reasons: the literature's legitimacy is no longer as much in question, which has prompted further examination into many phases of literary creativity, especially that which relates to its historical contextuality. Aside from the purely theoretical or comparative pieces in article form, much critical space in book-length manuscripts is devoted to the restoration of a literary legacy. New developments in this regard are slowly coming to fruition through original, even daring, groundbreaking scholarship, thus offering at times an oppositional view of American literary evolution, or at least complementing the latter's deficiencies with substantiated information while also challenging the culturally monolithic canon of American literature. The central motive is simply to claim a rightful place in this constellation of literary production vis-à-vis Anglo-American hegemony. Some might consider this mere revisionism, but in effect it denotes a revamping of biased criteria and exclusionary standards.

One key consideration that functions as a handicap has been language, often used as the first and fundamental determinant to either consider a work's value or relegate it to obscurity. Obviously, much of the early writings in Spanish only reached an audience of the same language group, thus limiting its later dissemination among Anglo-American literary historians. A linguistic ethnocentrism has traditionally been in operation, for example, as justified by Mabel Major and T. M. Pearce in *Southwest Heritage* (1938):

> Most Americans ... have read only books made in the tradition of Europe and written in the English language. (...) Moreover we shall frankly relate all other cultures in the Southwestern scene to our contemporary American life. There are good reasons besides expediency for our doing this. While civilization here is greatly enriched by contacts with other cultures and languages, today the dominant strain seems clearly to be Anglo-American, with its ever increasing tendency to spread its influence and to absorb its competitors. (2)

Language, then, like culture, has had political implications for the peoples who rivaled in their quest for domination and influence after the American conquest of half of Mexico in 1848. The degree of contempt toward the native cultures by the new settlers has had long-lasting repercussions in attempts to recover a legacy, in certain occasions using original archival documents as wrapping paper. Cleve Hallenbeck notes:

> Most of the provincial documentary material dealing with the Spanish period in New Mexico has forever disappeared. Complete records once existed in the archives at Santa Fe, for the Spaniards had a passion for preserving attested memoranda of every event, however insignificant. All the archives in the province . . . were destroyed in the great Pueblo Revolt of 1680. Then most of the archives covering the period 1693 to 1846 were burned or otherwise disposed by the early Anglo-American officials, who could not read Spanish. (viii)

III. Conceptualizing a Model: Problematics vs. Fleshing Out Its Application

The establishment of an adequate historical framework for early Chicano literature certainly has had its difficulties. There still remains the nagging question of when and where this literature originated, and the pertinent issue of overlapping with Mexican and American traditions. Few agree as to its exact historical inception because the people whom we study as producers of that literature have undergone a constant transformation of various nationalities, political borders and affiliations of identity: from indigenous to Spanish subjects, from Spanish to Mexicans, to Americans, to ethnic or Chicano and, for some, to Hispanic or Latino. Some critics suggest its beginnings at the point of initial contact between Europeans and Native Americans in what was the outer fringes of the northern frontier of New Spain. Luis Leal, Juan Bruce-Novoa and Francisco A. Lomelí refer to the early explorers such as Alvar Núñez Cabeza de Vaca in *Relaciones* (Reports, 1542) or Fray Marcos de Niza in *Relación del descubrimiento de las siete ciudades* (Report on the Discovery of the Seven Cities, 1539) as possible sources for implanting a written literary tradition in the region. As the Spanish language coalesced human experience from an Hispanic prism, there is undeniable proof that the indigenous world view and oral narrative culture also contributed significantly toward infusing a new expression. No wonder Cabeza de Vaca feels himself oscillating between two worlds after his extensive contact with various Indian groups, as if he were a transformed person, no longer only Spanish. To Juan Bruce-Novoa, this explorer intimates what a third culture would become, and by extension, what a Chicano would be.

To Luis Leal (1973), the psychological impact had less importance within the extant socio-historical forces as defined by the geopolitical interplay between Mexico and Anglo America. Instead, regionality and consciousness of race played primary roles in determining Chicano literary history. Therefore, the only requirement for a work to be considered under this rubric was for it to be written by a person of Mexican descent, no matter how remote or recent, regardless of status of the publication and/or dissemination (i.e. monograph, manuscript or oral transcription). This inclusive and flexible criterion encases a methodology based on a definite sense of regionality from which to measure a people's self-reflections through the imagination. Leal provided a macro-context of confluence, defined a power struggle between cultures, outlined specific trends applicable to Chicano-related events and unearthed titles and authors lost in the annals of dispersed documents.

In the process of erecting demarcations and parameters, one pivotal concern has emerged: how to grapple with the politics and poetics of reconstructing and/or appropriating a literary past. In doing so, is there in fact a danger of historical imperialism by adopting a work or author that supposedly pertained to another set tradition, or to no tradition at all? For example, by claiming Gaspar Pérez de Villagrá's *Historia de la Nueva México* (*History of New Mexico*, 1610) as a significant component of early Southwestern written tradition—applicable equally to Mexican as well as Chicano literatures—, are we committing historical piracy? How would we resolve the potential paradox of John Gilmary Shea's assertion in 1887 that Villagrá's work represents "The First Epic of Our Country?" If that is the case, how can we explain that it has remained one of the best kept secrets in the field of American literary historiography? Indeed, who appropiates what and when can be a puzzling dilemma. By subsuming or claiming something as our own, we are declaring that it is rightfully ours. In addition, we could be accused of fabricating a past for the sake of having one, or that we are randomly taking authors and works out of a hat or out of context. Accordingly, the accusation might emerge of being regarded as clever fabricators of an artistic reality that was never there. Is there in fact an attempt to create figments of our imagination to justify the purported vacuum of a past? Not only that, but it might be claimed that, to support our findings, we use others' materials to prove our arguments. How then can we verify a literary past that is truly our own? Besides, what might be the implications, if any, of claiming a proper literary history? Are autonomy and independence in these terms possible when various degrees of conquest, assimilation, mixture, cooptation, intermarriage and adaptation have taken place within a society partly responsible for erasing our past?

Gaspar Pérez de Villagrá

IV. Reclaiming vs. Appropriation: A Matter of Relativity or Two For the Price of One

The questions posed above offer numerous inferences difficult to unravel. First of all, it is not an easy task to rectify misconceptions about a people who historically have been labelled as non-generators of significant events or contributions, even if the facts bear out to the contrary. Recent revisionism now proves that a systematic approach toward eliminating Mexican influence was surreptitiously and overtly practiced since the nineteenth century. The objective was to replace Mexicans and their institutional apparatuses so as to Americanize them into a more 'modern' mold, eventually creating the impression that it had always been thus. The cinematographic projection of the Western frontier represents an illuminating example of the twentieth century techniques utilized to accomplish such a mission, and from there implant a whole new image of what actually occurred. This is considered rewriting history for the sake of promoting hegemony and conveniently justifying it. Therefore, Chicanos' reexamination of past events and the acknowledgement of an imposed social order becomes critical in dealing with a convoluted background that was not solely Chicanos' doing.

Reclaiming it is not only viable but necessary, even if it involves appropriating it. The procedure is not frivolous nor misguided because Chicanos have as much right to a past as any other people, whether it is recognized by others or not. Given the entanglements of double allegiance and mixed alliances through conquests and shifts in identity, it is not contradictory to regard one work as common to two national and/or ethnic literary histories. Few would quibble today about the classification of Alonso de Ercilla's *La araucana* (1569) as a foundational work of Chile—and by extension, Latin America—, although it was always claimed by Spain until modern times. Likewise, Alvar Núñez Cabeza de Vaca's *Relaciones* (1542), Don Pedro Baptista Pino's *Exposición sucinta y sencilla de la provincia del Nuevo México* (A Succinct and Simple Exposition of the Province of New Mexico, 1812), and Fray Gerónimo Boscana's *Chinigchinich* (1825?), as integral parts of early Hispanic regionalistic writings, clearly constitute a part of the written tradition from which Chicano literature would eventually emerge. These books no longer figure much in discussions on early Mexican works, existing marginalized in a type of limbo. Their regional construct makes them different and grounds them within a tradition of neglect on both sides of the border. Appropriation here, then, implies a reclamation project while properly making connections between a modern work and past literary production. Since it seems obvious that Chicanos did not spring up like mushrooms in the 1960s nor from the ashes of nothingness, by extension of that logic neither have their writings. In other words, a present-day work has an attachment to the immediate or remote past. Thus, bodies of literature possess an inviolable past, an historical source or backdrop from whence they derive, regardless if the self-identifier is evident or not. The point is adamantly clear: there is ample evidence of literature produced by peoples of Mexican descent even before the term Chicano—or for that matter, Mexican American—existed. Hypothetically, one author and his works could have experienced at least three changes in formal identity: a book from 1819 would be Spanish; another from 1831 would be Mexican; furthermore, another from 1849 could be termed American (in a matter of thirty years, note the differences); and after 1970 his works might be classified under the category of Mexican American or Chicano canon. This does not represent a far-fetched example, but rather a viable sample of the complexity involved in labelling works and authors. Literary history, however, does not meander as much as the herein presented transitory changes of nationality or rubrics.

Appropriation, consequently, becomes an indispensable methodology of revisionism and a medium for the reconstruction of origins, antecedents and background, all within a framework focusing on regional expression in the shadows of memory. Having been forgotten and ignored by Mexican circles—only as mere footnotes of frontier life—, they faced harsher times under the Americans through the politics of misunderstanding and poetics of indifference. It is essential for Chicano criticism to confront these thorny issues because it is best equipped to untangle webs of affiliation and belonging. Many of the early works embody an array of voices that fell through the cracks of legitimacy and real consideration for the chronicled perspectives contained within. Under Spanish and Mexican rule, they became lost voices in a silent desert; during American rule, they generally typified incomprehensible utterances of undecipherable sounds that registered little meaning. Their marginalization simply became compounded with time to the point of becoming a part of a general amnesia toward an Hispanic or Mexican presence in the Southwest. In this way, reconstructive literary history can be understood as a method by which to fill in gaps, reformulate nuances and recharacterize literary perspectives from the point of view of the people who created literature. Revisionism is crucial, but even more so is reconceptualizing basic questions to better appreciate the inner workings and underpinnings of a people in a state of flux and change in their world view. Early Hispanic material and discourse provide the type of insight rarely found in Anglo-American sources about the development of the Southwest as a unique regional entity.

V. The Regional Case Model: A Viable Point of Departure

Locating documents or materials, although still an adventurous task, is no longer an impossible feat because it does not imply working with a dearth of information. Quite the contrary, the over abundance demands new strategies for scrutiny and analysis. The main complication entails identifying, cataloging and handling dispersed sources and organizing them into some coherent fashion. It normally requires a detective's sense of perseverance and an archaeologist's willingness to pursue unorthodox clues. For instance, it is naive to expect most of the needed sources in a single centralized collection, neatly packaged; all options must be kept open to explore the most unlikely of places, turning over every stone. When researching the nineteenth century in a given region, for instance, we must approach such a period in the same way that it evolved, or at least in its own terms, while recognizing the primitive state of archival collections and library science. Counting on easy access tends to lead to quick disillusionment. It is perhaps best to examine the routes of trading and commerce, because books, newspapers, monographs and other pertinent documents travelled those same routes. This way, the researcher can piece together isolated bits of information from a wide variety of collections or sources to create a representative composite portrait of a desired period and/or region.

Efforts related to reconstructing a literary heritage imply resorting to creative research methods more within the confines of interdisciplinary studies. Fortunately, concentration on a specific geographical area offers many advantages and provides a focus with realistic parameters. General sources such as Hubert Howe Bancroft's volumes of historical compilations and chronicles (e.g. *Memorias* by Manuel Alvarez in 1825) might represent a start for a contextual groundwork. Beyond that, branching out into obscure sources becomes essential to unearth fragments of materials that have miraculously survived. Aside from isolated sources, monographs and specialized collections, much patience is advised to peruse with a clinical eye every possible newspaper collection, a natural informal repository. Many salient official documents mysteriously disappeared and most books vanished, but it became impossible to completely erase the chronicled quotidian experiences found in newspapers. Newspapers contain the live pulse of history in the making and therefore merit more serious consideration as a primary source for documenting a literary legacy. For that reason, it is still vital to index newspaper collections, ranging from the Historical Society in Kansas City to the Bancroft Library in Berkeley, or from the New Mexico Archives in Santa Fe to special collections in San Antonio. Within a region such as

New Mexico, it is just as important to examine the small town newspapers to evaluate cultural activity at a micro-local level. Only then can we uncover the dynamics of literary tastes of the times, including works read and discussed, and the type of organizational infrastructures, such as the famous *sociedades literarias* created to deal with literacy, rhetoric and aesthetics. The examination of these sources unveils a social and artistic reality much different from what is generally known, thus increasing our appreciation for the people who read and wrote during the harsh times of the frontier.

Despite the wealth of written materials that gives testimony to a reservoir of early poetic or fictionalized accounts, few critical paradigms have been proposed to study them. Scholarly indecisiveness has predominated, opting instead to focus on specific works, periods or genres. Few have hinted at a regional case model which might best permit conceptualizing a scope in a grander scale of interrelated and interdisciplinary data, including ethnographic and anthropological besides literary. Most approaches over specialize in dealing only with a parcel of the available materials with a limited contextual portrait. Much insight and discussion fall between the cracks. Some of the significant contributors are Rosaura Sánchez's monographic analysis of nineteenth-century novelist María Ruiz de Burton, Nicolás Kanellos' treatment of Hispanic theatre, Luis Leal's literary configuration of Aztlán, Genaro Padilla's discussion of autobiography, María Herrera-Sobek's and Tey Diana Rebolledo's vindication of the Chicana, and Clara Lomas' rediscovery of women writers.

Although these approaches provide invaluable results in Chicano criticism, the regional case model's distinction lies in being both diachronic and synchronic, eclectically dealing with written and oral sources. Concentrating on a single geographical area allows for viewing a complex network of interfacing data that provide a three-dimensional representation of a regional society. The cross-sectional stratification offers a more complete picture of trends, happenings and ideas. It encompasses historical revisionism, cultural anthropology, theories on culture, consciousness of race and class, partisan politics and literary theory. Besides, a region such as New Mexico, Arizona or Texas, appears to have an identity all of its own as shaped by the people, myths, historical gestation, interaction with others and their unique sense of cultural practices. Region functions as an immediate identifier, a cultural matrix or an insular feature to which people relate. In other words, region becomes the outer visible crust of what we study from within, providing the cultural elements of what is filtered through the creative literary act. Region is the *patria chica* (homeland) within all of us that somehow captures our essence or synthesizes what we believe ourselves to be.

In the case of New Mexico as a distinct geographical and cultural entity, it certainly possesses a series of unique qualities. A few stand out: permanence, marginality, remoteness and endurance. In addition, New Mexico was injected with an early enthusiasm and optimism after Juan de Oñate's expedition in 1598. Spanish explorers were hopeful to repeat their luck as they had with México-Tenochtitlan, the Aztec capital they conquered in 1521. Myths and legends about Quivira, Seven Golden Cities and other fantastic stories fertilized the Spanish imagination, often driven by fiction more than facts. The name of 'another Mexico' stuck but reality quickly set in when colonizers began to settle next to Indian pueblos, realizing the harshness of frontier life and the demands of the high desert. The new settlers became good students and in part imitators of the native peoples' lifeways through the necessity for survival. Contact was immediate, borrowing was expected and interrelationships were common. Because of isolation and distance from central Mexico, the region became a self-sufficient artery of civilization that developed with little outside influence. The sense of insularity and uniqueness grew with time to produce a network of pueblos and villages along the Río Grande that had to count on their own wits to survive. For that reason, New Mexico has viewed itself as a lost frontier (Lomelí 1988) from the rest of the world with a strong attachment to place.

It is not surprising that New Mexico would produce a deeply rooted literary tradition. Because of the region's believed potential, it attracted many visitors with a flair for hyperbole and adventure. Chronicles proliferated, diaries abounded, and accounts and *memorias* tried to persuade others of greatness. A literary tradition quickly prospered as it responded to an insatiable desire to dwell on fantasy, legend and larger-than-life happenings. This in part explains the first theatrical representation, Capitán Farfán's "Los moros y cristianos," along the Río Grande in 1598 and the early composition (1598–1604) and expeditious publication in 1610 of Gaspar Pérez de Villagrá's voluminous epic name, *Historia de la Nueva México*. These cannot possibly be perceived as literary flukes. The region developed a strong sense of itself and from there emerged numerous other incipient writings, including Miguel de Quintana's semi-mystical poetic renditions for which he was investigated, and finally exonerated, by the Inquisition (Colahan and Lomelí). Other writings, such as *Los comanches* (ca. 1777), attest to a consistent productivity, despite the circumstances under which many works were written. Although it would be exaggerated to declare New Mexico a literary hotbed during the Colonial period, nonetheless the variety of writings seems remarkable considering the region's major infliction of poverty and isolation.

By the time the printing press arrived in New Mexico by 1834, thanks to Father José Antonio Martínez, who spurred a notion of Hispanic pride and autonomy, New Mexico was a well established—though still poor—cultural entity. A literary tradition, both oral and written, and syncretically infused with Indo-Hispanic elements, was thriving. The printing press, along with the production of newspapers and the expeditious dissemination of information, simply added and enhanced what was already there. Newspapers, consequently, became publishing outlets for writers besides being instruments of fact and opinion. New Mexico's prominence grew dramatically in the 1880s and 1890s with the coming of the railroad, causing a renewed cultural vigor and economic prosperity. The written word gained even more importance as a tool of partisan struggle and as a rhetorical tool of carving the imagination. The result produced positive effects in the field of creativity, prompting a new age of latent writers to manifest themselves through the newspaper as forms of regional expression. Anselmo Arellano in *Los pobladores nuevo mexicanos y su poesía, 1889–1950* (The New Mexican Colonizers and Their Poetry, 1976) was one of the first contemporary anthologists to document the presence of past poetic voices who otherwise remained unacknowledged. Again, these are not isolated accidents of literary history, but rather mere examples of the vast collection of voices generally forgotten. When efforts such as Arellano's are combined with Erlinda Gonzales-Berry's edited collection of essays, *Pasó Por Aquí: Critical Essays on the New Mexican Literary Tradition, 1542–1988* (1989), the regional character and local artistic development gain a degree of coherence and unity. Such conceptualizations confirm the need to take into account more than mere titles and authors. The regional case model offers both an effective and practical approach to study literature in its proper cultural-historical context. A corollary contention is that if other critics concentrate on the literary production of other states of the Southwest, then we could authoritatively claim a much clearer concept of long-term Chicano/Hispanic aesthetics. An in-depth study of the four to five more Hispanic/Mexican states could potentially provide a broader mosaic of early Chicano creativity, establishing once and for all a rich legacy in these arid but hardly wretched wastelands.

In addition, there is the matter of dealing with artifacts from what might be regarded as the official folkloric culture. In the first half of the twentieth century, it became fashionable to collect and compile folkloric materials (see Espinosa, Otero-Warren, Campa, Rael, etc.), appropriating Hispanic music or rhyme or quaintness, but overlooking other artifacts with a politically sensitive content. Part of the objective involved reconciling past tensions with Anglos while romanticizing their own culture as a simple, pastoral society imbedded in superstition, myth and legend. This aura of hardy simpleness served as the discourse to camouflage difference and thus gain greater acceptance. It cannot be coincidental that New Mexico was reluctantly admitted into the American Union in 1912, only after lengthy discussions with regard to the sufficient Americanization and allegiance of the territory and its people.

Despite the rubric of folklorization that generally reigned, Chicano expression branched out into various other arenas and forms. Popular tradition continued but also evolved in conjunction with more sophisticated forms, often paralleling literary trends and developments of Latin America, Spain and Europe. In other words, a significant amount of carefully crafted writings were produced that attest to a serious intent in message, structure or language. Although anonymous folkloric samples might have sparked more interest, historical accuracy reveals this should be counterbalanced with a flourishment of individualized writings that bespeak of a rich tradition. Newspapers obviously reflect the phenomenon as it unfolded with thousands of poems, short stories, serialized novels or dramatic segments. Samples such as the herein mentioned are not a rarity; quite the contrary, they abound in a massive scale. Instead of being labelled as exceptions, they constitute the norm. The principal problem resides in unearthing, indexing, and cataloging them in order to place them in a framework that first explains a series of stratified misconceptions.

Beyond the writings themselves, we soon encounter an infrastructure that promoted their creation: increased newspaper subscriptions, more bookstores and libraries, renewed interest in monographs and an overall abundance of artistic activity. The figures are telling: between 1879 and 1900, 283 newspapers were launched in the state of New Mexico, and of these 44 alone correspond to the city of Las Vegas, New Mexico (Stratton 24), which served as the epicenter of a modest but important Hispanic literary renaissance (Lomelí 1988). Among some of the New Mexican authors to benefit from this resurgence are Eusebio Chacón's *Hijo de la tempestad* (Son of the Storm) and *Tras la tormenta la calma* (After the Storm the Calm) in 1892, Manuel C. de Vaca's (*Noches tenebrosas en el Condado de San Miguel* (Spooky Nights in the County of San Miguel) and *Historia de Vicente Silva y sus cuarenta bandidos, sus crímenes y retribuciones* (History of Vicente Silva and His Forty Bandits, Their Crimes and Retributions) from 1899 and 1896 respectively, Porfirio Gonzales' *Historia de un cautivo* (A Captive's Story) in 1898, and many others (Lomelí 1989). Perhaps the best way to measure the spiraling activity is by the number of new *sociedades literarias* founded in the northern part of the state, which functioned as centers of debates, poetic recitals and literary workshops, as well as institutes for rhetorical refinement in the art of political discourse, plus they provided mutual aid to people in need. There are claims that in Las Vegas, the hub of the renaissance, where six *sociedades* were founded in 1892 to add to the total

Eusebio Chacón (Miguel A. Otero Collection, Special Collections, General Library, University of New Mexico, Neg. No. 000-021-0168).

of eight for a city of 3,000 inhabitants. Activity was such that the following anonymous but prophetic comment appeared in *La Voz del Pueblo* on April 9, 1892: "cuando en un futuro lejano se haga la historia sobre la vida cultural de Las Vegas, se tendrá que afirmar que 1892 es el año de las sociedades literarias y de ayuda mutua."

Specialized approaches can be proposed to deal with such a diversity of materials and factors, but the regional case model is the only one to explicitly seek out comprehensiveness and interdisciplinarity. The complex nature of a region invites close examination of information, ranging from cultural politics to the studies of institutions, or from racial relations to governmental policies, or from infrastructural influences to the notion of imported ideas. This model presupposes social history as a dynamic process of change and interests, and literature is but one more contributing element within the larger picture. Since reality is stratified in multiple directions, consisting of long-term effects and one-time events, the composite is to be illuminated by explaining the relationship of the parts to each other. In this way, literary history becomes a science about origins, evolution, renovation, constants, dialectics and historical consciousness. It is perhaps the best way to know how a people has participated in history as well as how they have created it.

Works Cited

Arellano, Anselmo. *Los pobladores nuevo mexicanos y su poesía, 1889–1950.* Albuquerque: Pajarito, 1976.

Barrios, Ernie, ed. *Bibliografía de Aztlán.* San Diego: San Diego State Publications, 1971.

Bruce-Novoa, Juan. "Naufragios en los mares de la significación: de *La relación de Cabeza de Vaca a la literatura chicana.*" *Plural* 19.5. 221 (febrero 1990): 12–21.

Camarillo, Alberto. *Chicanos in a Changing Society: From Mexican Pueblos to American Barrios in Santa Barbara and Southern California, 1848–1930.* Cambridge: Harvard UP, 1979.

Campa, Arthur L. *The Spanish Folk Poetry in New Mexico.* Albuquerque: U of New Mexico P, 1946.

Candelaria, Cordelia. *Chicano Poetry: A Critical Introduction.* Westport, CT: Greenwood, 1986.

Chávez, Fray Angélico. "The Authentic New Mexican: A Question of Identity." *La cultura de Nuevo México.* Ed. Enrique Lamadrid. Albuquerque: n.d., 249–53.

Colahan, Clark and Francisco A. Lomelí. "Miguel de Quintana: An Eighteenth-Century New Mexico Poet Laureate?" *Pasó Por Aquí.* Ed. Erlinda Gonzales-Berry. 65–78.

Espinosa, Aurelio M. "Romancero nuevomexicano." *Revue Hispanique* 33 (1915): 446–560.

García, Eugene E., Francisco A. Lomelí, and Isidro D. Ortiz. *Chicano Studies: A Multidisciplinary Approach.* New York: Teachers College P, 1983.

Gonzales-Berry, Erlinda, ed. *Pasó Por Aquí: Critical Essays on the New Mexican Literary Tradition, 1542–1988*. Albuquerque: U of New Mexico P, 1989.

Hallenbeck, Cleve. *Land of the Conquistadores*. Caldwell, NM: 1950.

Herrera-Sobek, María. *Beyond Stereotypes; The Critical Analysis of Chicana Literature*. Binghamton, NY: Bilingual Press/Editorial Bilingüe, 1985.

Kanellos, Nicolás. *A History of Hispanic Theatre in the United States: Origins to 1940*. Austin: U of Texas P, 1990.

Leal, Luis. "Mexican American Literature: A Historical Perspective." *Revista Chicano-Riqueña* 1.1 (1973): 32–44.

————. Fernando de Necochea, Francisco A. Lomelí and Roberto G. Trujillo. *A Decade of Chicano Literature (1970–1979); Critical Essays and Bibliography*. Santa Barbara: Editorial La Causa, 1982.

Lomelí, Francisco A. "A Literary Portrait of Hispanic New Mexico: Dialectics of Perception." *Pasó Por Aquí*. 131–48.

————. "An Overview of Chicano Letters: From Origins to Resurgence." *Chicano Studies*. Eds. Eugene E. García, *et al.* 103–119.

————. "El caso de Nuevo México y su temprana emancipación literaria." *Culturas hispanas de los Estados Unidos de América*. Eds. María Buxó Rey and Tomás Calvo Buezas. Madrid: Cultura Hispánica, 1990. 599–606.

————. "New Mexico as a Lost Frontier: A Cultural and Literary Radiography." *La línea: ensayos sobre literatura fronteriza méxico-norteamericana/The Line: Essays on Mexican/American Border Literature*. Eds. Harry Polkinhorn, Gabriel Trujillo Muñoz and Rogelio Reyes. Mexicali/San Diego: Universidad Autónoma de Baja California and San Diego State U, 1988. 81–91.

————. and Donaldo W. Urioste. *Chicano Perspectives in Literature: A Critical and Annotated Bibliography*. Albuquerque: Pajarito, 1976.

López, José Timoteo, Edgardo Núñez and Roberto Lara Vialpando. *Breve reseña de la literatura hispana de Nuevo México y Colorado*. Juárez: Imprenta Comercial, 1959.

Major, Mabel and T. M. Pearce. *Southwest Heritage: A Literary History with Bibliographies*. Albuquerque: U of New Mexico P, 1972.

McWilliams, Carey. *North of Mexico: The Spanish-Speaking People of the United States*. Westport: Greenwood, 1949.

Ortego, Philip D. "Backgrounds of Mexican American Literature." Diss. U of New Mexico, 1971.

Otero-Warren, Nina. *Old Spain in Our Southwest*. New York: Harcourt Brace, 1936.

Rael, Juan B. *Cuentos españoles de Colorado y Nuevo México*. Stanford: Stanford UP, 1957.

Rojas, Guillermo. "Toward a Chicano/Raza Bibliography." *El Grito* 7.2 (1973): 1–56.

Saldívar, Ramón. *Chicano Narrative: The Dialectics of Difference*. Madison: U of Wisconsin P, 1990.

Shea, John Gilmary. "The First Epic of Our Country. By the Poet Conquistador of New Mexico, Captain Gaspar de Villagrá." *United States Catholic Society Magazine* 4 (April, 1987): 167–82.

Stratton, Peter A. *The Territorial Press of New Mexico, 1834–1912*. Albuquerque: U of New Mexico P, 1969.

Tatum, Charles. *Chicano Literature*. Boston: Twayne, 1982.

Nationalism and Literary Production: The Hispanic and Chicano Experiences

Ramón A. Gutiérrez

If one walks through the stacks of any major research library in the United States, searching the dusty recesses to recover the Hispanic literary past, one finds that the textual record documenting this heritage clusters into four major publication periods: 1) 1836 to 1897, 2) 1898 to 1945, 3) 1946 to 1966, and 4) 1967 to 1991. The boundaries that separate one period from another are rarely hard edges and straight lines, rather, these periods ebb and flow into each other. Nevertheless, the point to be made is that each period was uniquely characterized by a particular political configuration of power that resulted in the publication of certain texts and the relegation of others to obscurity. Similarly, this chronology focuses not on when a work was written, but when it was published and popularly disseminated.

So imagined, the first period of this history begins with the 1836 Texas Revolution and ends roughly around the 1890s, with the rather complete subordination of Mexicans to Anglo Americans in those areas of the United States that once belonged to Mexico. Most of the extant material from this period is largely autobiographical and thematically focused on the major political and social events of the day.

The second period begins very precisely in 1898, with Spain's loss of its last colonial outposts in Cuba, Puerto Rico and the Philippines as a consequence of the Spanish American War, and extends to the end of the Second World War. In the time-frame numerous texts were published that glorified Spain's past in the Americas. Much of this literature waxed and waned nostalgically about Spain's by-gone imperial greatness. It was produced as part of a global nationalist project launched by the Spanish state under the rubric of *hispanidad*, to ignite in its former colonial subjects memories of Spain's golden past. This period of textual revival saw the initial publication and translation of many of the heroic texts of America's colonial conquest.

The years 1945 to 1966 witnessed the development of Mexican, Puerto

241

Rican and Cuban immigrant communities in the United States. As persons from these communities assimilated, the literate among them wrote about their experiences as immigrants and workers, about their simultaneous negotiation of two cultures, and about their ambivalence as marginal members of American society. Whatever liminality writers in this period may have felt or expressed, writers who were active in the next period—from 1967 to the mid-1980s—expressed no such anxiety. Instead, theirs was a literary project of ethnic nationalism in which writers were sure of themselves, dug deeply into imaginary indigenous pasts for inspiration and reflected militantly, if not angrily, on the inequalities of life in the United States. These writers self-consciously labeled what they wrote "Chicano Literature," "Puerto Rican Literature," "Nuyorican Literature" and "Cuban-American Literature," literatures that historians often place under the generic rubric of American Ethnic Literature.

Surveying this large corpus of textual production as a whole, there are several regularities that seem to have structured the Hispanic literary impulse in the United States. In each of the four periods elaborated above, war was the structural force that impelled women and men to write. The *tejanos*, for example, reflected on the dispossession of their lands at the end of the Texas Revolution of 1836, much as the *californios* did in the years following the 1848 end of the U. S.-Mexican War.[1] In the seventeenth century, the Spanish conquistadors celebrated the heroism they had displayed in the Indian wars of colonial American conquest.[2] And Mexican-American veterans of the Second World War recounted their feats at Bataan and later on the battlefields of Korea and Vietnam (Morín).

Two major political tendencies, one integrationist and the other separatist, also characterizes this literary corpus. Integrationist writings have advocated basic civil rights and have sought political reform through peaceful appeals to the conscience of whites. This tendency prevailed when demands for equality were being partially accommodated, such as the two decades after the Second World War. The separatists, on the other hand, have employed nationalism and its various literary tropes as their main instruments, stressing community and national self-determination. Such writings have flourished in periods of virulent racism, years in which integrationist demands have been met with white apathy, such as the 1920s and 1960s.[3]

Much can be written about the Hispanic literature produced in each of these historical periods. What I would like to explore here more extensively are the similarities in the two periods that were marked by the ascendancy of literary nationalism: the period from 1898 to 1945, and the period from 1967 to 1991. The former period I have called Hispanic nostalgic literature, and the latter Ethnic Nationalist Literature. Literary historians have often seen these two periods of publication activity as having produced two very distinct literatures. Some characterize the temporal divide along class lines, as Hispanic "elite" literature versus Chicano, Cuban and Puerto Rican "folk" literatures. If viewed geographically, the division is sometimes imagined as that between Spanish or European literature and American "minority" literatures. And in some histories the division is between the literature of the colonizers and the literatures of the colonized.

Whatever epistemological closures, temporal or theoretical frames of reference one employs to make sense of this textual corpus, the division remains. Every literary history of the United States, be it from the margins or from the center, posits a division of one sort or another that cannot be bridged. My intention here is to explain how this division came into existence and to propose a way of bridging the gulf. My thesis is that Hispanic nostalgic literature and ethnic nationalist literatures really are more similar than different. Both created imaginary communities of readers who shared common assumptions about the meaning of the nation.[4] Both literatures were bred in political climates shaped by colonialism and neo-colonialism, and both were profoundly implicated in the generation of racial consciousness. Hispanic nostalgic literature was a nationalism from above, created by the Spanish state to instill national pride in a global community divided by a history of diaspora. Ethnic Nationalist Literature was a nationalism from below that imagined a community based on kinship, religion, language and terrain (Hobsbawm).

Hispanic nostalgic literature was born in 1898 when Spain lost its last morsels of colonial empire—Cuba, Puerto Rico, the Philippines—at the end of the Spanish-American War. In the years that followed this humiliation, Spain launched a massive world-wide campaign, known generally as the *hispanidad* movement, to recuperate culturally its former empire throughout Latin America, Africa and parts of the United States.[5] In the United States, the initial tangible fruits of the *hispanidad* movement were apparent shortly after the turn of the century when a whole variety of "Old Spanish Days" festivals were invented at places like Albuquerque, New Mexico and Santa Barbara, California to celebrate the heritage of the Spanish conquistadors and the legacy Spain had bequeathed to these areas. In Santa Fe, New Mexico, a "Spanish" festival was fabricated in the early 1900s to commemorate Don Diego de Vargas' reconquest of the city from the Pueblo Indian rebels in 1692. Here the intent was to project a heroic image of Spain's vanquishment of the Indians (Weigle and White). A similar motivation thematically inspired the 1915 Panama-California International Exposition held in San Diego, California's Balboa Park, to mark the opening of the Panama Canal. The Exposition's most visible display of culture was the construction of a

Spanish colonial town, complete with a Spanish baroque church. Mexico's proximity, only fifteen miles from Balboa Park, as well as its historic role in the development of Alta California, were totally ignored by the Anglo architects of the exhibition. What was emphasized was California's mythic Spanish past (Christman, Pray-Palmer).[6]

At the popular level, one can also see at the turn of the century the development of ethnic nomenclatures that emphasized things Hispanic. People of Mexican *mestizo* origin, at least in polite English-speaking circles, started referring to themselves as Spanish or Spanish-Americans, and deemed the label "Mexican" or "Mexican American" as pejorative. What was being emphasized at the cultural level in the invention of festivals, histories and ethnic labels was a fundamental connection with Spain's global culture and a rejection of Mexico and things Mexican.[7]

I suspect that one of the reasons the *hispanidad* movement became so popular in the Southwestern United States was that it coincided with a period of massive migration of Mexicans into the United States and consequently with the fears and anxieties that this movement provoked among Anglo Americans and which found expression in scientific racism and other nativist and xenophobic ideologies. Individuals of Spanish/Mexican origin living in the United States, by calling themselves Spanish and Spanish American, could distance themselves from the recent Mexican immigrant and thus assert a claim to social superiority (González, Gutiérrez, Metzgar, Chávez). The foundation of such assertions converged nicely with the basic tenets of scientific racism. European Aryan races were deemed to occupy the top of a complex chain of beings, with Indians and native peoples at the bottom of that hierarchy, close to animals. The whiter and more European one was, the higher was one's position in society. Individuals of Spanish/Mexican heritage living in the Southwest thus embraced their historic association with Spanish culture so that they would not be stigmatized by their Mexican Indian ancestry. The Mexican immigrants of the first third of the twentieth century were being discriminated against racially, and this is what the "Spaniards" and "Spanish Americans" of the U. S. Southwest were trying to avoid, allying themselves with a positively valorized European past rather than with the devalued indigenous past of the region.[8]

Examining the texts that were translated into English from the original Spanish-language sources, or simply published in the original, during the heydays of *hispanidad,* one notes that most of them contributed to the construction of a memory of Spain's glorious imperial past. What one finds in libraries published from 1898 to roughly the Second World War are translations of the *viajes marítimos* (ocean voyages), which glorify Spain's seaborne empire. There are numerous *crónicas de conquista* (chronicles of conquest), which relate the triumphs, the daring and the adventures of the Spanish conquistadors. And the *memorias* (memorials) and *visitas* (visitations) look at exotic lands in Spain's imperial trunk. Many of these books carry the imprint of The Quivira Society, an organization established in 1929 to translate the records of the Spanish expeditions of conquest and exploration in the United States. The Quivira Society published, to name but a few, the chronicles of Don Juan de Oñate, the *Historia* of Gaspar Pérez de Villagrá, and the *Memorias* of Fray Alonso de Benavides and Fray Juan de Morfi. It is clear, then, that the impact of *hispanidad* inspired publications in the Southwestern United States and to some extent in the Southeast.

These texts defined and fixed in extremely narrow terms what would be canonized as the Spanish literary history of the United States. Such literary histories as the *Literary History of the United States, The Cambridge History of American Literature* or *Columbia Literary History of the United States* all mention, in one way or another, that the documents produced by Christopher Columbus constitute the beginning of New World literature. Then, depending on the history, mention is made in passing of the texts produced by Álvar Núñez Cabeza de Vaca, Hernando de Soto or Francisco Vásquez de Coronado. But there the story virtually ends. Quickly the legacy of the English colonists of North America become hegemonic in these literary histories, and persons of Spanish, Mexican or Hispanic origin do not reappear again until after the Second World War when Mexican-American literature can no longer be ignored.

The legacy of such publication politics and literary canonization was to construct the Hispanic literary imagination in the United States as limited, fragmentary and defined by a short and transitory colonial period that was quickly supplanted by British supremacy. What literary histories fail to mention is that most of the chronicles of Spanish conquest and exploration were written by soldiers in order to ingratiate themselves to their monarchs. We now realize that the literary imagination of the Spanish colonists who settled in what is today the United States was rich and complex, and best examined in simple letters, homilies, diaries, songs, poetry and devotional literature. *Hispanidad* sponsored publications fail to mention how particular texts were being privileged; how masculine elite military culture and writing were being valued as superior to oral and popular cultural forms.

The second major legacy of Hispanic nostalgic literature was to establish firmly the superiority of metropolitan literary traits and aesthetic values over those developed in the peripheries of the empire, in such places as New Mexico, Texas and California. The literary culture of the Southwestern and Southeastern United States were deemed anemic reflections of a grander pure tradition. These ideas are very apparent in the literary archaeology of

Aurelio Espinosa, probably the best known and most prolific proponent of *hispanidad* in the United States. Espinosa's search for the Spanish literary tradition in the Southwest was expressed in the language of treasures and gems. Much as the Spanish conquistadors came to the Americas seeking gold, so too Espinosa found "true treasures," and "true gems," when he discovered what he deemed were pure and unadulterated variants of Spanish colonial literary forms. Espinosa's ideological mission, a goal he shared with other advocates of *hispanidad,* was to promote the idea that cultural mixing had not really occurred to any great extent. In New Mexico, California, Arizona, and Texas, one could find pure sixteenth and seventeenth century Spanish forms, or so Espinosa and others believed.

The hispanidad movement was successful in imposing from above a vision of the nation that included specific notions of what the Castilian language should look and sound like, of what aspects of Spain's history would be remembered and fixed textually, and what the contours of the nation's culture were. Against this grand standard, compatriots, dispersed about the globe, as bearers of an inferior anemic culture could aspire to the vigor and greatness of Spain's metropolitan past.

If the period 1898 to 1945 was characterized by state nationalism imposed from above to create patriotic citizens and loyal compatriots around the globe, the period from 1967 to 1991 was characterized by the inverse, a popular nationalism from below. In the United States the events that led to the end of neo-colonialism in Algeria, Cuba and Vietnam were marked by the development of nationalist movements against internal colonialism. Blacks, American Indians, Chicanos and Puerto Ricans all saw themselves as colonized peoples who sought territorial homelands and cultural and political self determination.[9]

Among Chicanos, Puerto Ricans and Native Americans, the political "decolonization" movement was fueled by a powerful cultural movement of self affirmation that, at least in literary circles, resulted in the construction of literary histories. Like those histories of Hispanic literature written several decades earlier by the *hispanidad* advocates, Chicano, Puerto Rican and American Indian scholars created a past that relied heavily on identifying key writers and key texts. In many ways there was very little difference between these scholars who sought the first Chicano novelist, the first Chicano poet, the first Chicano short story, and *hispanidad* scholars who sought the purest and earliest Spanish literary forms in the United States. Both groups were intent on creating a canon of sacred texts.

The histories of Chicano literature that were produced were premised on a monolithic concept of community and on the idea of political progress. Chicanos were Chicanos no matter whether they lived in Wisconsin or Texas, or whether they accepted this ethnic term or not. Chicano literature was getting better every day. Embedded in these histories too was a difficult, but nonetheless necessary, ideological conflation between aesthetics and politics. Chicano literary history began in 1848 at the end of United States-Mexico War. This date was chosen by Chicano scholars for very clear symbolic reasons. This date focused attention on racial and ethnic conflicts between Mexicans and Anglos, showing how Mexicans in the Southwest had resisted Anglo domination, and had forged an independent and autonomous culture. Why was 1836, the date of Texas Revolution not chosen as the beginning of Chicano literature? The answer was very simple. The lines of alliance were very complex during that rebellion. Mexican Texans united with Anglo Texans to overthrow what they deemed an oppressive Mexican state. One could also ask why Chicano literature did not start in 1540 when Francisco Vásquez de Coronado's expedition entered what is now the U. S. Southwest? Again, the cultural conflict represented in such literature would have been between Spaniards and Indians, and since the Chicanos glorified their *mestizo* heritage, obviously this was not the sort of tension the movement activists wanted emphasized.

Equally important to the Chicano literary movement was an intense interest in the authenticity of experience. Much of Chicano literature and criticism was preoccupied with "Who is the Chicano writer?" Were they born of a particular blood?[10] Was ethnicity dependent on surname? Or was it dependent on a particular type of childhood experience? These questions produced bitter debates over which much literary ink was spilt. Juan Bruce-Novoa, in "Canonical and Non-Canonical Texts," explored how some of these conflicts worked themselves out in the selection of the quintessential texts that were taught in Chicano literature courses. According to Bruce-Novoa, "The political identity [of Chicanos] was not allowed to be the sum of all possible parts of the community, but one restricted to those who fit into the ideological program. Identity was seen as a process of historical review carried out through an ideology of nation building which stressed several key points: retrieval of family and ethnic tradition, identification with the working class, struggle against assimilation, and the dire results if these efforts were not continued" (120). Thus Chicano homosexual authors, Chicana authors, authors who challenged the assumption that there was a monolithic Chicano "community," like Oscar Zeta Acosta, or who like Richard Rodriguez sought assimilation into the Anglo majority, were not allowed into the sacred pantheon of Chicano literature.

Thus far I have tried to argue that in the construction of literary canons, in the imagining of a national community and in the exclusionary visions of the world, Hispanic nostalgic literature had much in common with the ethnic nationalist literature of the last two decades. The principle difference was the locus of power, whether in the hands of the state or in the local political community. Hispanic nostalgic literature and American ethnic literatures are not anemic versions of robust European types. They were shaped in the American continent by different forces and must be understood as such and in their relationships to the peoples and places that inspired them.

Notes

[1]Jesús de la Teja recently prepared a new critical edition of Juan de Seguín's *Personal Memoirs* (1858), which deals with Seguín's role in the Texas Revolution, *A Revolution Remembered: The Memoirs and Selected Correspondence of Juan N. Seguín.* Other writers of the early Texas republic include, José María Rodríguez, *Rodríguez Memoirs of Early Texas*, and Antonio Menchaca, *Memoirs.* The Mexican side of the Texas Revolution has been recorded by Carlos E. Castañeda, ed. and trans., *The Mexican Side of the Texas Revolution, 1836, by the Chief Mexican Participants*; and José Enrique de la Peña *With Santa Anna in Texas: A Personal Narrative of the Revolution.* The published narrative reflections of the Californios can be found in: José del Carmen Lugo's *Vida de un ranchero*, serialized in English-language translations as José de Carmen Lugo, "The Days of a Rancher in Spanish California"; and "Life of a Rancher"; Angustias de la Guerra Ord, *Occurrences in Hispanic California*; Pío Pico, *Don Pío Pico's Historical Narrative.* The narratives of Eulalia Pérez, Carlos Híjar and Agustín Escobar appear in *Three Memoirs of Mexican California.*

[2]See for example the chronicle of Don Juan de Oñate's siege on the Indians of Acoma (Hammond and Rey).

[3]A very similar chronology seems to characterize the African-American experience in the United States (Genovese 55–72).

[4]On the importance of print capitalism in the construction of nationalism, see Benedict Anderson, *Imagined Communities: Reflections on the Origin and Spread of Nationalism.*

[5]On the history of the hispanidad movement see: Frederick Pike, *Hispanismo, 1898–1936*; Antonio Niño Rodríguez, *Cultura y diplomacia: los hispanistas franceses y España de 1875 a 1931*; Eduardo González Calleja, *La hispanidad como instrumento de combate*; Julio César Ycaza Tigerino, *Perfil político y cultural de Hispanoamérica.*

[6]The Panama-Pacific International Exposition held in San Francisco, California in 1915 also used Spanish culture as the park's main theme; see: Macober, *The Jewel City*; Barr, *The Legacy of the Exposition*; James, *Palaces and Courts of the Exposition.*

[7]On the invention of histories, festivals and ethnicities, see Hobsbawm and Ranger, *The Invention of Tradition*; and Werner Sollors, *The Invention of Ethnicity.*

[8]On scientific racism see Gould, *The Mismeasure of Man*; Bieder, *Science Encounters the Indian, 1820–1880*; and Keen, *The Aztec Image in Western Thought.*

[9]Robert Blauner has summarized these trends well in his *Racial Oppression in America.*

[10]One can see the hair-splitting levels that these debates reached when "Chicanesque writings" was coined as a way to refer to literature about Chicanos written

by individuals who were non-Chicanos; see Lomelí and Urioste, *Chicano Perspectives in Literature: A Critical and annotated Bibliography*; and Márquez, "Literature Chicanesque."

Works Cited

Anderson, Benedict, *Imagined Communities: Reflections on the Origin and Spread of Nationalism*. London: Verso, 1983.

Barr, James. *The Legacy of the Exposition*. San Francisco: J. H. Nash, 1915.

Bieder, Robert E. *Science Encounters the Indian, 1820–1880*. Norman: U of Oklahoma P, 1986.

Blauner, Robert. *Racial Oppression in America*. New York: Harper and Row, 1975.

Bruce-Novoa, Juan. "Canonical and Non-Canonical Texts." *The Americas Review* 14.3-4 (1986): 119-35.

Castañeda, Carlos E., ed. and trans. *The Mexican Side of the Texas Revolution, 1836, by the Chief Mexican Participants*. Austin: Graphic Ideas, 1970.

Chávez, John R. *The Lost Land: The Chicano Image of the Southwest*. Albuquerque: U of New Mexico P, 1984.

Christman, Florence. *The Romance of Balboa Park*. San Diego: Neyenesch, 1985.

De la Peña, José Enrique. *With Santa Anna in Texas: A Personal Narrative of the Revolution*. College Station: Texas A & M UP, 1975.

Elliott, Emory, ed. *Columbia Literary History of the United States*. New York: Columbia UP, 1988.

Espinosa, Aurelio M. *España en Nuevo Méjico*. New York: Scribner's, 1937.

————. *The Folklore of Spain in the American Southwest*. Norman: U of Oklahoma P, 1985.

Genovese, Eugene D. "Class and Nationality in Black America." *In Red and Black: Marxian Explorations in Southern and Afro-American History*. Ed. Eugene D. Genovese. New York: Random, 1971. 55–72.

González, Nancy. *The Spanish Americans of New Mexico: A Heritage of Pride*. Albuquerque: U of New Mexico P, 1969.

González Calleja, Eduardo. *La hispanidad como instrumento de combate*. Madrid: Centro de Estudios Históricos, 1988.

Gould, Stephen Jay. *The Mismeasure of Man*. New York: W. W. Norton, 1981.

Guerra Ord, Angustias de la. *Occurrences in Hispanic California*. Eds. Francis Price and William H. Ellison. Washington, D.C.: Academy of American Franciscan History, 1956.

Gutiérrez, Ramón A. "Unraveling America's Hispanic Past: Internal Stratification and Class Bounderies." *Aztlán: A Journal of Chicano Studies* 17.1 (1986): 79–101.

Hammond, George P. and Agapito Rey, eds. and trans. *Don Juan de Oñate: Colonizer of New Mexico, 1595–1628*. Albuquerque: U of New Mexico P, 1953.

Híjar, Carlos N., Eulalia Pérez and Agustín Escobar. *Three Memoirs of Mexican California*. Berkeley: Friends of the Bancroft Library, 1988.

Hobsbawm, Eric J. *Nations and Nationalism since 1780*. Cambridge: Cambridge UP, 1990.

————. and Terrence Ranger, eds. *The Invention of Tradition*. Cambridge: Cambridge UP, 1983.

Hodge, Frederick W., George P. Hammond and Agapito Rey, eds. and trans. *Fray Alonso de Benavides' Revised Memorial of 1634*. Albuquerque: U of New Mexico P, 1945.

James, Juliet. *Palaces and Courts of the Exposition*. San Francisco: California Book, 1915.

Keen, Benjamin. *The Aztec Image in Western Thought*. New Brunswick, NJ: Rutgers UP, 1971.

Lomelí, Francisco and Donald Urioste, eds. *Chicano Perspectives in Literature: A Critical and Annotated Bibliography*. Albuquerque: Parajito, 1976.

Lugo, José del Carmen. *'Vida de un ranchero,' a History of San Bernadino Valley*. San Bernadino, CA: San Bernadino County Museum Association, 1961.

Macober, Ben. *The Jewel City*. San Francisco: J. H. Williams, 1915.

Márquez, Antonio. "Literature Chicanesque." *A Decade of Chicano Literature (1969–1979)*. Eds. Luis Leal, et. al. Santa Barbara, CA: La Causa, 1982.

Menchaca, Antonio. *Memoirs*. San Antonio: Yanaguana Society, 1937.

Metzgar, Joseph V. "The Ethnic Sensitivity of Spanish New Mexicans: A Survey and Analysis." *New Mexico Historical Review* 49.1 (1974): 35–59.

Mortí, Fray Juan Agustín. *History of Texas, 1673–1779*. Albuquerque: Quivira, 1935.

Morin, Claude. *Among the Valiant: Mexican Americans in WWII and Korea*. Alhambra, CA: Borden, 1966.

Pérez de Villagrá, Gaspar. *History of New Mexico, 1610*. Los Angeles: Quivira, 1933.

Pico, Pío. Don Pío Pico's Historical Narrative. Glendale, CA: A. H. Clark, 1973.

Pike, Frederick. *Hispanismo, 1898–1936*. Notre Dame: Notre Dame UP, 1971.

Pray-Palmer, Lillian. *A Book of Memories for the Ages: A Pictorial Aftermath from the Panama-California Exposition*. San Diego: L. D. Gregory, 1925.

Rodríguez, Antonio Niño. *Cultura y diplomacia: los hispanistas franceses y España de 1875 a 1931*. Madrid: CSIC, 1988.

Rodríguez, José María. *Rodríguez Memoirs of Early Texas*. San Antonio: Standard Printing, 1961.

Seguín, Juan de. *A Revolution Remembered: The Memoirs and Selected Correspondence of Juan N. Seguín*. Ed. Jesús de la Teja. Austin: State House, 1991.

Sollors, Werner, ed. *The Invention of Ethnicity*. New York: Oxford UP, 1989.

Spiller, Robert E. ed. *Literary History of the United States*. New York: Macmillan, 1948.

Trent, William Peterfield, ed. *Cambridge History of American Literature*. New York: Macmillan, 1946.

Weigle, Marta and Peter White, eds. *The Lore of New Mexico*. Albuquerque: U of New Mexico P, 1988.

Ycaza Tigerino, Julio César. *Perfil político y cultural de Hispanoamérica*. Madrid: Cultura Hispánica, 1971.

PART IV
Literary Sources and Research Opportunities

Hispanic Literature: The Colonial Period

José B. Fernández

It was near the end of the fifteenth century when the nations of Europe set in motion the discovery and exploration of the Americas. The glory of discovering, exploring, conquering and colonizing this vast mass of land for more than a century and a half practically fell to one nation, Spain. The Hispanic heritage of what is now the United States begins in 1513 when the Spanish explorer Juan Ponce de León landed on the coast of Florida, ninety-four years before the British arrival at Jamestown. Although La Florida—the territory which extended from Florida northward to the Chesapeake and westward to Texas—was lacking in gold and silver, it was no cause for Spain to abandon her presence in this area. Her daring citizens explored and colonized this territory, and even expanded the Spanish domains as far west as California. Their observations, experiences and deeds were recorded in prose, poetry and drama.

Spanish colonial literature, produced in what became the United States, resembles the literature of the other Spanish colonies in the western hemisphere. The early literary period—covering the sixteenth and seventeenth centuries—contains plays, ballads and even epic poetry. Yet it was dominated by *relaciones*, *memoriales* and *cartas* that were written as official reports to the authorities and concerned incidents, results of reconnaissance outings, official acts of inspection tours, or the state and nature of the inhabitants of a particular region (Jackson 1). Most of the literature of this early colonial period is simple, utilitarian and practical, yet its contents reflect the exotic American scenery with its inhabitants, flora and fauna. It is not a literature for the sake of literature; it is a literature that provides information (Alarcón 2).

The literature encompassing the eighteenth century and the first twenty-one years of the nineteenth century contains its share of chronicles and *memoriales*, but it offers a more varied panorama, for it is rich in plays, ballads, lyric poetry, songs, short stories, *alabados* (morning songs), *pastorelas* (Christmas plays), *posadas* (shepherd plays) and folk tales. Most of these were in oral form, but they were collected and appear in publications such as Arthur L. Campa's *Spanish Folk Poetry in New Mexico*; Aurelio M. Espinosa's *Romancero nuevomejicano*, and Juan B. Rael's *Cuentos españoles de Colorado y de Nuevo México*. Unfortunately, American writers and literary historians have tended to minimize and even ostracize this Spanish colonial literature as part of the literary history of the United States primarily because it was written in Spanish (Alarcon 1). But as Professor Thomas Pearce stated in his "American Traditions and Our Histories of Literature": "Language does not seem to be a logical bar to recognition of non-English material as literature of the United States" (280).

Judging by Pearce's statement, Spanish colonial literature is indeed significant and worthy of study as part of the literature of the United States. Still, the few times that Spanish colonial literature appears in American literature textbooks, it appears as part of a foreign enterprise rather than as part and parcel of our American heritage.

In spite of America's linguistic chauvinism, attempts were made to extricate Spanish colonial literature from its desolate state. In 1929, for example, George P. Hammond, Frederick W. Hodge and Henry R. Wagner organized The Quivira Society for the purpose of a documentary publication series on the Spanish Southwest. Between 1929 and 1958, thirteen translations of Spanish colonial works and the impressive bibliography *The Spanish Southwest 1542–1795* were published by the society. Yet the series was inadequately financed; the editors received no compensation, and generally contributed compilations solely on what they were interested in, which often related to secondary works they had written. A systematic chronological series, such as those published by some of the eastern and midwestern states on their colonial periods, would have been more satisfactory (Beers 37). Fortunately, The Rockefeller Foundation has provided funding to undertake the project of Recovering the Hispanic Literary Heritage of the United States. Spanish colonial literature is included in this undertaking.

Selecting the colonial works to be edited, reissued and compiled is not an easy task, and mapping out the territory in a chronological and geographical fashion is also a difficult one. Nevertheless, I have tried to seek some possible venues.

I am of the opinion that an anthology of Spanish colonial literature of the United States, incorporating different literary genres arranged in either a chronological or topical manner will be of great value. It will be an important instrument for the literary scholar, linguist, folklorist, historian and anthropologist as well as the general public. In addition, it will provide additional insights for an understanding of the life of the early Spanish settlers in what later became the United States. Finally, this anthology will also offer an authentic panorama of the Spanish colonial heritage of the United States.

As to individual works, there is a definite need to prepare critical editions and translations incorporating the latest research findings. Following is an annotated bibliography containing selected works which I consider significant in Spanish colonial literature of the United States. Spelling and punctuation have been modernized.

1. Acuña, Juan de. *Reglamento para todos los presidios de las provincias internas de esta Gobernación, con el Número de oficiales y soldados que unos y otros habrán de gozar. Ordenanzas para el mejor gobierno, y disciplina militar de gobernadores, oficiales y soldados. Prevenciones para los que en ellas se comprenden: precios de los víveres, y vestuarios, con que a los soldados se les asiste y se les habrá de continuar. Hecho por El Excmo. Señor Marqués de Casa-Fuerte, Virrey, Gobernador y Capitán General de estos Reinos.* México: Imprenta de la Viuda de Miguel de Rivera Calderón, 1729.

A comprehensive set of regulations issued by Juan de Acuña, Marquis of Casa-Fuerte and Viceroy of New Spain to the Spanish garrisons north of the Rio Grande. The manuscript is the first series of regulations issued to the garrisons. It provides valuable information regarding the everyday life of the Spanish soldiers in the Southwest. It also contains interesting information regarding the interaction between Spanish soldiers and Indians.

2. Ascensión, Antonio de la. *Relación de la jornada que hizo el general Sebastián Vizcaíno al descubrimiento de las Californias en el año de 1602, por mandado del Excmo. Sr. Conde de Monterey, Virrey que era de Nueva España.* 1603.

One of several accounts written by Antonio de la Ascensión concerning the second expedition of Sebastián de Vizcaíno to California in 1602–1603. Superficial in terms of information concerning the inhabitants of California, but a moving account regarding the vicissitudes of the Spaniards. The original manuscript is in the Newberry Library in Chicago.

3. "Auto de la aparición de Nuestra Señora de Guadalupe." *Literary Folklore of the Hispanic Southwest.* Ed. Aurora Lucero-White Lea. San Antonio: The Naylor Company, 1953.

A religious Spanish play presented in New Mexico since Spanish colonial days. Written in octosyllabic verse, the play centers on the apparition of the Virgin Mary to the Indian Juan Diego in Mexico in 1531.

4. Benavides, Fray Alonso de. *Memorial que Fray Juan de Santander de la Orden de San Francisco, Comisario General de Indias, presenta a la Majestad Católica del Rey, don Felipe Cuarto Nuestro Señor. Hecho Por*

el Padre Fray Alonso de Benavides, Comisario del Santo Oficio y Custodio que ha sido de las provincias y conversiones del Nuevo-México. Madrid: Imprenta Real, 1630.

A simple and utilitarian account concerning the Franciscan missionary efforts in New Mexico. The *Memorial* gives an interesting portrait of the Pueblos and their relations with the Spanish colonizers. It also provides some of the early folktales of the Southwest. An original copy of the *Memorial* is in the Archivo General de Indias in Seville, Spain.

5. Castañeda de Nágera, Pedro de. *Relación de la jornada de Cíbola compuesta por Pedro de Castañeda de Nágera, donde se trata de todos aquellos poblados y ritos y costumbres, la cual fue en el año de 1540.* Sevilla, 1596.

A graphic account of Francisco Vázquez de Coronado's expedition to the Southwest (1540–1542), and a valuable source of information concerning the social, political, economic and cultural organization of the Indians of the Southwest. The original manuscript is in the Lenox Branch of the New York Public Library.

6. Castellanos, Juan de. *Elegías de varones ilustres de Indias.* Madrid, 1584.

A collection of octaves praising the deeds of the Spanish conquistadores. The poems offer a panoramic view of the Spanish conquest of the Americas. The "Canto Séptimo" concentrates on the deeds of Juan Ponce de León, discoverer of Florida.

7. "Coloquio de los pastores." *Literary Folklore of the Hispanic Southwest.* Ed. Aurora Lucero White-Lea. San Antonio: The Naylor Company, 1953.

Probably the most popular Nativity play in New Mexico. Its plot is as follows: A group of shepherds are going to visit the Child Jesus in Bethlehem but Lucifer tries to prevent the visit. The Archangel Michael appears and defeats Lucifer. After Lucifer's defeat, the shepherds continue their trek to Bethlehem bearing gifts to the newborn child. The play is rich in *coplas*, the most popular verse form of the Spanish Southwest. The play was probably brought to New Mexico by Spanish colonists during the eighteenth century.

8. Dávila Padilla, Fray Agustín. *Historia de la fundación y discurso de la provincia de Santiago de México de la Orden de Predicadores, por las vidas de sus varones insignes y casos notables de Nueva España.* Valladolid, 1596.

Written in 1596 by the personal preacher of King Philip II, the *Historia* narrates the ill-fated voyage of Father Luis Cáncer de Barbastro and four other Dominican missionaries to Florida in 1549. The missionaries were killed by the Indians shortly after their arrival. Dávila Padilla, however, forgives the Indians and denounces the conquistadores as abusers. The *Historia* is a worthy example of the use of irony in Spanish colonial literature of the United States.

9. Domínguez, Fray Francisco Atanasio, y Vélez de Escalante, Fray Silvestre. *Diario y derrotero de los R.R.P.P. Fray Francisco Atanasio Domínguez y Fray Silvestre Vélez de Escalante para descubrir el camino desde el Presidio de Santa Fe del Nuevo México, al de Monterey en la California Septentrional. 1776.*

A diary of the expedition of Fathers Domínguez and Escalante from Santa Fe to Monterey in 1776. It is one of the most interesting accounts of Spanish exploration of the Inter-mountain Basin and a tale of true adventure. It contains interesting observations concerning what is now the state of Colorado. A copy of the original is in the Archivo General de Indias in Seville, Spain.

10. Escalante Fontaneda, Hernando de. *Memorial de las cosas, costa e indios de la Florida.* Tomo 5 de la *Colección de documentos inéditos relativos al descubrimiento, conquista y colonización de las antiguas posesiones españolas de América y Oceanía.* 42 tomos. Madrid, 1864–1884.

Although not as thorough as Álvar Núñez Cabeza de Vaca's *La Relación*, the *Memorial* of Escalante Fontaneda contains notable observations concerning the inhabitants of Florida. Shipwrecked in 1551 at the age of thirteen, Escalante Fontaneda lived for seventeen years with the legendary Indian chieftain Carlos of southern Florida. He wrote the *Memorial* in 1567 after he was rescued by Spanish soldiers.

11. Escobedo, Fray Alonso de. *La Florida.* Madrid, ca. 1609.

Probably written in 1609, *La Florida* is considered to be Florida's first epic poem. Some even consider it to be America's first epic poem, although the specific date of composition casts a doubt on the claim. The 449 page original manuscript is in the Biblioteca Nacional in Madrid, Spain. The poem narrates the christianizing efforts of twelve Franciscan missionaries that came to Florida in 1587. It is worthy of study not only as a historical document, but also as an extraordinary piece of literature.

12. Espejo, Antonio de. *Relación del viaje, que yo, Antonio Espejo, ciudadano de la ciudad de México, natural de Córdoba, hice con catorce soldados y un religioso de la orden de San Francisco, a las provincias y poblaciones de la Nueva México, a quien puse por nombre la Nueva Andalucía, a contemplación de mi patria, en fin del año mil quinientos ochenta y dos.* México, 1584.

An account of the expedition led by Fray Bernardino Beltrán and Antonio de Espejo that went to New Mexico to rescue a number of Franciscan friars that remained behind after participating in the expedition of Francisco

Sánchez Chamuscado in 1581. The expedition failed to accomplish its goal, for the friars were killed by the natives prior to Beltrán and Espejo's arrival. Espejo's account started the myth of the Golden Lake in western Arizona.

13. Farfán de los Godos, Marcos. "Los Moros y Cristianos." *Literary Folklore of the Hispanic Southwest.* Ed. Aurora Lucero White-Lea. San Antonio: The Naylor Company, 1953.

Composed in 1598 by a captain in Juan de Oñate's expedition to New Mexico, the play was performed in the neighborhood of present day El Paso. The play commemorates the victory of the Spaniards over the Moors during the *Reconquista.* Captain Farfán, however, connected the subject matter with the conquest of New Mexico. Some consider it the first play in America's literary history.

14. Flores, Bartolomé de. "Obra nuevamente compuesta en la cual se cuenta la feliz victoria que Dios por su infinita bondad y misericordia fue servido de dar al ilustre señor Pedro Menéndez, Almirante y Capitán de la Gobernación de la Florida, contra Juan Ribao de nación francesa, con otros mil luteranos, a los cuales pasó a filo de espada. Con otras curiosidades que pone el autor de las viviendas de los indios de la Florida, y sus naturales facciones." Ed. José Toribio Medina. *Biblioteca Hispanoamericana.* Santiago de Chile: Impreso y grabado en casa del autor, 1898.

A lengthy and rather bombastic poem lauding Pedro Menéndez de Avilés' victory over the French Huguenots in Florida in 1565. Although the poem contains more fiction than fact, it represents a colorful picture of the conquest of Florida.

15. Gallegos, Hernán. *Relación y conclusión del viaje y suceso que Francisco Sánchez Chamuscado con ocho soldados, sus compañeros, hizo en el descubrimiento del Nuevo México en junio de 1581.*

An account of the journey of the Agustín Rodríguez-Francisco Chamuscado expedition to conduct missionary activities in New Mexico. Although the expedition never realized its objective, the account helped to maintain interest in the exploration of New Mexico. A copy of the original manuscript is located in the Archivo General de Indias in Seville, Spain.

16. Garcilaso de la Vega, el Inca. *La Florida del Inca. Historia del Adelantado Hernando de Soto, Gobernador y Capitán General del Reino de la Florida, y de otros heroicos caballeros españoles e indios.* Lisboa: Pedro Craasbeck, 1605.

La Florida del Inca is the lengthiest chronicle of Hernando de Soto's expedition to Florida and the Southeastern United States (1539–1542). Historians have questioned the chronicle's historical reliability for Garcilaso was never part of Hernando de Soto's expedition, nor was he ever in Florida. On the other hand, critics regard it as a literary masterpiece reminiscent of the contemporary romances of chivalry. Garcilaso, the first *mestizo* writer of the Americas illustrates the bravery of both the Spanish conquistadores and the Indians of Florida.

17. Gonzalez de Barcia, Andrés. *Ensayo cronológico para La historia general de La Florida.* Madrid: Nicolás Rodríguez Franco, 1723.

A chronological work detailing the Spanish, French and British colonial periods in North America with emphasis on the conquest of Florida by Pedro Menéndez de Avilés in 1565. The *Ensayo* also covers the expeditions of Pánfilo de Narváez, Francisco Vázquez de Coronado and Hernando de Soto.

18. Kino, Eusebio Francisco. *Favores celestiales de Jesús y de María Santísima y del gloriosísimo Apóstol de las Indias S. Francisco Xavier, experimentados en las nuevas conquistas y nuevas conversiones del Nuevo Reino de la Nueva Navarra de esta América Septentrional e incógnita, y paso por tierra a la California en 35 grados de altura, 1699–1710.*

A personal account of Father Kino's missionary works among the Pimas of Arizona and his vision for expanding the Catholic faith. It is a document of deep personal and spiritual development of the priest who spent twenty-four years with the Indians. A copy of the manuscript is in the Archivo de México.

19. León, Alonso de. "Historia de Nuevo León con noticias sobre Coahuila, Tejas y Nuevo México, por el capitán Alonso de León, un autor anónimo, y el general Fernando Sánchez de Zamora." Ed. Genaro García. *Documentos Inéditos o muy Raros para la Historia de México.* México, 1902.

A curious account dealing with Alonso de Leon's five expeditions to Texas (1686–1690). It is a valuable source of information regarding Franco-Spanish rivalry in the borderlands.

20. *Los Comanches.* Ed. Aurelio Espinosa. *University of New Mexico Bulletin*, Language Series, 1. (1907).

Composed of some 600 lines of octosyllabic verse, *Los Comanches* is a secular play that depicts the Spanish victory over the Comanche tribe in northern New Mexico and southern Colorado in the eighteenth century. The play glorifies both the Spanish victors and the vanquished Comanches. In addition, it offers interesting insights into the life of the Spanish colonists and their relationship with the marauding Comanches. The play was written in the latter part of the eighteenth century but the text first appeared in 1907.

21. Martire d'Anghiera, Pietro. *De Orbe Novo.* Alcalá de Henares, 1530.

Known in Spain as Pedro Mártir de Anglería, the author is considered to be the first historian of the Americas. Although written in Latin, his collection of decades contains a wealth of information on the Americas. Of special interest is the treatment of Ponce de León and the mythical Fountain of Youth and the expedition of Lucas Vázquez de Ayllón to present day South Carolina in 1520. The first edition of *De Orbe Novo* in Spanish did not appear until 1892.

22. Montoya, Juan de. *Relación del descubimiento del Nuevo México, y de otras muchas provincias halladas de nuevo. Venida de las Indias a España, y de allí mandada a Roma.* Roma: Bartolomé Bonfadino, 1602.

Although abundant in digressions, Montaya's *Relación* is the first published account of Juan de Oñate's expedition to New Mexico. It also contains the *Relación de las provincias descubiertas en el año 1598* written by Juan de Oñate himself.

23. Niza, Fray Marcos de. "Relación del Descubrimiento de las siete ciudades por el P. Fr. Marcos de Niza." Tomo 3 de la *Colección de documentos inéditos relativos al descubrimiento, conquista, y colonización de las antiguas posesiones españolas de América y Oceanía.* 42 tomos. Madrid, 1864–1884.

An account of Fray Marcos de Niza's expedition to New Mexico in 1537 that was given to the authorities in Mexico in 1539. Niza's sighting of the mythical and gold-laden Seven Cities of Cíbola is still a subject of controversy. The original manuscript is located in the Archivo General de Indias in Seville, Spain.

24. Núñez Cabeza de Vaca, Álvar. *La relación que dio Álvar Núñez Cabeza de Vaca de lo acaecido en las Indias en la armada donde iba por gobernador Pánfilo de Narváez desde el año de veinte y siete hasta de treinta y seis que volvió a Sevilla con tres de su compañía.* Zamora, 1542.

An account of the ill-fated expedition of Pánfilo de Narváez to Florida in 1528 and Álvar Núñez Cabeza de Vaca's wanderings on the North American continent (1528–1536). The *Relación* is a narrative of considerable literary merit and the prototype of the genre of true adventure. It provides excellent information on the flora, fauna and inhabitants of Florida and the present day American Southwest. Three copies of the original edition are in existence at the Lenox Branch of the New York Public Library, the British Museum and the John Carter Brown Library.

25. Palao, Francisco. *Relación histórica de la vida y apostólicas tareas del venerable Padre Fray Junípero Serra, y de las misiones que fundó en la California Septentrional, y nuevo establecimiento de Monterey.* México: Imprenta de don Felipe de Zúñiga y Ontiveros, 1787.

An account of the life and works of Father Junípero Serra, founder of the California Mission Trail. It is a moving biography and a document of value for those interested in the California missions.

CLa relacion que dio Aluar nu
ñez cabeça de vaca de lo acaeſcido enlas Jndias
enla armada donde yua poz gouernadoz pã
philo de narbaez deſde el año de veynte
y ſiete haſta el año ð treynta y ſeys
que boluio a Seuilla con tres
de ſu compañia.:.

The title page of the first edition of Cabeza de Vaca's *La relación*, 1542.

26. Pérez de Villagrá, Gaspar. *Historia de la Nueva México, del capitán Gaspar de Villagrá. Dirigida al Rey D. Felipe Nuestro Señor Tercero de este nombre.* Alcalá de Henares: Impreso por Luis Martínez Grande, 1610.

A poem of more than 12,000 hendecasyllable lines, *Historia de la Nueva México* is one of the most striking works in Spanish colonial literature of the United States and probably America's first epic poem. The poem begins with Oñate's march into New Mexico from Mexico City (1596) and concludes with the storming of the Acoma Pueblo by the Spaniards in 1599. The whereabouts of the original manuscript is unknown but a facsimile reprint was published in Mexico City in 1900 by the Museo Nacional de México.

27. Pino, Pedro Bautista. *Exposición succinta y sencilla del Nuevo México.* Cádiz, 1812.

An interesting report written by the first New Mexican Representative to the Spanish Cortes to acquaint the Spaniards with New Mexico. The *Exposición* calls for the Cortes to initiate a reform program in New Mexico. It depicts Spanish life in New Mexico and speaks well of the Navajos and Comanches.

28. Ranjel, Rodrigo. "Diario." *Historia general y natural de las Indias, Islas y Tierra Firme del Mar Océano.* Ed. Gonzalo Fernández de Oviedo y Valdés. Madrid, 1557.

A diary of Hernando de Soto's expedition written by De Soto's personal secretary. It contains interesting descriptions of the land as well as the characters of the inhabitants. The *Diario* is characterized by Ranjel's scathing comments regarding De Soto's cruel treatment of the natives.

29. Sáenz de San Antonio, Matías. *Señor, si el pastor no escucha el quejido de la oveja, si el padre no oye el llanto de sus hijos, si el Señor no atiende al ay de sus vasallos, no podrá compadecerse su obligación amorosa en las necesidades.* Madrid, 1724.

A witty and most exhilarating plea by a missionary in northeastern Texas begging the Spanish officials to send colonists to Texas. The author portrays Texas as an Arcadia. An original copy is located in the Archivo General de Indias in Seville, Spain.

30. San Miguel, Fray Andrés de. "Relación de los trabajos que la gente de una nave llamada Nuestra Señora de la Merced padeció, y de algunas cosas que en aquella flota sucedieron." *Dos antiguas relaciones de la Florida.* Ed. Genaro García. Mexico: J. Aguilar Vera y Cía., 1902.

An adventure filled account of a sinking Spanish ship off the coast of Florida and its survivors. The *Relación* narrates the Spaniards' ordeal and their lives among the natives of Florida's east coast. Although the event happened in the late sixteenth century, the account was not published until 1902.

31. Solís de Merás, Gonzalo. "Memorial que hizo el Dr. Gonzalo Solís de Merás, de todas las jornadas y sucesos del Adelantado Pedro Menéndez de Avilés, su cuñado, y de la conquista de la Florida, y justicia que hizo en Juan Ribao y otros franceses." *La Florida, su conquista y colonización por Pedro Menéndez de Avilés.* Ed. Eugenio Ruidíaz y Caravia. Madrid: Hijos de J. A. García, 1893.

Written in 1567, by Menéndez's brother-in-law, the *Memorial* is a personal but evaluative account of Menéndez's conquest of Florida. The chronicler is thorough and meticulous and the *Memorial* is considered to be Menéndez's best biography.

32. Torquemada, Fray Juan de. *Primera parte de Los veinte y un libros rituales y monarquía indiana con el origen y guerras de los indios occidentales, y de sus poblaciones, descubrimiento, conquista, conversión y otras cosas maravillosas de la misma tierra. Distribuidos en tres tomos compuestos por Fray Juan de Torquemada, Ministro Provincial de la Orden de Nuestro Seráfico Padre S. Francisco en la Provincia del Santo Evangelio de México en la Nueva España.* Sevilla: Matías Clavijo, 1615.

Although the majority of the *Monarquía indiana* is concentrated on providing information on the natives of Mexico, the book gives the accounts of the expeditions of Coronado, Oñate, Vizcaíno and Rodriguez and Chamuscado. Parts of the book narrate the Franciscan missionary activities in Florida, as well as the colonizing efforts of Tristán de Luna and Andrés de Villafañe in Florida and present day South Carolina prior to Menéndez's arrival.

33. Venegas, Miguel. *Noticia de la California y de su conquista temporal y espiritual hasta el tiempo presente, sacada de la historia manuscrita formada en México, año de 1739, por el Padre Miguel Venegas de la Compañía de Jesús.* Madrid: Imprenta de la Viuda de Manuel Fernández y del Supremo Consejo de la Inquisición, 1757.

This scholarly treatise depicts the works of the Jesuits in California during the first half of the eighteenth century. It provides a physical description of California as well as an account of the different Spanish attempts to settle California until the arrival of the Jesuit Order.

Works Cited

Alarcón, Jorge. "*Historia de la Nueva Mexico.* A Spanish Colonial Epic Poem of the Southwest." Unpublished essay, 1975.

Beers, Henry Putney. *Spanish and Mexican Records of the American Southwest.* Tucson: U of Arizona P, 1979.

Campa, Arthur L. *Spanish Folk Poetry in New Mexico.* Albuquerque: U of New Mexico P, 1946.

Espinosa, Aurelio M. "Romancero nuevomejicano." *Revue Hispanique* 33 (1915): 446–560.

Jackson, W. R. *Early Florida Through Spanish Eyes*. Coral Gables: U of Miami P, 1954.

Pearce, Thomas M. "American Traditions and Our Histories of Literature." *American Literature* 14.3 (November 1942): 277–84.

Rael, Juan B. *Cuentos españoles de Colorado y de Nuevo México*. 2 Vols. Stanford: Stanford UP, 1971.

Wagner, Henry R. *The Spanish Southwest*. 2 vols. Los Angeles: Quivira, 1937.

Memory, Language and Voice of Mestiza Women on the Northern Frontier: Historical Documents as Literary Text

Antonia I. Castañeda

> My father . . . came to Upper California with Captain Rivera, the first settler of the city of San Diego, and afterwards emigrated to Monterey, where I was born in 1793 . . . . I have witnessed every event which has transpired since that time, but, being a woman, I was denied the privilege of mixing in politics or in business. My education has been very limited, yet my memory is good.
>
> Dorotea Valdez, Monterey, California, 1874

A significant part of Spanish colonial literature consists of the chronicles of exploration, conquest and colonization written by missionaries, explorers and others who witnessed the events. The memories, words and interpretations of women who witnessed these and other events are not, however, part of the texts that historically have constituted the body of colonial literature of the Spanish borderlands (Jara and Spadaccini 9–50, Franco xi–xiv). Instead, the women who do appear in the literature of the colonial period are represented and interpreted by male writers (Virgillo and Lindstrom, Johnson). Precisely because gender, as well as social class and race, circumscribed the access of colonial women to literacy, their literary voice, with very few and notable exceptions, has been virtually silent.

According to Lynn Hunt (18) and Rolena Adorno (173–91), gender is a critical, in fact essential, line of differentiation in culture and society that must be included in any discussion of cultural unity and difference. Nevertheless, only very recently has gender become central to discussions and analyses of literature. For scholars of California's history, this lacuna is even more glaring. Few works chronicle representations of women in history, and fewer still study the literary voices of mestiza women in eighteenth- and nineteenth-century California.[1] To date, only one brief articles examining Spanish-speaking women's autobiographical voice in nineteenth-century California has been published (Padilla, " 'Yo sola aprendí' ... ").

Although historians have begun to examine the centrality of gender to the politics of New Spain's conquest and colonization, we still know almost nothing about gender differences in artistic and literary representations (Castañeda, *Presidiarias y Pobladoras* 63–113). How do racial and class distinctions affect representations of gender? How do ideas and images of gender differ for women and men? How do women imagine themselves? How do they imagine men? Do men imagine women differently than women imagine themselves? Contemporary Chicana/o literature certainly allows us to answer these questions for the twentieth century, but we do not know what mestiza women thought about or imagined or how they represented themselves during the eighteenth and nineteenth centuries in the Spanish borderlands.

One particularly important example of how men have represented women in Spanish colonial literature is their equation of woman with land (Todorov). Much has been written about women as a metaphor and emblem for land, as well as for nation. Both women and land are conquered, tamed, husbanded and seeded. The very name California, shrouded as it is in mystery and legend involving beautiful, black Amazonian women, is a prime example of the way in which women are perceived as a category of nature in men's minds.

The image of California as land and as woman first appeared in *Las sergas de esplandían* (1510), the chivalric novel by Garci Ordóñez de Montalvo. In this work, the Christian hero, Amadis of Gaul, meets Calafia—the beautiful but wild and ferocious black Amazonian queen—on California, an island situated next to the earthly paradise. Calafia and her army of black female warriors tame and mount fearsome flying griffins, wield weapons of pure gold and battle their male opponents while mounted on these flying creatures. The women feed the griffins the enemy men captured on the battlefield, sparing a few for purposes of procreation. When the children are born, the females are kept and the males immediately are killed.

The troops of Amadis and Calafia repeatedly engage in furious battles, and, although initially it appears that Calafia will win, the griffins turn on their mistresses, who eventually lose to the Christian heroes. Calafia is captured. She recants, converts to Christianity and marries one of Amadis' lieutenants. In this story, published ten years before the conquest of Mexico, the black Amazonian queen Calafia, like the land named for her, is conquered, Christianized and married to one of her Christian captors. The conquest of the beautiful but savage land—as woman—is complete.

Male representation of the land as female and of the females on the land—whether Amerindian or Mexican—as not only being conquered but participating in their own conquest, is a common theme in Spanish fiction, poetry and historical documents from the sixteenth to the nineteenth centuries, from Patagonia to California (Castillo, Castañeda, *Presidiarias y Pobladoras* 35–9). Tzvetan Todorov, in his examination of the writings of Bartolomé de las Casas and other sixteenth-century writers agrees, finding that las Casas, "just like Sepúlveda, identifies the colony with a woman; and there is no question of emancipation of either woman or Indians" (9). Moreover, Calafia is described as black, which in sixteenth-century Spain was a symbol for a non-Christian. As a woman, as a non-Christian, and as a person of dark skin, Calafia, in the minds of men, is the consummate symbol of the alien other.

Although much remains to be learned about how women are represented textually by men, the issue of most immediate concern here is how women represented and interpreted themselves. What discourses did mestiza women articulate in California? Did they change the way they represented themselves and others as reality changed from the mid-eighteenth century, when mestiza women arrived in Alta California under the auspices of Spanish colonization, to the mid-nineteenth century, when the United States conquered and colonized California?

What language, or languages, and what form—written, oral, material artifacts—did women use to express themselves? Which mediums of expression did women employ most often? When women are textually represented, are we reading their own voices or words that are mediated through male narrators? What was colonial women's consciousness in Alta California, and how was it expressed? How do the narratives of women depict hierarchy, domination and power? Did colonial women wage a struggle for interpretive power? If so, where and how? How does the concept of colonial literature as the "literature of conquest" apply to women, whose lives, irrespective of race or class, were circumscribed by gender hierarchies (Jara and Spadaccini).

Answering these questions with reference to the women of Spanish and Mexican California is not easy because few women were literate, and those who were generally did not leave written memoirs, diaries, essays, stories, poetry or novels. They left no works that fit the canonical genres of literary production. Nevertheless, I would like to propose here that through discourse analysis we can recover women's voices, language and representations (Jara and Spadaccini, Adorno 174–75). Rolena Adorno describes discourse analysis as "the study of interactive, relational, dialogic and synchronic cultural practices" (182–83). Discourse analysis enables us to examine historical documents generated, if not always written, by women as a basis for understanding women's subjectivities. We can also examine oral, visual and other non-written forms of expression and communication to help us understand how colonial women represented themselves. The following sections contextualize experiences of women in eighteenth- and nineteenth-century California, provide a socio-racial profile of mestiza women on the California borderlands, and discuss the kinds of historical documents that reveal women's multiple voices, memories and interpretations.

Context and Socio-Racial Profile
of Mestiza Women as Subjects

Although additional work on gender and gender difference may lead us to define new historical periods and new literary chronologies for the Spanish and Mexican far northern frontier, I examine documents written by or for women during standard historical periods: the Spanish colonial period (1769–1821), the Mexican national period (1822–48), and the early United States period (1849–1900) (Bean). Who were the Spanish-speaking women who migrated to and settled Spain's northernmost outpost, which was established as a religious and military frontier in 1769 and subsidized by the Crown through the Department of War and by the Church via the Franciscan College's Pious Fund? (Castañeda, *Presidiarias y Pobladoras* 114–73). Anna María Hurtado, her two teenage daughters and five other women who made the eighty-two-day sea voyage from San Blas in the winter of 1773-74, were the first group of Spanish-speaking women in Alta California. With their families, the eight women constituted the first artisan, administrative and professional group recruited to serve for six years in the missions and presidios of this remote colony. These women, who came from what may be considered the middle strata of eighteenth-century colonial Mexican society, did not remain or settle in Alta California because military officials failed to meet the terms of their contracts. Neither did women from the upper strata of colonial society remain in Alta California. The few Spanish- and American-born wives and kinswomen of colonial governors who came here returned to Spain or Mexico at the end of their husbands' terms.

Most of the women who settled Alta California were from New Spain's lowest socioeconomic classes (Bolton, Campbell, Mourhead). They were *mestizas*, the racially mixed and Amerindian wives, daughters and kin of leather-jacket soldiers who staffed the frontier presidios, of impoverished settlers who lived in the adjoining civilian pueblos and of convicts from

México City and Guadalajara sentenced to this remote military colony in lieu of other punishment (Bancroft, Campbell, Jones). Some of the impoverished soldier-settler families recruited and subsidized to colonize this frontier eventually became the elite "Californio" families of the Mexican period, including those of María Martina Castro, Josefa María Vallejo, María Petra Josefa Carrillo and Ana Joaquina Alvarado (Northrup 7, 99, 104, 350; Lynch).

In addition to the women of the soldier-settler families, their native-born mestiza daughters and the daughters of Indian women who married Catalán and mestizo soldiers, the Spanish-speaking female population in colonial California included the womenfolk related to lesser administrators, storekeepers and doctors.

The first *presidarias* and *pobladoras* were recruited to Alta California in three colonizing expeditions of soldier-settler families from Sonora and Sinaloa: the expeditions led by Fernando Rivera y Moncada in 1774 and 1781, and the expedition led by Juan Bautista de Anza in 1775–76. The wives of *reo-pobladores* (convict settlers) accompanied or followed their spouses. After the Yuma Indians closed the overland route in 1781, the government's settlement strategy shifted from recruiting families to recruiting single women of marriageable age. This strategy was not successful (Branciforte, Bancroft 603–06).

Mexican independence from Spain in 1821 provoked multiple changes in California, including the passage of new land laws, the development of private property and the secularization of the missions. These changes shifted the best land and Indian labor from the Catholic Church to privately owned ranchos, some of which were owned by women. The liberalization of colonization and trade laws spurred the development of merchant capitalism and brought a population of single European and American males— entrepreneurs, sailors, trappers, traders, adventurers—to Alta California. Some Californianas, often women whose families had entered into business or other alliances with foreigners, married them (Castañeda "The Political Economy," 233–34). These women, upon bearing children, added offspring who were half Anglo to the *mestizaje* of California.

During the Mexican national period, native-born Californianas were joined by Mexicanas who migrated both as members of large colonizing expeditions and as members of single families (Hutchinson, Vickery). Women journeyed from central Mexico with the Híjar-Padrés colony (1834) and with the de la Rosa party of Nuevo Mexicanos from Abiquiú (1843). Single families often migrated north from Baja California and sometimes moved back and forth between the two Californias. Although most of the women who migrated to Mexican California were mestizas, the class differentiation among colonists was greater during the national period than it had been during the colonial period.

Political instability in Mexico and the United States' imperial designs on Mexico's Pacific coast, was reflected in California: multiple political upheavals and intrigues occurred, and these often included the Euro-American husbands of Californianas. The struggle for California's political autonomy gave rise to complex, contradictory, conflictive realities for women in California, especially Californianas whose allegiances were claimed by multiple family lines that differed politically and warred with each other. Such conflicts did not lessen during the war between the United States and Mexico or in its aftermath, as the U. S. consolidated its conquest of California and the other territories of the Mexican cessation.

During the post-war era Mexican women in California, whether native-born or not, confronted displacement and subordination in ways both similar to and different from their male counterparts (Castañeda "The Political Economy"). Although few native-born Californianas rushed to the gold fields with their male kin, Mexican women were among the first and only women in the mining districts. Mexican women from Sonora journeyed to Alta California with their families as part of the migration to the mining district. These women and families left California when the passage of the First Foreign Miners Tax, and its attendant violence against non-whites, forced Mexican, Chinese and Chilean miners from the gold fields. The commonly advanced notion that women, due to their scarcity in the Mother Lode, were afforded moral, emotional and physical protection and respect by Anglo miners does not hold for Mexican women, who, as part of the conquered nation, were subject to the violence and lawlessness directed against Mexicanos in general. The only woman hanged during the gold rush was a Mexican. Juanita of Downieville was hanged for killing a white miner who had attempted to rape her (Secrest).

Historical Documents: Themes and Issues

Historical documents reveal the discourses of women writing and speaking from different social positions, but from the same gender position. Class divisions became more evident and social stratification more marked after Mexico became independent in 1821.

For the purposes of this essay, I have grouped the archival documents into broad categories and discuss them accordingly: petitions, court cases and land claims; and diaries, memoirs and oral histories. These categories are not fixed, and, depending on the nature of the documents and the source, other groupings may be more suitable. The linguistic practices revealed in these documents are of extreme importance. Words were—and remain—the instruments for transforming reality and often the instruments for negotiating power (González, Hunt 16–22).

Petitions, Court Cases and Land Claims

Women petitioned civil and military authorities for various kinds of assistance throughout the colonial period. Women whose husbands had been convicted of a crime elsewhere in New Spain wrote petitions asking the authorities to sentence their husband to the Alta California colony and to grant the family a subsidy so that it could be reunited there. In other cases, women petitioned authorities to release their spouses or sons from military duty, citing poverty or illness. In still others, wives, daughters and mothers sought military pensions upon the death of military officers in their family.

While some of these petitions contain the stories of women's migration to Alta California, others document and represent the conditions they faced on the frontier, especially the privations soldier-settler families endured. Other petitions tell the stories of women who remained in Mexico and other parts of Spain's colonial empire while their male kin served military duty in the presidios of California.

Women's voices and self-representations are also recorded in the documents of the criminal, civil and ecclesiastical courts. The criminal courts heard cases against property and persons, including sex crimes (fornication, rape, adultery and incest), as well as slander, theft and murder. Civil courts adjudicated suits over land, wills and contracts. Ecclesiastical courts adjudicated marital strife, including suits for divorce.

Civil, criminal and ecclesiastical court dockets, in which women were plaintiffs, defendants and witnesses, contain extensive descriptions of women's sexual behavior, marital and family relationships, including domestic violence. These documents also record instances of mestiza women's violence toward non-family members, as well as toward other women and Indian people. Women presented their notions of honor, justice, propriety and power in these records. Court materials also contain extensive information on the property owned by women, including both rancho and town lots, and on the property and goods willed by them, including information on whom they willed it to and why.[2] Women's words and actions, as recorded in court cases, belie the image of Spanish and Mexican women as passive, submissive victims so common in the American travel literature of the eighteenth and nineteenth centuries. The counter-image is particularly evident in the most celebrated California case placed before the ecclesiastical court: Eulalia Callis' suit for divorce from her husband, Pedro Fages, governor of the Californias.

In 1785 Eulalia Callis publicly accused her husband of infidelity and vowed never to sleep with him again. In her petition for divorce, Callis claimed that she had been arrested when she, against the advice of her priest and others, publicly continued to accuse Fages of infidelity. She stated that the forces arrayed against her would not "close the doors of my own honor and birth, which swing open in natural defense and protection." Callis then described how she was treated by the authorities; although ill, she was taken to Mission San Carlos, where she was kept incommunicado in a locked and guarded room, which she was only allowed to leave to attend daily mass in the chapel. She remained at the mission two or three months. While at the mission, she was excoriated from the pulpit by Father de Noriega, who threatened her with shackles, flogging and excommunication if she continued with her suit (77–86).

Eulalia Callis' actions directly challenged the political concepts and structures that were pivotal to the conquest and, as such, could not be tolerated. Her actions subverted the value system that required women to be subservient, meek and powerless. She publicly accused Fages of infidelity, refused him sexual relations, refused to acquiesce to the priest and military officers who counseled her to forgive her husband's transgressions. She refused to be *depositada* or *recogida* (deposited or sheltered) in the mission and had to be arrested and taken by force. She sued for divorce and defended her honor and birthright.

Pregnancy, childbirth, miscarriage and infection all too often spelled death for women. Callis, who was pregnant four times in six years, was all too familiar with the precariousness of female life. She gave birth to Pedrito in 1781, had a miscarriage at Arispe in 1782, traveled to California while pregnant and was ill after the birth of María del Carmen in 1784, and buried an infant daughter eight days after her birth in 1786. Thus, her "ploy" to get home may be interpreted as an effort to save her own life and the lives of her children. According to Fages, Callis fabricated the story of his infidelity with Indizuela to get him to resign his post in California and return their family to Mexico City. Callis, however, never admitted that this was so.

Historians have dubbed Eulalia Callis the "notorious gobernadora" (Bancroft 389–93). They have written, with tongue-in-cheek, about Fages' "domestic problems" and cast the gobernadora Callis as a fiery, tempestuous Catalán woman suffering from either a nervous breakdown or postpartum depression. Historians of early California have not examined either the lives of women on the frontier or the words with which women described their experiences, and thus cannot interpret Callis' language or her actions.

Almost a century later Californianas also inscribed their language and memories in the records of the Land Claims Commission, the tribunal established by the state of California in 1851 (Pitt 83-104). All recipients of Spanish and Mexican land grants were required to provide proof of ownership to this American tribunal. Individuals provided the tribunal with proof for their own land grants and served as witnesses in other land cases. Women testified before the tribunal as both grantees and witnesses. In an early study of women grantees, J. N. Bowman identifies about forty women, thirty of whom were native Californianas, who testified in the land grant cases (149–66). Carmen Cibrián, whom Bowman credits with having "a keen observation and retentive memory," testified in a record number of five cases (149–66).[3]

Diaries, Memoirs and Oral Histories

For the second half of the nineteenth century, particularly after the 1860s, scholars have identified and located oral histories, correspondence, diaries, journals, memoirs and at least two novels written by Californianas.[4]

Most of the collected oral histories, reminiscences, memoirs, diaries and journals that we know about are in the Bancroft Library in Berkeley, the California State Library in Sacramento, the California Historical Society Library in San Francisco and the Huntington Library in San Marino. County and city historical societies and museums throughout California, the West and Midwest are also rich sources of unmined material.

The best-known and most accessible collection of Californiana/o reminiscences was commissioned by Hubert Howe Bancroft in the 1870s. Bancroft's researchers collected the oral histories of approximately nine Spanish-speaking women and sixty-three men, all of which are available at the Bancroft Library on the Berkeley campus of the University of California. Some of these histories have been translated and published; most have not.[5] Among the unpublished narratives are those of Doña Catarina Avila de Ríos, Doña Apolinaria Lorenzana, Felipa Osuna de Marrón, María Inocenta Pico, Dorotea Valdez and Rosalía Vallejo de Leese. Published narratives include those of Angustias de la Guerra Ord, Eulalia Pérez, and Juana Machado Alipaz de Ridington.

Most of the women whose narratives were recorded in the 1870s were born during the Spanish colonial period and lived through the transition from Spanish to Mexican to United States rule. Thus, they experienced the change in status from colonizer to colonized, and their narratives describe and interpret those changes. Near the end of her lengthy narrative describing her work as the *llavera* (storekeeper and matron) at Mission San Diego de Alcalá, Eulalia Pérez stated that the Americans swindled her out of the two ranchos she had received in payment for years of service at the mission.

Rosalía Vallejo de Leese, in her brief narrative "History of the Bear Flag Party," tells her version of John C. Fremont's Bear Flag Revolt at Sonoma in June 1847. Fremont and his men arrested Vallejo's brother, Mariano G. Vallejo, and her husband, Jacob Leese, and threatened to burn her house with her family inside if she did not cooperate with him and his men. Vallejo, pregnant at the time, did as those "outlaws and cowards" demanded because "I feared for the life of my unborn child and my female kin." Vallejo de Leese ended her story with the remark that: "those hated men inspired me with such a large *dosis* of hate against their race, that although over twenty-eight years have elapsed since that time—I have not yet forgotten the insults they heaped upon me, and not being desirous of coming in contact with them I have abstained from learning their language."

In addition to undertaking the research, translation, and publication of women's eighteenth- and nineteenth-century oral histories that have been recorded in written form and are contained in known collections, scholars need to research, collect and publish the various manifestations of women's creative oral expression. This, I believe, requires that we rethink and reconceptualize notions of oral literature. Various forms of oral expression that merit consideration include, among others, personal *oraciones* and *rezos* (prayers) that women composed for special, difficult, or tragic moments in their lives; *historias* (personal accounts) that women related or narrated to family members and that later became part of the family history and lore; and *mitos y cuentos* (myths and legends) that were women-centered.

Certainly, folk songs, including lullabies and nursery rhymes, should also be examined for the insights they provide into women's emotional lives and consciousness. The exchange in "Levántese niña," a folk song from nineteenth-century California, communicates a young wife's feelings about housework:

Levántese niña	Get up, girl,
Barra la cocina	and sweep the kitchen
Atice la lumbre	Light the fire
Como es su costumbre	like you're supposed to
Yo no sé barrer	I don't know how to sweep
Yo no sé tizar	or make the fire
Yo no me casé	I didn't get married
Para trabajar	to work! (Morehouse 77)

While some folk songs from the eighteenth and nineteenth century have survived and may still be heard throughout the Southwest, others have disappeared but were written and are now held in various collections and archival repositories, such as the Charles F. Lummis Collection at the Southwest Museum. Still other forms of oral expression that may have been documented in writing and collected include the more formal, formulaic poetry intended to be recited publicly on national, religious and other holidays or at family gatherings. Although most of the *declamadores* (reciters) were male, female *declamadoras* historically existed in our communities as well. We have yet to examine extant archival collections with gender-centered questions that would lead us to identify women's voices and interpretations in these and other materials.

Women on the Spanish borderlands inscribed their memories, voices and interpretations of events and of their own place in society in a myriad of written documents. They also left women-centered forms of oral expression in the memory and oral traditions of their communities. Although not yet part of the traditional literature of the colonial period, their voices and self-representations are beginning to be discovered by women and other scholars who are studying the historical documents in which women speak for themselves. Women participated in and witnessed the changes taking place on the borderlands during the colonial period. We, as scholars, must begin to rethink our concept of history and of literature so that, in recovering their voices, we reclaim our literary heritage in its fullness, complexity and power.

Notes

[1] I use the terms *mestiza* and *Spanish-Mexican* women to refer to the same population of women: racially mixed women who came to Alta California under the auspices of Spanish colonialism (1769–1821), their femal descendants and other mestizas who lived in California during the Mexican national period (1822–1848).

[2] For eighteenth- and nineteenth-century California, see Castañeda, "Presidarias y Pobladoras" 43–44. For nineteenth-century New Mexico, see Deena J. González, *Refusing the Favor: The Spanish-Mexican Women of Santa Fe.*

[3] I started to go through women's testimonies several years ago but have not returned to them. I plan to do so in the near future and would welcome a collaborative effort. They merit close examination, especially the testimonies of Carmen Cibrián. In 1854, she testified about the condition of land grants between 1822 and 1839, including the homes built, the corrals, cattle, fields, gardens, fruit trees and details about the boundaries.

[4] Rosaura Sánchez has recently completed a critical edition of *The Squatter and the Don* by María Amparo Ruíz de Burton.

[5] I am currently translating the Californiana narratives from the Bancroft and other collections and am preparing a bilingual edition of these narratives.

Works Cited

Adorno, Rolena. "New Perspectives in Colonial Spanish-American Literary Studies." *Journal of the Southwest* 32 (1990): 173–91.

Bancroft, Hubert Howe. *History of California*, Vol. 1. San Francisco, 1886–88.

Bean, Walton. *California: An Interpretive History*. New York: McGraw, 1973.

Bolton, Hubert E. *Anza's California Expeditions*, Vol. 3. Berkeley: U of California P, 1930.

Bowman, J. N. "Prominent Women of Provincial California." *Historical Quarterly of Southern California* 39 (June 1957): 149–66.

Branciforte, [Viceroy]. "Sobre envío de mujeres para pobladores," letter to the Governor of the Californias, 15 January, 1798. *Archives of California, 1767– 1849*, Vol. 10. Bancroft Library, Berkeley, California. 19–20.

Campbell, Leon G. "The First Californios: Presidial Society in Spanish California, 1769-1822." *Spanish Borderlands*. 106–18.

Castañeda, Antonia. *Presidiarias y Pobladoras: Spanish-Mexican Women in Frontier Monterey, Alta California*, 1770–1821. Diss. Stanford U, 1990.

———. "The Political Economy of Nineteenth Century Stereotypes of Californianas." *Between Borders: Essays in Mexicana/Chicana History*. Ed. Adelaida del Castillo. Los Angeles: Floricanto, 1990. 213–36.

Callis, Eulalia. "Ynstancia de Doña Eulalia Callis, muger de Don Pedro Fages, gobernador de Californias, sobre que se le oyga en justicia, y redima de la opresión que padece," 23 de agosto de 1785. *Archivo General de la Nación, Provincias Internas*, Vol. 120: 66–81. Bancroft Library, Microfilm Collection.

Castillo, Adelaida del. "Malintzín Tenépal." *Essays on la Mujer*. Ed. Rosaura Sánchez. Los Angeles: Aztlán, 1979. 124–49.

Franco, Jean. *Plotting Women: Gender and Representation in Mexico*. New York: Columbia UP, 1989.

González, Deena J. *Refusing the Favor: The Spanish-Mexican Women of Santa Fe, 1820–1880*. Oxford and New York: Oxford UP, forthcoming.

Guerra, Angustias de la. *Occurrences in Hispanic California*. Trans. Frances Price and William H. Ellison. Washington, D.C.: Academy of Franciscan History, 1956.

Hunt, Lynn, ed. "Introduction." *The New Cultural History*. Berkeley: U of California P, 1989.

Hutchison, C. Alan. *Frontier Settlement in Mexican California: The Híjar- Padrés Colony and Its Origins, 1769-1835*. New Haven: Yale UP, 1969.

Jara, René and Nicholas Spadaccini, Eds. "Introduction: Allegorizing the New World." *1492–1992: Re/Discovering Colonial Writing, Hispanic Issues*. 4 (1989): 9–50.

Johnson, Julie Greer. *Women in Colonia Spanish American Literature: Literary Images*. Westport: Greenwood, 1983.

Jones, Oakah L., Jr. *Los Paisanos: Spanish Settlers on the Northern Frontier of New Spain*. Norman: U of Oklahoma P, 1979.

Lynch, Henry. "Six Families: *A Study of the Power and Influence of the Alvarado, Carrillo, Castro, De la Guerra, Pico, and Vallejo families in California, 1769– 1846*. Thesis, California State U, Sacramento, 1977.

Machado Alipaz de Ridington, Juana. "Times Gone by in Alta California: Recollections of Doña Juan Machado Alipaz de Ridington." Trans. Raymond

S. Brandes. *Historical Society of Southern California* 61 (September 1959): 195–240.

Moorhead, Max L. "The Soldado de Cuera: Stalwart of the Spanish Borderlands." *The Spanish Borderlands.* Ed. Oakah L. Jones, Jr. Los Angeles: Lorrin L. Morrison, 1974. 85–105.

Morehouse, Theresa, ed. *Singing Gold: Songs and Verses from Early California.* Sacramento: The Sacramento Bee, 1977.

Northrup, Marie. *Spanish-Mexican Families of Early California: 1769–1850,* Vol. 1. Burbank: Southern California Genealogical Society, 1984.

Padilla, Genaro. " 'Yo sola aprendí': Contra-Patriarchal Containment in Women's Nineteenth-Century California Narratives." *The Americas Review* 16:3-4 (1988): 91–109.

————. "The Recovery of Chicano Nineteenth-Century Autobiography." *American Quarterly* 4 (1988): 286–306.

Pérez, Eulalia. "Una vieja y sus recuerdos/An Old Woman and Her Recollections." *Three Memoirs of Mexican California.* Berkeley: Friends of the Bancroft Library, 1988. 71–106.

Pitt, Leonard. *The Decline of the Californios: A Social History of the Spanish-Speaking Californians, 1846–1890.* Berkeley: U of California P, 1966.

Ruiz de Barton, María Amparo. *The Squatter and the Don.* Eds. Rosaura Sánchez and Beatrice Pita. Houston: Arte Público, 1992.

Secrest, William B. *Juanita: The Only Woman Lynched During Gold Rush Days.* Fresno: Saga West, 1967.

Todorov, Tzvetan. *The Conquest of America: The Question of the Other.* Trans. Richard Howard. New York: Harper, 1976.

Valdez, Dorotea. *Reminiscences of Dorotea Valdez.* Manuscript Collection, Bancroft Library, U of California, Berkeley.

Vallejo de Leese, Rosalía. "History of the Bear Flag Party." Manuscript Collection, Bancroft Library, U of California, Berkeley.

Vickery, Joyce Carter. *Defending Eden: New Mexican Pioneers in Southern California, 1830–1890.* Riverside: Dept. of History, U of California, Riverside, 1977.

Virgillo, Carmelo and Naomi Lindstrom, eds. *Woman as Myth and Metaphor in Latin American Literature.* Columbia: U of Missouri P, 1985.

Nineteenth-Century Californio Narratives: The Hubert H. Bancroft Collection

Rosaura Sánchez

About a hundred years ago, in 1890, Mariano Guadalupe Vallejo died at his home "Lachryma Montis" in Sonoma, California. By then fifteen years had passed since this once wealthy landowner and former Commander-General of the California territory had written his *Memoirs*, dictated to his friend Enrique Cerruti for the Hubert H. Bancroft House historiography project. In his five-volume handwritten manuscript, Vallejo had not only reconstructed the past but had recognized and been driven by a perceived duty to counter hegemonic versions of the Spanish and Mexican periods of California history. As a historian and as a Californio, he also addressed his future readers and asked that they too assume the task of narrating the U. S. invasion of California and the reduction of the Californios to the status of a conquered people. By the time he died, penniless and forgotten, Vallejo must have foreseen the marginalization and subordination that the Californios and their descendants would continue to suffer during the coming century. He probably would not have thought, however, that his history would still lie unpublished in the Bancroft Collection at the University of California, Berkeley. Mined like a rich vein by numerous historians who would read his work and borrow excerpts and information to suit their own purposes, the Californio would not be allowed to have his own words see the light of day in print, that is, to speak for himself. His, like that of many other Californio men and women, is a silenced voice, the voice of the subaltern.

Vallejo's experience as an unpublished Californio writer is not unique. It has always been the condition of the subaltern to be silenced by the dominant classes, for publication, that is, cultural reproduction, is generally in the hands of those who control its technologies and markets. In the nineteenth century, as before and after, editorial houses determined what was printed, unless, of course, one was independently wealthy or able to borrow the money for publication, as María Amparo Ruiz de Burton, another Californio

279

author, would have to do to publish her second novel. If one represented hegemonic ideologies that encouraged trade, settlement or even invasion and occupation of California by North Americans, it was easy to get published. These published and much-reprinted nineteenth-century writers would be amongst a number of travellers, merchants, trappers and sailors coming to Alta California, before and after 1846. The diaries and recollections of these visitors to Mexican California are today considered to have contributed significantly to the annals of history. Alfred Robinson, for example, who spent several years exploiting the hide and tallow trade, provided in his *Life in California*, published in 1846, first-hand observations of his nine years as merchant and son-in-law of one of the wealthiest Californios after marrying the youngest daughter of José de la Guerra y Noriega of Santa Barbara. Richard Henry Dana in his *Two Years Before the Mast*, published in 1840, and William Heath Davis' *Sixty Years in California*, published in 1889, provided additional information on the hide and tallow trade and on Anglo settlers in California during the Mexican period. It would be their hegemonic views of the Californios as indolent and anarchic and their support for annexation of California that would gain currency and attract attention. There were also accounts in print by individuals who had not even visited California, like the Englishman Alexander Forbes, whose history (1939) was based on the reports of others (Bancroft 1964, 145), or by travelers who had visited only briefly, like Thomas Jefferson Farnham, who stopped off in Monterey and Santa Barbara in 1840 on his way to Mexico. Even Bancroft would describe the work of the latter as "worthless trash" and his views on the Californios as "a tissue of falsehoods" (137; see Farnham, Forbes). But the memoires or historical accounts of the Californios themselves, those accounts that represented the views of the conquered, interested no one except as raw material to be appropriated by U. S. historians manufacturing California history.

Yet we have to acknowledge that it is to one such entrepreneurial researcher and publisher that we owe even the existence and accessibility to us today of a number of manuscripts narrated by the Californios themselves. Like Vallejo's manuscript, there exist in the Bancroft Library's Collection housed at University of California, Berkeley, a number of other testimonials encoding the process of territorialization and deterritorialization that began with the Spanish settlements in Alta California in 1769. These testimonials reveal not only the everyday practices of these settlers but also allude to the demographic shifts that brought early on a slow increase in the population of white/mestizo/mulatto settlers, to the decimation of the Indian population and to the political changes that transpired with Mexican independence in 1821 and thereafter.

These early Californio narratives were dictated in the 1870s, nearly thirty years after Alta California was invaded by United States forces. Other than these testimonials and official documents, letters, diaries and some poetry, we have no material published in Alta California before 1846. While this failure to procure a press is noteworthy, one would have to consider that the Spanish-Mexican period was relatively short—a mere 78 years—and that printed material arrived in California from Europe and Latin America via Mexico itself. Sometimes print material had to be smuggled into California because of the Church's ban on books considered immoral, anti-clerical or atheistic. We know that such materials did arrive on trading vessels and were quickly read by young Californios like M. G. Vallejo, Juan Bautista Alvarado and José Castro. Perhaps this accounts in part for the fact that there was little interest in the acquisition of a printing press before 1833. This lack however did not impede communication between the pueblos, missions and presidios, as a "pony express" system of sorts was available whenever necessary. The first printing press that did arrive had been ordered in Boston, not for California but for a Honolulu trader. When the Sandwich Islander changed his mind about purchasing the printing equipment that arrived on the ship "Lagoda," it was returned to the ship which sailed for home via Monterey, where the ship docked to trade her cargo for hides, a cargo which included the press purchased by Agustín Vicente Zamorano, a Mexican Army officer and the executive secretary of the California territory for the years 1825–1836. Zamorano established California's first printing press in 1834. Prior to that time all official documents were handwritten, although it is thought that by 1825 there may have been a small seal press for the purpose of stamping and imprinting government seals on official papers and documents. It was only after 1834 that a number of official documents and three school textbooks on basic arithmetic operations and grammar were printed. No newspapers, however, were published in California before 1846. Ironically, this same printing press would serve the U. S. invaders to publish the first newspaper in California, the *Californian*, which first appeared on August 15, 1846 (Fahey 1956, Kemble 1962). After 1846 only a handful of Spanish-language newspapers would be established to serve the now minority population (Kemble 1962). These bear witness not so much to the rapid subordination of the previously dominant population as to their linguistic resistance.[1]

The nineteenth century California narratives that are the focus of this essay are housed at the Bancroft Library. Hubert Howe Bancroft was a wealthy book dealer, publisher and businessman who established the Bancroft House in San Francisco. Between 1859 and 1880 he acquired several private libraries and numerous publications for a personal collection that focused on the U. S. Southwest, Central America, Mexico and the U. S. Northwest and Alaska. Bancroft's ambitious master plan was to write and publish a number of histories on each of these areas. He began the first project of what later would be considered a controversial method of "cooperative authorship" by hiring a number of writers, none of them professional historians, to write the various histories, which he then published under his own name, without by-lines or mention of the real authors. In harmony with his entrepreneurial outlook, Bancroft assumed that, because he paid his assistants, he had a total right and claim to their work. For this reason he would later be severely criticized throughout the nation, especially after some of the writers in this cooperative enterprise of history-writing publicly asserted their authorship (Caughey).

One of Bancroft's principal research projects was on the history of California, for which reason he acquired as many official documents, records and letters from the Spanish-Mexican period as were available. If he was unable to obtain the documents themselves, he at least had them copied for his library. Bancroft sent out agents to contact California pioneers, as the early Anglo settlers were called, and Californios, the Mexican/Spanish settlers of the territory, not only to procure whatever documents they might possess, but also to interview them if possible. Two men fluent in Spanish were responsible for the interviews made during the decade of the 1870s of about 160 old residents, half of them of Mexican or Spanish origin. The two men were Thomas Savage, a Yankee who had been born and raised in Cuba and had done consular service in Havana and Central America, and Enrique Cerruti, an Italian who was fluent in several languages and had traveled throughout Latin America. In his notes on the bibliography of California history, Bancroft indicates that his reporters took dictations of personal reminiscences of individuals from all walks of life, including twenty-four men who had occupied prominent public positions in the north and in the south. Bancroft further notes that eleven of those interviewed were women. In addition to these dictations, Bancroft acquired over 500 other manuscripts, including diaries, journals, official reports by military and religious officers, regulations, *expedientes* and the like, as well as additional narratives provided by both men and women of Californio origin that were not dictated or written expressly for the historical project but which came to be part of the Bancroft Collection (Caughey 189, Cerruti).

These interviews or testimonials are narratives and can be considered as intertextual as any novel. Each one tells about California, its people, its problems and often narrates the informant's own recollections of everyday practices or observations of noteworthy events. Each testimonial provides an ideological perspective on social and political practices within a particular segment of time. These narratives, while differing widely among themselves in terms of form, content and ideology, can be subdivided into several subgroups, but for purposes of classification they can all be said to share the following characteristics.

1. Oral compositions

These narratives were initially produced orally as part of an interview carried out by Bancroft's agents or their assistants who took notes and later transcribed the dictation in long hand. It is important to note, and it is clear as well from the texts, that the informants' declarations were in response to questions posed by the interviewers. In some cases the questions have also been recorded, but generally these have been omitted from the transcriptions.

Most of the dictations are the product of informal conversations, often conducted and noted down over a drink and sweets, as Cerruti enjoyed making the interview as pleasant to the informant as possible, especially if the person being interviewed was of modest means. It should be noted that the type of responses such interviews elicited were very much influenced by the informant, in terms of the atmosphere created and the willingness to please not only the interviewer at hand, but the larger audience, that is, Bancroft himself.

In the case of Mariano Guadalupe Vallejo's narrative, acknowledged by Bancroft to be "the most extensive and in some respects the most valuable of all," the dictation to Cerruti represents in this regard a different case, for it followed not the interviewer's but Vallejo's plan, his notes, his documents and his editing. Whenever, after reading the text of the copied dictation, Vallejo found that he did not like what had been transcribed, he would tear it up and do it over, much to Cerruti's chagrin. The fact that Vallejo previously had written a history of California, which had been destroyed in a fire at his house, indicates a previously conceived plan for the composition of the history, a pre-existing text as it were. Thus unlike most of the other dictations, which are an aggregate of responses to interviewers' questions, Vallejo's memoirs and those of Juan Bautista Alvarado are fully controlled by the narrators, who saw it as within their purview to dictate the conditions of the sessions. When Cerruti tried to hurry Vallejo, the General responded:

> My friend, you seem to be in haste. I should take you for a Yankee rather than for an Italian. Do you expect me to write history on horseback? I do not approve of this method. I am willing and ready to relate all I can remember, but I wish it clearly understood that it must be in my own way, and at my own time. I will not be hurried or dictated to. It is my history and not yours, I propose to tell. Pardon me, my friend,

> for speaking thus plainly, but I am particular on this point. If I give
> my story, it must be worthy of the cause and worthy of me. (Bancroft
> 1890: 343)

Because of the extensive nature and particular dynamic involved in the
Vallejo interview, this particular "dictation" took an entire year, whereas
most of the others in the Bancroft Collection took a few hours. Another
testimonial that evinces at least partial authorial control is that of Doña Angustias Guerra de Ord, who, after reviewing what had been transcribed by
Thomas Savage, was allowed to add footnotes in which she corrected or
expanded various points. However she was not allowed to change the original text. Once dictated, she lost the right to her own words and it became
Savage's, and ultimately Bancroft's text.

Other lengthy testimonials include those of Juan Bautista Alvarado, Salvador Vallejo, Jesús Vallejo, Pío Pico, and Antonio Franco Coronel, all of
which took several hours, days and sometimes months to transcribe, as in
the case of Alvarado's. The longer narratives cannot then be placed in the
same category as the shorter "dictations," not only because of their length
and consequently their form and content, but also, as we shall see shortly,
because of the particular dynamic involved in their production.

2. Double-voiced discourse

Because these narratives are orally produced, the dialogical component
is clearly marked in the text. But the fact that these are the product of a
dialogue, and that, like all narratives, are heteroglossic is not the only aspect
of their production that needs to be remarked. Most important is the fact that
these narratives were filtered through the interviewer (never a neutral or inert
medium), who then wrote down what was being said. Modern interviews
make use of tape recorders, in which cases fidelity to the original can always
be checked, although it rarely is. But with the Californio narratives what we
have are the handwritten manuscripts plus the reports of Cerruti and Savage
of the work they accomplished. To what extent can we gauge the degree of
accuracy and consequently trust that there was no alteration of the text in
taking dictation or in recopying it? Savage, who, for example, did most of
the interviews in Southern California, also used a number of assistants, all of
them native Spanish speakers and supervised by Savage himself, to interview
the Spanish-speaking Californios. In some cases the names of the actual
recorders appear on the titlepage of the handwritten dictations. The degree
to which they could all take dictation of a conversation conducted at normal
speed is, of course, not known. Cerruti, who worked largely with informants
in the North, used no assistants and was proud of the fidelity with which he

transcribed the recollections of the old Californios. We know, however, that in some of his earlier work, before he began recording Vallejo's history, he translated the dictations into English before submitting them to Bancroft. Thus, for example, the lengthy interview of Salvador Vallejo, brother of Mariano Guadalupe Vallejo, appears in English. Modern translations of the testimonials likewise have led to problems of fidelity, as is the case in the Guerra de Ord text, dictated in 1878, and translated by Price and Ellison in 1956. With this testimonial it is easy to compare the two versions, as Genaro Padilla has indicated in his comments on her work. But when there is no original Spanish version of the narrative, we have no means of comparing the two texts against each other.

The reader and scholar of these histories, then, must bear in mind that the interviewer assumes an agencial role in the interaction, not only because he transcribes and in some cases translates the dictation, but also because he determines to some extent the style and language variety, the focus and direction of the conversation and the degree of openness and spontaneity of the interaction. Outside of these interactional constraints, the interviewer/informant dynamic figures prominently in another exceedingly important fashion. The transcriber evidently functioned as an editor, a fact that becomes all-too-obvious in Cerruti's transcription of his conversation with Isidora Filomena, wife of the Indian Chief Solano. This particular dictation, recorded in Spanish, changes from an informal Spanish style to a non-native style after about two pages of transcription. With the shift comes a loss of number and gender agreement and a failure to conjugate some verbs in Spanish, which for Isidora Filomena was a second language acquired after many years of contact with the Californios. At the end of the dictation Cerruti acknowledges the clear shift in the text stating that he thought it preferable to let Isidora Filomena express herself in her own words, invoking the consideration that she was due given her husband's multiple services to settlers in Sonoma. What is clear, however, is that he initially thought it best to follow what was standard procedure for these dictations, editing her remarks as they were put down in writing. For whatever reason, in at least this one case it was thought preferable to let Isidora Filomena tell her story in her own voice, through a construction of her own discourses.

What the Filomena episode makes clear, and what for purposes of the analysis of these texts makes them extremely interesting indicators of the dynamics of textualization at work, is that the interviewers took notes during the interview, then retired elsewhere to produce a clean copy of the notes taken during the actual interview. Most testimonials are thus a construction or re-construction of the verbatim transcriptions. Bancroft's agents probably used a form of shorthand or note-taking technique which, when transcribed and given form, required grammatical and stylistic changes. In one case an individual named Estolario Larios of Los Angeles, whose uncle had not been interviewed by Savage, sent the Bancroft House a copy of an interview that he himself had conducted with his uncle. Someone on Bancroft's staff subsequently recopied the dictation and edited it. In some cases sentences that began in a rambling way were crossed out and then expressed in a different form, as if the copier had at first merely been copying and then proceeded to revise and edit. What this calls attention to is an additional intervention—beyond that of the interviewers—during the editing and copying of the texts by Bancroft's staff in San Francisco.

In reading the narrations of several women included in Bancroft's Collection, I began to find that the style of what were ostensibly "dictations" was very similar, as if the very same woman had dictated all of the recorded interviews, although of course the content varied. The sentences were long and flowed without any asides or veering off in tangents, which is so characteristic of oral interviews. Such style may have been elicited in response to particular questions, which do not appear in the text, or editorially when sentences were rewritten either in transcribing or recopying. The longer texts, like those of Alvarado and M. G. Vallejo do, on the other hand, include many asides, which are placed within parentheses so that the exact same sentence from which the speaker deviates is continued after the closing of the parentheses. Whether the interviewers intervened to lead the informant back to his previous thought or whether the interviewer later re-organized the material cannot be established.

What I will term double-voicing is especially evident in the translated dictations, in that the original voice is totally filtered through the interviewer's pen, reproducing both the voice of the informant and that of the interviewer. In the particular case of Rosalía Vallejo de Leese, who hated the North Americans and refused to speak English, the fact that her testimonial exists only in English translation is thus especially abominable. In other cases, however, not all is "lost" in translation; in some, the translations are not always totally diluted, as is evident in the case of Salvador Vallejo's narration. Here Cerruti, who translated the interview, managed to retain in the English version the speaker's bravado, sarcasm and bitter invective against the Missourians, as he called the Anglos, perhaps because he himself was Italian and was able to preserve what could perhaps be termed a distinctive Latin flavor, even in translation.

Some of these testimonials must also be viewed as multi-voiced or heteroglossic because of the subsequent intervention by Bancroft's staff. I have already mentioned that submitted testimonials were edited by the staff. The procedure followed with submissions of this type to the Bancroft House would lead to one particular incident that triggered Cerruti's indignation and rage. It seems that on one occasion the staff in San Francisco copying Vallejo's personal documents poked fun at the Californio's grammar and spelling. After overhearing them, Cerruti precluded Bancroft's minions from having to copy Vallejo's work by persuading the General to donate his papers and documents *in toto* to the Bancroft historiography project. Cerruti thus indirectly gained his revenge by ensuring that the copier who had made fun of his friend would be let go, as there was no longer a need for so many copiers. Of course, once in the Bancroft House these manuscripts were always re-copied and carved up by topics, periods, etc., to create files of notations, excerpts and documents for the various writers hired to write Bancroft's California history.

3. Hegemonic and Counter-Discourses

One cannot assume that because these narratives are the discourses of a conquered people, deterritorialized and marginalized, that they are all contestatory. Whether genuinely felt or not, in some cases the informants assume the perspective of the oppressors and conquerors and posit the political and economic changes taking place to be beneficial for all concerned. In some cases the discourses of the Californios are racist and classist and reveal not only their contempt for Native Americans but for Mexico and the lower-classes in California. What is particularly interesting for the tracing of the history of contestatory positions in California history is that some of these narratives do in fact offer a network of counter-discourses and point to an awareness and identification with a collectivity, be it on the basis of nation, language, region, gender or religion. These discourses are antagonistic to hegemonic structures and the dominant classes, and sometimes reveal the Californios to be self-critical of themselves as a collectivity. No testimonial can be said, then, to be characterized by one ideological perspective alone for individual manuscripts often shift from one perspective to another, according to the content being dealt with and historical moment being addressed.

In most cases the class and caste perspectives of the informants is obvious, for the majority of those interviewed were either members of the Californio elite or were administrators or middlemen/middlewomen for those in power. As is often the case, the voices of the disenfranchised were neither sought out nor recorded, although in his bibliographic notes Bancroft indicates that dictations were taken "from all classes and in the aggregate fairly represent the Californian people." Nevertheless, one needs bear in mind that, by the time these interviews were conducted, many of the Californios were older, retired persons. Many of them had fallen on hard times and had lost their lands. These individuals, with few exceptions, had been part of California's oligarchy, those leading families that controlled the political and economic system in Mexican California, including ex-government officials and presidio officers like Alvarado, the Vallejos, Pío Pico and Coronel. Divisions among these ruling families, who were all related through ties of blood and marriage, are clear in the testimonials. In many cases their discourses favor either a federalist, liberal and anti-clerical stance or a centralist, conservative and pro-Church perspective. Their representation of their own political perspectives during the Mexican period is especially interesting given their subsequent reactions to invasion and domination, because, of course, they did not all react in the same way.

The class status of these informants is an important element to consider in an analysis of these ideological discourses, although naturally not the only one. Gender, class and religious discourses, for example, combine in a testimonial like that of Angustias Guerra de Ord, daughter of a wealthy Santa Barbara Presidio commander who served as treasurer for the missionaries. The articulation of class and politics are necessarily special considerations in an analysis of the discourses of wealthy landowners and merchants like M. G. Vallejo, Juan Bandini, José María Estudillo and Pío Pico. Among the Californios, one can also distinguish a "middle-class" population, an intermediary group that served the interests of the dominant agencies. Take, for example, Doña Apolinaria Lorenzana, "la Beata" (the pious woman), who came to Alta California as an orphan, worked in several homes, and from early adulthood until the period of the United States invasion worked at the San Diego Mission. There she held a position of power as teacher, nurse and later housekeeper, supervisor of Indian seamstresses and official purchaser of goods for the mission. She was moreover the owner of three ranches. Doña Eulalia Pérez, said to be the oldest person in California in 1878, likewise served as the official housekeeper of the richest mission in California, the San Gabriel Mission, where she was in charge of all the Indian labor attached to domestic chores, of the storeroom and of the distribution of goods. Both women served in managerial or administrative capacities for the missionaries and facilitated their exploitation of the neophyte Indians. Gender and class also played an important role in the case of women who were interviewed, primarily because they were married to or were the daughters and sisters of important foreign merchants, mission administrators, wealthy landowners, and government officials. This is the case in the testimonials of Avila de Ríos, Carrillo de Fitch, Vallejo de Leese, Guerra de Hartnell, Machado de Ridington, Osuna de Marrón and Pico de Avila.

Caste also plays an especially important role in all of these interviews, for as "gente de razón"—the rational ones—all of these Californios looked down on the Indians as an inferior and dangerous caste, despite the fact, or perhaps precisely because the Indians did all the work on the ranchos, haciendas, presidios and missions and mission ranchos.

By the time the Bancroft interviews were conducted all of these individuals had lost their positions of power, except those who married into the new ruling classes. For this reason these Californio narratives are in great measure marked by overt and other times implicit resentment and a sense of displacement and dispossession. But the testimonials cannot be assumed to be marked exclusively by contestatory discourses, for as can be seen quite blatantly at times, there is a great deal of ideological accommodation intersecting this resentment.

4. Historiography

The interviews which led to the production of these narratives were conducted by Bancroft's agents to garner individuals' recollections of the past and specific information on some particular event. Day-to-day customs and the cultural traditions of the Californios were also of interest to the researchers. The informants often were cognizant of their role as repositories of a disappearing history and generally were interested in recounting their first-hand experiences to elucidate the past. In some of the narratives, particularly those of the Vallejos and Alvarado, there is also a clear discursive strategy: to deconstruct the dominant view of California's history and to reconstruct a Californio version of it. In a letter to his son Platón, M. G. Vallejo expressed the need to have someone tell their side of the story, to make their version of history known. At that time Vallejo thought that Bancroft would be that historian, but later he came to regret having participated in the project (Brown Emparán). The reconstruction of history is a strategy that characterizes not only these nineteenth-century narratives, but is as well one of the principal thrusts of Chicano literature today.

5. Genres and Subgenres

The narratives that we can call "testimonials" (Roberts 1991),[2] as opposed to Bancroft's "dictations," can be subdivided further according to length, scope, time frame, focus, style and structure, narrative perspective, and inter-textuality. Although all are narrated in first-person, not all the testimonials deal exclusively with the life of the individual being interviewed. Antonio Berreyesa, for example, was interviewed for his recollection of the Fremont episode in which his uncle José de los Reyes Berreyesa and the two young Haro brothers were shot to death on their way to Sonoma by John Fremont's men. First the details of the killing are presented and witnesses cited since the narrator was not present. We then learn of the after effects of these killings on Nicolás Berreyesa, the narrator's father, who went mad from suffering one disaster after another, losing lands, cattle, horses and finally even family members to the Anglo invaders.

In many cases it is the individual's participation in a particular event that interests the interviewer. Josefa Carrillo Fitch and María Teresa Guerra Hartnell, for example, were interviewed for what they might say about their husbands, Henry Delano Fitch and William Hartnell, respectively, who were of interest to Bancroft. These dictations are thus short and limited to short biographies. In the longer memoires, the narratives are really macro-texts encompassing many shorter narratives about particular events—like accounts of Indian insurrections, kidnappings, internecine conflicts between the North and the South in California, scandals, conflicts and skirmishes between Mexicans and Californios—as well as sketches of individuals, discussions of classes or castes, relations between nations or individuals, social change, the economic system and the organization and operation of the missions. These macro-texts sometimes incorporate official documents and manifestos, poetry, lyrics of songs and even the recollections of other Californios. The structure of these memoires is thus necessarily fragmented and lends itself to excerpting for publication. Many include personal recollections in which they describe personal events and their own lived experience of pre-1848 California. Some provide third-person chronicles of events relating to the collectivity in general or to other persons in particular. Some, like that of Coronel, also provide sketches of what occurred after 1846 in the mines and with the bandits, as the invasion of Anglo settlers increased.

The Bancroft Collection, it should be stressed, also served as a sort of clearinghouse, which, even in the nineteenth century, attracted materials produced long after Bancroft's history of California was written. Such are the sketches provided by Platón Vallejo at the turn of the century in which he reviewed California's history, narrated events from his father's life in Sonoma, and provided short stories about the capture of the Russian Princesss Helene by the Suysunes, the Bear Flag Revolt, the arrival of Anglo settlers from the east and stories told to him as a boy by the Suysun Indians.

Together these nineteenth-century testimonials provide a collective reconstruction of a crucial period in Chicano history. Other Californio writers, like the novelist María Amparo Ruiz de Burton, would further disarticulate the social practices of this time-space, which marks the beginnings of American imperialism, the loss of half of the Mexican territory to the United States, a shift in the mode of production in the Southwest and the beginning of the

Mexican population as a national minority, as a subordinated group displaced economically, politically, linguistically and culturally. This period also marks the beginning of our cultural production as a marginal ethnic group. If we hope to prepare for the future, as well as to grasp the present better, we will have to understand the past. But even more importantly, if we hope to make ourselves heard, we will have to enable previously silenced voices to speak. The subaltern of the late nineteenth century in California, as much mestizo and Indian as criollo, must speak through us.

Notes

[1]Edward C. Kemble notes that only a handful of Spanish-language newspapers were established in California after 1846. These bear witness to the rapid subordination of the previously dominant population and to their linguistic resistance.

[2]Term used by Roberts as translation of "testimonio" in *"Just the facts, M'am": Mediated Testimonials*.

Works Cited

Bancroft, Hubert H. *Literary Industries*. San Francisco: The History Co. Publishers, 1890.

———. *Pioneer Register and Index*. Baltimore: Regional Publishing, 1964.

Brown Emparán, Madie. *The Vallejos of California*. San Francisco: The Gleeson Library Associates, 1968.

Caughey, John W. *Hubert Howe Bancroft*. Berkeley: U of California P, 1946.

Cerruti, Henry. "Ramblings in California." Bancroft Collection, Ms. 1874.

———. *Pioneer Register and Index*. Baltimore: Regional Publishing Co, 1964.

Farnham, Thomas Jefferson. *Travels in the Californias and Scenes in the Pacific Ocean*. New York: Saxon and Miles, 1844.

Forbes, Alexander. *California*. London: Smith, Elder, 1939.

Fahey, Herbert. *Early Printing in California, From its beginning in the Mexican Territory to Statehood*. San Francisco: The Book Club of California, 1956.

Guerra de Ord, Angustias. *Occurrences in Hispanic California*. Trans. F. Price & W. H. Ellison. Washington: Academy of American Franciscan History, 1956.

Kemble, Edward C. *A History of California Newspapers*. Los Gatos, CA: Talisman, 1962.

Padilla, Genaro. " 'Yo sola aprendí': Mexican Women Nineteenth-Century Californio Personal Narratives." *The Americas Review* 16.3-4 (1988): 91–109. Rpt. in *Revealing Lives: Autobiography and Gender,* Eds. Marilyn Yalom & Susan Groag Bell. Albany: State U of New York P, 1990. 115–31.

Roberts, Rebecca. *Just the Facts, M'am." Mediated Testimonials*. MA thesis, U of California, San Diego, 1991.

Robinson, Alfred. *Life in California*. New York: Da Capo, 1969.

Ruiz de Burton, María Amparo. *The Squatter and the Don*. San Francisco: Samuel Carson, 1885.

———. *Who Would Have Thought It?* Philadelphia: J. B. Lippincott, 1872

Testimonials/Memoires
(Available at Bancroft Library)

Alvarado, Juan Bautista. "Historia de California," vol. I–V. 1876.
Avila de Ríos, Catarina. "Recuerdos." 1877.
Bandini, Juan. "Historia de California." n.d.
Berreyesa, Antonio. "Relación." 1877.
Carrillo Fitch, Josefa. "Narración." 1875.
Coronel, Antonio Franco. "Cosas de California." 1877.
Estudillo, José María. "Datos Históricos."
Fernández, José. "Cosas de California." 1874.
Filomena, Isidora. "Recuerdos de Solano." 1874.
Guerra de Hartnell, Teresa. "Narrativa de la distinguida matrona californiana," 1875.
Larios, Estolario. "Vida y aventuras de mi padre, don Manuel Larios." 1878.
Lorenzana, Apolinaria. "Memorias." 1875.
Machado de Ridington, Juana. "Recuerdos: los tiempos pasados de la Alta California." 1875.
Osuna de Marrón, Felipa. "Recuerdos." 1878.
Pérez, Eulalia. "Recuerdos." 1877. (See also: Carlos N. Híjar, Eulalia Pérez and Agustín Escobar. *Three Memoirs of Mexican California.* Berkeley, CA: Friends of the Bancroft Library, 1988).
Pico, Pío. "Narración histórica." 1877.
Pico de Avila, María Inocencia. "Cosas de California." 1878.
Valdez, Dorotea. "Reminiscencias." 1874.
Vallejo, José de Jesús. "Reminiscencias históricas de California." 1874.
Vallejo, Platón. "Memoires of the Vallejos." n.d. (ca. 1906).
Vallejo de Leese, Rosalía. "History of the Bear Party." 1874.
Vallejo, Salvador. "Notas históricas sobre California." 1874.
Vallejo, Mariano Guadalupe. "Recuerdos históricos y personales tocante a la Alta California," vol. I–V. 1875.

The Articulation of Gender in the Mexican Borderlands, 1900–1915

Clara Lomas

I have the honor to report increasing activity of the very intelligent class of Mexican exiles in the Cities and Towns along the Mexican-American Border line, between the Gulf and the Pacific Ocean . . . [They] are busily engaged [in] writing and publishing inflammatory articles intended to educate up to date, in new revolutionary ideas, the thousands of Mexicans now on the American side of the Border line, and as many as possible of those on the Mexican side.

—Luther E. Ellsworth, US Consul in Mexico

. . . [P]ienso que a Cármen ni siquiera le importaron las cuestiones patrióticas—aunque esto mueva a escándalo—sino que iba más allá, como suele acontecer con muchas vidas femeninas que no se han estudiado bien. Había en ella una solidaridad generosa, la conmovía el dolor de la miseria, la arrebataba la injusticia, la apasionó la piedad humana, nada más.

(I think that Carmen was not a bit preoccupied with patriotic matters, although this may sound scandalous. She was beyond this, as is usually the case with many women's lives that have not been studied well. There was a generous solidarity in her: she was moved by the pain of misery; injustice enraged her; human compassion impassioned her; nothing more.)

—María de los Ángeles Mendieta de Alatorre

The US-Mexico border area, especially the urban centers of Laredo, San Antonio, El Paso and Los Angeles, served as center stage for a vital part of

293

the precursory work of the Mexican revolution of 1910. At the boundaries of these two nation-states, issues of liberalism, anti-clericalism, anarchism, nationalism, class and race were addressed with revolutionary fervor and articulated through the over 200 Spanish-language newspapers published in the Southwest during the historical moment (Valadez 1–8). Within the counter discourses articulated by the divergent factions of the precursor movement, a small but significant number of Spanish-language periodicals not only expounded concern for women's emancipation, or subverted patriarchal authority by including women as part of struggle for justice, but manipulated gender for their particular revolutionary ends. Within the precursor movement, *El obrero* (The Worker), *La voz de la mujer* (The Woman's Voice), and *Pluma roja* (Red Pen) articulated the need to disrupt the social formation. Under the apparent leadership of women, together these periodicals revealed the articulation and manipulation of gender issues within the Mexican revolutionary movement.

Established in San Antonio, Texas, in 1909, by Teresa Villarreal, and aimed at the proletariat, *El obrero* called for the involvement of all, men and women, in the new social order. *La voz de la mujer*, founded in El Paso, in 1907, under the directorship of Isidra T. de Cárdenas, published, as US Consul Ellsworth contended, "inflammatory articles intended to educate" the public about the oppressive and exploitative regime of Porfirio Díaz. *La voz de la mujer* also attempted to affirm through its publication that women were intellectually and morally engaged in the revolutionary effort against the Díaz dictatorship. *Pluma roja*, edited by Blanca de Moncaleano in Los Angeles from 1913–1915, placed the emancipation of women at the center of its anarchist agenda. These periodicals were produced as part of the precursor movement that led to the 1910 Mexican Revolution, which began with the downfall of the Porfiriato, the three-decade-old Porfirio Díaz dictatorship (Cockcroft xiv). From 1900 to 1910, the movement to unseat Díaz was initiated by San Luis Potosi's Club Liberal "Ponciano Arriaga," which advanced traditional Liberal ideals (democracy, anticlericalism and free enterprise). But the movement rapidly grew, including workers and peasants, as well as the anti-reelection campaigns of the Partido Liberal Mexicano (PLM, 1905–1911), headed by Ricardo Flores Magón, and the Partido Nacional Anti-reeleccionista (1910–1911), lead by Francisco I. Madero (Cockcroft xiv-5).

One of the most powerful tools against the dictatorship was the alternative press, and, as such, it was constantly subjected to government repression. The offices of newspapers such as *Regeneración* (Regeneration), *Renacimiento* (Renaissance), *El porvenir* (The Future), *El hijo del Ahuizote* (The Emperor's Son), *El Paladín*, *El Demófilo* (The Demophile), were raided

Ricardo Flores Magón (1884–1922) and brother Enrique in Leavenworth Federal Penitentiary in 1922. The Magóns began publishing *Regeneración* in 1914. (Courtesy of the *Los Angeles Times*).

and closed down. Their journalists were beaten, jailed and often murdered. In 1903, threats of imprisonment and death prompted several leaders of the San Luis Potosí Club Liberal "Ponciano Arriaga"—Camilo Arriaga, Antonio Díaz Soto y Gama and Juan Sarabia—to seek refuge in the United States. As these newspapers were shut down, other more militant periodicals were founded in their place. *Vésper* (Eve), established by journalist Juana B. Gutiérrez de Mendoza and schoolteacher Elisa Acuña y Rosetti, was one such newspaper.

Ricardo Flores Magón and other opposition journalists were jailed for several months in 1903. After their release in early 1904, they also went into exile in Texas and from there tried to re-establish their opposition newspaper *Regeneración*, to create liberal clubs (PLM groups) and to launch a revolutionary movement in Mexico. Persistent harassment by President Díaz's foreign agents forced these radicals to flee to St. Louis, Missouri (Valencia).

PLM activity nonetheless persisted and spread throughout the U. S. Southwest, to Texas, Arizona, New Mexico and California. Headquarters for the PLM leadership were established in San Antonio in 1904 and in El Paso in 1906, where more oppositional newspapers were published: *Humanidad*, *La reforma social*, *La democracia*, *La bandera roja* (The Red Flag), *Punto rojo* (Red Point), and *La voz de la mujer*. The principal propaganda organs of the PLM in Los Angeles were *Revolución* in 1907 and *Libertad y trabajo* (Liberty and Work) and *Regeneración* from 1910 through 1918. Out of approximately 200 newspapers that were published in the Southwest during the period between 1900 and 1920—the majority of which supported the dictatorship of Mexico's President Porfirio Díaz—, more than thirty were founded by PLM members or sympathizers (Valadez 1–8, Griswold Del Castillo 42–7).

The years between 1907–1910 were ones of intense activity for the PLM. While their leaders were being arrested in California and Arizona, the forty to sixty-four PLM groups organized on both sides of the border were attempting to foment rebellion in Mexico and escape arrest by U. S. and Mexican authorities. By the time most of the PLM leaders were released from prison in 1910, the political situation in Mexico had dramatically changed. After two unsuccessful armed efforts to establish "local political revolutionary hegemony" in Baja California and Texas in 1911 and 1913, respectively, and a very successful campaign launched by Mexican consular agents to discredit them as traitors, the PLM lost their influence in the border communities (Gómez-Quiñones 52–6). By the time Blanca de Moncaleano published *Pluma roja*, the PLM faction in Los Angeles shared the periodical's anarchist ideals. The feminist agenda set forth by the newspaper, however, added a new demension to the politics of the revolutionary struggle. *El obrero*, *La voz de la mujer* and *Pluma roja* imploded the nationalist and anarchist discourses of the times by articulating gender issues.

El obrero

On December 15, 1910, Teresa Villarreal, director of *El obrero: periódico independiente*, San Antonio, published the eighth issue of the periodical intended to educate the proletariat along the U. S.-Mexico border.[1] In her article, "El Partido Anti-reeleccionista," Villarreal cited an incident of female bravery as an illustration of the heroism found within the Anti-Reelection Party, and urged PLM members and sympathizers to demand guarantees of democracy and justice from the next president. Her narrative of an incident in Puebla, on 18 November 1910, subverts the official account of the event. Additionally, her concern for Mexico's destitute population reveals the importance she gave to issues of human dignity over those of patriotism.

Villarreal recounts the heroic deeds of the Serdán family who, on 18 November 1910, defended their house in Puebla, Mexico, with gun fire as the police chief attempted to arrest them for sedition. According to official history, Aquiles Serdán, along with some eighteen people, including three women and two children, was in a house fully equipped with arms and ammunition, prepared for the first day of the revolution, 20 November 1910. In their attempt to arrest the revolutionaries, Police Chief Miguel Cabrera and his men were surprised when Aquiles Serdán received them pointing a rifle at Cabrera. Cabrera shot at Aquiles, who shot back, mortally wounding Cabrera and initiating the revolution two days early.

What is particularly interesting about Villarreal's narrative of this event is that, contrary to the official record which attributes the first shots to Aquiles Serdán, Villarreal credits a woman with the killing of the despised police chief. She writes:

> Recordamos con verdadero entusiasmo la escena que tuvo lugar en Puebla en la casa de Cerdán [sic], donde contestaron con balas a los polisontes, los serviles que por asegurar un salario trabajan en pro del despotismo, y nos regocijamos de que en México aún existan heroínas que sepan levantar su mano para desafiar a los tiranuelos mercenarios. Una mujer, sin tener las fuerzas del hombre, pero de una alma viril [sic] y heroica mató al jefe de la policía, a Miguel Cabrera, el hombre degenerado que cometía crímenes para obedecer las órdenes de un gobierno despótico . . . (1)

> (We remember with true enthusiasm the event that took place in Puebla at the Cerdán house, where the inhabitants retaliated with bullets against the police, those subservient men who work for despotism in order to secure a salary. We rejoice that Mexico still has heroines who

know how to raise their fists to defy the mercenary tyrants. A woman, lacking the strength of a man, but with a virile and heroic soul, killed Police Chief Miguel Cabrera, the degenerate man who would commit crimes following the orders of a despotic government . . .)

The narration continues citing the heroic behavior of the unidentified woman as the example for all to follow:

> Hombres degenerados e indiferentes que soportáis los ataques de la Dictadura y vosotras mujeres mexicanas, hijas de México, de esa bella patria donde han nacido héroes valientes y heroínas sin tacha; imitad el ejemplo de esa mujer que ha muerto pero como mueren los valientes: desafiando a los verdugos. Unamos todos los mexicanos nuestras fuerzas . . . (1)

> (You, degenerate and indifferent men, who tolerate the dictatorship's attacks, and you, Mexican women, daughters of Mexico, that beautiful country where valiant heroes and heroines without fault have been born, imitate the example of that woman who has died as brave people do: defying the tyrants. Let us unite our strengths . . .)

It is noteworthy that Villarreal should attribute the action that intitiated the overthrow of the dictator to a woman. Her praise of that action undermines, to some extent, rigid patriarchal notions that relegated women to the domestic sphere and demanded considerable more modesty of them. The vast majority of historical accounts still credit Aquiles Serdán as having taken the first shots that started the Mexican Revolution.

According to historian Angeles Mendieta Alatorre, however, there is an undecipherable mystery with regard to the events of 18 November 1910 at the Serdán house. Alatorre suspects that Carmen Serdán, Aquiles' sister, shot Cabrera when he was about to attack Aquiles:

> Históricamente, la presencia de Carmen Serdán en la vida pública dura escasamente cuatro horas . . . Quizá fue ella misma la que dio muerte a Cabrera cuando iba a atacar a Aquiles —las primeras versiones dijeron que fue una mujer— ya que éste era zurdo y torpe en el manejo de las armas que ella fue tan certera como acaece con los que disparan por primera vez . . . Empero, de esas mismas horas, poco también hay que decir, hubo un misterio que la Familia Serdán se encargó de guardar con esa fidelidad leal con la que se guardaban los secretos de familia (1971: 199)

> (Historically, the presence of Carmen Serdán in public life lasts scarcely four hours . . . Perhaps it was she who killed Cabrera when he was going to attack Aquiles—the first versions of the incident said it was a woman—because he was left handed and careless with guns. On the other hand, she could have had the sharp aim of those who shoot for

the first time . . . But there is little to say of those four hours. There
was a mystery that the Serdán family decided to keep with the loyalty
used to keep family secrets.)

Mendieta Alatorre was convinced that "Algo extraño, profundamente
conmovedor fue sacado a la conciencia pública" (Something strange, profoundly moving, was removed from the public conscience, 199). Perhaps
Carmen Serdán herself chose to ascribe the act to her own dead brother.
We can speculate that either Villarreal received the incorrect information or
that, given the choice, she decided to educate her readers by crediting the
revolutionary act to a woman.

In the second part of the article, Villarreal urges the members of the PLM
to support the reelection campaign in order to construct an effective force
against the dictatorship. She also cautions her readers that the reelection
must yield a new president capable of providing economic, educational, and
cultural improvement for the masses.

> Debemos aspirar al mejoramiento económico de las masas y queremos
> que México figure como un pueblo culto entre las naciones del mundo
> civilizado. Esa debe ser la aspiración que nos aliente a todos en la
> lucha contra la Dictadura actual. Luchemos en pro de la civilización
> y el adelanto moral y material del proletariado mexicano. (*El obrero*
> 15 December 1910: 4)

> (We should aspire for the economic improvement of the masses. We
> want Mexico to stand as a cultured country among the nations of the
> civilized world. That should be the aspiration that inspires us all in
> the struggle against the present dictatorship. We struggle on behalf
> of civilization and the moral and material progress of the Mexican
> proletariat.)

Evidently both Villarreal and the principal character in her narrative shared
the conviction that their participation in the revolutionary effort was essential, whether with the rifle or with the pen. Clearly, Villarreal's narrative of
a woman's heroism inscribed itself in the social text of the borderlands quite
differently than did the official account in central Mexico.

La voz de la mujer

Founded in El Paso, Texas, to function as a propaganda tool for the
PLM, *La voz de la mujer* struggled in 1907 against threats and harassment
from President Díaz's secret agents, as did many other PLM periodicals.[2]
On its front page *La voz de la mujer* identifies a staff consisting primarily
of women: "Isidra T. de Cárdenas—Directora; María Sánchez, Redactora

en Jefe (Chief Editor); María P. García, Administradora; León Cárdenas, Secretario de Redacción."

The publication explicitly states that its primary purpose is: "Semanario Liberal de Combate, Defensor de los Derechos del Pueblo y Enemigo de las Tiranías" (Combat Liberal Weekly, Defender of the People's Rights and Enemy of Tyrannies). The newspaper's logo summons women's participation in the revolutionary struggle by exhorting their duties and rights: "La mujer forma parte integrante de la gran familia humana; luego tiene el deber y el derecho de exigir y luchar por la Dignificación de su Patria" (Women are an integral part of the great human family; therefore, it is their duty and right to demand and struggle for the Dignification of their Country).

Purporting to be the voice of women, the majority of the articles and commentaries in *La voz de la mujer* are written in the first person plural, "nosotras, las madres" (we, mothers), "las esposas" (wifes), "las hermanas" (sisters), "las hijas" (daughters), none individually signed. From the outset, the newspaper establishes a communal identity and assumes a collective female voice. Most of the writings are political essays that strongly attack Mexico's autocracy. Its tone is militant, fearless, combative, similar to the tone of Ricardo Flores Magón's writings. Its style is that of revolutionary romanticism. The newspaper vehemently attacks the harshness and brutality of the regime, passionately denounces the exploitation of the proletariat, and calls for reform within the confines of the nation, as did the PLM during the early phase of their work in exile.

The article, "Unifiquémonos: trabajemos en favor de la Junta de San Louis, Mo." (Let us unify: let us work for the Saint Louis, Mo. Junta), asserts:

> *La voz de la mujer* surgió al estadío de la prensa liberal, defendiendo el principio de libertad; coadyuva con nuestros hermanos de ideales en defensa del pueblo oprimido; sus trabajos son limpios por eso hablamos claro; no somos serviles, por eso fustigamos a los protervos; no tememos despertar su encono, por eso denunciamos sus maldades. (*La voz de la mujer*, October 27, 1907, n.p.)

> (*La voz de la mujer* emerged to the stage of the liberal press to defend the principle of liberty; to contribute with our brothers' ideals in the defense of the oppressed people. Its work is clean and so we speak clearly. We are not servile, and so we sharply reprimand the perverse. We are not afraid of wakening their anger, and so we denounce their corruption.)

La voz de la mujer follows in the tradition established by journalist, poet and political radical Juana Belen Gutiérrez de Mendoza with her newspaper

Vésper, founded in 1901 in Guanajuato (Macías 26). Their language had been characterized as "viril" (manly), "estilo en pantalones" (long-pants style) (Mendieta Alatorre 33). Through the use of an extremely metaphoric language, *La voz de la mujer* attempts to expose the criminal face of the so-called "Mexican peace" and to unveil the bestiality of the Díaz government. In an article entitled "Apocalipcis de la tiranía" [sic] (Apocalypses of the Tyranny), which comments on the dictator's iron hand of repression against the PLM, the bourgeoisie are identified as the "sanguijuelas del erario" (leeches of the treasury), the mercenaries as "los peletas alquilados" (hired canines) and the consulates as "las emponsoñadas víboras"[sic] (poison snakes). An article which exposes the exploitation of farmworker, warns of the coming upheaval: "[La labor] ha tenido una cosecha de exasperación que ya se manifiesta con el descontento general que ha venido madurándose, y solo bastará con un beso del viento para que desprenda su fruto" (*La voz de la mujer* 28 July, 1907, 3) (Labor has had a harvest of exasperation. This already manifests itself with the general discontent which has been maturing. A kiss of the wind will be sufficient to let go of its fruit).

Some of the most intriguing pieces in the newspaper sum up and comment on the current political events, in the tradition of the Mexican ballad. "¡Loor a los mártires traicionados!" a heroic romance, celebrates the betrayed Mexican Liberal Party heroes' feats when captured by the dictator's secret police, who are assisted by Pinkerton detectives and United States immigration officers. The final stanza addresses the oppressed people directly:

> ¡Pueblo! tu deber es rebelarte
> Contra ese mito que de sangre vive:
> Si mártires te sirven de baluarte,
> ¿Por qué consientes que tu pena avive?
> Convierte abyección en rebeldías
> Y alcanzarás el medio de salvarte . . .
>
> (People! Your duty is to rebel
> against that myth which lives of blood:
> if martyrs serve as your bastion,
> why allow your sorrow to intensify?
> Transform abjection into rebellion
> and you will find the means to liberate yourself)

Through the poetic piece, the readers of *La voz de la mujer* are challenged to raise their level of social consciousness and not remain apathetic to the realities of their circumstances.

The extant issues of *La voz de la mujer* do not address the specific condition of women. Their situation is alluded to within the context of the proletariat conditions. There are moments in the articles, however, which pay special attention to how women are affected differently by the new upheaval. The article "Conviene prevenirse: iniciativa" (It is in our best interest to prepare ourselves: initiative) reports that due to their oppositional discourse the rebels are being imprisoned. Among them, women run a greater risk as they are always in jeopardy of also being raped: "como respuesta a sus demandas, son arrancados de sus hogares y por la fuerza se les deporta a los cuarteles, lugar de tormento para los espíritus que no abdican sus derechos y persisten en reivindicar su dignidad, máxime y con mayor abundancia cuando algún miembro femenino de esos REBELDES despierta la lujuria de algún cacique vulgar" (*La voz de la mujer*, 28 July 1907, 4) (as a response to their demands, they are violently taken from their homes to the prison quarters, a tormenting place for those spirits that do not give up their rights and persist in recovering their dignity. This is especially true when a vulgar cacique is attracted to a female member of the rebels).

Although the newspaper does not analyze women's condition, it does address itself to women, encouraging them to rouse their men to fight against peonage and for liberty: "Hoy el dilema es otro: tomar lo que se necesita, ¡libertad! Y ésta sólo se conquista con rebeldías. ¡Hay que ser rebeldes! Primero morir, antes que consentir que nuestros hijos lleven el estigma de la esclavitud. A nosotras, madres y esposas, hermanas o hijas, toca encausar este dilema" (28 July 1907, 4) (Today the dilemma is another: to take what is needed, liberty! Liberty can only be conquered through rebelliousness. It is up to us, mothers and wives, sisters or daughters, to confront this dilemma).

La voz de la mujer counsels women to assume new duties within the public sphere: to form mutualist societies to raise funds for families of soldiers, as well as to accept posts men are not willing to assume. Within the domestic sphere, it urges women to send their sons off to war with blessings and words of valor and to expect nothing but heroism from their husbands. It is important to note, however, that women's incorporation into the public sphere was ultimately intended for the benefit of the state and, therefore, limited within the constraints of nationalism.

Two aspects of the newspaper had the potential of consciously, or subconsciously, affecting the gender politics of their readers. The first of these was the newspaper's gendering of political positions. In the article, "La prensa honrada? Redactado por pseudo-independientes" (The Honest Press? Published by Pseudo-Independents), which promotes the alternative press' position against the state, the ambiguity of the so-called "independent presses" is attacked through gender rhetoric:

> Sirviendo de estribillo que provoca náuceas [sic], a diario vemos en
> cierta prensa, que por sí y ante sí se hace los honores de llamarse hon-
> rada, independiente, instructiva, un cúmulo de ataques infamatorios

contra la prensa de oposición al gobierno mexicano; ataque que nunca ha justificado, porque si bien es cierto que emplea frases ofensivas contra sus adversarios, es más verdad que jamás justifica tales calificativos aunque haga derroche de elocuencia hasta hipnotizar a los lectores con vastos conocimientos en retórica, con un lleno completo en gramática, para expresar conceptos sublimes que conmuevan a todo continente.

(Daily, we see in a certain press—which depends on a tautology that provokes nausea and attempts to honor itself by calling itself honest, independent, instructive—a series of attacks against the press in opposition to the Mexican government. These attacks are never justified. Instead it employs offensive phrases against its adversaries without qualifying them. Through eloquent use of rhetoric and grammar, it seeks to hypnotize its readers with sublime concepts meant to move the entire continent.)

La voz de la mujer does not tolerate the ambiguity of those who purport to be between the political Right and Left. "Estos parásitos" (These parasites), it points out, "son editores que pertenecen al género neutro" (are editors which belong to the neuter gender). Evidently, through this publication, it is the women who speak out for the oppressed in opposition to the state. Those who take an ambivalent attitude are neutered. By inference, the male is equated with autocracy. *La voz de la mujer*, then, claims to be the voice of the oppressed. All who are exploited are imagined as the oppressed sex. They are impoverished, their basic needs and rights denied and their existence dehumanized.

The other aspect of the newspaper that draws attention to women's social position is manifested through the title of the newspaper, *La voz de la mujer*. The collective voice of women is not only vigorous, decisive and vital, but it calls for the restructuring of society. Readers, the vast majority men, were likely to be prompted to react to women's appropriation of the written word and to their intellectual and revolutionary activity.

Further research on this periodical has revealed a letter regarding the gender of the production staff, which problemizes the issue of authority and raises the question of manipulation of gender by the author of the letter.[3] Dated 11 August 1907, addressed to Antonio I. Villarreal and signed by the secretary, "Leonor," the letter claims that this weekly was not produced by women at all:

Efectivamente que puede suceder una acusación como Ud. lo prevee al aparecer yo como secretario de *La Voz de la Mujer*, a ello me he visto obligado porque nuestro amigo Don Lauro [Aguirre] está temeroso de que se crea que él escribe el semanario aludido y esto lo hacía estar inquieto, y además que las damas que en él figuran, sólo tienen un corazón muy grande para trabajar por la causa, pero nada pueden expresar ellas porque no son capaces de escribir y en este caso sólo tomo el nombre de ellas como un impulso para la causa porque supongo que muchos hombres al aparecer señoras en el periódico, deben sonrojarse al encontrarlas en puestos que ellos deberían desempeñar; así, repito, lo que *La Voz* dice, no lo escriben ellas pero con su abnegación expresan más de lo que se asienta en imprenta. (López and Cortés 194–5)

(Surely, an accusation such as the one you have foreseen could be made since I appear as the secretary of *La voz de la mujer.* I have been forced to do so because our friend Don Lauro [Aguirre] is afraid that someone may think he is the one writing the weekly and this made him feel quite uneasy. Moreover, the ladies that appear as the writers only have a big heart for the cause: they cannot express anything because they are incapable of writing. In this case, I only take their names as an impulse for the cause. I suppose that having women appear as writers of the newspaper will make men blush as they find them in positions men should be holding. I reiterate, what *La voz* says is not written by women, nonetheless, with their devotion, they express more than what goes down on print.)

One can surmise that this letter was written by León Cárdenas. If we take at face value his claim that the weekly was not written by women, thereby depriving women of any authority, we would then have to address the issue of manipulation of gender by the proponents of the social revolution. Instead of women's appropriation of the written word, we may have here the appropriation of women's "voices" by men. This may explain why the narrative voices in *La voz de la mujer* are not at all different from those of the male precursors of the revolution, why the newspaper lacks an analysis of women's condition and why attempts are made therein to develop women's sense of state nationalism. This manipulation of gender buttresses Emma Pérez's critique of the PLM's ideology on women. As Pérez has pointed out, "*Regeneración* helped to politicize Mexican women in the Southwest, but women were politicized to serve a nationalist cause—the Mexican revolution" (459–82).

León Cárdenas rationalizes that his manipulation of gender in the newspaper's pages is a way both to humiliate and to motivate men. He suggests that the periodical's call for women's participation in the revolution was a very specific one: to arouse their men's civic pride by overthrowing the dictator. If Cárdenas was correct, it is important to note that his manipulation of gender in the pages of the newspaper also allowed him to have access to the women's private sphere, the home, as did the priests from the pulpit.

Nonetheless, we should not forget that León Cárdenas was responding to an accusation. We cannot therefore rule out the possibility that he very well could have been responding defensively, inaccurately, and perhaps cleverly, in order to protect his masculine pride.

Pluma roja

Whereas in the 1900s Andrea and Teresa Villarreal and Sara Estela Ramírez defied the well-established Catholic ideology, and *La voz de la mujer* called for liberal democracy through a revolution, in the following decade *Pluma roja* proposed Anarchism as the solution to oppression.[4] Founded in Los Angeles during the second phase of the Revolution, *Pluma roja* was edited and directed by Blanca de Moncaleano from 1913–1915. Although there are no indications that this publication was founded as a political organ of the PLM, it was established to network with the international anarchist movement in which Ricardo Flores Magón participated.

Although little is known about Blanca de Moncaleano, John Hart writes that "In early June 1912, Juan Francisco Moncaleano, a Colombian anarchist and political fugitive sought by the Colombian military [and 'his dynamic wife'], arrived in Mexico after a brief stay in Havana ['inspired by the news of the Madero led revolution']" (11–13), A university professor in Colombia, Francisco Moncaleano founded the newspaper *Luz* in Mexico City, which according to Hart, "was a remarkable newspaper. Moncaleano used it to publicize the hopeless cause of Flores Magón and the Partido Liberal Mexicano, the anarchist program of which he enthusiastically endorsed and whose leader he deeply admired" (113). As Moncaleano prepared the opening of the La Casa del Obrero in September of 1912, the Madero regime succeeded in arresting him and expelled him from the country. The few issues of *Pluma roja* located and consulted for this study indicate that the Moncaleanos continued their anarchist work crossing still another border.

Unlike the nationalist ideology of *La voz de la mujer*, *Pluma roja* did not believe in national borders. It adopted instead José Martí's concept of one united America. "[Hay que demostrar] que las fronteras son un mito" (We should demonstrate that borders are a myth), appeared in its pages. For *Pluma roja*, the need to recode the position of women in society was at the center of the struggle for social, political and economic freedom, and was an integral part of the ideal of anarchism, as it had been for Emma Goldman during that same historical moment. For *Pluma roja*, unquestioned patriarchal authority, upheld by religion and the state, was the target of its red pen.

Many of the articles that appeared in the newspaper were directed specifically at women who were encouraged to break their chains through the acquisition of knowledge. The anarchist program, as defined by *Pluma roja*, searched for an egalitarian society in which women would be fully emancipated. It proposed women's freedom from their three oppressors: the state, religion and capital.

As editor and director, Blanca de Moncaleano not only addressed women but men as well, urging them to convert their obedient enslaved women into thinking "compañeras." For example, although the title, "Hombre, educad a la mujer" (Men, Educate Women), appears to be a call for men to educate women, in essence the article addresses the issue of the importance of allowing women to educate themselves: "Dejen los hombres que la mujer se instruya, que piense y reflexione por sí sola" (1 February 1914: 1) (Men, allow women to learn, think, and reflect by themselves).

The articles signed by Blanca de Moncaleano are perhaps the most vehemently critical of those men involved in the struggle for liberation and who were least conscious of their own suppression and enslavement of women. "Engolfados los hombres en su supuesta superioridad, fatuos por su ignorancia, han creído que sin la ayuda de la mujer, pueden llegar a la meta de la emancipación humana ... " (*Pluma roja* 27 June 1915: 1) (Lost in the suppostion of their superiority, stupefied by their ignorance, men have believed that, without the assistance of women, they can reach the goal of human emancipation ...). Confronting apathy from her male counterparts, she denounces the source of their power, "El hombre no ha sido otra cosa que el verdadero ladrón de los derechos naturales de la mujer" (Men have been nothing but the true theives of women's natural rights). Moncaleano expounded her firm, militant stance through the newspaper's motto: "Ante mí la estrella del ideal. Tras de mí los hombres. No miro atrás." (Before me, the star of ideal. Behind me, men. I do not look back).

El obrero, *La voz de la mujer* and *Pluma roja* all had an impact on their audiences as they articulated gender issues. It is highly probable that their audiences consisted of PLM activists and partisans described by Gómez-Quiñones as:

> 1) the large audience composed of Chicano-Mexicano general sympathizers and intermittently active, for the most part lower middle class, artisans and laborers; 2) the local cores of leadership, in the majority Chicano, district organizers, chapter officers, local journalists who were transmitters and interpreters of PLM policy usually active for prolonged periods; 3) the bi-national leadership, well educated, self taught or as a result of professional training, they were the policy makers and were mostly Mexicano but with some Chicanos ... (27)

Whether that public read privately or listened to someone reading in groups at gatherings, the articulation of gender issues within an environment of revolutionary change, must have encouraged rethinking of women's role in society. While we now know that the Mexican revolution was a catalyst for the women's movement in Mexico, we know little of its repercussions for women's lives in the U. S. Southwest (Macías 49). Recovery of periodicals such as *Pluma roja*, research of its impact on various communities and of women's social history, should reveal the history of the development of feminist consciousness in the borderlands. The voices and pens of these women articulate a passionate rebelliousness whose documentation long has been absent from both Mexican and United States cultural theatres.

Notes

[1]I located one issue of *El obrero* at the Secretariat of Foreign Relations in Mexico City.

[2]From the Silvestre Terrazas Collection at the Bancroft Library and the International Institute of Social History in Amsterdam, I have retrieved five issues of *La voz de la mujer*: number 5 (July 28, 1907); number 7 (August 11, 1907); number 9 (September 6, 1907); and number 13 (October 27, 1907). I am grateful to Rafael Chabrán for alerting me to this Institute's holdings of *La voz de la mujer* and *Pluma roja* (see n. 4).

[3]I am grateful to Victor Nelson-Cisneros for indicating the materials which lead to this correspondence.

[4]At the International Institute of Social History in Amsterdam, I was able to locate five numbers of *Pluma roja*: number 1, (5 November 1913); number 3 (14 December 1913); number 4 (1 February 1914); number 11 (15 June 1915); number 13 (27 June 1915).

Works Cited

Cockcroft, James D. *Intellectual Precursors of the Mexican Revolution, 1900–1913*, 2nd ed. Austin, TX: U of Texas P, 1976.

Ellsworth, Luther E. "Dispatch from Ciudad Porfirio Díaz, Mexico to the Secretary of State, Washington, D.C., 12 October." *Documents on the Mexican Revolution.* Ed. Gene Z. Hanrahan. Salisbury, NC: Documentary Publications, 1910.

Gómez-Quiñones, Juan. *Sembradores Ricardo Flores Magón y el Partido LIberal Mexicano: A Eulogy and Critique.* Los Angeles: U of California, Los Angeles Chicano Studies Center, 1973.

Griswold del Castillo, Richard. "The Mexican Revolution and the Spanish-Language Press in the Borderlands." *Journalism History* 4.2 (1977): 42–47.

Hart, John. *Anarchism & the Mexican Working Class, 1860–1931*, Austin: U of Texas Press, 1987.

Hernández, Inés. "Sara Estela Ramírez: The Early Twentieth-Century Texas Mexican Poet." Diss. U of Houston, 1984.

López, Chantal and Omar Cortés. *El Partido Liberal Mexicano (1906–1908).* México, D.F.: Antorcha, 1986.

Macías, Anna. *Against All Odds: The Feminist Movement in Mexico to 1940.* Connecticut: Greenwood, 1982.

Mendieta Alatorre, María de los Ángeles. *Carmen Serdán.* Mexico: Bohemia Poblana, Edición del Centro de Estudios Históricos de Puebla, 1971.

————. *La mujer en la revolución mexicana*. México, D.F.: Biblioteca del Instituto Nacional de Estudios Históricos de la Revolución Mexicana, 1961.

Pérez, Emma. "A la mujer": A Critique of the Partido Liberal Mexicano's Gender Ideology." *Between Borders: Essays on Mexicana/Chicana History* Ed. Adelaida R. Del Castillo. Encino, CA: Floricanto, 1990.

Raat, Dirk. *Revoltosos: Mexico's Rebels in the United States, 1903–1923*. College Station: Texas A&M UP, 1981.

Soto, Shirlene. *The Mexican Woman: A Study of Her Participation in the Revolution, 1910–1940*. Palo Alto, CA: R&E Research, 1979.

Valadez, José. "Más de cuatrocientos periódicos en Español se han editado en Estados Unidos." *La prensa* (13 February 1938).

Valencia, Tita. "Ricardo Flores Magón y el periodismo subversivo mexicano en EUA." *The Americas Review* 17.3-4 (1989): 169–78.

The UCLA Bibliographic Survey of Mexican-American Literary Culture, 1821–1945: An Overview

Ramón A. Gutiérrez

In 1988 Professor Raymund Paredes received a National Endowment for the Humanities grant to undertake an historical and bibliographic survey of Mexican-American literary culture in the United States from 1821 to 1945. Literary culture was defined broadly to include all the traditional literary genres—poetry, short stories, novels, plays, personal narratives—as well as those oral expressions sometimes categorized as "folkloric"—legends, tales, songs and ballads.

The bibliographic survey took 1821 as its initial date because this year marked the end of Spanish colonial rule and the beginning of a proliferation of settlements in what is now the U. S. Southwest. The survey ended in 1945 with the appearance of a distinct Chicano literature. The project's immediate and still pending goal was to produce three research and bibliographic guides on Mexican-American literary culture: 1) a guide to published and unpublished Spanish-language periodical and archival literature; 2) a guide to English-language periodical literature; and, 3) a guide to Mexican-American folklore collections. The project's ultimate end is to integrate knowledge about Mexican-American literary culture into the curricula of educational institutions throughout the country.

The work of the bibliographic survey progressed through several stages. First a survey questionnaire was created and mailed to some 200 libraries, archives, museums and research centers throughout the country. Responses were analyzed. Specific collections and holdings that seemed particularly rich in material were studied further. Eleven institutions ultimately were selected for on-site inventory: The Huntington Library (San Marino, California), The Southwest Museum (Los Angeles, California) The Bancroft Library (Berkeley, California), The Strachwitz Collection (El Cerrito, California), The Latin American Collection at the University of Texas (Austin), The Texas State Library (Austin), The New Mexico State Records Center and Archives (Santa Fe), The Museum of New Mexico's History Library (Santa Fe), The Special Collections Sections of the University of New Mexico Library (Albuquerque), The Newberry Library (Chicago), and The Library of Congress.

Some of the highlights of the UCLA Survey are listed below, particularly those collections that are important in tracing the literary culture of Mexican Americans in the United States.

1. The Newberry Library

The Newberry Library has two collections that contain extensive Mexican-American material. The Everett D. Graff Collection of Western Americana is a major source of primary documentary materials on the American West, from its initial exploration by the Spanish to the present. Over 125 items were inventoried from this collection. Among these are several Californio narratives from the 1820s and 1830s, which originally appeared in *The Century Illustrated Monthly Magazine*, *The Overland Monthly* and *Esquire*. María Antonia Pico, the mother of General Manuel B. Castro and Juan B. Castro, describes the 1818 arrival in California of an Anglo pirate named Hippolyte Bouchard in her article "A California Lion and a Pirate." Brígida Briones, in "A Carnival Ball at Monterey in 1829," and "A Glimpse of Domestic Life in 1827," chronicles the daily activities of Mexican and Indian women. Amalia Sibrián focuses on relations between Californios and Anglo Americans in "A Spanish Girl's Journey from Monterey to Los Angeles." And in Prudencia Higueras' "Trading with Americans," one reads about early mercantile activities in California.

The Graff Collection also contains several diaries and autobiographies that describe life in the Southwest during the second half of the nineteenth century. Exemplary is José Policarpo Rodríguez's autobiography, *José Policarpio Rodríguez: "The Old Guide," Surveyor, Scout, Hunter, Indian Fighter, Ranchman, Preacher. His Life in His Own Words.* Rodríguez was a lieutenant in the Texas Army from 1849 to 1861, a period of profound changes. This collection also contains the journals and logs of military and scientific expeditions to the Southwest.

The Edward E. Ayer Collection has three archival groups that help chronicle various aspects of the Mexican-American experience in the United States. The Archives of the State of Matamoros, Mexico, contains photographic reproductions of material on early settler movements in Texas and New Mexico, the 1836 Texas Revolution, the 1846–48 war between Mexico and the United States, and border relations between the two countries to 1880.

The Mexico Archives in the Ayer Collection contains documents on the early history of Texas, and on Spanish Louisiana and New Mexico. In these archives one also finds the Richman Collection, which are materials on California's history culled from the British Museum and various Mexican archives.

Finally, the Nacogdoches Archives consists of documentary reproductions from 1729 to 1836, describing Indian-White relations and migration in and out of Texas during Spanish, Mexican and American rule.

2. The Southwest Museum

The Southwest Museum contains eighteen collections of folkloric material that are particularly rich. The Charles F. Lummis Collection of Wax Cylinders contains 340 *canciones* (songs) from the early twentieth century, as well as the original and yet unpublished poems and folksongs of José de la Rosa, a Mexican printer who took up residence in California in 1833. The folksongs in the Eleanor Hague Collection come from all of Latin America, but there are some here of Mexican-American provenance from Los Angeles and Ventura counties in California. The Manuela García Collection contains approximately 159 of her songs that date from 1850 to 1904 and which were recorded onto wax cylinders by Charles Lummis in 1904. The Lenora Curtin Collection of folkmusic contains some 50 *inditas, corridos, alabados, romances* and *canciones*, which she recorded and transcribed in the New Mexican towns of Taos, Santa Fe and Chimayó from 1890 to 1950. The Lalo Guerrero Collection primarily documents this musician's life through recordings and audio cassettes produced between 1945 and 1985.

3. The Strachwitz Collection

The Strachwitz Collection of commercial phonographic recording by popular Mexican and Chicano musicians is a private and yet uncataloged collection owned by Chris Strachwitz. While there are miscellaneous letters, photos, films and promotional materials in this collection, its bulk consists of some 12,000 recordings from the 1920s to the present. Bluebird, Brunswick, Columbia, Decca, Edison, Folk Lyric, Folkways, Odeon, Oken, Pathé, Peerless, Universal, Victor and Vocalion are but some of the record labels contained in this collection.

4. The Huntington Library

The Huntington Library is home to the personal papers of several individuals that were important to the development of the U. S. Southwest: Mary Austin, Henry Castro, José de Gálvez, the Guerra Family, Charles Lummis, William Gillet Ritch, Reginaldo Valle, Mariano Vallejo. The Huntington's large collection of broadsides, portraits and sketches includes images of Joaquín Murieta, Vicente Lugo, Antonio Maná, Pío Pico, Father Junípero Serra, Concepción Argüello and Manuel Domínguez. The Library owns a copy of Pedro Baptista Pino's 1812 *Exposición sucinta y sencilla del nuevo méxico*, and Antonio Barreiro's 1832 *Ojeada sobre nuevo méxico, que da una idea de sus producciones naturales, y de algunas otras cosas que se consideran oportunas para mejorar su estado, é ir proporcionando su futura felicidad.*

5. Special Collections, University of New Mexico Library

The Special Collections at the University of New Mexico's Zimmerman Library has two parts. The first, the Clinton P. Anderson Collection, was gathered by the late U. S. Senator to chronicle the history and ethnology of the American West. Most of these materials are in printed form: books, pamphlets, magazine excerpts. The second part, the Coronado Collection, focuses primarily on Native-American and Hispanic materials. The Coronado Collection has extensive microfilm archives which contain *The Spanish Archives of New Mexico*, *The Mexican Archives of New Mexico*, *The Territorial Archives of New Mexico* and *The Archives of the Archdiocese of Santa Fe*. Also housed here are the photographic copies of all the documents relating to New Mexico gathered by Professor France V. Scholes during the 1940s, in such Spanish, Mexican and American repositories as the Archivo General de Indias (Seville), the Archivo General de la Nación (Mexico City), the Parral Archives (Durango), and the Béxar Archives (Austin). The Coronado Room contains numerous personal collections of New Mexicana, among them the papers of Beltrán Osorio, which is particularly rich with early New Mexican literary materials.

6. The Bancroft Library

The initial collection that formed the Bancroft Library was gathered by Hubert Howe Bancroft, a wealthy San Francisco entrepreneur and publisher, who wrote a seven-volume *History of California* (1884–1889). As part of this project, Bancroft and a team of assistants gathered some two-hundred original narratives from native and pioneer Californians that are particularly important sources for the study of Mexican-American literary culture. For a more extensive discussion and list of these "Californio Personal Narratives," see the essays in this anthology by Genaro Padilla and Rosaura Sánchez.

7. Benson Latin American Collection, University of Texas Library

The Benson Latin American Collection contains eleven collections that vividly document Mexican-American literary activity in the United States. These collections are catalogued as: Carlos Villalogín, Carlos Castañeda, Catarino Garza, Eleuterio Escobar, Eustacio Cepeda, Jovita Gonzáles Mireles, Lalo Astol, Rómulo Munguía, Seferino Vela, the Migrant Border Ballad Project and the Tafolla Family Papers. Particularly noteworthy is the Catarino Garza Collection, which contains his unpublished journal, *La lógica de los hechos o sean observaciones sobre las circunstancias de los mexicanos en Texas desde el año de 1877 hasta 1889.* In this manuscript Garza describes the discrimination Mexicans and Mexican Americans suffered in Texas between 1877 and 1889.

8. The Museum of New Mexico's History Library

The historical collections in this library primarily focus on New Mexico's Native-American and Hispano heritage. The library has all the standard primary and secondary published works on the state's history. Though the collection of personal papers is small, it does include some material that is infrequently consulted. For example, The Abeyta Family Papers is a collection of folksayings, songs and recollections of life in nineteenth-century New Mexico. The Adolph Bandelier Collection contains several copies of the "Legend of Montezuma" and Bandelier's unpublished translation of Gaspar Pérez de Villagrá's *Historia de la Nueva México* (1610). The library also owns a complete collection of transcribed interviews on New Mexican folklife and culture conducted by the Works Progress Administration during the 1930s.

9. Library of Congress

The Library of Congress has a wealth of material on Mexican-American literary culture that is too extensive to describe in any adequate way here. Particularly important, but frequently overlooked is the Mexican-American Folksong and Music on Field Recordings section, which is contained in the Archives of Folkculture. This is an extensive collection of recorded music (including transcriptions) collected in Texas, New Mexico and California from the early 1940s to the present.

Contributors

Edna Acosta-Belén is a Professor of Latin American and Caribbean Studies, Women's Studies and Director of the Center for Latin America and the Caribbean at the University at Albany, SUNY. She has authored/edited *The Puerto Rican Women: Perspectives on Culture, History, and Society; The Hispanic Experience in the United States* (with B. Sjostrom), *Researching Women in Latin America and the Caribbean* (with C. Bose), *Integrating Latin and Caribbean Women into the Curriculum and Research* (with C. Bose), and *In the Shadow of the Giant: Colonialism, Migration, and Puerto Rican Culture* (forthcoming).

Antonio I. Castañeda is an Assistant Professor of Women's Studies and Chicano Studies at the University of California, Santa Barbara. Her scholarly work is on *mestizas* in eighteenth- and nineteenth-century California.

Rodolfo J. Cortina is a Professor of Spanish at Florida International University. His publications include the anthology *Cuban American Theater* (Houston: Arte Público, 1991), *Hispanos en los Estados Unidos* (Madrid: Cultura Hispánica, 1988), *"El Mutualista" (1947–1950): A Facsimile Edition of a Milwaukee Hispanic Newspaper* (Milwaukee: SSOT, 1983), and other books, articles and reviews. He heads the RUSHLH Bibliographic Database Project.

José B. Fernández is Professor of History and Spanish at the University of Central Florida. A specialist in Spanish colonial letters, Fernández is the author of three books on the Spanish explorer Álvar Núñez Cabeza de Vaca.

Juan Flores, Professor, Department of Latin American Studies, City University of New York, and Research Director and consultant Center for Puerto Rican Studies, Hunter College, is the author of the recent *Divided Borders: Essays on Puerto Rican Identity* (1992). Other publications and editions include *On Edge: The Crisis in Contemporary Latin American Culture* (1992), *Memoirs of Bernardo Vega: A Contribution to the History of the Puerto Rican Community in New York* (1984), and *Divided Arrival: Narratives of the Puerto Rican Migrations (1920–1950)* (1987).

Erlinda Gonzales-Berry is Professor and Chair at the Department of Spanish and Portuguese at the University of New Mexico. She is editor of *Pasó por Aquí: Critical Essays on the New Mexico Literary Tradition* and author of a novel, *Paletitas de Guayaba*.

Ramón A. Gutiérrez is a MacArthur Fellow and Professor of History and the founding chair of the Ethnic Studies Department at the University of California-San Diego. He is the author of *When Jesus Came, the Corn Mothers Went Away; Marriage, Sexuality and Power in New Mexico, 1500–1846*, as well as numerous articles on colonial Latin American and American history.

María Herrera-Sobek is Professor at the Department of Spanish and Portuguese, University of California, Irvine. Her publications include: *The Bracero Experience* (1979), *The Mexican Corrido* (1990), and *Northward Bound: The Mexican Immigrant Experience in Ballad and Song* (1993). She has edited several books on Chicana literature.

Nicolás Kanellos is Professor, Department of Hispanic and Classical Languages and Director of Arte Público Press, University of Houston. Winner of the American Book Award (1989), his *A History of Hispanic Theatre in the United States: Origins to 1940* (1990) received the Texas Institute of Letters Book Award (1991) and the Southwest Conference on Latin American Studies Book Award (1991). He is also the author of *Mexican American Theatre: Legacy and Reality* (1987), *A Bio-Bibliographic Dictionary of Hispanic Literature of the United States* (1989) and editor of *Las aventuras de Don Chipote o Cuando los pericos mamen*, by Daniel Venegas.

· Luis Leal is Professor Emeritus, University of Illinois, Champaign-Urbana, Distinguished Lecturer, University of California, Santa Barbara, and Visiting Professor, Stanford University (1991–93). He has published extensively on Mexican and Chicano literatures. His works include *Juan Rulfo* (Twayne, 1983) and *Aztlán y México* (Bilingual, 1985). In 1987 he received the Distinguished Scholar Award from the National Association for Chicano Studies (NACS), and in 1991 the "Aztec Eagle" from the Mexican Government.

Clara Lomas, Associate Professor at the Department of Romance Languages, The Colorado College, has contributed chapters to *Multi-Ethnic Literature of the United States*, *Longman Anthology of World Literature by Women, 1895–1975*; *Estudios Chicanos and the Politics of Community*, and *Chicana Voices: Intersections of Class, Race, and Gender*; and has co-edited *Chicano Politics after the 80s*. She is currently working on a book on the intellectual production by women in the Mexican borderlands at the turn of the century.

Genaro Padilla is an Associate Professor of English at the University of California-Berkeley. He is the author of numerous essays on Chicano autobiography and culture. His book *History, Memory and the Struggles of Self-Representation: The Formation of Mexican Autobiography* is forthcoming from University of Wisconsin Press.

Raymund A. Paredes is a Professor of English and Associate Vice Chancellor for Academic Development at UCLA. He has published widely on Chicano literature and culture. He is co-editor of the *Heath Anthology of American Literature*. Associate Vice Chancellor, Academic Development, University of California, Los Angeles. His publications include "Diversity and Admission Policy in the University of California," in the *Los Angeles Times* (July 1, 1990), "Cultural Collisions and the Emergence of Chicano Literature" in the *Humanities Network* (1990), and "The Promise of diversity" in *CAIP Quarterly* (1990).

Charles Tatum is Professor and Head of the Department of Spanish and Portuguese at the University of Arizona. He is the author of *Chicano Literature* (1982), published in translation in 1986 in Mexico. He is co-founder and co-editor of the journal *Studies in Latin American Popular Culture*. Tatum recently edited three volumes of *New Chicana/Chicano*